PENGUIN REFERENCE BOOKS

WHO'S WHO IN THE ANCIENT WORLD

BETTY RADICE read classics at Oxford, then married and, in the intervals of bringing up a family, tutored in classics, philosophy and English. She became joint editor of the Penguin Classics in 1964. As well as editing the translation of Livy's *The War with Hannibal* she translated Pliny's Letters, Livy's *Rome and Italy*, the Latin comedies of Terence, *The Letters of Abelard and Heloise* and Erasmus's *Praise of Folly*, and also wrote the Introduction to Horace's *The Complete Odes and Epodes* and *The Poems* of Propertius, all for the Penguin Classics. She also edited and introduced Edward Gibbon's *Memoirs of My Life* for the Penguin English Library. She edited and annotated her translation of the younger Pliny's works for the Loeb Library of Classics, and translated from Italian, Renaissance Latin and Greek for the Officina Bodoni of Verona. She collaborated as a translator in the Collected Works of Erasmus in preparation by the University of Toronto. Betty Radice was an honorary fellow of St Hilda's College, Oxford, and a vice-president of the Classical Association. She died in February 1985.

WHO'S WHO IN THE ANCIENT WORLD

A HANDBOOK TO THE SURVIVORS OF THE GREEK AND ROMAN CLASSICS

SELECTED WITH AN INTRODUCTION BY

BETTY RADICE

WITH FIFTY-SIX PLATES

PENGUIN BOOKS

PENGUIN BOOKS

Published by the Penguin Group
Penguin Books Ltd, 27 Wrights Lane, London W8 5TZ, England
Penguin Books USA Inc., 375 Hudson Street, New York, New York 10014, USA
Penguin Books Australia Ltd, Ringwood, Victoria, Australia
Penguin Books Canada Ltd, 10 Alcorn Avenue, Toronto, Ontario, Canada M4V 3B2
Penguin Books (NZ) Ltd, 182–190 Wairau Road, Auckland 10, New Zealand

Penguin Books Ltd, Registered Offices: Harmondsworth, Middlesex, England

First published in Great Britain by Anthony Blond 1971
First published in the USA by Stein & Day Publishers 1971
Revised and published in Penguin Books 1973
13 15 17 19 20 18 16 14

Printed in England by Clays Ltd, St Ives plc
Set in Monotype Bembo

In Memoriam

Catherine Lucy Radice

1947–1968

sunt apud infernos tot milia formosarum

CONTENTS

LIST OF ILLUSTRATIONS

PREFACE

A book on a subject like this can only be selective and perhaps idiosyncratic, but this one has a full INDEX.

It covers everything which is entered under another heading and is intended for use as a starting-point in a search for information.

There is a short bibliography of books which helped me and which would be useful for following up individual subjects. I have not included standard authors, current translations of the classics nor illustrated books on artists, but I have referred to nothing which I have not seen in a gallery or museum or in some accessible book.

When attitudes to the past have changed in the process of history I have generally dealt with them chronologically, Greek and Roman, medieval, Renaissance and post-Renaissance on to the present day. I doubt if I have done justice to the eighteenth century, but in a period when the classics provided an accepted framework for almost any creative work, it is difficult to know where to start or stop. I hope that where I stop someone else will start – putting me right, filling in gaps, or tracking the more agreeable of the red herrings in his path.

I should like to thank Michael Alexander, Rae Dalven, Kimon Friar, Peter Green, Harold Isbell and Peter Jay for quotations, Arthur Cooper, Michael Haslam, Andrew Kimmens, William Radice, Jacob Simon and Edward Watling for their help, and Wing Commander R. F. Pemberton for the index.

Highgate, 1970 **B.R.**

INTRODUCTION

In 1944 T. S. Eliot told the Virgil Society:

> We need to remind ourselves that, as Europe is a whole (and still, in its progressive mutilation and disfigurement, the organism out of which any greater world in harmony must develop), so European literature is a whole, the several members of which cannot flourish, if the same blood-stream does not circulate throughout the whole body. The blood-stream of European literature is Latin and Greek – not as two systems of circulation, but one, for it is through Rome that our parentage in Greece must be traced.
>
> (*What is a Classic?*)

Twenty years later George Steiner gave a more urgent warning:

> From Chaucer to *Sweeney among the Nightingales* much of English poetry has relied on a code of instantaneous recognition. Where the code lapses, where classical literacy becomes, in the strict sense, marginal, a good deal of the poetry may lapse also.
>
> (*Arion* iii, 4, 1964)

Such pronouncements might equally well have been made about most of the artistic achievements of Western civilization, where the two great influences have been the legacy of Greece and Rome, and the Christian Church, which also owed its circulatory system to the Roman Empire.

This reference book is compiled as an attempt to foster classical literacy in its wider sense. It assumes that a few known facts about a creative work, its subject, setting and genesis, as well as its date and author, help rather than hinder our appreciation. The subject of an opera on Orpheus or Dido, the words of a Schubert song about Ganymede or Prometheus are relevant. Visiting any gallery of European art whose works range from late antiquity to the nineteenth-century Impressionists, we must have a minimum knowledge of the Bible and the Christian saints, and be able to answer questions posed by a compelling picture with a laconic title, such as *Danaë* or *The Triumph of Scipio*. If we travel in Greece we really need to know why Apollo was important at Delphi and Delos, or why we keep coming across Lapiths battling with centaurs. There are Roman monuments everywhere: what exactly is a temple of Mithras or the purpose of Hadrian's Wall?

Even at the lowest level, the commonplaces of current metaphor, the classics still seem to be with us whether we welcome them or not. A mere fortnight's check on *The Times* in 1970 produced the following: Purcell was called the English Orpheus, the Prince of Wales a dedicated Thespian, and Queen Christina of Sweden a hyperborean Minerva (though admittedly by a professor of history). A member of the Conservative Party spoke of the years 1951–64 as a Golden Age, and someone else compared Dr Vorster and his African policy to Sisyphus and his stone. A would-be Indian immigrant from Kenya came to the end of her Odyssey, and more recently, the name 'Ulysses factor' was given to the urge men have to attempt the impossible. (This suggests some conflicting assumptions about Odysseus/Ulysses.) During the same fortnight the *Radio Times* showed that the B.B.C. offered a solo aria by Handel called 'Lucrezia'; an 'Overture to *Pygmalion*' by Rameau; *The Gordian Knot Untied* by Purcell; *Pan and Syrinx* by Nielsen; and *The Breasts of Tiresias* by Poulenc.*

Some magic we can't hope to recapture. Too much commentary would silence the music of Milton's lines in *Comus* which for him were singing with Homeric echoes and overtones of Virgil and Ovid. For us they are lovely names, for him the nereids and sea-creatures of antiquity:

> Listen, and appear to us,
> In name of great Oceanus,
> By the earth-shaking Neptune's mace,
> And Tethys' grave majestic pace;
> By hoary Nereus' wrinkled look,
> And the Carpathian wizard's hook;
> By scaly Triton's winding shell,
> And old soothsaying Glaucus' spell;
> By Leucothea's lovely hands,
> And her son that rules the strands;
> By Thetis' tinsel-slippered feet,
> And the songs of Sirens sweet;
> By dead Parthenope's dear tomb,
> And fair Ligea's golden comb,

* A similar check in 1971 was no less rewarding. A Health Visitor's task is still Sisyphean; Lord Hill complained of letters demanding a clean-up of the Augean Stables of the B.B.C.; Mr Wedgwood Benn made a Fabian speech which opened a veritable Pandora's box; and a book reviewer described the late Robert Kennedy as the Marcellus if not the Titus of his country. Meanwhile the B.B.C played the music from Rameau's *Castor et Pollux*, revived von Kleist's *Penthesilea*, and produced Mozart's early *Mitradate Re di Ponto*.

Wherewith she sits on diamond rocks
Sleeking her soft alluring locks . . .

But I am not as pessimistic as some about losing the classics altogether. I think it is more likely that we are beginning to be afraid of doing so, and to revalue and appreciate our heritage. No one is likely to say again that the study of Greek literature 'not only elevates above the vulgar herd, but leads not infrequently to positions of considerable emolument', as was pronounced from the pulpit of Christ Church by Dean Gaisford, the Professor of Greek in Oxford in the early nineteenth century. Science and an expanding universe, and an increased sense of social responsibility, have their proper claims on the young and their educators. But the classical curricula have had a good shake-up, and the classicists lived to see new standards of literary criticism applied to their ancient texts, so that they are coming to see themselves as taking part in a continuously developing process. More people travel, and many of them more intelligently, thanks to an awakened interest in the past which has been helped by television and even the colour supplements; photography has kept pace with improved techniques in archaeology. Schliemann's discovery of Troy is a landmark for all time, but possibly more people knew and cared about Ventris's decipherment of 'Linear B' as Greek, and about the theory that the eruption on the island of Santorini, greater than that of Krakatoa, was the cause of the collapse of the Minoan civilization, or that the fortress of Masada has been shown by recent excavations to be the last stronghold of the Jews against the Romans, just as Josephus describes it.

And so translations abound, both those which are intended to help us with texts, and the creative imitations of the kind Ezra Pound sparked off in his *Homage to Sextus Propertius*, so that a new 'imitation' by Robert Lowell of Aeschylus's *Prometheus* is rightly hailed as an event, and comparative translation is beginning to be taken seriously. Ancient history and politics are being looked at in the light of twentieth-century experience, and rightly so, for however eloquently presented and however influential the metaphysics behind it, Plato's Republic can be judged as a totalitarian state in which apartheid and censorship played an integral part. It may be that, apart from the professional classical scholars on both sides of the Atlantic who were never better, we are going to be brought up on little Latin and less Greek and a second-hand knowledge of ancient civilization, but I don't see this need be necessarily debased. The classics of the 70s will be different from those of the 30s or even of the 50s, but hasn't this always been so? When George Steiner attacks the post-Freudian French playwrights, Anouilh, Cocteau, Gide, Giraudoux and Sartre, for their manipulation of ancient legends for their purposes,* he finds in them frivolity, perversion, and a travesty of symbolism, and he may be right. But I think we should see them as coming near the end of a long line of selectors and adaptors which started with the Greeks themselves; indeed with Homer, who selected what he thought fit for his epics and set aside a great deal of cult myth which the Athenian dramatists seized on and the Alexandrian poets and their Roman counterparts dealt with in their own ways. It is easy to forget that between the Homeric *Hymn to Demeter* and Claudian's *Rape of Proserpine* there is a span of about a thousand years with frequently shifting values. And if we go back a thousand years from today, we are back in the Dark Ages, with so much to come – Dante, Chaucer, *Ovide moralisé*, the Renaissance allegorists, the great Venetian and the baroque artists, Rubens and Poussin and the Neoclassicists, Goethe and Shelley, the Greek ideal of the nineteenth century, *The Golden Bough*. Every generation brings a new attitude to the classics, often one in reaction against a preceding one, and with the accretions of time the subject becomes increasingly complex.

A simple *Who's Who in the Ancient World* begins to be elusive. What it can offer is more like who *was* who – and when and how and why and for whom – since the more a personality has been discussed throughout the ages, the more it becomes apparent that, though there may be a discernible tradition which persists through various modifications, there may also be another interpretation which conflicts with it, or even several interpretations due either to certain moral attitudes prevalent at a particular time or to an individual presentation which is powerful enough to leave its stamp on future impressions. For example, Orpheus to many music-lovers means Gluck, and that means a Eurydice restored to him forever by grace of the gods. But this is not the ancient tradition. Joyce's Ulysses is basically Homer's Odysseus; he is not Sophocles' Odysseus nor Virgil's Ulysses, and still less is he in the tradition which started with Dante and moves through Tennyson to Kazantzakis's mammoth epic and Dallapiccola's opera. This can be true even of historical persons. Marcus Junius Brutus is an obvious instance. The professional historian tries to interpret the known facts about one of the leaders of the conspiracy which murdered Julius Caesar in 44 B.C. He is unlikely to think of him as Shake-

* *The Death of Tragedy*, p. 324 ff.

speare's Brutus, who is also Plutarch's idealist and liberator and generally accepted as such in popular imagination. And there still remains Dante's Brutus, consigned to the lowest circle of Hell along with Cassius and Judas Iscariot as an arch-traitor and destroyer of the appointed secular order, just as Judas was the enemy of the divine order. This is not a political or historical judgement, and has to be seen in the context of Dante's purpose; Brutus has become a symbol of treachery and subversion.

It is a commonplace to talk of the treasures of antiquity, though difficult to know how else to describe what has enriched so many generations. Even with all our losses – so many marble statues crumbled to dust in the lime-kilns, every Greek painting destroyed, seventy plays by Aeschylus lost, every poem by Gallus gone and most of Sappho and Ennius – the treasures are still rich and worth seeking:

> It may be we shall touch the Happy Isles
> And see the great Achilles, whom we knew.
> Tho' much is taken, much abides; and tho'
> We are not now that strength which in old days
> Moved earth and heaven; that which we are, we are...

And we are in fact the inheritors of a legacy from Greece and Rome which has come down to us in the form of artefacts which are of interest and beauty in themselves because they bear the stamp of the masters who created them. Our judgement of the Roman poet Statius, for instance, is coloured by the discovery that he was so much admired by Chaucer, and chosen by Dante to replace Virgil as a guide on the last stage of the journey to Paradise; he looks as different in this setting as a Roman cameo mounted on an early crucifix. And though a great painter is great whatever his subject, and in that sense it is immaterial whether Titian paints a Holy Family or an Actaeon, I think we understand more about Titian if we know that he took a rather horrific episode in Greek mythology and made a magnificent picture out of it, and surely we look at Actaeon's legend with a new concern if we wonder why it has always meant much to sculptors and painters through the ages, Titian among them.

Some of these problems raise questions which range too far for any one book to answer, and all that is possible is to offer one person's pointers to some of the classical names which have kept their vitality for some reason – as a symbol for a poet, a subject which caught the imagination of a dramatist, a painter or a composer; as an author who will always be read or the builder of a monument still standing; or even as part of a metaphor which is now no more than an unconscious assumption on which western literacy still rests.

Our legacy starts, as it did for the classical Greeks, with Homer. He made his two epics out of themes taken from a great mass of saga and legend, some of it going back to the Mycenean Age, which collapsed before the Dorian invasions about 500 years before he created the *Iliad* and the *Odyssey*. His heroes are armed with the leather body-shields and the bronze thrusting-swords of the pre-Iron Age, and there are many echoes from a distant past. Old Nestor has a Mycenean-style gold cup, and in his youth had fought for Theseus against the centaurs. The tale of Meleager and the Calydonian Boar-hunt is told as ancient history, and so is the story of Bellerophon, who is without his winged horse Pegasus. Homer's version of the fate of Oedipus is also different from that of the dramatists, and Clytemnestra is a woman to be pitied rather than condemned. Nor does he let himself be sidetracked into recording irrelevant details of an abnormal nature. Nestor twice mentions the Molione twins whom he met in a chariot race and again in a battle where they were rescued by Poseidon, but Homer is not interested in saying that they were a celebrated pair of Siamese twins: this we know from more than one early geometric vase-painting, where they are always shown with one large body-shield protecting them both. There is no Minotaur in Crete, and the labyrinth which was depicted on the shield Hephaestus made for Achilles is a dancing floor 'which Daedalus made for Ariadne of the lovely hair in the wide town of Knossos', where there are ritual dances and acrobatic displays by young men who are recognizably Minoan. This Ariadne is the Minoan Lady of the Labyrinth, a goddess of prime importance, someone quite different from the Ariadne of classical mythology, where the emphasis has moved to the god Dionysus.

When Aristotle in the *Poetics* gives his highest praise to Homer, for creating epics with an internal unity of structure, he says that the *Iliad* and the *Odyssey* could not be used as source material by the tragedians because they are complete dramas in themselves. He then names the loosely constructed episodic sagas which incorporated what Homer rejected and are known to us only from such references and occasional quotations, and the fact that the dramatists found their plots in them: the *Cypria*, *Little Iliad*, *Sack of Troy*, *Returns* and several others now grouped under the name of the Epic Cycle. (The best of them in Aristotle's view was the *Thebais*, the source of all the plays about the ill-starred House of Labdacus.) Hesiod in his *Theogony* had tried to coordinate myths about the gods, and early poets like Stesichorus (who provided Euripides with his variant treatment of Helen) and the Homeric Hymns add to the literary tradition of gods and heroes which is also in general the artistic tradition. But there was always the cult tradition which was very variable and localized, and still alive in Pausanias's day; indeed his *Guide to Greece* is the best guide we have to rituals and shrines of local heroes, to which belong Tree-Helen, Duck-Penelope and Demeter with a horse's head. There were also the powerful mystery rites, of whose close-guarded secrets we have only hints.

It is impossible to reconcile the humanized literary treatments with the cult rituals, and the Greeks themselves did not attempt to do so. Nor were their attitudes uniform. There was certainly articulate criticism of the amorality of the Olympian gods as early as Xenophanes, in the late sixth century B.C. Yet this was the heyday of the Delphic Oracle, and the archaic statues have a simplicity and strength which is never quite the same in the classical fifth century. A small bronze centaur dating from 540 B.C. [1]* convinces me as the work of someone who saw a centaur as a genuine living creature, something natural, however strange; not as a tutor to heroes or embattled with Lapiths as a symbol of primitive life which Hellenism had overcome. Some of the early black-figure vases have the same immediacy; Odysseus blinds Polyphemus, Perseus beheads Medusa, and the facts are recorded without doubts. The poetry of the period is too fragmentary for comparison, but I think the gods still walk alive among men in Pindar, later in date though not in spirit.

The intellectual ferment of the fifth century throws out questions of every kind. Apollo stands as a true god of power and authority on the west pediment of the temple at Olympia in a rather cold and terrifying way, and one wishes that the gods and goddesses from the Parthenon were in a better state for comparison. The frieze in the Elgin Marbles is a superbly conceived sacrificial procession for a great civic and religious festival, but we can't know now what Athene meant to the average man. Pericles who planned the building of the Parthenon was accused of having atheist friends; but he was also the friend of the dramatist Sophocles, a deeply religious man. Euripides and Aristophanes are paradoxes in themselves; it is Euripides who has been called the rationalist and sceptic and yet gives us *The Bacchae*, with all the Dionysiac forces unleashed, and Aristophanes

* Numbers in square brackets indicate illustrations throughout.

whose irreverence seems to spring from a deep emotional belief in the old gods. For the most part, the gods in their statues are human, and in the Attic red-figure vases they can even be domesticated among the conversation pieces of symposia and athletes' dressing-rooms.

The sculptured relief of Orpheus, Eurydice and Hermes of the late fifth century [2], known from several Roman copies, is perhaps typical in its ambiguity. The relaxed pose of the figures, the delicately traced drapery of the clothing recalls the Parthenon frieze and some of the tomb monuments; Orpheus has his conventional Thracian cap and lyre and Hermes his broad messenger's hat. The sculptor has chosen not to give him his traditional winged shoes and caduceus – we don't know why. And why is Hermes there at all? In the common version of the legend Orpheus goes alone to the Underworld in search of Eurydice and brings her back alone. He is forbidden to turn and look at her on the way back, he does so, loses her for ever and is distraught with grief. But these lovers seem to show a wistful resignation, which suggests that the scene represents a different literary tradition in which Orpheus was told that he could have her back but only for a day. The day has ended, Hermes has come to claim her for the shades, the lovers' gesture is that of a final and anticipated farewell.

The emotion is only lightly indicated here, but in the next century there is a great surge forward into the representation of movement and strong feeling. Though the Hellenic humanized gods become the rather sentimentalized Hellenistic ones – the Hermes of Praxiteles gives way to the Apollo Belvedere – this is the time of the Laocoön, the Niobids, the Winged Victory. There is more purely decorative use of the human form and its swirling draperies: in the Nereid Monument, for example, or the sculpture from Pergamum. The vase-paintings pose many of Keats's questions:

> What leaf-fring'd legend haunts about thy shape
> Of deities or of mortals or of both,
> In Tempe or the dales of Arcady?
> What men or gods are these? What maidens loth?
> What mad pursuit? What struggle to escape?
> What pipes and timbrels? What wild ecstasy?

At the same time there is greater sophistication among the poets, and the kind of erudition we find in Callimachus, for which Alexandria is famous, as well as the literary romanticism of Apollonius Rhodius. There are still perfect short lyrics among the epigrams of the *Greek Anthology*, but there is also a great deal of expert, decorative verse. There begins to be a feeling of a need for a younger stimulus, and this came with the Roman conquest of Greece.

All the accumulated past had its impact on Rome from the mid first century B.C.; an inherited civilization is like a snowball, growing and growing as it rolls on. *Graecia capta ferum victorem cepit*,* but we should not underestimate what the Romans themselves contributed. They are known as the trans nitters – Greek philosophy through Cicero and Seneca – and the copyists – all those Roman marble copies of Greek bronzes which exhaust the footsore visitor to European galleries. We should in fact be forever grateful for these copies. Without them we should know none of the statues of Polyclitus and Myron, and Hellenistic painting would be as completely lost as that of Polygnotus and Zeuxis if we had not the superb frescoes of Herculaneum, Pompeii and Rome. They were perhaps great craftsmen rather than great artists, and part of their contribution is an inheritance from yet another civilization, that of the Etruscans who were deeply conscious of grave ritual and the needs of the dead. In the Romans this produced the splendid tombs and decorated sarcophagi which passed on into the Christian Church, and also the fine realistic portrait busts of the dead and the famous, which put an end to Hellenistic stereotyped prettiness. They brought *gravitas*, a sense of responsibility, *iustitia*, a sense of justice, *pietas*, a man's duty to his country, his gods, his dead and his living dependants: these were qualities which would hardly have been understood in Greece, and which created that triumph of organization and communications, the Roman Empire. And for all its ironing-out of democratic liberties, the Empire did make it possible for Hellenism in its widest sense to develop for several centuries and eventually to reach us today, bringing with it the Latin language and some great works of literature. I don't think anyone now would compare Virgil adversely with Homer; we see him more as Dante and Milton did, *il nostro maggior poeta*. Lucretius too, struggling to find Latin words for Greek concepts, Catullus, Propertius, Horace with his self-deprecatory wisdom, Juvenal and his *saeva indignatio* could only have been bred in Rome.

What of the gods and heroes? The whole Olympian hierarchy was taken over and grafted where possible on to the indigenous Italian gods. How much it meant either to the articulate intelligentsia or to the simpler

* 'Greece enslaved made a slave of her rough conqueror.' Horace, *Epistles* II.1.156.

country people is again impossible to know. Tibullus can write wistfully of the rural gods, and one suspects that the family deities, the Lares and Penates, and the odd festivals and rituals described by Ovid in the *Fasti* had a warmer emotional meaning than the amours of Olympians which he set out with such expertise in the *Metamorphoses*. And there were the secret Mysteries too, as in Greece, of Cybele, Isis and Bacchus, so that by far the most disturbing work of Roman art is the great frieze of the Bacchic initiation rites in the House of the Mysteries, Pompeii. But the silver Mildenhall Dish from the British Museum [3] seems to me to tell more of the pagan world which was coming to an end than any other work of art. It is worked by a superb craftsman, and it dates from about A.D. 350, when the Empire was already officially proclaimed Christian under Constantine the Great. It was found among a hoard of imported silver objects, all beautiful, in Suffolk, which is still a rural corner of England, and was then an obscure part of a remote and never thoroughly Romanized province of the Empire, at a time when the frontiers were already under pressure. And it is in the long tradition of Hellenistic art, with the grave bearded head of Neptune in the centre, surrounded by the tritons and floating nereids, the dolphins and horses of the sea, while all round the rim are the familiar figures of the Bacchic procession, the maenads and satyrs, the dancing nymphs and piping shepherd.

It was to be another hundred years before Attila and his Huns sacked Rome, and the Western Empire fell into the hands of rival claimants, few of whom were as appreciative of what they found in Italy as Theodoric the Ostrogoth. After Justinian's fight to recover it was spent, the West was almost entirely cut off from the Byzantine Empire of the East. This was the period, rightly named the Dark Ages, of break-up and stagnation and illiteracy, in which the flame of continuity was kept alight only by the Catholic Church. The early Christian Fathers had a sort of love–hate relationship with the ancient world, St Jerome fretting lest he were a better Ciceronian than a Christian, St Gregory said to have had whole libraries destroyed in case pagan works distracted men's minds from the holy scriptures. But the Latin language was faithfully preserved as the only means of civilized communication, and in the monasteries manuscripts were lovingly copied and recopied. Some of the fourth- and fifth-century manuscripts of Virgil belonging to the Vatican are illustrated in recognizably Roman style, and the manuscripts of Terence were copied with similar classical illustrations until about 1200. The first real dawning of the light came in 800 with the crowning of Charlemagne in Rome as the head of a new Holy Roman Empire. This is the period of the Carolingian revival, and it is to Alcuin, whom Charlemagne had brought over from York, and the scribes Alcuin taught that we owe the majority of the Latin texts we have now, for they are copies of the beautiful clear Carolingian script. Charlemagne also had his own chapel at Aix-la-Chapelle (Aachen) modelled on the church of San Vitale which he had admired in Ravenna.

There was another long period of stagnation, but by the twelfth century people educated in the monastic schools knew something of Virgil, Horace, Ovid, Lucan, Statius and Terence, and Seneca's prose, some Cicero and Livy and Sallust. A scholar like John of Salisbury had read Petronius; Abélard could also quote Juvenal, and give the references to classical allusions in Jerome. Hélöise reluctantly took the veil with a cry of self-reproach which is a quotation from Pompey's wife Cornelia in Lucan's *Pharsalia*. At the same time Ovid and Virgil were wizards locally in Salmona and Naples, and the pagan myths are illustrated in some odd ways. What was lacking was a sense of historical perspective, though a 'historian' like Geoffrey of Monmouth does try very hard to account for the generations between the British and their Trojan ancestor Brutus. Where literary texts were copied and illustrated by monks who had never seen a pagan work of art, the ancient world appears in medieval guise, Thisbe sitting by a Gothic tomb, Mars in full armour on a charger, and in an illustration [4] from a fourteenth-century French translation of Livy, there are four engaging contemporary scenes, one of Aeneas and his men landing in Italy, complete with crossbows and standard bearing his name, another of Romulus and Remus tightly swaddled and conveniently labelled, the building of Rome in the style of a turreted early French château by masons with picks and trowels and a sort of primitive scaffolding, and a battle of Sabines and Romans in full contemporary armour. Still odder are some of the representations of the gods whose names had been given by the Greeks to constellations and planets and who had then been taken over by the Arabs and given an oriental appearance. As the Middle Ages knew of Aristotle and Ptolemy only through Latin translations of Arabic versions, there are examples of medieval copies of works on astronomy with the gods reproduced in orientalized form.

An even more powerful influence was that of astrology, in which the planets and stars were believed to govern men's lives. The Greeks had taken it from the Babylonians in Hellenistic times, and by the end of the Republic it was important in Rome; there are many references in the satirists to the casting of horoscopes and the fears they preyed on. It determined the form of ancient medicine through its emphasis on 'humours', and it was a major opposition to the teaching of the early Church, for if our future is determined at birth by the stars, it cannot wholly be subject to God's will. It allowed nothing to man's efforts – a pair of star-crossed lovers is doomed from the start. By this time the planets were wholly identified with the gods after whom they were named, and so when the early Christian Fathers are concerned with expelling 'demons' they often mean the pagan gods whose evil influences were felt through their astrological powers, and against whom men looked to professional magicians to help them. To some extent the Church reached a compromise by teaching that Venus, Mars, Saturn and the other planetary powers could only be signs of God's intentions, and the gods achieve respectability among the representations of the Virtues and Sciences in Giotto's Campanile in Florence. Here again their appearance is generally medieval.

Throughout the Middle Ages there was also a tendency to present the pagan gods as symbols of the vices, Venus in particular as Sensuality or Lewdness, and Mars as Fury; it also needed more than a Hrotsvitha, the tenth-century nun who rewrote Terence in Christian terms, to make a great deal of Ovid acceptable to the pious. The answer came in the vast French poem of about 1320, *Ovide moralisé*, and the Latin prose *Ovid moralisatus* of 1342, on which was based a shortened handbook on the gods which was used by Chaucer, among other authors. Not that Chaucer has any use for the book's elaborate explanations, such as the one which turned Daphne into the Virgin Mary, loved by him who is the true Sun, who crowns himself with a laurel to indicate that he put on the body of his mother. But anything which was in one of these moralizing works was thereby purged of immorality, and *Ovide moralisé* was doubtless the reason why Ariadne and Philomela appear in *The Legend of Good Women*, and Alcestis there has been noted to share some features with the Virgin Mary.

If we except Dante, who is so great a poet that he could make his own use of the ancient world to present the reality of his Christian vision in terms which are both Virgilian and symbolic, we could perhaps say that medieval man's attitude to the classics was confused and often fearful, that what he read he could not interpret as belonging to a wholly different world, and what he saw (outside Italy) was likely to be only coins and cameos, which were in demand as amulets, or an occasional mosaic or statue left by the Romans which might well be nude and a sin to look at. The schoolmen of the universities could take examples from Cicero and Seneca, just as Chaucer and Gower can select an edifying tale and tell it well, but classical antiquity was something that should be useful, and useful only if it was somehow made safe, either by transformation into a medieval image or by moralizing allegory. What makes the Renaissance proper different from all the earlier 'renascences' is that its humanists saw antiquity in better perspective, from a distance, with nostalgia even, and not necessarily with any thought of utilizing it for moral purposes.

There was no uneasiness about the early leaders of the Renaissance. The feeling of rebirth, of escape from the stereotyped Byzantine discipline in painting, and of breaking away from the fetters of medieval scholasticism, which started in Italy with Petrarch and Boccaccio in the later fourteenth century and spread steadily across western Europe to gather in writers as different as Machiavelli and Erasmus, and artists as far removed from each other as Botticelli and Jan van Eyck, Raphael and Dürer, gave the Renaissance its name. It was a long time before its brightness faded. Petrarch died only about fifty years after Dante, but his eager search for classical manuscripts, his infectious enthusiasm for discovery of a new world in antiquity, is something totally different from Dante's steady conviction, strengthened by his emotions as an Italian, that there was a thread of continuity linking the classical past with the Christian present. And it was not only a rebirth, it was a return to Nature and a vindication of Man as a rational being sharing in life on earth with other living things. It was a time when men worked for men as their patrons; the great families like the Medici in Florence, the Gonzagas in Mantua and the d'Estes in Urbino could offer as much – and more in the way of independence – as the Church.

Yet it was also a time during which Galileo clashed with the Church and Erasmus worked all his life to bring the classics into the service of Christianity but died knowing he had failed. It is difficult perhaps for us to enter imaginatively into the tensions created by the confrontation of the Church's teaching with the new humanism. Ovid was still the sourcebook for the painters, but the pagan gods and goddesses had shed their medieval symbols, and most of their clothes as well. Somehow pagan nudity had to be made acceptable, and also the use of pagan images generally, even when classically draped or in contemporary dress. When Sigismondo Malatesta had the church of San Francesco in Rimini (the Tempio Malatestiano) decorated with reliefs of the planetary gods in classical form among the saints and angels, he was accused by Pope Pius II of filling it with pagan work so that it looked more like a temple of heathen worshippers of 'demons' than a Christian church (*ut non tam Christianorum quam infidelium daemones adorantium templum esse videretur*).

There will always be rare characters as strong as Michelangelo, who was a match for the equally masterful Pope Julius II, and great individualists like Piero di Cosimo who could withdraw into his private eccentricity and continue to paint the mythological past as he saw it. But a great many artists at this time were glad to replace *Ovide moralisé* by Boccaccio's *Genealogy of the Gods* and similar manuals of mythology, where the emphasis was on allegory. The images from antiquity become much more acceptable when they represent the virtues and vices, and this accounts for the many pictures of Mars and Venus (War and Hatred yielding to Love), Battles of Love and Chastity (Venus versus Diana), and Apollo with the Muses. In the case of the Florentine painters, a further strong influence was the neoplatonist teaching in the Platonic Academy of Florence by such philosophers as Marsilio Ficino, Politian and Lorenzo Valla. Legends like that of Ariadne, Daphne, Marsyas and Psyche could all be interpreted as the progress of the soul towards divine love. Here again then we have interpretations of the classical past according to an individual's reaction to the spirit of his own age.

An extreme example is Botticelli's *Primavera* [5], perhaps the best known picture of the early Renaissance, and the most discussed. We know that it was a companion picture to the less puzzling Birth of Venus, and that both literally and figuratively, Venus Genetrix is the central figure.* At the right is a scene taken directly from Ovid's *Fasti*, book 5; Zephyr, the wind of Spring, pursues the nymph Chloris who is in the act of fading away with flowers coming out on her breath, until she is transformed into Flora, herald of Spring, stepping firmly on to the earth. Symbolically this could be Beauty created by Passion working on Chastity. The trio is balanced by the Three Graces, who dance formally, their arms raised to heaven; they traditionally represent Pleasure, Chastity and Beauty, and it is to be noted that the vigorous blindfold Cupid above directs his burning arrow directly at Chastity, who looks withdrawn and sad, gazing wistfully in the

* This interpretation is mainly that of Edgar Wind in *Pagan Mysteries in the Renaissance*, pp. 113 ff.

direction of Mercury. Now he is the recognized leader of the Graces, but here he is aloof, looking upwards, and in the original picture it can be seen that he is dispelling some wisps of clouds in the trees with the tip of his staff. This too is allegorical, for the Neoplatonists saw Mercury as the mediator between the aspirations of the human mind and the divine wisdom. This the hesitant Grace can attain only through submitting to the initiation of Love (Cupid); and over the whole Venus presides, hand raised either in permission or as a check on Cupid's ardour. The whole picture then is an allegory of her power over Celestial and Earthly Love.

It may well be said that thousands see this picture every year in Florence and thousands more know it in reproduction without bothering about any of this, and perhaps explanations are less important in the case of a picture as great as the *Primavera*. But this sort of intellectual treatment of the classics can be very frustrating in lesser painters – even Bronzino's *Venus and Cupid and Folly and Time* in the National Gallery can be irritating if one is too conscious that a key is needed to unlock its problems. Fortunately the Venetian painters were less concerned with elaborations of philosophic allegory. Titian's paintings of Danaë, for instance, don't look at all like a soul about to be redeemed by divine love, and though we are told that Tintoretto's classical series in the Doges' Palace is intended to glorify the Republic of Venice, we don't really have to think of the Cyclopes in his *Vulcan's Forge* as making arms for her service.

Nothing can go on being a rebirth or remain new for ever, and inevitably as pagan antiquity became more widely known through printed books and the recovery of such classical works of art as the Laocoön, it lost its bloom and became more of a convention. This is clearly seen in the Elizabethan masques (the counterpart of Italian *trionfi*) and the facility of a lot of Elizabethan love-poetry and madrigal verse, as well as in the countless decorative frescoes and ceilings of the Italian palazzi and the French châteaux, which are often great baroque mythologies, or apotheoses of royalty and nobility with elaborate classical trappings. From the sixteenth century onwards what I have called the rolling snowball of inherited antiquity is more like a solid mountain which is simply *there* – to be climbed. And as all the educationalists of the western world until very recently have been primarily concerned with leading their charges up the lower slopes, these have been trodden into well-marked paths. A little higher comes the reward, the pleasant walks and vistas enjoyed by cultivated men, nothing more arduous than the Arcadia or Parnassus of the eighteenth century. But there have been the great climbers too, who have brought their genius and energy to the task of scaling the formidable heights, and it is from them that we can learn what the ancient world could mean at different periods to men who chose to make it their inspiration. There is Ronsard, greatest of the sixteenth-century Pléiade, and Racine; Titian, Bernini and Palladio; Rubens and Poussin, Gluck and Berlioz, Goethe and Rilke, Milton and Dryden and Gibbon – everyone has someone who has given him an insight into some aspect of antiquity, and the names I quote are only a selection from my personal preferences.

Rubens, who lived from 1577 to 1640, was surely the greatest of the baroque artists, breathing life into everything he worked on, portraits, religious paintings, landscapes of the Flemish countryside, as well as the superb classical subjects which he painted in Antwerp after he had seen the Titians and Raphaels in Madrid and the other painters of the High Renaissance in Italy. For he was also an active diplomat in the service of the Spanish governors of the Netherlands; he was twice married, both times happily; and he was a sincere Catholic who refused to discriminate between his religious and his secular paintings, and took a firm stand against Protestant gloom and Spanish-Catholic asceticism alike. At a time when the baroque painters in Italy are lost in clouds of symbolism and the classics are often no more than a stage setting for court ballets and masques, Rubens paints a picture like his *Rape of the Daughters of Leucippus* [6], a masterpiece of sensuous joy and at the same time a balanced composition which is firmly controlled. It is moreover a subject which was unrepresented in Renaissance painting, so it is wholly original. Those two delicious girls, Hilaera and Phoebe, are being carried off by the Dioscuri, Castor and Pollux, a pair of magnificent young men, and though 'rape' is an ugly word now, there is no cruelty here; the girls look startled but not seriously alarmed, and the little Cupid smiles as he clings precariously to the bridle. The horses rear up into a cloud-swept northern sky, but they paw the earth which is part of a landscape as solid as that of the Château de Steen.

Rubens of course belongs to his age, but what he brings to bear on the classical past is the experience of a complete and balanced man who was also a painter of genius. Poussin, who died twenty-five years after Rubens, is a more prolific painter of classical subjects and a great one in a very different way. He is an artist of strict logic and intellectual discipline, and also of heroic ideals; his series on the Plutarchian story of Phocion, for instance, is the counterpart of the dramas of Corneille. He places the myths in an Arcadia which is entirely his own, and seems to look at antiquity with a nostalgia for lost innocence. The *Bacchanalian Revel before a Herm of Pan* [7] in the National Gallery of London is not an interpretation of the Dionysiac spirit as the Greeks knew it, not even as Titian expressed it in an equally famous picture, and there is nothing sinister about Pan in the form of a bust on a pillar. But the formal dignity of the so-called revellers, controlled by Poussin's personal views of harmony of composition and pictorial architecture, has given us a Golden Age which is a perpetual revelation and delight. Hazlitt puts it well, in a comment on Wordsworth's admiration of Poussin which illuminates both painter and poet:

> We have known him enlarge with a noble intelligence and enthusiasm on Nicolas Poussin's fine landscape-compositions, pointing out the unity of design that pervades them, the super-intending mind, the imaginative principle that brings all to bear on the same end; and declaring he would not give a rush for any landscape that did not express the time of day, the climate, the period of the world it was meant to illustrate, or had not this character of *wholeness* in it.
>
> ('Mr Wordsworth' in *The Spirit of the Age*)

Poussin's natural complement is his contemporary Claude, who lived and worked in Rome most of his life and gave classical titles to many of his greatest paintings – *Ascanius Shooting the Stag*, *Aeneas at Delos*, *Acis and Galatea*—though the imagined romantic landscapes matter more than the delicate foreground figures, and everything is subordinated to the pervading golden light. It is of Claude that Kenneth Clark writes:*

> The world of his imagination is so clear and consistent that nothing obtrudes, nothing is commonplace, nothing (least of all) is done for effect. As with Racine's plays, which give the same feeling of devotion to an ideal whole, this is not so much the result of self-discipline – an act of will – as of a natural habit of mind.

Preoccupation with light and its effects is what makes Turner the spiritual descendant of Claude, and it was perhaps because Turner admired both Poussin and Claude in youth that a good many of his paintings have romantically conceived classical subjects; there are several on Aeneas and Dido and the building of Carthage, for example, and *Ulysses Deriding Polyphemus* was reproduced to hang in countless English drawing-rooms. But Turner was first and last a painter, with no real literary interests or classical education, so I have never felt that he has reinterpreted antiquity; any more than the English pre-Raphaelite painters did in their carefully

* *Landscape into Art*, p. 64.

contrived classical paintings which are indistinguishable from their romantic scenes of medieval chivalry. And the eighteenth-century portrait painters used classical names light-heartedly in a way which does no more than indicate the fashionable tastes of the time. George Romney, for instance, painted Lady Hamilton in various guises, as a bacchante, as Cassandra, and as Circe.

In the literary tradition, throughout the seventeenth and eighteenth centuries, the Latin classics predominate, moulding the shape of English prose through Cicero, providing satirists with models in Horace and Juvenal, filling the lines of the poets with allusions which can range from the artificial and conventional to what can still illuminate or delight. We can pick and choose from the anthologies:

When we have run our passions' heat
Love hither makes his best retreat:
The gods, that mortal beauty chase,
Still in a tree did end their race:
Apollo hunted Daphne so,
Only that she might laurel grow:
And Pan did after Syrinx speed
Not as a nymph, but for a reed.

And here is Venus Genetrix again:

Lo! where the rosy-bosom'd Hours,
  Fair Venus' train, appear,
Disclose the long-expecting flowers
  And wake the purple year!

Or there is Arion's escape from drowning, and perhaps Leucothea's help to Odysseus after his shipwreck:

Eight times emerging from the flood
She mew'd to every watery God
  Some speedy aid to send:—
No Dolphin came, no Nereid stirr'd,
Nor cruel Tom nor Susan heard –
  A favourite has no friend!*

But if we look for a poet whose natural nourishment was drawn from the classical past and who could somehow integrate the ancient world with his profound Christian beliefs, rather in the same sort of way that Rubens

* Andrew Marvell, *Thoughts in a Garden*; William Collins, *Ode on the Spring*; Thomas Gray, *Ode on the Death of a Favourite Cat, Drowned in a Tub of Goldfishes.*

does, I think we always come back to Milton. No later poet seems to use the language of antiquity to give positive shape to his vision as Milton could. His early works of course are full of classical echoes – his masque *Arcades*, *Comus* which deals with the old theme of the triumph of Chastity over Vice in an Arcadian setting, *L'Allegro* and *Il Penseroso* with their references to Orpheus and Eurydice:

> Such strains as would have won the ear
> Of Pluto to have quite set free
> His half-regained Eurydice.

Lycidas is perhaps the most inspired poem in the pastoral genre in any language, and it is a commonplace to say that *Samson Agonistes* is the nearest approach we have to a Greek tragedy. It is *Paradise Lost*, the epic in which Milton set out to 'justify the ways of God to man' which comes so close to the ancient world as Milton saw it. The beautiful stylized sentences are often Latin in structure, the cadences Virgilian, the Homeric similes often, but not always, taken from the classics, and yet there is something deeper than that, which Hazlitt discerned when he wrote that 'Milton's learning has the effect of intuition', and on his intensity of imagination that 'the strongest and best proof of this, as a characteristic power of his mind, is that the persons of Adam and Eve, of Satan, etc. are always accompanied, in our imagination, with the grandeur of the naked figure; they convey to us the ideas of sculpture'. Of Satan, Hazlitt* says 'the poet has not in all this given us a mere shadowy outline; the strength is equal to the magnitude of the conception. The Achilles of Homer is not more distinct; the Titans were not more vast; Prometheus chained to his rock was not a more terrific example of suffering and of crime.'

After Milton we have another fine imaginative classicist in Dryden, but throughout the so-called Augustan Age of the eighteenth century there was an increasing emphasis on precision and refinement, and a conviction of maturity and superiority to all previous ages which inevitably bred critics of anything considered uncouth or eccentric. Dr Johnson in his English Dictionary set out to provide a canon of correct language, and so he ignored some of the Elizabethan verbal extravagances which would be unworthy of his times. In his *Lives of the Poets* he censured Dryden for 'freedom' and poor taste, Donne for 'ruggedness', and Milton's *Lycidas* 'because the diction is harsh, the rhymes uncertain, the numbers un-

* 'On Shakespeare and Milton' in *Lectures on the English Poets.*

pleasing'. 'Poetic diction' set a standard of words which should be neither too familiar and vulgar nor too remote and obscure. It can be seen at its best in the poetry of Pope, but it could also be used to produce a great many heroic couplets whose facility and polish are their weakness. A select use of the Latin authors was the accepted basis of a gentleman's education, as we see clearly in the letters to his son by the fastidious and cultivated Lord Chesterfield. He is too intelligent a man not to realize that these should be reinforced by some history and modern languages, especially French, if the Graces are to be cherished, for 'Since barbarism drove them out of Greece and Rome, they seem to have taken refuge in France, where their temples are numerous, and their worship the established one' (18 November 1748). But Shakespeare is not recommended, since his beauties are marred by 'extravagances and nonsense'.

In the end such restrictions were no longer bearable, and there was a violent reaction against both poetic diction and the whole convention of classical imagery. Coleridge was eternally grateful to an enlightened schoolmaster of Christ's Hospital who taught him English composition:

... He showed no mercy to phrase, metaphor, or image, unsupported by a sound sense, or where the same sense might have been conveyed with equal force and dignity in plainer words. Lute, harp and lyre, Muse, Muses, and inspirations, Pegasus, Parnassus, and Hippocrene were all an abomination to him. In fancy I can almost hear him now, exclaiming 'Harp? Harp? Lyre? Pen and ink, boy, you mean! Muse, boy, Muse? Your nurse's daughter, you mean! Pierian spring? Oh aye! the cloister-pump, I suppose!' (*Biographia Literaria*, Chapter 1).

Keats has a passionate outburst against the English followers of the French purist Boileau:

The winds of heaven blew, the ocean roll'd
Its gathering waves – ye felt it not. The blue
Bared its eternal bosom, and the dew
Of summer night collected still to make
The morning precious: Beauty was awake!
Why were ye not awake? But ye were dead
To things ye knew not of, – were closely wed
To musty laws lined out with wretched rule
And compass vile; so that ye taught a school
Of dolts to smooth, inlay, and clip, and fit,
Till, like the certain wands of Jacob's wit,
Their verses tallied.

(*Sleep and Poetry*)

Wordsworth's attack on 'gaudiness and inane phraseology' and defence of his 'selection of the real language of men in a state of vivid sensation' in his *Preface to the Lyrical Ballads* (second edition, 1800) is famous as a manifesto of the English Romantic movement, especially in the form it took among the Lakeland poets, Wordsworth and Coleridge and their followers, whose inspiration was their idealized view of Nature, and their worship of natural, not man-made, beauty. In one sense they were the spiritual descendants of the French philosopher Rousseau, but in their rejection of the classics as a source of inspiration as well as a standard of diction and sentence structure, unlike Byron, Keats and Shelley, they put themselves outside the main European stream. True, Wordsworth's belief in the harmony of man and nature and God was essentially that of the Roman Stoics, whose teaching, especially in Seneca, he knew and admired, and his mature views on duty and self-discipline were also stoical. Coleridge owed some of his rather rambling metaphysics to his interest in Neoplatonism. But they set their faces against the long tradition of using classical subjects and symbols, as part of their search for natural simplicity, and they had their counterparts in English art in Turner, Constable, Morland, the Norwich School and a long line of lesser watercolourists.

On the continent *le grand siècle*, which created Corneille and Racine, moved over into the eighteenth century with its more frivolous aristocratic tastes. Similarly in place of the great baroque painters Rubens and Poussin we have the rather fragile gaiety of a painter like Watteau, whose *Embarkation for Cythera* is a masterpiece of sensibility but classical only in name (Cythera is the island of Venus and love), and the more carefree, less disciplined rococo painters, the greatest of whom is the Venetian Tiepolo. Rococo decorative art never appealed to the English, and by mid-century reaction came in France with the Age of Enlightenment, and its artistic expression in the movement later known as Neoclassicism. This was essentially a search for simplicity in place of novelty and virtuosity, the 'noble simplicity' of Gluck instead of the display of vocal agility in opera, a more puritanical morality to replace cynicism and flippancy, and a stoic and reasoned discipline to put against the teachings of a Church which seemed to stifle original thinking and had lost its hold. It had a very marked effect on the way men interpreted antiquity, for in seeking for a natural rather than a sophisticated code of morals many believed they found it in the virtues of the old Roman Republic as set out by Plutarch in his *Lives* *of Famous Men*. David's *Oath of the Horatii*, which was painted in 1785, only fifteen years after the death of Tiepolo, is always quoted as a landmark in art history. For centuries pagan mythology had been of prime importance. As Hugh Honour puts it:*

> The gods of Greece and Rome had been condemned as demons or converted into saints by early Christians, rescued as links with Imperial Roman grandeur at the court of Charlemagne, allegorized by the schoolmen of the Middle Ages, metamorphosed into symbols by Renaissance humanists, and drummed into service of Church and State in the Baroque period. By the time they reached the eighteenth century they were fit for nothing better than a voluptuous dream world...

Now the Age of Enlightenment proceeded to explain them away as inventions or symbols, and the Neoclassicists on the whole ignored them. Moreover, if the Roman Republic stood for the simple virtues, the more sophisticated Empire was looked upon as decadent, a view which was reinforced by the discovery of the wall-paintings of Herculaneum and Pompeii in all their sensuous abandon, to say nothing of the erotica still to be seen only on request in the Naples museum or behind locked doors at Pompeii. Here we have a good instance of the way people have often shut their eyes to what they disliked in antiquity and looked only for what suited their presuppositions. These paintings may be copies of Hellenistic originals, but no one now who has seen them *in situ* or in the museums of Naples can fail to admire their technique and subtlety of colour. Yet very few took notice of them at the time, and even the abstract wall-decorations of Nero's Golden House and the houses of Herculaneum and Pompeii were not accepted for some years. They then set the short-lived fashion of the Etruscan style in classically simple furniture and in English pottery from Josiah Wedgwood's factory, which he called Etruria. After Robert Adam visited Diocletian's great palace at Spalato (Split) and published his drawings in 1764, many English stately homes had an 'Etruscan Room' designed by him or his imitators.

But even more influential than the Neoclassicists' admiration for the virtues of republican Rome was their dedication to Ideal Beauty in the Platonic sense, a theory which had been applied to art as far back as Zeuxis and the elder Pliny. It was now taught by the German critic and dramatist Lessing and the art historian Winckelmann, some of whose judgements we now find very surprising. Lessing could see the *Laocöon* as

* *Neoclassicism*, p. 43.

a model of classic restraint; Winckelmann believed that the spiritual qualities he sought in Greek art, 'noble simplicity and calm grandeur', were supremely expressed in the Apollo Belvedere. It would seem now that in their reaction against artificiality they evolved the theory that 'Beauty is Truth' and that Truth was to be found in the ideal order and harmony which lay at the heart of Nature itself. Man is an element in Nature, the Greeks had been pre-eminent in their study of man and sculpture, which had created the ideal beauty, and so the hidden truth of Nature could best be discerned through study of 'the antique'. By this was meant Greek statues, or, very often, Roman copies of Greek statues. The weakness of any strong theory about antiquity is that it tends to ignore conflicting evidence or to lump too much together, and the differences between archaic, Hellenic and Hellenistic sculpture are great. But the 'ideal art' theory does at least raise artists above slavish imitation. Canova's *Theseus and the Dead Minotaur* is a genuine recreation of great power and austerity, and his *Cupid and Psyche* is as idealistic in its way as David's sublimation of Roman republican morality.

The extent of the revolution in approach to the classics can be illustrated by contrasting two great paintings, Tiepolo's *Antony and Cleopatra* [8] and Ingres's *Oedipus and the Sphinx* [9]. The Tiepolo is a study for the central scene in a series of frescoes for the Palazzo Labia, Venice. Even in a reproduction without its glorious colour contrasts – the pale green of Cleopatra's dress, the red of Antony's cloak and plumes, the golden prows of the Roman galleys and billowing white sails against a pale blue-and-white sky – this can be seen as rococo painting at its best, vital and free, its atmosphere created by every detail of Cleopatra's proud bearing and the expressions of the onlookers, her own attendants and Antony's men. Birds high in the sky and a black slave with a large hound in the foreground are all integrated into a sweeping composition on a high romantic theme. The fact that Cleopatra is depicted as a Venetian aristocrat of Tiepolo's own time is a convention we readily accept.

Ingres, who was a pupil of David, has been called the last of the Neo-classicists. Right up to his death in 1867 he adhered firmly to his belief in precise observation, discipline of design and clarity of line. The two versions he painted of this celebrated picture are stripped bare of any supporting detail or extraneous persons; even the Sphinx is only dimly outlined against the shadowy background. The naked Oedipus stands out like a statue in an attitude which is both challenging and heavy with foreboding, a statue no more like a Greek statue than those of Canova's uncompromising purity and intellectualism. This is Ingres's personal recreation of an episode in mythology which has had firm hold on men's imaginations from Homer and Sophocles to the present day. Oedipus is going to answer correctly the question put by the Sphinx, and he has already killed his father and will marry his mother when he becomes king of Thebes. In the old versions of the legend he has no inkling of what awaits him, but Ingres's Oedipus is Cavafy's:

> – and now
> he no longer fears her for he has
> the solution ready and he will win.
> And yet he does not rejoice over this victory.
> His glance, full of melancholy,
> is not on the Sphinx; far off he sees
> the narrow path that leads to Thebes
> and will end at Colonus.
> And his soul clearly forebodes
> that there the Sphinx will accost him again
> with more difficult and more baffling
> enigmas that have no answer.
>
> *Oedipus*, translated by Rae Dalven

This is a picture which has been seen as standing on the watershed between the strict neoclassical approach and that of the Romantic painters like Géricault and Delacroix, who were virtually Ingres's contemporaries. The disciplined design and statuesque poise of the central figure are the link with David and Canova; the unmoralizing subject and sense of pending issues suggest the *Leda* of Géricault. But I think we can find a latent romanticism throughout this period of enlightenment and classic idealism, in its rejection of artificiality in poetic diction or in artistic convention, its withdrawal from orthodox Christianity and its cult of Nature, its cultivation of sensibility, its moral earnestness, and, above all, its dedication to the ideal of freedom. Winckelmann had taught in the middle of the eighteenth century that true art could only flourish in conditions of liberty, and the liberal Romantics of the next generation, Goethe, Byron and Shelley, the French poet André Chénier and the Italian dramatist Vittorio Alfieri, were all ardent for freedom and looked to the Greek spirit for its realization. This is not the place to attempt a discussion of the relationship between the Age of Enlightenment, the French Revolution and the Romantic movement, but the idealization of Greece, the devotion to a Hellenic ideal which was to a large extent of their own creating, is a characteristic of the Romantic spirit.

Keats, as we are always told, had no formal classical education but found his Greece (which for him meant beauty) through translations such as the Elizabethan George Chapman's translation of Homer, in Lemprière's Classical Dictionary, and in the Elgin Marbles which had recently arrived in London. Byron had evidently been less fortunate in his teachers at Harrow than Coleridge at Christ's Hospital – or De Quincey at Manchester Grammar School; the *Confessions of an English Opium Eater* pays warm tribute to the encouragement he found there for his literary interests. But, when not expressing violent contempt for 'the drilled dull lesson, forced down word by word/In my repugnant youth', Byron shows himself as sensitive to the classical past of Greece and Italy, where he was widely travelled, and he died in the Greek War of Independence fighting for his ideal of restored liberty for Greece. Shelley had a really good classical education at Eton, and one which fed his enthusiasm for Greek literature. He read and reread Homer, and translated some of the Homeric Hymns. His favourite among the dramatists was Aeschylus; *Hellas* was modelled on *The Persae*, a play in which a free nation makes a stand against aggression, and *Prometheus Unbound* was designed as a continuation of Aeschylus's *Prometheus Bound*, where a tyrant is defied. In the preface to *The Cenci* he mentions his interest in the Oedipus plays, and the book in his pocket when he was drowned was a volume of Sophocles. He was also an enthusiastic Platonist, translating the *Symposium* and some of the *Republic*. 'He loved to idealise reality', as Mary Shelley wrote in her preface to the posthumous first edition of his poems, but we should hardly go on to agree with her that he was a kindred spirit to Plato. Carried away by his enthusiasms, by his self-absorption and his indulgence in rather nebulous philosophizing, Shelley rarely created anything with the kind of stark lucidity and perceptive insight which we think of as Greek, and when in his preface to *Hellas* he writes of the modern Greek as 'the descendant of those glorious beings whom the imagination almost refuses to figure to itself as belonging to our kind', one is left wondering whether these glorious beings have much in common with Socrates or Pericles or Sappho or Phidias, or any Greek who lived an intense precarious life warmed by the Mediterranean sun.

The whole Romantic ideal of Greece as a land of youth and energy, toleration and intellectual freedom, love of beauty released from any inhibitions about nudity, is as selective and unhistorical as many earlier concepts of antiquity. It could only conceivably apply to Athens, and to the period of Athenian democracy which had defeated the Persians, produced the great dramatists and built the Parthenon, and it ignored some very uncomfortable facts such as slavery, the Spartan restrictive régime, the growth of Athenian imperialism, the atrocities of the Peloponnesian War, and the trial and death of Socrates. In English education it has had a long life, though as R. M. Ogilvie shows,* serious study of Greek did not start until the reforms in the English public-school system made by Dr Thomas Arnold, headmaster of Rugby School from 1828 to 1842. He reorientated the classical curriculum away from the study and imitation of Horace and Ovid and towards Greek history and philosophy, concentrating on Thucydides, who had a special appeal for the Victorian empire-builders, and Plato, whose educational programme in the *Republic* of 'music' (which in Greek includes literature) and 'gymnastic' (athletics generally) was designed for a ruling-class élite. The later nineteenth century produced many of the great works of European scholarship and a more critical evaluation of historical sources and editing of texts, and classical students will long remember names like Benjamin Jowett, Theodor Mommsen and Richard Jebb with the respect they feel for the lexicographers Liddell and Scott, Lewis and Short. But the ordinary man today would look at Jebb's text-cum-translation of Sophocles only in order to enjoy fully A. E. Housman's famous parody:

Chorus O suitably-attired-in-leather-boots
Head of a traveller, wherefore seeking whom
Whence by what way how purposed art thou come
To this well-nightingaled vicinity? . . .
Alcmoen I journeyed hither a Boeotian road.
Chorus Sailing on horseback, or with feet for oars?
Alcmoen Plying with speed my partnership of legs . . . †

And the high moral tone of Victorian classical education appeared to lay a dead hand on the literature of Greece and Rome for creative writers. Certainly Tennyson's *Lotus-Eaters*, *Tithonus* and *Ulysses* are among his

* 'Plato, Thucydides and the Victorians': chapter 4 in *Latin and Greek*.

† Printed in *Apes and Parrots*. An Anthology of Parodies collected by J. C. Squire, Herbert Jenkins Ltd, London.

best poems, and Matthew Arnold bids a moving farewell to Arcadia in *The Scholar Gypsy* and *Thyrsis*; there are long classical poems by William Morris and Swinburne, now largely unread, and Walter Pater's mannered *Plato and Platonism*, written as an attack on Victorian materialism, is an attempt to interpret Plato in purely aesthetic terms. But there is nothing in English literature corresponding to the French Parnassian movement. For nineteenth-century poetry which draws its imagery from Greece and Rome in a manner which is both imaginative and disciplined we have to go to *Les Trophées* of de Heredia and *Poèmes antiques* of Leconte de Lisle.

There were of course powerful counter-sources of inspiration in England in the Gothic Revival and Ruskin's influence, and in the widespread enthusiasm for ballads and tales of Arthurian chivalry and Teutonic legend which found expression in Tennyson, in Morris, and in the pre-Raphaelite painters. But one wonders whether the classics lost their imaginative appeal at the time simply because they were so strictly selected for their uplifting qualities and censored where these were found wanting. Some authors (Petronius or the Hellenistic novelists) could not be read at all, others (Juvenal or Martial) only in suitable 'selections'. School editions (some of which are still reissued) were prepared with bits of Terence rewritten and great chunks of Aristophanes left out. (We have not seen the end of such bowdlerization. The Loeb Library of Classics still issues an Aristophanes published in the 1920s in which the Greek text is rewritten in places to be accommodated to the censored translation, and has only recently revised its Martial, originally published in 1919 with a sentence in the Introduction to explain that 'All epigrams possible of translation by the use of dashes or paraphrases have been rendered in English, the wholly impossible ones only in Italian.') No one could maintain a rigid belief in the purity and nobility of the 'Greek spirit' without excluding a great deal of literature that was judged 'unworthy' and even a potentially corruptive influence if made generally known.

The damaging effect of such a theory is brought out by the Slade lectures* given in Cambridge by the art critic Roger Fry (1866–1934), who had been responsible for the first post-Impressionist exhibition in England in 1910, in which he attacked Greek art for its intellectualism, its lack of vitality and sensibility, and compared it adversely with Chinese and primitive Negro art. Most of us would see this now as a curious aberration

* Posthumously published with an introduction by Kenneth Clark in 1939: *Last Lectures* by Roger Fry, Cambridge University Press and Beacon Press, New York.

in Fry's perceptive judgement. But the explanation is in Fry's own words about his boyhood:

> . . . Even in homes where art was in true Victorian fashion thoroughly despised, Greek art was supposed to have some mysterious educational value, and the young were taken periodically to be exposed to the influence of Greek sculpture in the dingy rooms of the British Museum . . . We learned to take Greek art for granted while still believing that, as we had been told, it was the greatest art in the world . . . Although Greek art meant quite different things at different times, the idea that Greek art was the supreme canon of *all* art remained unchallenged.

The challenge was necessary; Kenneth Clark comments that those 'who are persuaded by these lectures to look at Greek art with a free and innocent eye will experience one of the great pleasures of life, liberation from an unconscious insincerity'.

Respectable Academicians such as Sir Lawrence Alma-Tadema and the sculptor G. F. Watts continued to be inspired by lofty classical ideals into the twentieth century, and they had their continental counterparts and lesser followers, as any provincial gallery will show. But in its very nature the French Impressionist movement was a reaction against traditional concepts of composition, and as we move through the galleries of post-Impressionist painters, the Cubists and Surrealists and the abstract artists of our own technological age, we might well decide that the classical dictionary can go back on to its shelf and stay there. Then we find Rodin; and after him another giant, Picasso.

Auguste Rodin claimed with justification to be a disciple both of Phidias and of Michelangelo, and he has also been called the spiritual heir of the great romantic painter Delacroix. He shares with Rubens the power of breathing new life into a much-handled theme. In his case it is his tragic view of life and his compassion which add a new dimension to our own attitude to a classical subject. His creation of figures half-emerging from unworked stone emphasizes their struggle for existence and also their identification with the natural elements; Orpheus with his lute is a part of the rocks he can move, Icarus lies, fallen to his death, the Danaïd has given up, exhausted by her hopeless task. And *The Fallen Caryatid Bearing her Stone* [10] is a sharp reminder of our inferior sensitivity, for though we know those sturdy firm-necked figures of the Erechtheum and the Siphnian Treasury at Delphi, and may even know some of the legends devised to explain why they are punished by having to stand holding up such a weight of stone, have we ever thought of them as human or put ourselves in their place? Through Rodin's eyes we can now see what it is like to be a tired caryatid, and though his is a view which would certainly have surprised the Greeks, it shakes us out of complacency and opens out our minds.

Any such opening-out process can only be of benefit, and the most encouraging thing about classical scholarship of the last hundred years is that scholars themselves now take much wider views. Teaching is no longer concentrated on fifth-century Athens as a Golden Age of Greece or on Cicero as a writer of the 'best' Latin; even more important, along with Victorian stuffiness was blown away a good deal of snobbishness about a classical education largely confined to a thorough knowledge of Greek and Latin. Greece and Rome are no longer the scholars' *hortus conclusus*, and the scholars are the ones who have broken down the walls. I don't think Yeats could say of them now

> . . . All shuffle there; all cough in ink;
> All wear the carpet with their shoes;
> All think what other people think;
> All know the man their neighbour knows.
> Lord, what would they say
> Did their Catullus walk that way?
>
> (*The Scholars*)

Proof of this is the widespread interest in Homer, which was started off in the late nineteenth century by German scholarly interest in the origins of epic, and the inspired amateur archaeology of the wealthy German grocer's son, Heinrich Schliemann, who found ancient Troy beneath modern Hissarlik by studying the terrain on the spot, *Iliad* in hand. He then went on to excavate Mycenae, and Sir Arthur Evans followed on with his excavations at the Palace of Minos in Crete. Another classical amateur, the architect Michael Ventris, cracked the code of Linear B, and expert work continues in Pylos, on the island of Santorini, and in Crete. The publications of these findings are naturally learned and specialized, but knowledge spreads through travel and popular media, and it is surely no coincidence that the more is known of the pre-Homeric Bronze Age reflected in the poems, and also of the technique of bardic poetry through field work in Yugoslavia, the more translations come out, to be eagerly received. Since the biblical prose of Butcher and Lang and Lang-Leaf-Myers we have had the 'plain prose' of Samuel Butler, T. E. Lawrence and E. V. Rieu, verse of varying kinds from Richmond Lattimore, Edward Fitzgerald and Christopher Logue, and a mixed verse and prose from Robert Graves in a wayward moment, to name a few.

It must be as true of today as it ever was that men's attitude to antiquity is largely determined by the spirit of their age. What determines today's spirit? Scientific archaeology, an increasing interest in the social and economic problems of the ancient world tending to a change in historical values and a general widening of horizons. We are readier to see Rome as a development out of Greece, and Western civilization as a continuation of the same process, and the symbols we use have a new and searching intensity. In the past there were creative works which served as landmarks pointing the way to new attitudes, and there are certainly two such boundary stones which mark off the modern approach from any preceding ones. First, J. G. Frazer's *The Golden Bough*, published in eleven volumes between 1890 and 1915, a classic of comparative mythology which may not be much read today, but which was followed by Jane Harrison and Gilbert Murray and the people whom I once heard a very conservative old classicist dismiss as 'Covent Garden mythologists, all talk of corn kings and spring queens'. It was Frazer who led the way to a more penetrating examination of the Mysteries, the rituals of death and rebirth, and their association among primitive peoples with the seasonal cycle and the fruits of the earth on which human life depends. He also wrote commentaries on Pausanias and on Ovid's *Fasti*, where we have specific details on the survival of primitive festivals, often barbarous and apparently incompatible with rationalized beliefs. But we can't ignore what we don't like or what does not seem to square with preconceived ideas about fifth-century Greeks, and no one now would wish to do so. And the Greek and Roman achievement is surely seen as all the greater if we accept that these conflicting elements were always there. It also makes it possible to put them into a historical perspective – there are common elements, for example, in Hesiod's *Theogony* and the mythology of Anatolia. We are a long way now from Shelley's 'glorious beings'.

The irrational was also the concern of the second major influence on our times, that of the psychoanalyst Sigmund Freud, whose theory of the unconscious was illustrated by parallels drawn between certain myths and the symbolism of dreams, with special emphasis on the instinctive sexual conflicts in the developing child. (Plato had also remarked that in their dreams men were free from rational restraints and could dream of sleeping with their mothers.) It was Freud who coined the terms narcissism, Oedipus complex and Electra complex, now often so loosely used, and from him stemmed what T. S. Eliot once called 'a curious Freudian-social-mystical-rationalistic-hypercritical interpretation of the Classics', which is seen in its most extreme form in Cocteau, Gide and contemporary French authors, and also in the operas of Richard Strauss (with von Hofmannsthal's libretti), and in certain recent continental films on classical subjects. The Oedipus and Orpheus myths have been worked threadbare – or have they? It could be argued that since the great tragic myths embody deep-lying truths, this is how they should now be reinterpreted for a post-Freudian world; that Shakespeare and Dryden were doing the same sort of thing in their day when they made contemporary plays out of Antony's relations with Cleopatra. Perhaps the test should be whether yet another selective approach enriches understanding of the past or diminishes it by gimmickry.

Today the French symbolist writers and painters belong to the immediate past and their preoccupation with the psychology of the Greek heroes is dated. There is a steady output of serious classical novels, most of them analysing character in depth since Robert Graves set the fashion in *I, Claudius*. Sulla, Spartacus, Caesar, Hadrian and Julian, Sappho, Pericles and Theseus are some of the well-known personalities who have been treated, sometimes with considerable imaginative insight. But if one looks at the poets and writers who have made significant use of classical imagery and are likely to remain a living influence, the two great Europeans, the Austrian Rilke and the Alexandrian Cavafy, died in 1926 and 1933; Eliot, Yeats, Joyce, and now Forster have gone, and Pound's best work was written long ago. They have all taken from antiquity's wealth and left us artefacts enriched by themselves – Tiresias, Philomela, Helen, Leda, Ulysses, Cynthia: these are names which demand our recognition if only because of what has been made of them.

Of contemporary European artists, Michael Ayrton alone draws deeply from the classical world in his long preoccupation with Daedalus and Icarus, the Minotaur and the labyrinth. And there is one great figure still alive when I write this who has never ceased to gather up the past as well as the present and recreate it for the future. Pablo Picasso, born in 1881, had a recent exhibition of drawings in London which showed that he was still captivated by the half-wild fauns, satyrs and centaurs of the ancient world, though his illustrations for the *Metamorphoses* of Ovid were made as far back as 1931. The hundred etchings of the *Vollard Suite* were made between 1930 and 1937. Here in *The Sculptor and Statue of Three Female Dancers* [11] we have the three naked Graces poised in their formal dance, watched by the relaxed bearded sculptor in a scene of almost classical serenity. The Graces had had a long history when Botticelli saw in them a symbol of aspiration to celestial Love. They have come a long way since then – or have they gone back to their first conception as embodiments of natural beauty and the early representations which look no further than themselves?

Finally there is the Minotaur [12], sensuous, amorous, awkwardly beautiful, drawn with tenderness and love, and in the scenes of his death in the arena or blinded and helplessly led by a child through the night, with disturbing intensity. What Minotaur is this, drinking to the woman who is going to accept his love? Not the bull-headed deity of pre-Hellenic Crete, nor a priest-king wearing a bull's mask; not the monstrosity killed by Theseus in an ancient legend, and still less Dante's symbol of perversion. He might look forward to Gide's languorous erotic symbol, but he is no passive lover. Perhaps it suffices to say no more than that he is Picasso's Minotaur, and that through a great artist's instinct and insight a new myth is created for one of the oldest – and hitherto least-loved – figures of antiquity.

I began by saying that I thought we should not lose interest in the classics altogether as long as we care about our inheritance of constantly changing attitudes towards Greece and Rome. But we shall be the poorer if the poets and painters never draw from them again, and they cease to provide a common language and a range of living symbols. If this book can add to our awareness of the past, it has its justification; yet I should like to continue in the hope that the future will fill out its pages.

SELECT BIBLIOGRAPHY

John Boardman, *Greek Art*, Thames & Hudson, 1964.

R. R. Bolgar, *The Classical Heritage and its Beneficiaries*, Cambridge University Press, 1954.

Ernle Bradford, *Ulysses Found*, Hodder & Stoughton, 1963.

Hermann Broch, translated by J. S. Untermayer, *The Death of Virgil*, Routledge & Kegan Paul, 1946.

C. P. Cavafy, *The Complete Poems*, translated by Rae Dalven, Hogarth Press, 1961.

Kenneth Clark, *Landscape into Art*, John Murray, 1949;
The Nude, John Murray, 1956 and Penguin Books, 1967.

E. R. Dodds, *The Greeks and the Irrational*, Berkeley, 1951.

Patrick Leigh Fermor, *Mani*, John Murray, 1958.

S. Gilbert, *James Joyce's Ulysses*, Penguin Books, 1952.

Robert Graves, *The Greek Myths*, Penguin Books, 1955.

Gilbert Highet, *The Classical Tradition*, Oxford University Press, 1949.

Hugh Honour, *Neoclassicism*, Penguin Books, 1968.

N. Kazantzakis, translated by Kimon Friar, *The Odyssey; a Modern Sequel*, Simon & Schuster, 1958.

Peter Levi, S. J., *Pausanias's 'Guide to Greece'* (translation and notes), Penguin Books, 1971.

C. S. Lewis, *The Allegory of Love*, Oxford University Press, 1936.

Amedeo Maiuri, *Roman Painting*, Skira, 1953.

R. M. Ogilvie, *Latin and Greek: A history of the influence of* The Classics *on English Life 1600–1918*, Routledge & Kegan Paul, 1964.

The Oxford Classical Dictionary, Oxford University Press, 1949; second edition, 1970.

Erwin Panofsky, *Meaning in the Visual Arts*, Doubleday, 1955 and Penguin Books, 1970;
Renaissance and Renascences in Western Art, Paladin, 1970.

Gisela Richter, *A Handbook of Greek Art*, Phaidon, 1959; paperback 1969.

Martin Robertson, *Greek Painting*, Skira, 1959.

Fritz Saxl, *A Heritage of Images*, Penguin Books, 1970.

George Seferis, translated by W. E. Keeley and P. Sherrard, *Collected Poems*, Cape, 1967.

Jean Seznec, *The Survival of the Pagan Gods*, Warburg Institute, 1940 (in French); Harper Torchbook, 1961.

Wolfgang Stechow, *Rubens and the Classical Tradition*, Harvard, 1968.
T. J. B. Spencer, *Shakespeare's Plutarch*, Penguin Books, 1964.
George Steiner, *The Death of Tragedy*, Faber & Faber, 1961;
Language and Silence, Faber & Faber, 1967 and Penguin Books, 1969.
T. B. L. Webster, *From Mycenae to Homer*, Methuen, 1958.
Roberto Weiss, *The Renaissance Discovery of Classical Antiquity*, Basil Blackwell, 1969.
Mortimer Wheeler, *Roman Art and Architecture*, Thames & Hudson, 1964.
L. P. Wilkinson, *Ovid Recalled*, Cambridge University Press, 1955.
Edgar Wind, *Pagan Mysteries in the Renaissance*, Faber & Faber, 1958 and Penguin Books, 1967.

Achates
The faithful friend of Aeneas in Virgil's *Aeneid*, in the heroic tradition of Patroclus's relation to Achilles and Pirithous's to Theseus. '*Fidus Achates*' then becomes synonymous with loyalty.

Acheron ('woeful')
An actual river of northern Greece which ran underground in several places and so was thought to lead to the Underworld. In the literary tradition of Homer, followed by Virgil, it is the principal river of Hades, with Cocytus, Phlegethon and Styx its tributaries. It is then the river encircling Dante's Hell across which the souls of the dead must be ferried by Charon, and it is one of the 'four infernal rivers' of Milton's *Paradise Lost*: 'sad Acheron of sorrow, black and deep'.

Achilles
A Greek hero, son of PELEUS king of Thessaly and the nereid THETIS. In the *Iliad* he has brought fifty ships to Troy with his Myrmidons, after capturing many Trojan cities, including Lyrnessos, where he took Briseis captive. The action of the *Iliad* centres on his anger and mortification when Agamemnon insults him by taking the girl for himself (→ CHRYSEIS). Achilles 'sulks in his tent' and comes out to fight again only when his close friend Patroclus borrows his armour, leads out the Myrmidons, and is killed. Achilles then storms out to rout the Trojans and kill Hector after chasing him round the walls of Troy. He drags the mangled body behind his chariot back to the Greek camp, but after the funeral of Patroclus he gives it back to Priam, king of Troy and father of Hector. Throughout the *Iliad* he knows he is doomed to early death, and in the *Odyssey* his shade is already in the Underworld, still envious of the living. In the non-Homeric epics of the Troy saga, of which few fragments remain, he killed the Trojan prince Troilus, the Amazon queen Penthesilea, and the Ethiopian king Memnon, and many other legends grew up around him. He was said to have been dipped in the river Styx by Thetis and made invulnerable except for the heel she held, and so when Paris killed him, it was by a poisoned arrow in the heel (hence the expression 'Achilles' heel' for a vulnerable spot, and in anatomy the Achilles tendon). This episode is first mentioned by the Roman poet Statius, but presumably he found it in material lost to us. He was also said to have been educated by the centaur Chiron, and when the Greek fleet was assembling for the Trojan War he was dressed as a girl by his father and hidden on the island of Scyros, where he was recognized by Odysseus and the other envoys sent to look for him. This story, and his love for Patroclus probably account for the late tradition of his effeminacy – which Shakespeare follows in *Troilus and Cressida*. A famous wall-painting from Pompeii, which may be a copy of an original by Polygnotus, shows the recognition scene at Scyros. On the other hand, DEIDAMIA was also a popular figure in legend, and she bore him a son, Neoptolemus. None of this can be reconciled with the Homeric hero, who is magnificently barbarian in his

outbursts of rage and love and grief. In classical art he is the conventional armed warrior, and an 'Achilles painter' is so called from a red-figure vase of the fifth century B.C. from Vulci which shows Achilles preparing for battle.

Acis

In late legend he is the young son of Faunus and a river-nymph, and lover of the sea-nymph GALATEA. He was killed by his jealous rival, the Cyclops Polyphemus, and turned into the river which still bears his name at the foot of Mount Etna. This bit of Sicilian folklore, which is first mentioned by Theocritus, was well known to the Renaissance from Ovid's *Metamorphoses*, and later inspired a painting by Poussin and a landscape by Claude, but Acis is generally remembered through Handel's opera, *Acis and Galatea.*

Actaeon

A famous legendary huntsman, grandson of Cadmus, king of Thebes, who inadvertently came upon Artemis bathing naked, was turned by her into a stag, and torn to pieces by his own hounds. This poignant illustration of the belief that the gods did not allow themselves to be seen without permission (cf. SEMELE) is Hellenistic in its detail, though Actaeon's cruel death is also known from the fragments of Stesichorus and from examples in Greek classical art, notably a red-figure vase of the fifth century B.C. by the 'Pan painter', and a metope from a temple of Hera of the same period in Selinus, Sicily [13]. In the earlier version he was punished either because he was a better hunter than Artemis or wanted to marry her. OVID suggests that the error which led to his own banishment was comparable with Actaeon's, and he tells the story at length in the *Metamorphoses.* Consequently Actaeon was well known from the Renaissance onwards, and constantly painted. There are several versions of his death by Titian and by Veronese, frescoes by Parmigiano in Parma, and paintings by Poussin, Rembrandt and Gainsborough – one of his rare classical subjects.

Adonis

A beautiful youth of Cyprus, born of incest between father and daughter, loved by Aphrodite (Venus), and in the legend told by Ovid, killed by a boar while out hunting. His name is Semitic, meaning 'Lord', and he is very like the Syrian Thamuz (→ PAN); the cult of a mother-goddess and her mortal consort was common throughout the Middle East. Adonis was a vegetation god, and his rites included the mourning of women followed by rejoicing at his rebirth. The festival in Alexandria is described by Theocritus in *Idyll* 15. In Athens the *Adonia* was a midsummer festival, and pots of short-lived flowers and herbs ('Gardens of Adonis') were used in its celebration; these appear in a wall-painting of the first century B.C. from Boscoreale, near Pompeii. Shakespeare's poem *Venus and Adonis* (probably his first published work) follows Ovid's account of Adonis's death, while Shelley's *Adonais*, an elegy on the death of Keats, takes its title from the pastoral poet Bion's *Lament for Adonis.* Adonis was often painted by post-Renaissance artists, notably by Titian, by Veronese in three versions, and by Poussin in two scenes of Venus lamenting his death.

Adrastus
A king of Argos who led the 'Seven against Thebes' in an ill-fated expedition to restore Polynices, son of Oedipus, to the throne of Thebes (→ ETEOCLES). He was the sole survivor, thanks to his magic horse Arion, and ten years later he led back the sons of the Seven (*Epigoni*) to avenge their fathers and sack the city, but died of grief when his son Aegialeus was killed in the fighting. These Theban sagas refer to a time before the Trojan War and are mentioned by Homer. They provided subjects for tragedies by the great dramatists and for later epics, and the Theban cycle was known to the Alexandrian scholars to consist of three epics, the *Story of Oedipus*, the *Thebais* and the *Epigoni*. Nothing survives but a few quotations.

Aeacus
Son of Zeus, father of Peleus, grandfather of Achilles and Ajax, and king of Aegina; in late legend, for his virtues, he was made one of the judges over the souls of the dead with Minos and Rhadamanthys.

Aegeus
King of Athens, married to the daughter of Pittheus, king of Troezen, and by her the putative father of THESEUS. He died by throwing himself into the sea (called after him the Aegean) when Theseus forgot to change his black sails to white as a sign of his victory over the Minotaur. With Theseus he is the centre of a complex of legends, most of which are set out in Plutarch's *Life* of Theseus and in two modern novels (*The King Must Die* and *The Bull from the Sea* by Mary Renault).

Aegisthus
The son of Thyestes, seducer of his cousin Agamemnon's wife Clytemnestra, and murderer of Agamemnon; then killed by Orestes. See genealogical tree of the House of Pelops, p. 187.

Aeneas
A Trojan hero, son of Anchises and Aphrodite. In the *Iliad* he plays only a small part, but later legend made him escape with his family from burning Troy and sail to Italy where he was the founder of Rome. He is thus the hero of the AENEID, though not in any romantic sense. For Virgil he is always *pius Aeneas*, a man devoted to his father and his gods and conscious of being an instrument of the destiny which was to make Rome great.

Aeneid
Virgil's twelve-book epic in honour of Rome's glorious past and of the new era of peace and prosperity he hoped to see under the Emperor Augustus. It describes the wanderings of Aeneas after the fall of Troy, his landing in Carthage and love for Dido, the funeral games in Sicily for his father, his descent into the Underworld to find his father's spirit, his arrival at the mouth of the Tiber, and his wars with the Latins and their allies in Italy until the Rutulian prince

Turnus is defeated and Aeneas unites both peoples by marrying the Latin princess Lavinia. Virgil's model was Homer. Though he left the *Aeneid* unrevised at his death (and is even said to have given orders for its destruction), it is not only his supreme poetic achievement but perhaps the most profound of all 'literary' epics, and has influenced writers of similar works ever since – for example Statius, Dante, Spenser, Tasso and Milton. Dryden's translation of 1697 is a great poem in its own right, and the most successful recent verse translation is that of C. Day Lewis. →→ VIRGIL.

Aeolus
The god of the winds, ruling the Aeolian Islands. In the *Odyssey* he gives Odysseus the contrary winds tied up in a bag, but the sailors let them out and the ship is blown off course, which further delays the return to Ithaca. The present Aeolian Islands are part of the Lipari group off the north-east coast of Sicily, but Ernle Bradford (*Ulysses Found*) thinks that the single 'floating isle' described by Homer is the volcanic island of Ustica, some eighty miles west.

Aeschines (*c.* 397–*c.* 322 B.C.)
Athenian orator and, as leader of the party wishing to preserve peace with Philip of Macedon, the political opponent of DEMOSTHENES.

Aeschylus (525/4–456 B.C.)
The great Athenian tragic dramatist, author of at least eighty plays, of which seven survive: *Persians* (→ DARIUS), *Suppliants* (→ DANAIDS), *Seven against Thebes* (→ ETEOCLES), *Prometheus Bound* (→ PROMETHEUS), and the trilogy *Oresteia*. Aeschylus is known to have fought at the battle of Marathon, but the tale of his death by a tortoise dropped on his bald head by an eagle is apocryphal. He was one of the founders of Greek drama, introducing a second actor to allow dramatic dialogue and action independent of the chorus. All his plays are permeated by deep religious feeling, and show how destiny is worked out through the conflict of man's human passions with divine purpose, and he was already famous in his own times for the free use of soaring metaphor and the sonorous language which Aristophanes caricatured in *The Frogs*, and which later was admired by Shelley. (→ AGAMEMNON, ELECTRA, ORESTES).

Aesop
The creator of the genre of fable in Greece is said by Herodotus to have been a slave from Samos and lived in the sixth century B.C. These brief anecdotes (usually of animal life) which point a moral have never lacked imitators. Through the Roman poet Phaedrus (*fl.* first century A.D.) and in a later Latin prose version they were popular in the Middle Ages and reached greater sophistication in seventeenth-century France in the *Fables* of La Fontaine, and in our own times from James Thurber's variation on the theme.

Agamemnon
Son of Atreus, brother of Menelaus (→ HOUSE OF PELOPS, p. 187), king of Mycenae (and in later legend, of Argos).

He led the Greek forces in the Trojan War, and his quarrel with Achilles is the main subject of the *Iliad*. On his return he was murdered by his wife Clytemnestra and her lover Aegisthus, and later avenged by his son Orestes: a drama which inspired Aeschylus's trilogy *Oresteia*, and has captured the imagination of later playwrights, notably Eugene O'Neill in *Mourning Becomes Electra*, T. S. Eliot in *The Family Reunion* and Sartre in *Les Mouches* ('The Flies'). So too in Eliot's *Sweeney among the Nightingales* the birds

> sang within the bloody wood
> When Agamemnon cried aloud,
> And let their liquid siftings fall
> To stain the stiff dishonoured shroud.

One of the great moments of archaeology was when Heinrich Schliemann uncovered six tombs of a circle in Mycenae and telegraphed to King George of the Hellenes, 'I have gazed upon the face of Agamemnon.' But the beaten gold 'mask of Agamemnon' now in Athens is several centuries earlier than the Homeric king. →→ IPHIGENIA.

Agathon
Athenian tragedian of the late fifth century, satirized by Aristophanes for effeminacy in his play *The Poet and the Women* (*Thesmophoriazusae*), and a leading figure in Plato's *Symposium*. Only fragments of his plays survive, but he was ranked high by Aristotle.

Agricola, Cnaeus Julius (*c.* A.D. 40–93)
His upbringing in Forum Julii (Fréjus) and his distinguished career, civil and military, are fully described in the *Life* written by his son-in-law Tacitus, whose avowed intention was to show that 'even under bad emperors [i.e. Domitian] there can be good men'. Agricola's governorship of Britain is of great interest, both for his sympathetic relations with the native British and his campaigns in Wales and the Highlands of Scotland. He also sailed round the north of Scotland and sighted Ireland.

Agrippa, Marcus Vipsanius (*c.* 63–12 B.C.)
The leading supporter of Octavian (later Emperor Augustus) in defeating Mark Antony, in organizing the provinces of the Empire, and also in restoring and improving the city of Rome. It was he, rather than Augustus, who 'found Rome brick and left it marble'. He was responsible for reconditioning the sewers, adding two new aqueducts, building public baths in the Campus Martius, and for the Pantheon, which still carries an inscription with his name and the date (27 B.C.). This must have been replaced by Hadrian when he rebuilt the Pantheon. It is the only ancient building with its dome intact and had great influence on later architects like Palladio. Agrippa also set up the naval base at Misenum and the harbour known as the Portus Julius at Cumae (for which → AVERNUS).

Agrippa I, called 'Herod' in Acts xii, where he arrests the apostle Peter, was the grandson of Herod the Great and a popular king of Judaea; after his death in A.D. 44 the Emperor Claudius made his kingdom a Roman province.

Agrippa II, his son, was made ruler of several principalities in northern Palestine by the Emperors Claudius and Nero, and was loyal to Rome in A.D. 66 when he tried to check the Jewish rebellion. He is the 'King Agrippa' of Acts xxv–vi who meets St Paul in captivity at Caesarea and hears his account of his conversion to Christianity.

Agrippina the Elder (*c.* 14 B.C.–A.D. 33)
Daughter of M. Agrippa and Augustus's daughter Julia, wife of GERMANICUS and mother of the Emperor Caligula, she was banished by Tiberius and starved to death.

Agrippina the Younger, her daughter (A.D. 15–59), was the wife of Cnaeus Domitius Ahenobarbus and mother of the Emperor Nero. She was later the wife of her uncle Emperor Claudius, whom she was suspected of poisoning after she had ensured Nero's succession in the place of Claudius's own son Britannicus. She was murdered on Nero's orders. Her horrifying crimes are the subjects of Racine's *Britannicus* and of Robert Graves's two novels of the period, *I, Claudius* and *Claudius the God*.

Ahenobarbus ('Red-beard')
A surname in the Domitius family, a member of which was Cnaeus Domitius Ahenobarbus who supported Antony in the war against Octavian but deserted him before the Battle of Actium. He is the Enobarbus of Shakespeare's *Antony and Cleopatra*.

Ajax (Greek, **Aias**)
(i) Greek hero, son of Telamon king of Salamis, depicted in the *Iliad* as doggedly courageous but rather stupid. In later legend he recovers the body of Achilles but competes with Odysseus for Achilles' armour, and loses; he then goes mad and kills himself. This is the theme of Sophocles' *Ajax*, and is described by Ovid in the *Metamorphoses*. Local legend in Salamis said that flowers sprang from his grave marked AI; → HYACINTHUS.
(ii) Another Ajax, son of Oileus king of Locris, leads his troops in the *Iliad*, and in non-Homeric legend dragged Cassandra from the altar of Athene and was punished for his sacrilege by being drowned in a storm sent by the goddess on his voyage home to Greece. In historic times up to the first century A.D. the Locrians sent two virgin girls annually to Ilium (refounded Troy) to serve as priestesses of Athene in expiation of this crime.

Alaric
The chief of the Visigoths who invaded Italy in A.D. 408 and sacked Rome in 410, the first time the 'eternal city' had been occupied since the Gauls invaded Italy in 390 B.C. The episode is dramatically described by Gibbon in chapter 31 of his *Decline and Fall of the Roman Empire*. The Goths later moved on to Spain and after Alaric's death came to terms with the Romans. → CLAUDIAN, STILICHO.

Alcaeus
Greek lyric poet of Mytilene in Lesbos, *fl. c.* 600 B.C., friend of Sappho and, as

an aristocrat, a consistent opponent of the reigning tyrants (→ PITTACUS). A good picture of the turbulent political life of his time is given in Peter Green's novel *The Laughter of Aphrodite*. The four-lined alcaic metre often used by Horace is called after him. Only fragments of his songs of love and war survive.

Alcestis

Daughter of Pelias, and wife of Admetus, king of Pherae in Thessaly, she was the only person willing to die in place of her husband, but was brought back from the Underworld by Heracles. This is the theme of one of Euripides' best-known plays, and of Gluck's opera *Alceste*, which was modelled on it (though here Alcestis is rescued by Apollo). Euripides seems to have been the first person to cast doubts on Admetus's character, but Alcestis is traditionally the model wife, and in medieval literature she speaks for all true lovers, as she does in Chaucer's *Legend of Good Women*. Rilke's *Alcestis* is a revelation of what Admetus has lost by rejecting the gods' offer of death. In Eliot's *The Cocktail Party* Celia/Alcestis prefers to return to death as the greater reality.

Alcibiades (*c.* 450–404 B.C.)

Athenian politician and general, brought up by Pericles and a pupil of Socrates. In the Peloponnesian War between Athens and Sparta his charm and brilliance won him the leadership of the democratic party after Pericles' death, but his ambitions to extend Athenian imperialism in the West made him suspect. Though he succeeded in organizing and leading the ill-fated expedition to Sicily in 415 he was recalled on the charge of impiety after the mutilation of the HERMAE. He escaped to Sparta and gave valuable advice on the conduct of the war, but lost Spartan confidence, went over to Asia Minor and tried (unsuccessfully) to engineer his return to Athens in 411 by winning Persian support for the oligarchic revolution in Athens. However, the Athenian fleet at Samos made him general, and after a series of successes in the Hellespont he returned to Athens in triumph in 407. He was then given a new command in Ionia, but could not succeed against the combination of the Spartan Lysander and Cyrus of Persia, and his enemies moved again; he retired to Phrygia where he was murdered by emissaries of the Thirty Tyrants. Alcibiades features prominently in Thucydides' history, and also in Plato's *Symposium* and Plutarch's *Lives*, from which material has been drawn for several recent novels on his complex character: notably Peter Green's *Achilles His Armour* and Mary Renault's *The Last of the Wine*.

Alcinous

King of the mythical Phaeacians in Scheria, grandson of Poseidon and husband of his own sister Arete. He entertains Odysseus in book 6 of the *Odyssey*, and in later legend receives the Argonauts on their return from Colchis and refuses to return Medea to her father. Scheria or Phaeacia has been identified since classical times with Corfu.

Alcmaeon

The son of AMPHIARAUS and Eriphyle, and one of the heroes of the Theban cycle of early epics (→ ADRASTUS). He led the Successors (*Epigoni*) and captured Thebes, but was then pursued by the Furies and forbidden to settle on ground which had witnessed his matricide of Eriphyle, in vengeance promised to his father. He finally settled on new alluvial soil at the mouth of the river Achelous, in western Greece, and married the river-god's daughter. She asked him to give her his mother's ill-fated necklace which he had given to his first wife, Arsinoë. He tried to recover it for her, but was murdered by Arsinoë's brothers. He was regarded as the ancestor of the Athenian noble family of the Alcmaeonidae, to which Pisistratus, Clisthenes and Pericles belonged, and the tale of his madness and death was known to the tragedians, but does not seem to have roused much interest in later times. Late legend said that the necklace was dedicated at Delphi and brought nothing but bad luck to the thief who stole it.

Alcman
An early Greek lyric poet, probably late 7th century B.C., who may have come from Sardes in Lydia and settled in Sparta at a time when the city was still aristocratic and cultivated. He wrote in the Laconian dialect on nature and on simple pleasures with genuine feeling, and was famous in antiquity for songs to be sung by two choirs of girls. The major part of one such song, the *Parthenion* ('maiden-song') was discovered in 1855.

Alcyone (or **Halcyone**)
The wife of Ceyx, legendary king of Trachis. When she heard of his death by drowning she threw herself into the sea and was changed into a bird along with her husband. They keep the waters of the Aegean calm while they build and sit on their nest; hence the term 'halcyon days'. Their story is told by Ovid in book 11 of the *Metamorphoses*, and appears in Chaucer's *Book of the Duchess*.

Aldobrandini Wedding
A famous Roman frieze-painting [14] dating from the beginning of the first century A.D. and showing preparations for a wedding. It is named after the cardinal who was its first owner when it was discovered about 1605, and is now in the Vatican library. It has been copied by many painters, notably Poussin, Rubens and Van Dyck.

Alexander the Great (356–323 B.C.)
King of Macedon, son of Philip II and Olympias, and educated by Aristotle, he succeeded his father in 336. He first aimed at maintaining his father's dominant position in Greece, then at removing Persian domination in the Mediterranean and controlling all the Greek cities in Asia Minor. He defeated Darius III at Issus, then consolidated his position in Syria and Egypt and founded Alexandria. In 331 he defeated Darius again at Gaugamela near the river Tigris, destroyed Persepolis, and took the Persian title of Great King. The next few years were spent penetrating into the Hindu Kush and the Punjab until his troops refused to go further than the Indus delta. Chapter 1 of the first *Book of the Maccabees* describes briefly how he 'went through to the ends of the earth',

and also gives the length of his reign accurately as twelve years. He died of fever in Babylon at the age of thirty-two; his body was brought to Alexandria and buried wrapped in gold in a glass coffin in a vast tomb at the cross-roads in the centre of the city, so that Alexander could be its protective deity. This has never been located, and up to the present century there have been rumours that his body has been seen intact in its coffin in some underground chamber.

Alexander's empire then broke up among the rival claimants known as the Successors, but his conquests had spread Greek culture widely in the Middle East and central Asia, and his influence lingered for centuries; a Hellenistic style of portraiture is marked in north Indian Buddhist statuary and he features in Persian and Indian miniature paintings.* Some historians have thought that he hoped to create a multi-racial state, and may have conceived of the essential unity of mankind, though whether he saw himself as a universal monarch is still debated. And though he encouraged his worship as a god (and appears on coins as the god Apollo) it is not known if he believed in his own divinity. Others have seen in him primarily a military commander of superb versatility and strategy who wore himself out by his restless ambition for personal glory and by what the Greeks called *pothos*, an overruling desire to press on into the unknown. His virtues and vices were on the heroic scale; cf. the Homeric ACHILLES.

Alexander's *Life* was written by Plutarch, and his campaigns recorded in the *Anabasis* of the Greek historian Arrian in the second century A.D., both drawing on contemporary records. Popular stories about him were common: → DIOGENES, GORDIAN KNOT. In Plutarch's day there was still an oak tree by the river Cephisus called Alexander's Oak, because it was said that his tent had once been pitched under it. Folklore in Greece remembers him; Patrick Leigh Fermor in *Mani* and J. E. Flecker in his poem *Santorin* describe how the two-tailed mermaid of the Aegean will appear to sailors and ask 'Where is Alexander?', to which the proper answer is 'He lives and reigns.'

The *Alexander Romance*, a work of the second century B.C. attributed to Callisthenes the nephew of Aristotle, added a wealth of romantic and miraculous detail to the historical accounts of Alexander. It was the main source of the medieval poems written when Alexander was a favourite subject for fantasy. He regularly appears among the Nine Worthies (see Chaucer's *Monk's Tale*, and *Love's Labour's Lost*). In particular, the long *Roman d'Alexandre* written in twelve-syllable lines gave its name to the French Alexandrine metre. The twelfth-century Latin *Alexandreis* was translated into Icelandic prose, and the resulting *Alexander's Saga* ranks high in medieval Icelandic literature.

Apart from Hellenistic coins and statues, Alexander is commemorated in the famous Alexander Mosaic. This was originally a pavement in a house in

* Illustrated in Peter Green, *Alexander the Great*, Weidenfeld & Nicholson, 1970.

Pompeii, and is now in Naples. It is a copy of a Greek painting (probably by APELLES) of the fourth century B.C., of great skill and subtlety, and shows the victory of the young Alexander over Darius at the battle of Issus in 333 B.C. In post-Renaissance art and literature he features less than one might expect. There is a series of scenes by Sodoma in Rome, a set of tapestries designed by Rubens's pupil Jordaens, and another in the Bishop's Palace at Würzburg, Altdorfer's *Alexander's Victory* which was one of Napoleon's favourite pictures, and the great Veronese of *The Family of Darius before Alexander* [15] in the National Gallery, London. He is the subject of an early play by Racine and of Dryden's Pindaric ode *Alexander's Feast* (on the burning of Persepolis), and his early life is the subject of Mary Renault's novel *Fire from Heaven.*

Amalthea

One of the nurses of the infant Zeus in Crete, later transformed into the star Capella. In some versions of the legend (→ KRONOS) she is a she-goat, and one of her horns when broken off became the Cornucopia, or 'horn of plenty', which is common in art, particularly as a decorative feature of stone- and woodcarving. It is also held by Roman reclining statues of river-gods: the Nile and Tiber, for example, in the Piazza del Campidoglio, Rome. As a patron nymph of shepherds she appears in a statue in the eighteenth-century grotto behind the Queen's Dairy at Versailles, and as a goat in an early statue by Bernini and two paintings by Poussin.

Amazons

A race of mythical female warriors in south-west Asia; their name was interpreted in antiquity as meaning that they amputated their right breasts (*mazos* in Greek) to make it easier to hold a bow in battle. They have given a name to a militant type of woman. In the *Iliad* they are said to have been warred on by Priam and Bellerophon, and in post-Homeric legend they come to aid Troy after Hector's death under their queen Penthesilea, who was killed by Achilles. Heracles also made war on them to capture the girdle of Hippolyte, who became the wife of Theseus. Fighting Amazons are often represented in Greek art, notably on the fourth-century B.C. frieze of the Mausoleum at Halicarnassus [16] and the late fifth-century frieze of the temple of Apollo at Bassae in Arcadia. The 'Amazon sarcophagus' from Tarquinii shows Etruscan paintings of the late fourth century B.C. Neither Arrian nor Plutarch believed the story that an Amazon queen brought troops to join Alexander, but ancient writers all thought that Amazons had existed in the past, and that the Greek victories represented a triumph of civilized over primitive peoples.

Ammon

The Egyptian god Amun appears in this Greek form after his cult at the Siwa oasis became known to the Greeks in the seventh century B.C. He was identified with Zeus by Pindar, and the oracle of Zeus Ammon was repeatedly consulted, notably by Alexander the Great whom the priests greeted as the son of Zeus. Zeus Ammon is shown on coins of Cyrene and in sculpture by a head with curling ram's horns, and Alexander often wore a similarly horned helmet.

Amphiaraus
Greek prophet who accompanied the Argonauts and foresaw the failure of the Seven against Thebes (→ ADRASTUS). He refused to take part until persuaded by his wife Eriphyle, who had been bribed to do so by Polynices who gave her a magic necklace, which had been made by the god Hephaestus for Harmonia, wife of CADMUS. Before setting out he charged his children to avenge his expected death (→ ALCMAEON) but was saved by Zeus, who opened the ground for him and his chariot to enter at Oropus in Boeotia. There he had a famous oracular shrine, described by Pausanias, where dreams were interpreted and the sick healed. Remains of a later theatre, temple and colonnade can still be seen.

Amphitryon
King of Thebes, husband of Alcmene, impersonated by Zeus who begot Heracles, while Amphitryon begot Iphicles later the same night, after Hermes had been instructed to delay the dawn for Zeus to take his time. The comic possibilities of this situation have appealed to dramatists of all periods, to Greek New Comedy, to Plautus, and after him to Molière, to Dryden (with music by Purcell); and to Jean Giraudoux, whose *Amphitryon 38* claims that thirty-seven versions have preceded his, and makes a delightfully human and resourceful character out of Alcmene.

Anacreon
Greek lyric poet of the mid sixth century B.C., whose chief patrons were Polycrates of Samos and Hipparchus of Athens. A full-length portrait statue of him dating from the mid fifth century is known from a Roman copy. The surviving fragments of his work are mainly concerned with love, wine and the pleasures of life, and were much liked by Byron in his friend Thomas Moore's translation of 1800. For Goethe too he is the 'happy poet' of sunny days in *Anakreons Grab*, popular in its setting as a song by Hugo Wolf.

Anadyomene ('rising')
A title of Aphrodite rising or born from the sea, first used by the Hellenistic artist Apelles for a famous (lost) painting in Cos. Aphrodite (Venus) Anadyomene appears too on the sculptured reliefs of the LUDOVISI THRONE [35], in Roman paintings reclining on a shell, and later in Botticelli's *Birth of Venus* and in paintings by Titian and Ingres.

Anaxagoras (*c.* 500–*c.* 428 B.C.)
Greek philosopher from Clazomenae in Ionia, the first to live in Athens, where he was the friend of Pericles. He believed in infinitely divisible 'seeds', which conglobulated to form solid bodies through centrifugal force directed by a supreme Mind (*nous*); Mind was also the animating principle behind animal and plant life. He denied that the heavenly bodies were divinities, and explained them as stones torn from the earth, the sun red-hot through motion, and its light reflected by the moon. For this he was charged with impiety, and

retired to Lampsacus in the Troad where he founded a school. Aristotle confirms his high reputation in antiquity.

Anchises
A Trojan shepherd (or prince) loved by Aphrodite who bore his son, Aeneas. He features mainly in Virgil's *Aeneid*, where he is carried from burning Troy on his son's back, dies in Sicily, is buried at Eryx, and appears among the blessed spirits in the Underworld to foretell the future greatness of Rome. *Aeneas Carrying his Father* is an early group by Bernini.

Androcles
A common Greek name, best remembered from the story told by Aulus Gellius of the runaway slave who removed a thorn from a lion's paw and was later recognized by the lion and not eaten in the Roman arena. In G. B. Shaw's *Androcles and the Lion* he is a Christian.

Andromache
Wife of the Trojan Hector and mother of Astyanax. She provides two of the most touching scenes in the *Iliad*, when she parts from Hector and again when she mourns his death, and she stands for all women who suffer in war. *Andromache Mourning Hector* is one of David's heroic paintings. In non-Homeric legend Astyanax is flung from the city walls at the sack of Troy and Andromache taken as a slave by NEOPTOLEMUS. In the version followed by Euripides and by Virgil (Aeneas meets her with Helenus in Epirus) Andromache has a son by Neoptolemus and is threatened by his wife Hermione, whose passionate jealousy is the main theme of Racine's *Andromaque*. → → HELENUS.

Andromeda
Daughter of Cepheus king of Ethiopia and of Cassiope, who angered Poseidon by boasting that her daughter was more beautiful than the nereids. He sent a sea-monster to destroy the land, which could only be placated by the sacrifice of Andromeda. She was therefore chained to a rock but rescued by PERSEUS. This theme of knight-errantry has naturally been popular with painters. There are two famous frescoes from Pompeii [17], and later versions by Titian, Piero di Cosimo – with a particularly fearsome monster – Rubens and Ingres.

Andronicus, Livius (*c.* 284–*c.* 204 B.C.)
Early Latin poet, probably a Greek freedman from Tarentum, who translated the *Odyssey* into Latin and produced the first Latin comedy and tragedy, both modelled on Greek originals. We know from Horace that he was read and learned by heart in Roman schools, but few fragments of his work survive.

Antaeus
A giant of Libya, son of Poseidon and Earth (Ge), and an unbeatable wrestler until Heracles realized that he was made stronger by contact with his mother, held him up in the air and squeezed him to death. The best known representations of him in Renaissance art are the bronze group [19] and the painting by Pollaiuolo in Florence.

Antigone

The daughter of Oedipus king of Thebes and his mother Jocasta. She and her sister Ismene played no great part in the Theban saga until Sophocles wrote his Theban trilogy. In *Oedipus at Colonus* she looks after her blinded father in his self-imposed exile, and in the *Antigone* she has returned to Thebes and defies her uncle Creon by insisting on burying her brother Polynices who had tried to seize the city from his brother ETEOCLES. Condemned to burial alive, she forestalls her fate by suicide. The conflict of principles – of conscience and family loyalty versus the law – in this play is of perennial interest, and is debated again in an *Antigone* by Cocteau, and in another by Anouilh written during the German occupation of France.

Antilochus

The son of Nestor king of Pylos, mentioned in the *Iliad* several times as a brave fighter and charioteer. In post-Homeric legend he is killed by Memnon while defending his father, and for later poets his death was a symbol for the tragedy of children dying before their parents.

Antinous

(i) in the *Odyssey*, the most prominent and insolent of Penelope's suitors who is killed by Odysseus on his return home.

(ii) The young favourite of the Roman Emperor Hadrian, born in Bithynia *c.* A.D. 110 and drowned in the Nile in 130 – how or why is unknown. He was deified by Hadrian and the site of his death marked by the founding of the city Antinoöpolis. His head was stamped on coins of Mantinea, where he had a temple, and almost any museum of Roman antiquities has a statue or bust of this beautiful, soft-looking boy [23]. Hadrian's personal tragedy is the basis of a recent historical novel, *Memoirs of Hadrian* by Marguerite Yourcenar.

Antiope

A Theban princess, loved by Zeus in the shape of a satyr, to whom she bore twin sons, Amphion and Zethus. Her father put the children out to die on Mount Cithaeron, but they were reared by a shepherd, and later on Amphion was given a lyre by Hermes and helped Zethus to build the walls of Thebes by making stones move to his music. Antiope fled from her father but was later brought back by her uncle Lycus and his wife Dirce and kept in prison. Eventually she escaped and was avenged by her sons (→ DIRCE). The amours of Zeus were well known to the Renaissance through Ovid's account, and there are several paintings of him in satyr form with Antiope, notably two by Titian and others by Correggio and Watteau.

Antoninus Pius (Roman Emperor A.D. 137–61)

A senator of good family, Antoninus was adopted as the successor to Hadrian. His reign was distinguished by peace and orderly government, and so he was much admired by Gibbon, who compares him with NUMA and says that 'His reign is marked by the rare advantage of furnishing very few materials for history; which is, indeed, little more than the register of the crimes, follies, and misfortunes of mankind.' Of him and his successor MARCUS AURELIUS Gibbon also says that 'Their united reigns are possibly the only period of history in which the happiness of a great people was the sole object of government.'

He extended the British frontier north, and the Wall of Antoninus was built of turf and clay, thirty-seven miles long, between the Firths of Forth and Clyde in Scotland in his reign. It had to be abandoned before the end of the century.

Antonius, Marcus (*c.* 82–30 B.C.)
Best known as Mark Antony, he is the most famous member of a prominent family in the Roman Republic. He supported Julius Caesar and was consul with him in 44 B.C. After Caesar's death he was violently attacked by Cicero in his *Philippics* as a traitor to the cause of liberty. He joined Lepidus and Octavian to form a triumvirate which sentenced many prominent republicans, including Cicero. After the defeat of Brutus and Cassius at Philippi he controlled the forces of the Eastern Empire and began his liaison with CLEOPATRA [8]. He then married Octavian's sister, and the triumvirate was renewed for five years in 37, but Antony returned to Cleopatra, and his gifts of territory to her and their children after his annexation of Armenia made him suspected of disloyalty in Rome. Open war between him and Octavian broke out in 32, and he was decisively defeated at the naval battle of Actium. He returned to Egypt and committed suicide.

The picture Shakespeare gives (in *Julius Caesar* and *Antony and Cleopatra*) of his colourful personality is largely drawn from Plutarch's *Life*, which he knew from the translation of Sir Thomas North, though what Plutarch sees as an infatuation unworthy of a great soldier Shakespeare (and, later, Dryden) transforms into a great tragedy of love. Plutarch tells how Antony liked to be associated with the god Dionysus and claimed descent from Heracles, and the legend that the gods failed him before Actium is repeated in Shakespeare (*Antony and Cleopatra*, IV, iii) and worked into the poem by C. P. Cavafy, *The god abandons Antony*.

Apelles
Greek painter of the fourth century B.C., a native of Colophon near Smyrna, who became official painter at the Macedonian court and was the only man allowed to portray Alexander the Great. Nothing of his work survives, but we have glowing descriptions from the ancient writers, who thought him the greatest painter of his age. His most famous paintings included Aphrodite ANADYOMENE, Alexander as a god with a thunderbolt, the original of the Alexander Mosaic, and an allegorical painting in which Calumny as a female figure preceded by Envy, Intrigue and Deception drags her victim before a man attended by Ignorance and Superstition, while Repentance and Truth follow after them. This was described in detail by Lucian, and followed by

Botticelli in his late picture, *The Calumny of Apelles.*

Aphaia

A goddess identified with the Cretan BRITOMARTIS and worshipped in the island of Aegina, where the ruins of her temple still stand. The sculptures from the pediments of heroes fighting in the Trojan War (*c.* 500 B.C.) are now in Munich, heavily restored in the nineteenth century by the sculptor Thorwaldsen.

Aphrodite (Roman **Venus**)

The Greek goddess of beauty, love and reproduction, worshipped all over Greece but particularly at Paphos in Cyprus, Cythera and Corinth, and on Mount Eryx in Sicily. In one primitive legend she is born of the sea-foam and washed ashore at Paphos after the castration of KRONOS' father Uranus; in others she is the daughter of Zeus and Dione. She is the wife of Hephaestus and lover of Ares in the popular tale told in *Odyssey* 8, and by her mortal lover the Trojan Anchises she is the mother of Aeneas. By Ares she is the mother of EROS. Her association with Adonis shows her as a mother-goddess with close affinities with the Semitic Astarte. In Greek literature she is often not much more than a personification of love or sexual desire; for her later, more romantic treatment, → CUPID, VENUS.

The most famous statues of Aphrodite in antiquity were (i) the Aphrodite of Cnidos, the most celebrated work of the sculptor Praxiteles, made about 350 B.C., which is known to us only through coins of Cnidos and the many Roman copies – forty-nine full-size replicas are known, the best being the 'Capitoline Venus' in Rome; (ii) the Aphrodite of Melos (Venus de Milo), which is based on it. This marble of the second century B.C. is one of many Hellenistic statues of the goddess and was found on Melos in 1820 with other marbles intended for a lime-kiln; it is now in the Louvre, Paris. A 'Crouching Aphrodite' by her bath is also known from Roman copies, and one in the Vatican suggested the pose of Rubens's *Venus Frigida.* The Aphrodite of Arles [45] is also a Roman copy of an original by Praxiteles.

Apicius

A celebrated Roman gourmet (or two, or more, whose personalities have been conflated) under the early Empire, though the cookery book bearing his name is at least two centuries later. This was edited and translated for practical use by B. Flower and E. Rosenbaum under the title *The Roman Cookery Book* in 1958.

Apollo

One of the 'Twelve Olympian' Greek gods, a symbol of light (when he is often given the epithet of Phoebus, 'shining'), of youthful manly beauty and of reason, He is also associated with music. archery, medicine, the care of flocks and herds and with prophecy, and consequently there are an enormous number of legends which deal with his many functions. The island of Delos was sacred to him from earliest times, as it was there that Leto gave birth to him and his sister Artemis; so too was the

DELPHIC ORACLE, where he had the title 'Pythian' after killing the monster which guarded it. This myth is told as early as the Homeric *Hymn to Apollo* and represents the triumph of the Olympian gods of light over the chthonic deities of darkness: see also MARSYAS. Of the many statues of him in antiquity the most famous originals are perhaps the one dating from the mid fifth century from the west pediment of the temple at Olympia, and the Etruscan 'Apollo of Veii' of *c.* 510 B.C. →→ COLOSSUS OF RHODES.

In the Middle Ages Apollo is usually pictured as a doctor or scholar in contemporary dress, but from the Renaissance onwards he appears in all paintings about PARNASSUS, the MUSES, the arts generally, or in his special relationships (e.g. Daphne, Hyacinthus). The Galérie d'Apollon in the Louvre was painted by Lebrun for Louis XIV, whose emblem was Apollo, le Roi Soleil. He appears again with the Muses in Stravinsky's ballet *Apollo*. For Nietzsche's view, → DIONYSUS.

The Apollo Belvedere [24] is a marble copy of a Hellenistic bronze found in Rome in the late fifteenth century and now in the Vatican Museum. Dürer based his proportions for the 'ideal male' on it, and for over three hundred years critics were unanimous in their praise for this romantic concept of the god, overlooking its flabbiness and structural weakness which now seem all too obvious. It was described in ecstatic terms by the German antiquarian of the eighteenth century, Winckelmann, and by Byron in *Childe Harold's Pilgrimage*:

The God of life, and poesy, and light –
The Sun in human limbs array'd, and
  brow
All radiant from his triumph in the
  fight . . .

Byron's own features were compared with the Apollo's by his biographer Thomas Moore. A very different conception of Apollo is found in Rilke's poem, *On an Archaic Torso of Apollo*.

Apollonius Rhodius

Alexandrian poet of the third century B.C., so called because he retired to Rhodes. He was head of the famous library in Alexandria, and as a poet, the rival of CALLIMACHUS. His *Argonautica* (*Voyage of the Argo*), a four-book epic dealing with Jason's quest for the Golden Fleece and Medea's love for Jason, is the first classical work to treat love romantically from the woman's point of view, so that it had great influence on later poets such as Ovid, on Valerius Flaccus (first century A.D.), who also wrote an *Argonautica* in Latin, and in the nineteenth century on William Morris's *Life and Death of Jason*.

Apollonius of Tyana

A Pythagorean philosopher of Cappadocia who was also a wandering holy man and miracle worker. All that is known of him comes from the *Life* written by Flavius Philostratus, a philosopher of the early third century A.D., who was a member of the literary circle of Julia Domna, wife of the Emperor SEPTIMIUS SEVERUS. It is clear from this that Apollonius lived in the first century A.D., for he was in Rome at intervals during the reigns of Nero and Nerva, and he was cultivated by those who saw in his visions and miracles a counterblast to Christianity. His travels took him to India, and he has much in common with Indian fakirs. Robert Burton recalled one episode in the *Life* in his *Anatomy of Melancholy*, and this in its turn inspired Keats's *Lamia*. There a beautiful woman of Corinth vanishes when Apollonius enters her home on her wedding night and detects her as a Lamia, the serpent woman of Greek folklore who is still to be feared as a child-stealing witch. The strange fascination of the *Life*, written so long after the death of its subject, inspired Cavafy's poem *If Dead Indeed.*

Apuleius, Lucius (?)

Roman writer, born *c.* A.D. 123 in north Africa, educated at Carthage and Athens, widely travelled and famous as a poet, philosopher and orator. The best known of his surviving works is the *Golden Ass* or *Metamorphoses*, the only complete Latin novel to survive. This describes the adventures of Lucius, a sorcerer's apprentice, who is accidentally turned into an ass and finally restored to human form by the goddess Isis. It contains a moving description of the Mysteries of Isis, and the story of CUPID and PSYCHE, and has been much translated, notably by William Adlington in 1566 and by Robert Graves.

Arachne

In a legend told by Ovid she is a Lydian girl who challenged Athene to a tapestry-weaving contest, and when the angry goddess destroyed her work she tried to hang herself and was changed into a spider (Greek *arachne*). This is a good example of the popular feeling that the gods resent human competition; cf. MARSYAS, NIOBE, SALMONEUS.

Aratus (*c.* 315–*c.* 240 B.C.)

Greek poet from Cilicia, who came to Athens, where he learned Stoicism from Zeno and became a friend of Callimachus, and then lived at the court of the Macedonian kings. His most famous work was his *Phaenomena*, a long astronomical poem on the fixed stars and constellations and the myths attached to them, and also on weather signs, for which he made use of HESIOD. It includes fine passages of description on the Golden Age and on a storm at sea. It influenced Lucretius and Virgil, and the parts that were translated into Latin by Cicero were widely read in the Middle Ages. It was a fifteenth-century manuscript of Aratus which inspired Dürer's famous Skymap of 1515, the first printed chart of the heavens in which the gods of the stars began to be restored to their classical images instead of appearing in medieval or even Arabic guise. And who but Ronsard could have started a long poem

> *'J'ay l'esprit tout ennuyé*
> *D'avoir trop estudié*
> *Les Phaenomènes d'Arate*

– and ended it with a call to his servant to go out and buy wine and melons, strawberries and cream?

Arcadia

A central region of the Greek Peloponnese, traditionally the home of the primitive god Pan to whom Mount Maenalus was sacred: a wild and mountainous terrain which later became idealized as the home of pastoral poetry and song, with nymphs and satyrs, shepherds and their loves all living an idyllic life of innocence and simplicity. Arcadia in this sense is the setting for Theocritus's idylls, though the scenery he describes is that of Sicily and south Italy, for Hellenistic romances such as *Daphnis and Chloe*, and for Virgil's *Eclogues*. The pastoral genre was enthusiastically developed in the Renaissance after the circulation in translation from the Italian of Jacopo Sannazaro's *Arcadia* of 1481, and has been constantly reinterpreted. Marlowe's *Passionate Shepherd*, Shakespeare's *As You Like It*, Spenser's *Shepherd's Calendar*, Milton's *Comus* and *Lycidas*, Shelley's *Adonais*, Matthew Arnold's *Thyrsis* are all variations on the theme; so too are Bach's *Peasant Cantata* and *Phoebus and Pan*, Mallarmé's and Debussy's *L'Après-midi d'un faune*, Ravel's *Daphnis and Chloe* and Delibes's *Sylvia*. The ideal landscapes of Poussin and Claude are Arcadian, and so is the landscape-gardening of the eighteenth century or the rustic artificialities of Marie Antoinette at the Petit Trianon. The Arcadian Society founded in Rome in 1690 by Queen Christina of Sweden in her retirement was only the first of many such; it lasted two hundred years. Arcadia still haunts E. M. Forster's novels, and perhaps any urge to escape from formal or urban society carries with it the idealization of a natural life.

Et in Arcadia ego (Even in Arcadia I am found) refers to Death, and is first used as a title for a picture by Guercino, best known from two copies by Poussin [21], of Arcadian shepherds looking at a skull and a tomb – perhaps that of Daphnis who dies for love in Virgil's *Eclogue* 5. This has been misquoted or at least mistranslated as 'I too have lived in Arcadia', i.e. have known a happier life, from the German romantic poets onwards.

Archilochus

Greek elegiac poet of Paros of the mid seventh century B.C. (he described a total eclipse of the sun in 648). He was the bastard son of a slave woman and an aristocrat, and was famous among the Greeks for his bitter satire and anti-heroic, anti-romantic personal opinions. Among the surviving fragments of his poetry his poem about throwing his shield away in battle in order to escape with his life was often quoted, and his work was the model for Horace's *Epodes*.

Archimedes (*c.* 287–212 B.C.)

Greek scientist of Syracuse, the greatest mathematician of the ancient world. He studied in Alexandria and then returned to Syracuse as adviser to King Hiero II, designing catapults and grapnels to help in the city's defence under siege. He was killed when the Romans took Syracuse. Archimedes calculated the value of π and his name is associated with several principles of geometry and mechanics, e.g. 'Archimedes' screw' as a means of raising water, 'Archimedes' problem' for calculating the volume of a sphere, and 'Archimedes' principle', whereby a body immersed in fluid apparently loses weight equal to the weight of water displaced, from which can be calculated the volume of the body. This he was popularly said to have discovered in his bath while trying to work out whether a crown made for Hiero was pure gold or alloyed with silver. He ran out into the street crying 'I have found it!' (*heureka*). He was also quoted for his boast that he could move great masses by a small force: 'Give me a place to stand and I will move the earth.' He designed his own tomb, a sphere inside a cylinder, to commemorate his proudest mathematical discovery, i.e. that the sphere occupies two-thirds of the space. Cicero was sad to find it overgrown and neglected by the Syracusans. He also saw Archimedes' planetarium, which had been moved to Rome.

Ares

The Greek god of war, possibly imported from Thrace, and never very popular in myth. In the *Iliad* he supports the Trojans, in *Odyssey* 8 in the song of the minstrel Demodocus he is the lover of APHRODITE, and elsewhere he is the father by her of Eros. For his post-classical treatment, → MARS.

The Areopagus, or Hill of Ares, north-west of the Athenian Acropolis, was the meeting place of the Council of Elders, originally acting as advisers to the kings, but in historic times reduced in powers. It tried cases involving homicide and treason; → ORESTES. The hill is the 'Mars' Hill' of Acts xvii, 22 from which St Paul addressed the Athenians.

Arethusa

A nymph of Elis whom the river Alpheus pursued when she was bathing in his waters. Artemis then opened a passage under the sea through which their mingled waters flowed until they rose as a spring on the island of Ortygia in Syracuse. This is the subject of Shelley's *Arethusa* and the starting-point of Swinburne's play in the style of a Greek tragedy. On Syracusan coins of the fifth century Arethusa's head appears in profile surrounded by dolphins [31.2], and it was said that objects thrown into the Alpheus could be recovered from the spring. This was still local belief in A.D. 397 when STILICHO defeated the Goths by the Alpheus and the news reached Sicily when the waters of Arethusa ran red – with their blood. The Fontana Aretusa is indeed still to be seen, a rather grimy pool planted round with bamboo, but its waters are now salt; according to Baedeker as the result of earthquakes in the past.

Argo, Argonauts

The ship *Argo* was the first longship ever built and carried the Greek heroes (the Argonauts) who sailed with JASON to Colchis on the Black Sea to recover the Golden Fleece (→ PHRIXUS). This is one of the oldest of Greek legends, known to Homer, and possibly based on a real exploit of the prehistoric Minyan people from Orchomenus in Boeotia, though it is also rich in detail of the traditional adventure-voyage kind. Later accounts of the voyage took the Argonauts up the Danube and down the Rhône as well as to Lake Tritonis in Libya. It inspired Pindar's greatest ode

(*Pythian* 4). → APOLLONIUS RHODIUS. In Seferis's *Argonauts* the voyage is symbolic of the soul's search for self-discovery; yet it is described by someone uncomprehending of its purpose.

Argus

(i) An Argonaut, who built the *Argo* with the help of Athene.
(ii) In the *Odyssey*, the faithful dog of Odysseus who recognized his master after twenty years and then died.
(iii) A hundred-eyed giant, set to watch IO when Zeus turned her into a heifer: hence the expression 'argus-eyed' for the carefully watchful. He was killed by Hermes and turned into a peacock. →→ SYRINX.

Ariadne

The daughter of Minos king of Crete, who guided Theseus through the labyrinth by means of a ball of thread so that he could escape after killing the Minotaur. He took her away with him but abandoned her on the island of Dia (later identified with Naxos). There she was found by Dionysus (Bacchus) who married her and gave her a crown of seven stars which became a constellation after her death. Ariadne's betrayal by the ungrateful Theseus is one of the themes of Catullus's longest poem (64) and she is a natural subject for one of Ovid's romantic *Heroides*, which accounts for her appearance in Chaucer's *Legend of Good Women*.

She was also well known to Hellenistic writers and artists. The statue known as the 'Sleeping Ariadne' in Rome is copied from a Hellenistic original. But though she could express for Catullus his personal sufferings in love, for the Renaissance she became more a symbol of life through death because she was gathered up into the divine ecstasy brought by Bacchus. His arrival was painted by Titian in his *Bacchanal* (which Poussin copied) and in *Bacchus and Ariadne* [20]; Tintoretto and Raphael also painted Ariadne and her divine lover. This concept was revived in the opera *Ariadne auf Naxos* by Hugo von Hofmannsthal and Richard Strauss, where the classical story is the play within the play; Ariadne abandons herself to death only to find new life in the god. For Gide's view, → THESEUS.

Arimaspi

A fabulous people of the Scythian steppes bordering on the HYPERBOREANS, said by Herodotus and Pausanias to be one-eyed and to be perpetually fighting to gain a hoard of gold from the griffins which guard it; they and the griffins belong to Asiatic folklore. They are mentioned by Aeschylus in a description of the wanderings of IO, and after him in a famous simile in Milton's *Paradise Lost*, 2.943–5:

As when a gryphon thro' the wilderness
With winged course o'er hill or moory
  dale
Pursues the Arimaspian...

Herodotus (4.13) also says that an epic poem was written about them by Aristeas, who was a servant of Hyperborean Apollo and a native of Marmora on the Black Sea. (A few lines of this are quoted by Longinus.) His brief account is of special interest because Aristeas is recognizable as a shaman, able to separate soul from body, appear in two places at the same time, reappear after death, and assume the form of a raven.

Arion
A Greek poet of the late seventh century B.C. who developed the type of choral song called the dithyramb as a literary composition. He left his native Lesbos for the court of Periander of Corinth, and then toured successfully in Italy and Sicily. On his voyage back to Corinth he was thrown into the sea by the crew of the ship, but was brought safely back to Corinth on the back of a dolphin. This sounds like folklore but is told by Herodotus and was widely accepted. A man with a lyre on a dolphin can be assumed to be Arion: e.g. in a Roman mosaic at Ostia. In Mantegna's ceiling painting in the ducal palace at Mantua Arion appears with his dolphin, as do the guilty sailors brought before Periander.

Aristaeus
A minor Greek hero, whose cult originated in Thessaly where, according to Pindar, he was the son of Apollo and a Lapith girl, Cyrene. He was the protector of cattle and fruit trees and patron of bee-keepers. Virgil in *Georgic* 4 says that Cyrene was a nymph, and tells a tale unknown elsewhere, that Aristaeus was punished by the death of all his bees for pursuing Eurydice and indirectly causing her death when a snake bit her. Cyrene helps him to get advice from PROTEUS, and acting on this he sacrifices cattle to placate the, nymphs and finds new swarms in the carcasses nine days later. This too sounds like folklore – a similar story about bees is told in connection with the Hebrew hero Samson. Virgil's account of Eurydice's death is followed by Niccolo dell' Abate in his painting called *The Story of Aristaeus.*

Aristides (*c.* 520 or earlier–*c.* 467 B.C.)
Athenian statesman and general, a prominent leader in the war against the invading Persians, and then responsible for creating the Delian League which was to become virtually an Athenian empire. Plutarch contrasts him with Themistocles, but the two worked together over rebuilding the walls after the Persian wars. Aristides' reputation for honesty became proverbial, and the story is often told how a citizen voted for his ostracism simply because he was tired of hearing Aristides called 'the Just'. He was in fact banished in 482 (but recalled a year later) by this system of popular vote, then recently instituted in Athens, and fragments of broken pottery (Greek *ostraca*) have been found bearing his name.

Aristogiton
The Athenian tyrannicide, who with Harmodius planned to kill the tyrants Hippias and Hipparchus in 514 B.C. Only Hipparchus was killed; Harmodius was killed by Hippias's guards and Aristogiton was executed later. Three years later the tyranny was overthrown, and the two were regarded as liberators and founders of Athenian democracy. The famous group of statues in their honour which Pausanias saw in the Athenian agora had been carried off to

Persia by Xerxes and restored long afterwards by Alexander. It is known from numerous Roman copies, the best known in the museum at Naples. Brutus and Cassius had a similar image in Roman history, and when they came to Athens after Caesar's murder their statues were commissioned to stand by those of the tyrannicides.

Aristophanes (*c.* 450–*c.* 385 B.C.)
Greek comic dramatist, the only writer of 'Old Comedy' of whom any complete plays survive. From his immense output (forty titles are known) we have eleven to illustrate his inventive wit, gift for parody and satire, dramatic sense and poetic sensibility. Above all he was a creator of words in a way no one has matched, except the Irishman James Joyce. His plays are topical, dealing with Athenian policies and politicians, contemporary poets and the philosophers such as Socrates, and attitudes current in his day, with an underlying seriousness leaning towards conservatism in both literature and politics. The best known of his plays in modern translation are perhaps *The Birds*, *The Frogs* and *Lysistrata*.

Aristophanes of Byzantium (*c.* 257–180 B.C.)
Head of the library at Alexandria and a remarkable scholar, who produced a critical edition of Homer and Hesiod and the first collected and annotated editions of the works of Pindar, the lyric and tragic poets, and the comedies of Aristophanes. He also wrote studies on Greek grammar and dialects, and introduced the system of accents and breathings that was adopted in Byzantine times and is still used in modern Greek and in our texts of ancient Greek works.

Aristotle (384–322 B.C.)
Greek scientist and philosopher who was born at Stagira in Thrace and studied in Athens under Plato until Plato's death. He then left to travel in the eastern Mediterranean, and for a short time lived at the Macedonian court at Pella as tutor to the young Alexander. He returned to Athens in 335 and set up the Lyceum where he taught until his retirement a year before his death. His school of philosophy is sometimes called the Peripatetic School from the covered arcade (*peripatos*) among the buildings where he taught. His works were collected and edited as early as the first century B.C.; those extant seem to be in the form of memoranda for lectures, and cover every branch of science and philosophy known in his day. They were eclipsed by the popularity of Stoic and Epicurean philosophy, but were rediscovered in the Middle Ages, largely through the work of Arabic scholars such as Averroës, and in a Latin version were widely known, especially after St Thomas Aquinas incorporated Aristotle's philosophy into Catholic theology. (In a painting by Gozzoli, Aristotle and Plato are grouped with Aquinas.) For Dante he was '*il maestro di color che sanno*' (the master of those who know), and all western thinking has made use of his system of classification and terminology. A combination of close observation with acute reasoning and an

orderly exposition of facts mark all his work, whether he was writing on politics, ethics, physics or biology, and his main characteristic has been defined as 'a sort of inspired common sense'. In the Renaissance his works were translated more than those of any other pagan author because they were common ground for scholastics and humanists. But as Plato's higher flights of imagination grew in appeal, Aristotle became identified with the arid scholastic logic used by the sort of theologian Erasmus condemned, and his creative work was forgotten or became scientifically out of date.

The dramatic Unities of Time, Place and Action, which were a rigid rule for the French classical dramatists, were thought to derive from Aristotle's *Poetics*, but were in fact based on a misinterpretation which can be traced to Italian renaissance scholars and, in particular, to the *Poetics* of Julius Caesar Scaliger. Aristotle is not laying down rules, he only comments on the practice of the theatre he knew when he contrasts epic and tragedy by saying that one has no fixed limit of time, the other 'generally tries to keep within a single revolution of the sun, or not much more'. He also points out that epic can cover events in many places whereas a play is limited to one stage and the parts of the actors. What he does insist on is 'unity of plot', which can be found in the Homeric epics just as much as in a play. The *Poetics* also contain Aristotle's theory of catharsis, i.e. that tragedy purges the emotions through the sensations of pity and fear. → DIONYSUS.

Artemis

Greek goddess, probably pre-Olympian in origin, but from Homer onwards said to be the daughter of Zeus and Leto and twin sister of Apollo. She was worshipped with him at Delos, and her most important sanctuaries were at Brauron in Attica and at Ephesus. She was a virgin huntress, associated with uncultivated places and wild animals (→ ACTAEON, CALLISTO, HIPPOLYTUS), and often conflated with Hecate, or with Selene, the moon goddess; she was also sometimes a primitive birth goddess, and in Sparta merged with the Dorian goddess Orthia. With her arrows she brought natural death, and also punished impiety (→ NIOBE). The Romans identified her with the Italian goddess DIANA. Consequently the reference in the New Testament (Acts xix) to the Temple of Diana of the Ephesians, when St Paul's arrival causes a riot outside, is really to the great Artemisium at Ephesus, one of the Seven Wonders of the Ancient World. A celebrated statue of Artemis was there, covered all over with breasts to mark her connection with childbirth.

Ascanius

The son of Aeneas and, according to Virgil, of Creusa, who escaped with his parents and grandfather Anchises from burning Troy. Another tradition makes his mother the Latin princess Lavinia. He succeeded his father as second king and made his capital at Alba Longa (on the site of Castelgandolfo). He was also called Julus by Latin writers, and the Julian family claimed to be descended from him and also from his divine grandmother, Venus (→ ANCHISES). 'Ascanius shooting the Stag of Silvia' has been a popular subject with painters, and there are beautiful examples by Claude. This comes from an episode in *Aeneid* 7. Juno sends the Fury Allecto to stir up trouble between the Trojans, newly arrived in Latium, and the Rutulians, allies of the Latins. She directs Ascanius's arrow at the pet stag of the royal herdsman's daughter, and a pitched battle ensues.

Asclepius

Greek hero and god of healing. In Homer he is mortal and has been taught medicine by the centaur Chiron; in later mythology he is said to be the son of APOLLO and CORONIS, and was associated with Apollo as a god of healing. His cult was widespread, each shrine having its sacred snakes, and baths and a gymnasium for therapeutic treatment, though the most important element was the ritual act of sleeping in the temple to await visitation from the god. His main sanctuaries were on the island of Cos, where HIPPOCRATES and his disciples took over his work, and at Epidaurus, the Lourdes of the Greek world. There was also one on the slopes of the Athenian Acropolis. There is still much to be seen at Epidaurus, but not the statue described by Pausanias of Asclepius with his staff and sacred snake. It was copied on the coins of Epidaurus. Plato quotes the last words of Socrates, that he owed a cock to Asclepius – the traditional sacrifice for a cure, which to Socrates meant death as the supreme 'cure' for life.

Asclepius was brought to Rome after a plague in 293 B.C., by order of the Sibylline Books, and according to Livy and Ovid the sacred snake which embodied the god chose the present Isola Tiberina for its home. There a temple and sanctuary were set up and the cult was modelled on that of Epidaurus. The god was then worshipped there under the Latinized name Aesculapius.

Asinius Pollio, Gaius (76 B.C.–A.D. 5)
Roman general and statesman who fought for Caesar and then for Antony in the Civil Wars, but afterwards retired from politics and became a patron of the arts. He founded the first public library in Rome, of which VARRO was librarian. He knew Catullus in his youth, was a friend of Horace and Virgil, and wrote poetry himself as well as speeches and a history of the Civil War: none of it survives. As a critic he is remembered for his jibe about Livy's *patavinitas*, i.e. the provincialism of the historian's native Padua (Patavium).

Aspasia

The mistress of the Athenian statesman Pericles, born in Miletus and living with him in Athens from about 440 B.C. She was famous for her intellectual attainments at a time when Greek women were uneducated, and acted as hostess to Pericles' political friends. Consequently she was attacked by his enemies and tradition says that she was prosecuted, unsuccessfully, for 'impiety' in 431, though this is unconfirmed. Her son by Pericles was legitimized by special decree, and after Pericles' death she married the democrat Lysicles and had another son.

W. S. Landor's *Pericles and Aspasia* is a series of imagined letters discussing topics of artistic and literary interest.

Atalanta

An Arcadian heroine, disowned by her father and suckled by a bear sent by Artemis, with whom she seems to be identified: she grew up to be a famous huntress, vowed to virginity, and took part in the hunt of the CALYDONIAN BOAR. There Meleager fell in love with her and gave her the boar's skin. In some versions she had a child by Meleager, in others she made her suitors compete against her in a footrace, and was eventually beaten by Milanion (or Hippomenes), who dropped three golden apples one by one which she stopped to pick up. This story was well known in the Renaissance from Ovid's *Metamorphoses* 10, and was painted by Poussin, closely following Ovid. Atalanta also attracted Swinburne, who first became known through his poetic drama *Atalanta in Calydon.*

Até

In Homer *até* is no more than the sort of blinded judgement which makes AGAMEMNON take Achilles' mistress or GLAUCUS make a bad bargain, and it carries no moral reproach. The man who does something misguided admits responsibility and says only that it was sent by FATE – i.e., that it had to be, though he cannot explain why. The concept of *até* as an infatuation which makes men provoke the gods and destroy themselves comes later, when Hesiod makes her the daughter of Strife and Lawlessness, and in the dramatists *até* is linked with the presumption (*hubris*) which leads to NEMESIS.

Athene (In Greek, more correctly, **Athena**)

The Greek goddess of war, the patron of the arts and crafts and the personification of wisdom, identified in all her roles with Minerva by the Romans. Early legends say she sprang fully armed from the head of Zeus, and she competed with Poseidon for the ownership of Attica. Poseidon produced the horse, Athene the olive, which was judged the more useful gift, so Athens was called after her and she was its special patron. She was worshipped on the Acropolis 'in the house of Erechtheus' according to Homer, i.e. in the former Mycenean palace, and the Parthenon was built in her honour as a virgin goddess (*parthenos*, virgin). This contained the famous gold-and-ivory statue by PHIDIAS known to us from copies. His thirty-foot bronze statue of Athene the Warrior stood by the Propylaea, the great marble gateway at the west end of the Acropolis. She is commonly shown in ancient art with helmet, spear and shield, particularly in vase-paintings, though she is also patroness of all arts and crafts. She was widely worshipped all over the Greek world; Syracuse Cathedral, for example, incorporates pillars from a temple of Athene. In Homer she supports the Greeks, especially Odysseus throughout his wanderings, and sometimes takes the form of a bird; her stock epithet *glaucopis* could mean either 'bright-eyed' or 'owl-faced', but the owl is not specifically associated with her until classical times when it marked the coins of Athens [31.1]. 'Owls to Athens' was a saying equivalent to 'coals to Newcastle'.

Atlantis

About 1450 B.C. an eruption on the volcanic island of Santorini (ancient Thera) destroyed Knossos, covered eastern Crete with ash, and could well be the basis of the story which Plato (in his *Timaeus*) says was told to Solon in Egypt about the lost Atlantis – a large island which had attempted to enslave the Mediterranean world but had been defeated by Athens and then destroyed in a tidal wave. Atlantis was later popularly located west of the straits of Gibraltar, and confused with the islands of the HESPERIDES. Seneca describes a continent beyond the seas in a chorus of his play *Medea*, a passage which is said to have impressed Columbus before his voyage of discovery.

Atlas

A Titan, condemned to stand in the west holding up the sky on his shoulders, except for a short time when Heracles took over the burden while Atlas fetched him the golden apples of the Hesperides. In another early legend he is visited by Perseus, turned into stone by the Gorgon's head, and so identified with Mount Atlas in north-western Africa. These are popular explanations of why the sky does not fall. In Homer he is the father of Calypso, but usually his daughters are the Pleiades because the mountains bring rain. He appears with Heracles in a metope of the mid fifth century from the temple of Zeus at Olympia, and is fairly common in Hellenistic sculpture, either supporting a sphere or adding decoration to a pillar, as a caryatid does: in architecture, atlantes are the male counterparts of CARYATIDS. In the Middle Ages Atlas was believed to have taught men astrology, through his association with the sky and stars. Then he became a symbol of endurance, until by the time of Heine's poem which Schubert set to music it is a world of sorrows which he must bear.

Atreus

King of Mycenae, son of PELOPS, father of Agamemnon and Menelaus, husband of Aerope who was seduced by Atreus's brother Thyestes. In revenge Atreus served up the flesh of the incestuously begotten children to Thyestes, at which the sun turned back on its course with horror and Thyestes cursed the whole family of Atreus. See genealogical tree of House of Pelops, p. 187. The so-called 'Treasury of Atreus' at Mycenae is the largest circular-vaulted tholos tomb in Greece, built *c.* 1350 B.C.

Attalus

The name of several kings of Pergamum from the third to the first century B.C. Attalus I (269–197) won a victory over the invading Galatians and set up a famous triumphal monument in Pergamum (see DYING GLADIATOR). He supported the Romans in the second Macedonian War against Philip V of Macedon, and was an able diplomat as well as a patron of the arts and benefactor to Athens. Attalus II (220–138) continued his father's patronage of the arts and built the Stoa of Attalus on the east side of the agora or marketplace of Athens. This was a two-aisled colonnade nearly 400 feet long with small shops behind and an upper storey, and it stood until it was burnt by invading Celts in A.D. 267. It was rebuilt in its original form in 1956 by the American School of Classical Studies in Athens, and now houses a small museum of finds upon the site.

Atticus, Titus Pomponius (109–32 B.C.)
A Roman businessman of great wealth and wide cultural interests, who was long resident in Athens – hence his surname. He took no part in politics on his return, but he was a close friend of Cicero and a recipient of many of his letters. There seems to be no real proof for the idea that he sponsored the posthumous publication of the letters he received.

Attila (*c.* A.D. 404–53)
King of the Huns and known as *flagellum dei*, the 'Scourge of God'. He and his army of Tartars ravaged the Eastern Empire for several years until the Emperor Theodosius bought peace with him, and then Attila turned to the West. He was defeated at Châlons by the Roman general Aetius in 451, but then invaded northern Italy as far as the Po; there he was met by Pope Leo and agreed to leave Italy in return for the princess Honoria and her vast dowry, but died suddenly soon after. All this is vividly described by Gibbon in chapters 34–5 of the *Decline and Fall*, where he also refers to the painting by Raphael in the Vatican in which Leo is helped in his mission by apparitions of St Peter and St Paul, 'one of the noblest legends of ecclesiastical tradition'. Attila and his hordes were also painted by Delacroix. Attila is the Etzel of medieval German saga and is a prominent character in the *Nibelungenlied*. In Norse saga he is Atli. In the guise of tragic hero he is also the central figure in Corneille's *Attila*.

Attis
Originally, like Adonis, a vegetation god, with a spring festival of death and resurrection which originated in Phrygia. There he was the young male consort of the goddess CYBELE. In one version of his myth he castrates himself in a religious frenzy and becomes the leader of Cybele's eunuch priests; the horror of his self-mutilation pervades one of Catullus's greatest poems (63).

Augeas
A king of Elis, remembered chiefly for the filthy state of his stables. Cleaning them was one of the labours of Heracles, who did so by diverting the river Alpheus through them. Augeas then refused to pay, so Heracles killed him and gave his kingdom to his son. 'Augean stables' became proverbial.

Augustine, Saint (A.D. 354–430)
Bishop of Hippo Regius (Bizerta) in north Africa, and one of the most influential Fathers of the Christian Church. His output of theological and

critical writing was enormous (six times that of Cicero); the best known are his autobiography (*Confessions*), which gives a moving account of his conversion to Christianity after hearing the sermons of St Ambrose, Bishop of Milan, and *The City of God*, where he contrasts the two worlds of heaven and earth. The *Confessions* inspired Petrarch's personal confessions (*Secretum*) which take the form of three dialogues between himself and St Augustine.

He is not to be confused with the first Archbishop of Canterbury, sent by Pope Gregory to convert the Saxons in 597.

Augustus (Gaius Julius Caesar Octavianus, first Emperor of Rome 27 B.C.–A.D. 14)

This was the title taken by Octavian, great nephew and adopted son of Julius Caesar, and also his heir. With Mark Antony and Lepidus he was the victor in the Civil War against his uncle's murderers, Brutus and Cassius. (As 'Octavius Caesar' this is the part he plays in Shakespeare's *Julius Caesar*.) He subsequently fell out with Antony and defeated him in 31 B.C. He was then effectively in sole command of Rome, backed by his able supporters AGRIPPA and MAECENAS. He based his constitutional position on the traditions of the old Republic, though there was no question of his restoring the democratic liberties which in his view had led to the political factions and fighting of the last two generations. His character has been variously assessed, but in the eyes of contemporary writers such as Livy, Horace and Virgil he brought internal peace and prosperity to Rome and security to the provinces of the Empire. His achievements (*res gestae*) are set out in Greek and Latin on the famous Monumentum Ancyranum which was found in 1555 at Ancyra (Ankara), a copy on stone of the record which, as we know from Suetonius, Augustus had deposited with the Vestal Virgins to be read out in the Senate after his death. Perhaps the most impressive monument of his reign is the Altar of Peace (*ara pacis*) which was set up in 13 B.C. in the Campus Martius to commemorate his safe return from Gaul and Spain. The sculptured slabs of this show a sacrificial procession and members of the imperial family in a relaxed design of real beauty. The title of Augustus was borne by all subsequent Roman emperors and by those of the Holy Roman Empire.

Aurora

The Roman goddess of the dawn, identified with the Greek EOS. Aurora driving her chariot and horses across the sky was a natural subject for the baroque ceiling-painters, and there are fine examples in Roman palaces by Carracci, Guercino and Guido Reni.

Ausonius, Decimus Magnus (*c.* A.D. 310–*c.* 395)

A Gallo-Roman teacher of rhetoric and provincial governor, a native of Bordeaux, and also a prolific poet. He was a baptized Christian, but his poems are more Virgilian than Christian in tone. His best poem is *Mosella* (the river Moselle), a poetic guidebook to the river, its fish and surrounding vineyards, in which the literary echoes of Virgil are combined with a perceptive love of nature.

Autolycus
The maternal grandfather of Odysseus, renowned for his trickery and thieving. He was taught by Hermes, who in some versions of his legend was his father. His name became synonymous with roguery; hence the character in Shakespeare's *The Winter's Tale*.

Avernus
A deep sulphurous lake N.W. of Roman Puteoli (Pozzuoli), still called Lago Averno, which in ancient times was generally thought to be one of the entrances to the Underworld and never visited by birds (Greek *a-ornos*). This is the way Aeneas is told to go by the SIBYL of near-by Cumae, in *Aeneid* 6. AGRIPPA connected it with the Lucrine lake during the construction of his harbour at Portus Julius. By now the area has been much changed by volcanic eruptions and building development. But the lake with its surrounding woods (painted by Claude and Richard Wilson) is still 'suggestivo'.

Bacchants (or **Maenads**)
Women roused to ecstatic frenzy by the god DIONYSUS, as described by Euripides in *The Bacchae*. They are liberated from all human fears and conventions, and roam the mountains, living like animals, uprooting trees and devouring raw flesh. There were famous passionate bacchants in statues of the fourth century B.C. (one by Scopas is known from a copy) but the tendency was to show them in more formal ritual dance, as in the frescoes of the Villa of the Mysteries, Pompeii, or on the silver Mildenhall Dish of the mid fourth century A.D. [3], until they became purely decorative. They are often shown in a frieze on the side of a sarcophagus. In the paintings of the Renaissance there is little to distinguish them from dancing nymphs, though Titian in his two Bacchanal paintings catches their sensuous abandon. Poussin's *Bacchanal* was copied by Picasso with disturbing effect.

Bacchus
A title of the Greek god DIONYSUS, his usual name in Latin; consequently this is the form more often found in post-Renaissance art and literature. Michelangelo's statue shows him typically as a youth crowned with vine-leaves and grapes, with a hermaphroditic suggestion which was noted as early as the sixteenth century by the critic Vasari, and among other paintings there is a splendidly sensuous Correggio. See also ARIADNE. His upbringing by the nymphs, like that of the infant Zeus, was also painted several times by Poussin. Piero di Cosimo has two scenes of *The Discovery of Honey* and *The Discovery of Wine* by Bacchus, both drawn from Ovid's *Fasti*, book 3.

Bacchylides
Greek lyric poet, born on the island of Ceos at the end of the sixth century B.C., the nephew of Simonides and rival of Pindar. He settled in the Peloponnesus, and for a time lived at the court of

Hiero I of Syracuse. Most of his surviving poems, victory-odes and choral hymns, were discovered on Egyptian papyri as late as 1896. They include a fragment of a splendid dithyramb on the hero Theseus.

Barbari

Often mistranslated as 'barbarians', this is the term applied by the Greeks to all non-Greek-speakers, as an onomatopoeic description of an unintelligible language. Its contemptuous use comes much later.

Baucis

The wife of Philemon, a countryman of Phrygia. This virtuous old couple is known from Ovid's account (which was translated by La Fontaine and by Dryden). They entertained Zeus and Hermes in their cottage when the gods were travelling in disguise and were refused hospitality elsewhere. In return they were told to climb a mountain to escape the flood which overwhelmed their impious neighbours, and afterwards served the temple of Zeus, died together, and were changed into intertwining trees. They inspired a splendid landscape by Rubens and a late picture by Rembrandt of the old people in their hut with the gods.

Belisarius

The famous general of the Emperor Justinian, whose exploits are recorded by his secretary Procopius (and are the subject of Robert Graves's novel *Count Belisarius*). He is first heard of in A.D. 526 in Justinian's war against Persia, but his greatest achievements were as leader of a small force sent to recover Africa from the Vandals and Italy from the Goths. He occupied Sardinia and Corsica, Sicily, Naples and Rome, and then the Gothic capital of Ravenna in 540. The jealousy of his fellow generals led to his recall to Constantinople, though he emerged from retirement to defend the city against the Bulgars in 559. He was then arrested on a charge of conspiracy against the emperor and imprisoned in his own palace in 562. He was reinstated next year and died in 565, but later stories said he died blinded and a beggar. This is how the neoclassicist French painter David painted him in the first of his great heroic pictures, *Give Belisarius a Penny*.

Bellerophon(tes)

Son of Glaucus, grandson of Sisyphus, and the hero of a very old legend of Corinth, recounted by Homer in the *Iliad*, book 6. Most of his adventures are very like those of Heracles or belong to the common stock of folklore. At the court of Proetus king of Argos he repelled the queen's advances and was denounced by her (cf. PHAEDRA). Proetus then sent him to his father-in-law, the king of Lycia, bearing a sealed letter demanding his death. There Bellerophon was set some tasks likely to kill him, such as killing the Chimaera, a fire-breathing monster 'lion in front, serpent behind, goat in the middle'. Bellerophon did everything successfully and married the king's daughter. Later legend says he was helped by his magic winged horse PEGASUS. Afterwards he incurred the wrath of the gods by trying to ride Pegasus to heaven, was driven mad and died a wandering outcast. He was the grandfather of the Homeric hero GLAUCUS.

Berenice

The most famous of many Berenices is the daughter of Herod Agrippa, who was born in A.D. 28, married to her uncle, and then lived incestuously with her brother. (She is the 'Bernice' of Acts xxv who is present when Agrippa hears St Paul defend himself.) She supported the Romans in the Jewish War and became the mistress of the Emperor Vespasian's son Titus when he was in command in Judaea in 67–70. Later she joined him in Rome and lived openly with him, but was dismissed – unwillingly – by him when he became emperor in 79. This is the theme of Corneille's *Tite et Berenice* and Racine's *Berenice*.

'The Lock of Berenice' is a constellation referred to in a poem by Callimachus, on which Catullus's poem 66 is so closely modelled as to be virtually a translation. This Berenice was born in 273 B.C. and married Ptolemy III. She dedicated a lock of her hair against her husband's safe return from war in Syria. The lock disappeared, but was happily discovered as a group of stars by the royal astronomer. In Pope's *The Rape of the Lock* the heroine's curl of hair also becomes a new star.

Bion

Greek pastoral poet, living in Sicily about 100 B.C. The best known of his few surviving poems is a 'lament for Adonis', perhaps intended for a festival of ADONIS.

Biton and Cleobis

Heroes of Argos, sons of a priestess of Hera, who drew their mother's chariot several miles to the temple of the goddess when no oxen could be got. She prayed for the best gift possible as their reward, and they died in the temple. The story is told to Croesus of Lydia by Solon in Herodotus's history to illustrate the paradox 'call no man happy until he is dead'. There are archaic statues *c.* 600 B.C. of the brothers at Delphi.

Boadicea

The usual English form of **Boudicca**, the queen of the Iceni, a tribe settled in East Anglia. After her husband's death in A.D. 61 the Romans annexed her kingdom, and she then led a rebellion, sacking Colchester, London and Verulamium. She was defeated by the general Suetonius Paulinus and took poison. Her story is told by Tacitus. There is a statue of her in her chariot at the corner of Westminster Bridge in London by the sculptor Thomas Thornycroft, and a painful experiment in galliambic metre by Tennyson:

So the Queen Boädicéa, standing loftily charioted,
Brandishing in her hand a dart and rolling glances lioness-like,
Yell'd and shriek'd between her daughters in her fierce volubility . . .

Boethius, Annius Manlius Severinus

(*c.* A.D. 480–524)

Roman statesman and author of several treatises on music, mathematics and philosophy which had wide influence in the Middle Ages. His Latin translations of Aristotle meant that there was continuous knowledge of Aristotle in the West. He held high position at the court of the Gothic Emperor Theodoric in Ravenna, but was charged with treason, for some reason unspecified, and finally tortured to death. While in prison he wrote his famous *Consolation of Philosophy*, a dialogue in prose and verse between himself and a personified Lady Philosophy. This was translated into English by Alfred the Great, by Chaucer, and by Queen Elizabeth I, and was more frequently translated into European languages in the Middle Ages than any other book except the Bible. Troilus's Hymn to Love in book 3 of Chaucer's *Troilus and Criseyde*, is a translation of *Consolation* book 2, stanza 8, and his discussion of the conflict between predestination and free will is taken from book 5, prose 3. For Dante, Boethius is *l'anima santa* and he is set in Paradise beside the Venerable Bede. His local veneration as a saint in Pavia was officially recognized by the Catholic Church in 1883. →→ EURYDICE.

Bona Dea

A Roman fertility goddess worshipped only by women, particularly at an annual all-night ceremony presided over by the wife of the chief magistrate. Details of this are well known from Cicero's writings on the occasion when his political enemy CLODIUS contrived to enter dressed as a woman.

Boreas

The north or north-east wind in Greece, the Roman *aquilo*, like all the winds sometimes appearing in horse form, and begetter of horses – perhaps because of the popular belief quoted by Virgil in the *Georgics* that mares can be impregnated by the wind. He was also said to have carried off the nymph Orithyia, the daughter of the early King Erechtheus of Athens. On the so-called Tower of the Winds at Athens he is shown as a scowling, bearded old man.

Briareus

A monster who with his three brothers helped Zeus in his battle against the Titans. Homer and, following him, Virgil give him a hundred hands and he sometimes also has fifty heads; but Statius follows a tradition which makes him no more than a savage giant, and he is with the giants in the Ninth Circle of Dante's Hell.

Britomartis

A Cretan nymph or goddess, identified locally with Artemis. When pursued by King Minos she leapt into the sea and escaped to the island of Aegina, where she was worshipped as APHAIA. In the third book of Spenser's *Faerie Queene* Britomart is Chastity personified, and it seems likely that Spenser knew her story from a poem attributed to Virgil, the *Ciris*.

Brutus

The mythical ancestor of the Britons, great-grandson of Aeneas, exiled from Italy for accidentally killing his father Silvius; after a variety of adventures in Greece he collects a party of Trojans, is told by the goddess Diana that he is destined to found a second Troy 'beyond the setting sun', and sails off through the Pillars of Hercules. After more adventures in France (which include the founding of the city of Tours) he lands at Totnes in Devon and makes his way to the Thames to build his Troia Nova. The name is soon corrupted to Trinovantum, i.e. Roman London. This fantasy is told in the twelfth century by Geoffrey of Monmouth in his *History of the Kings of Britain*. He either found Brutus in some earlier medieval pseudo-history or invented him.

Brutus, Lucius Junius

According to Roman tradition, recounted by Livy, he led the Romans to overthrow the monarchy of the Etruscan Tarquins after the rape of LUCRETIA, and became the first consul of Rome in 509 B.C. He was also famous for his stern sense of justice. He condemned both his sons to death for suspected treason – the subject of one of David's classical pictures.

Brutus, Marcus Junius

The descendant (85–42 B.C.) of Lucius Brutus, who took the side of Pompey in the civil war between Pompey and Caesar, but was pardoned by Caesar after Pompey's defeat and death and given high office. He was then influenced by Cassius to lead the conspiracy to murder Caesar, with the idea of following his famous ancestor and restoring the republic. He fled to Greece after Caesar's death and committed suicide after his defeat at Philippi. Brutus was long remembered in history as an idealist and a tyrannicide, and impressed Plutarch by his moral seriousness. For Shakespeare, following Plutarch, he is 'the noblest Roman of them all', and the same concept is evident in Michelangelo's portrait bust. But Dante, in *Inferno* 34, put him with Cassius and Judas Iscariot in the lowest circle of Hell for his betrayal of Caesar's friendship.

Bucephalus

The favourite horse of Alexander the Great which died after the battle of the Hydaspes in 326 B.C. and was commemorated by the founding of the town Bucephala (modern Jhelum in Pakistan). Plutarch tells the popular story of how it was given to Alexander by his father, Philip of Macedon, because the boy was the only person able to break it in and ride it.

Cacus

A fire-breathing giant, son of Vulcan, in some legends with a sister Caca, living in a cave on the Palatine hill in Rome; they would seem to be the primitive fire-god and goddess of the Italians. Virgil in *Aeneid* 8 locates the cave on the Aventine, and tells the tale of how Cacus stole the cattle of Geryon from Heracles and dragged them backwards into his cave. Heracles heard them mooing, tracked them to the cave and killed Cacus. Christian humanist writers saw in this a symbol of triumph over the forces of evil, and this is how Heracles' victory appealed to painters like Poussin. There is a statue group of Heracles struggling with Cacus by Bandinelli in the

Signoria, Florence, which is famous for Cellini's abuse of it, a painting by Domenichino in the Louvre, and an engraving by Dürer.

Cadmus

The legendary founder of the city of Thebes, son of the Phoenician King Agenor, who was sent to look for his sister Europa after she had been carried off by Zeus. He consulted the oracle at Delphi and was told to found a city where a cow lay down; this led him to the site of Thebes, beside a spring, where he killed its guardian dragon and sowed the dragon's teeth. A crop of armed men sprang up who fought each other until five only were left; in historical times these were held to be the ancestors of the Theban nobility. The ancient acropolis of Thebes was called the Cadmeia, and it held out against the attack of the Seven against Thebes (→ ETEOCLES) at such a cost that a 'Cadmeian victory' was proverbial in Greece (cf. PYRRHUS). Cadmus married Harmonia, daughter of Ares and Aphrodite, and had several children, including SEMELE. As a wedding gift Harmonia was given a necklace made by Hephaestus which was to play a fatal part in Theban saga. See AMPHIARAUS. Eventually he and his wife retired to Illyria and were changed by Zeus into snakes. The Greeks believed that he introduced their alphabet from Phoenicia into Greece. Most of the stories about Cadmus were well known later from Ovid, and Pausanias has much of interest to say about early Thebes. In his day only the Cadmeia was inhabited.

Caelius Rufus, Marcus (83–48 B.C.)

The protégé of Cicero and friend of Catullus, whom he supplanted as lover of Clodia; later he quarrelled with her and was successfully defended in a famous speech of Cicero's (*Pro Caelio*) on the charge of violence which she instigated against him. His letters to Cicero during the latter's governorship of Cilicia are collected in book 8 of Cicero's *Letters to his Friends* and provide a brilliant commentary on political and social life in Rome. Caelius took Caesar's side against Pompey, but was soon disillusioned by Caesar's unwillingness to cancel debts. He then helped to foment a debtors' insurrection, but was captured and executed. His name has always been associated with the 'smart set' of Rome in the late Republic.

Calchas

A seer and priest of Apollo, who accompanies Agamemnon's army in the *Iliad* and foretells the length of the war. In post-Homeric legend he is also associated with the sacrifice of IPHIGENIA and the building of the Wooden Horse. After the Trojan War he is said to have died of mortification when he found that there was a better seer than himself in Mopsus – a shadowy figure whose legends range over several generations, for if he sailed with the Argonauts he can hardly have been alive to confound Calchas.

Caligula ('Little Boot')

The popular name of the Emperor Gaius (C. Julius Caesar Germanicus, ruled A.D. 37–41) who was born while his father Germanicus was serving on the Rhine and was dressed by his mother in miniature soldier's uniform, including boots. Ancient and modern historians alike have generally believed that he was mentally unbalanced (see also Robert Graves's *I, Claudius*, and Albert Camus's *Caligula*, where he finds a sort of rapture in killing); and if for nothing else he is remembered as the emperor who gave a consulship to his horse.

Callimachus (*c.* 305–240 B.C.)
Hellenistic poet of Cyrene, who settled in Alexandria, where he worked at the famous library and produced a critical catalogue in 120 volumes. He was distinguished both as a scholar and as a poet of originality (he is credited with having written 800 volumes), and the surviving fragments of his work justify his reputation. Fragments of his *Aetia* ('Origins') include his *Lock of Berenice*, which was closely imitated by Catullus, and his shorter personal poems had great influence on Propertius, who thought of himself as the Roman Callimachus. His refusal to write epic conforms with Callimachus's dictum *mega biblion mega kakon* (a big book is a big evil). Callimachus took the view that the epic form was outdated, and this provoked his quarrel with Apollonius Rhodius. →→ HERACLITUS.

Callisto
Originally perhaps an alternative name for Artemis, who was associated with bears – at least at Brauron in Attica, where young girls acted as bears in a festival of Artemis; cf. ATALANTA. Callisto is an Arcadian goddess or nymph in late legend who was one of the loves of Zeus and bore him a son, Arcas, the eponymous hero of Arcadia. Either Artemis or Hera then turned her into a bear, and she was killed, in one version by her own son. Zeus turned her into the constellation called The Great Bear, and Arcas into the star Arcturus. The Renaissance painters knew her story from Ovid, and Titian painted two pictures of her being condemned by Artemis (Diana). *La Callisto*, an opera of 1651 by Cavalli, has recently been revived.

Calpurnia
The wife of Julius Caesar, remembered for her devotion and her warning to him not to attend the fateful meeting of the Senate on the Ides of March, 44 B.C. (so Shakespeare, following Plutarch).

Calydonian Boar
A wild boar sent by Artemis to ravage the territory of Oeneus king of Calydon because he had not offered her proper sacrifice; for the boar-hunt in which it was destroyed, → ATALANTA, MELEAGER. This was the subject of a lost early epic which may have been known to Homer. Pausanias has an odd story of tusks three feet long at Tegea, which were locally believed to be those of the boar, seen by the Roman Emperor Augustus and taken to Rome. Presumably they belonged to a prehistoric mammoth.

Calypso
A nymph, daughter of Atlas, living on the remote island of Ogygia where she

keeps Odysseus for seven years until ordered by Zeus to send him home to Ithaca. Her name means 'hidden' and she seems to be a death-goddess – she promises Odysseus eternal youth, but he stoutly prefers real life. Post-Homeric legend gives her two sons by Odysseus. Ogygia has been conjecturally identified with Malta. Calypso appears, surprisingly, in Webster's Dictionary, which derives the dance-form from her name via 'island nymph' and 'West-Indian island'.

Camillus, Marcus Furius
A personality in the early history of Rome whose exploits were later exaggerated by tradition, but who was always remembered as the saviour and refounder of Rome after its occupation by the Gauls in 387 B.C. He levied an army, pursued the Gauls, recovered the booty they had taken, and successfully opposed the suggestion that the surviving population of Rome should be transferred nine miles away to the Etruscan city of Veii – which he had captured himself in 396. Plutarch adds a good deal to the stories told by Livy, and it is from him that Poussin took the subject for his picture *Camillus and the Schoolmaster of Falerii*, as an example of the Roman sense of justice he so much admired. When the Romans were besieging Falerii the local schoolmaster brought the children in his care to the Roman camp and suggested they should be used as hostages for handing over the town, but Camillus refused to take advantage of his treachery and sent the children back, whipping their master before them.

Capaneus
One of the legendary heroes of the Seven against Thebes and the husband of Evadne. He boasted that nothing should stop him scaling the walls of Thebes and was killed by Zeus's thunderbolt. His name became a symbol of defiance of the gods which met its just punishment, and it is as the arch-blasphemer that he appears in the burning sand of Hell in Dante's *Inferno* 14.

Caracalla (a Celtic cloak)
Popular name of the Roman Emperor Marcus Aurelius Severus Antoninus (ruled A.D. 211–17). He succeeded his father Septimius Severus with the support of the army when Severus died at York, returned to Rome, and murdered his brother Geta and thousands of his supporters. In Caracalla's reign was issued the famous edict giving Roman citizenship to all free subjects of the Empire, but he is chiefly remembered for his wanton acts of cruelty and his extravagance. The ruins of the Baths of Caracalla in Rome still bear witness to his grandiose building schemes, though the great bare walls are less romantic than they were when Shelley climbed them to look at the view of the Campagna and write *Prometheus Unbound*:

> This poem was chiefly written upon the mountainous ruins of the Baths of Caracalla, among the flowery glades, and thickets of odoriferous blossoming trees, which are extended in ever winding labyrinths upon its immense platforms and dizzy arches suspended in the sky. The bright blue sky of Rome, and the effect of the vigorous awakening spring in that divinest climate, and the new life

with which it drenches the spirits even to intoxication, were the inspiration of this drama. Shelley's *Preface*.

Caractacus

The popular but incorrect form of Caratacus (Welsh 'Caradoc'), the son of Cymbeline (Cunobellinus), king of south-eastern Britain. After his father's defeat and the Roman capture of Camulodunum (Colchester) in A.D. 43 he went west and rallied the Welsh tribes, but was defeated; he then fled to the Yorkshire Brigantes, but was handed over to the Romans. Tacitus says that his life was spared by the Emperor Claudius, and he lived on as an honoured exile in Rome.

Caryatids

Columns carved in the shape of draped women supporting a roof or cross-beam on their heads; the best known example is that of the porch of the Erechtheum on the Athenian Acropolis. There are fragments of early caryatids among the ruins of the treasuries of Cnidos and Siphnos at Delphi. They were adapted for Hadrian's Villa at Tivoli, and later often copied; for example, in the Salle des Caryatides with sixteenth-century sculpture in the Louvre, Paris. VITRUVIUS explains them by an episode in the Persian wars when the Greek state of Caria (or, in another version, the Laconian city of Caryae) supported the Persians. After the Persian defeat the Greeks killed off the Carian men and enslaved the women, and architects of the time used their statues to carry a heavy burden as a record of their sin for posterity [10].

Casca

Two brothers with this surname joined the conspiracy against Julius Caesar, of whom one (Publius Servilius Casca) is said to have been the first to strike him down. This seems to be the tradition followed by Shakespeare ('Speak, hands, for me!'), though he has only one Casca. Both died when Brutus was defeated at Philippi.

Cassandra

One of the daughters of King Priam of Troy, and according to Homer the most beautiful of them all. He knows nothing of her prophetic gifts, but they are taken for granted by the time of Pindar and of Aeschylus. The most common legend is that she was given the power of prophecy by Apollo, but was then doomed to be disbelieved because she refused him her love. Virgil follows this tradition in *Aeneid* 2, where Cassandra vainly tries to warn the Trojans against the Wooden Horse. After the sack of Troy she was brought to his home by AGAMEMNON and murdered with him. Her awareness and helplessness add to the mounting horror of Aeschylus' *Agamemnon*. 'Cassandra-like warnings' are proverbial. She was also known as Alexandra, and gave the title to a long poem about her prophecies which is generally attributed to the Alexandrian poet Lycophron. It has the reputation of exceeding any other Greek poem in obscurity and inconsistency.

Cassius Longinus, Gaius

(i) The murderer of Caesar. He commanded part of Pompey's fleet in the

Civil War, but afterwards came to terms with Caesar and held high office in Rome. He was one of the leaders of the conspiracy against Caesar in 44 B.C., with Brutus, whose sister he had married. He committed suicide after his defeat at Philippi. Shakespeare follows the ancient authorities, particularly Plutarch, in making him more calculating and ruthless than the idealist Brutus:

Yond Cassius has a lean and hungry look;
He thinks too much; such men are
dangerous.

Medieval writers tended to conflate the two tyrannicides; Chaucer, for example, in the *Monk's Tale* refers to 'Brutus Cassius'.

(ii) The distinguished Roman jurist of the early Empire, whose pronouncements on civil law are often quoted in Justinian's *Digest* and by other jurists.

Castor and Pollux (Greek **Polydeuces**)

They are often called the **Dioscuri** ('Sons of Zeus'), and are twin bothers of Helen and sons of LEDA, wife of Tyndareus, king of Sparta. In some legends they are hatched from an egg, after Zeus visited Leda in the shape of a swan, in others they are the sons of Tyndareus, or Polydeuces comes from the egg and Castor is fathered by Tyndareus. Among their many exploits they took part in the Argonauts' expedition; and they were allowed to enjoy immortality on alternate days after Castor was killed (→ LEUCIPPUS and illustration 6). This is the subject of the opera *Castor et Pollux* by Rameau. They were later identified with the constellation Gemini ('the Twins') and one of their functions was to protect sailors at sea. In Acts xxviii St Paul sails from Malta in a ship 'under the sign of Castor and Pollux'. They were also associated with horses from Homeric times, and it was as horsemen that they appeared and fought on the Roman side against the Latins in the battle of Lake Regillus in 484 B.C., after which, according to tradition, their cult was introduced in Rome. (See Livy, book 2 and Macaulay's *Lays of Ancient Rome*.) It was always associated with the ceremonial parade of the Roman *equites* or knights. Three columns from their temple still stand in the Roman forum, and in the Piazza del Quirinale is a statue group of them with their horses, a fine Roman copy of a Greek original, and one of the few ancient works of art which were to be seen in medieval times; they were thought to have been wizards who advised the emperors. Their statues also stand at the head of the steps leading to the Campidoglio (Capitol).

Catiline (Lucius Sergius Catilina, *c.* 110–62 B.C.)

Roman politician and impoverished patrician, who after his failure to be elected consul for 63, when Cicero defeated him, produced a programme of cancellation of debts and revolutionary reform calculated to appeal to any discontented person. After a second defeat he increased his following and embarked on a serious conspiracy in which Cicero was to be killed and the city occupied. Cicero was informed, and took active steps to suppress the rising and frighten Catiline into leaving Rome and joining his army in Etruria. There he was defeated and died. His severest critics, Cicero and Sallust, allow him courage and qualities of leadership (cf. Ben Jonson's *Catiline*), but he was prompted by reckless ambition rather than any genuine wish to champion the oppressed.

Cato

Of the many members of the Porcius family bearing this surname, the most famous are:

(i) Marcus Porcius Cato, 234–149 B.C., known to posterity as 'the Censor', and a byword for austerity and puritanism. He was active in the war against Hannibal and in politics, his policy being based on the idea of a return to the simpler Roman society of the previous century; hence his suspicion of the infiltration of Hellenistic ideas and moral laxity, and his persistent demand for the destruction of a resurgent Carthage (*Delenda est Carthago*). Cato was also one of the founders of Latin prose style, and his most famous work in antiquity was his *Origines*, on the history of Rome from earliest times to his own day. His practical manual *On Agriculture* survives.

(ii) His great-grandson, Marcus Porcius Cato, 95–46 B.C. He was brought up as a Stoic and maintained the family reputation for obstinacy and rectitude. In the Civil War he supported Pompey, and after Pompey's defeat joined the Pompeians who were holding out in northern Africa. He committed suicide at Utica when they were defeated by Caesar at the Battle of Thapsus and he saw that the cause was lost. This made him a hero to LUCAN and to all with republican sympathies, helped by a virulent attack by Caesar in his pamphlet *Anticato* which roused public feeling for the losing side.

Both Catos were well known later from Plutarch's *Lives*. Dante makes the younger Cato guardian of the approach to Mount Purgatory and the path to spiritual liberty because of his devotion to political freedom. His stand for liberty also inspired Addison's tragedy *Cato*.

Catullus, Gaius Valerius

(*c.* 84–*c.* 54 B.C.)

Roman poet, born in Verona. He came to Rome as a wealthy young man and quickly joined the fashionable younger set. He had a passionate love-affair with Clodia, the Lesbia of his poems, who threw him over for Cicero's young friend CAELIUS. After attacking Caesar in some of his earlier poems he was reconciled to him, but very little is known of his life except what can be found in his poems; e.g. he went to Bithynia on the staff of the governor, Gaius Memmius, saw his brother's grave in the Troad, and returned by sea, perhaps on his own yacht. He had a villa at Sirmio on Lake Garda, but the ruins shown at Sirmione today are certainly very much later in date. Catullus was the leading figure of the new poets of the late Republic, breaking with the tradition of Rome's past and finding his models in Greek poetry, both in the polished Alexandrian style and in the direct lyricism of Sappho. His style is immensely versatile and whatever he writes is his own, so that he is one of the greatest of all poets, and an influence on lyric poets from the time of Petrarch. At the same time he is perhaps the most modern-sounding poet for us today. And he was nearly lost. The texts we have all stem from a single codex, now lost, traditionally said to have been found in Verona at the end of the 13th century, being used to bung up a wine barrel.

Cecrops
The mythical first king of Athens, often represented as a serpent below his waist to indicate that he was a son of earth (cf. ERECHTHEUS). He was believed to have been a benefactor of mankind and the judge in the contest for the ownership of Attica between Athene and Poseidon.

Centaurs
A tribe of wild creatures, half-human, half-horse, living on wooded mountains, particularly in Thessaly. They are of very early origin, probably pre-Homeric, and for the Greeks they represented primitive desires and anti-social habits, by getting drunk and chasing women and fighting – all expressed in their battle with the LAPITHS at the wedding of Pirithous [22]. This is a popular subject for vases and sculpture from early times; e.g. the François Vase, the metopes of the Parthenon and the sculptures on the west pediment of the temple of Zeus at Olympia. There are also vigorous small bronzes of centaurs of the seventh and sixth centuries B.C. [1], and a famous Roman wall-painting from the House of the Centaur at Pompeii. In Hellenistic art they often appear with the followers of Dionysus and become more purely decorative. The tradition continues into the Middle Ages, with a centaur on one of the capitals of Winchester Cathedral. Some centaurs have their special legends: → IXION and NESSUS. One was civilized as early as Pindar and gained fame as a medicine man and teacher of heroes; → CHIRON. Patrick Leigh Fermor in *Mani* has a fascinating chapter on centaurs and the other 'divine maquisards', and sees in the 'kallikantzaroi' of Greek folklore a mixture of centaur and satyr. Centaurs reappear in the latest drawings of Picasso.

Cephalus
An Attic hero, husband of Procris and one of the loves of Eos (Aurora), the Dawn. His story is told as early as Hesiod, but in much greater detail by Ovid. Aurora releases him, but makes Procris jealous of the time he spends hunting, so she follows him to the woods, hears him praying for a breeze (*aura*) and supposes this is his mistress. She comes closer and is killed by his spear which never misses. From Ovid's account this becomes a popular subject for Renaissance painters; → FAUNUS. There are also well-known pictures by Poussin and Claude. Their names appear in garbled form as Shafalus and Procrus in the 'Pyramus and Thisbe' section of *A Midsummer Night's Dream*.

Cerberus
The monstrous dog which guards the entrance to the Underworld. Hesiod gives him fifty heads, but in classical art

and literature there are three. He has to be brought up from Hell by Heracles as one of his Twelve Labours for Eurystheus: this is painted on two large sixth-century water-pots from Etruscan Caere (Cervetri), where Eurystheus is shown taking refuge in a large jar. Orpheus also has to charm him with music when he goes in search of Eurydice, and Aeneas is told to drug him with a cake soaked in honey and narcotics: hence the expression 'sop to Cerberus'. In Dante's Hell he gnaws at the gluttonous in the Third Circle (*Inferno* 6), and he is popular in medieval art.

Ceres

The ancient Italian corn-goddess, worshipped in historic times in a temple on the Aventine hill, with games in her honour and the popular spring festival of the *Cerialia*. She was early associated with DEMETER, and her daughter Proserpina with Persephone or Kore, but as always, the Roman names are the ones known in the Renaissance and traditionally used since. Ceres, for example, comes to sing her blessing in the masque at the end of Shakespeare's *The Tempest.*

Cestius, Gaius

A public official during the reign of the Emperor Augustus whose tomb was set up in 12 B.C. near the old Ostian Gate in Rome, the present Porta San Paolo. This is a pyramid of brick faced with marble, 120 feet high, in the square Egyptian style. In spite of the inscription setting out the career of Cestius and the fact that Marcus Agrippa was his heir, it was believed to be the tomb of Remus, brother of Romulus, throughout the Middle Ages and even by Petrarch. It was romantically painted by many people, including Piranesi, and is visited now because it stands at the corner of the Old Protestant Cemetery and near it, at his own request, was buried John Keats in 1821:

... And gray walls moulder round, on which dull Time
Feeds, like slow fire upon a hoary brand;
And one keen pyramid with wedge sublime,
Pavilioning the dust of him who planned
This refuge for his memory, doth stand
Like flame transformed to marble; and beneath
A field is spread, on which a newer band
Have pitched in Heaven's smile their camp of death
Welcoming him we lose with scarce extinguished breath.

Shelley: *Adonais*

Charon

The ferryman of Greek mythology who takes the dead in his boat across the river Styx if the funeral rites have been properly performed and the fare (an obol, a small coin) put in the mouth of the corpse. He is unknown to Homer, but prominent by the sixth century B.C. and often represented on Etruscan and Greek vases. As a disagreeable old man he plays a part in the *Frogs* of Aristophanes, and his role is also satirized by Lucian. In modern Greek folklore he is still spoken of as a synonym for death. In post-classical times he is pictured as Virgil describes him in *Aeneid* 6 – unkempt white hair, fierce burning eyes (*canities inculta iacet, stant lumina flamma*)

– and so he appears in Dante, where he has to be ordered by Virgil to take the living Dante into his boat (*Inferno* 3). He is painted by Michelangelo on the ceiling of the Sistine Chapel, Rome.

Charybdis
A whirlpool in a narrow channel of water, traditionally in the Straits of Messina, where the currents can be strong and dangerous. In *Odyssey* 12 it is opposite the monster SCYLLA so that Odysseus is presented with a choice of evils, and the two have become proverbial to describe a situation with equally unattractive alternatives.

Chimaera
The fabulous fire-breathing monster killed by BELLEROPHON which features with him or alone on many early Greek vases. There is also a famous bronze chimaera in Florence which is Etruscan work of the fifth century B.C. From being a lion-headed monster with a goat's body and serpent's tail, the chimaera develops into any fantastic beast, often winged, and lastly into the word 'chimera', which means a fanciful notion.

Chiron
One of the centaurs, who in later myths is given Kronos for a father, and unlike his fellows becomes wise and kindly, the teacher of heroes such as Jason, Achilles and Asclepius, and famous for his knowledge of archery, music and medicine. He ends as the constellation Sagittarius (the Archer) after being accidentally killed by Heracles. Botticelli's allegorical painting of *Pallas and the Centaur* which is sometimes said to represent violence checked by wisdom is more likely to show Chiron, for his face of wistful melancholy suggests that he knows that his instinctive knowledge is inferior to Pallas's heaven-sent wisdom.

Chryseis (Cressida)
In the *Iliad*, the daughter of Chryses, priest of Apollo at Chryse near Troy. Before the epic starts he has been captured and given to Agamemnon. When he refuses to let her father ransom her, Apollo sends a plague on the Greek camp. Calchas explains this, Chryseis is returned to Troy, but Agamemnon takes Achilles' girl Briseis for himself, and the famous quarrel begins. The medieval *Roman de Troie* first tells the story of Troilus and his love for her, and how she left him for the Greek Diomedes, and this is developed by Boccaccio in his poem *Filostrato*. It is the source of Chaucer's *Troilus and Criseyde*, which in its turn was the source for Shakespeare's *Troilus and Cressida*. After this her name is synonymous with faithlessness, though Chaucer says only that she was 'tendre-herted, slydynge of corage'.

Cicero, Marcus Tullius (106–43 B.C.)
A 'new man' from Arpinum, Cicero was educated in Rome and Athens and quickly rose to be recognized as the greatest orator of his day. As consul he put down the Catiline conspiracy, and this was his supreme political hour, though his hopes of permanently reconciling the interests of upper- and middle-class citizens were not realized. He

supported Pompey in the Civil War, but was pardoned by Caesar, and after Caesar's murder attacked Antony, so that he was proscribed and put to death by Antony and Octavian. As well as many political and legal speeches Cicero wrote verses and books on oratory and philosophy. In these he introduced Greek philosophic theories to the Romans and created a Latin vocabulary and style suitable for expressing abstract ideas. He was also a master of witty riposte, and his letters are spontaneously written in a free colloquial style. They are an invaluable commentary on the restless political and social life of his day.

Cicero had great influence on the early Christian writers both as a Latinist and a thinker. St Jerome even had a vision in which he saw himself being accused of being a Ciceronian rather than a Christian, and St Ambrose modelled his book on Christian morals on Cicero's *On Duties*. Cicero's expressed view that virtue was the outcome of human effort and not of divine grace also appealed to the followers of Pelagius. It was as a philosopher and transmitter of Greek philosophy that he was known all through the Middle Ages. In 1345 his letters were discovered by Petrarch in Verona and copied out by him, and they became a model for Petrarch's own Latin letters, as well as for other humanist writers. From then on Cicero was valued as an individualist as well as thinker and stylist. Erasmus even had to write his *Ciceronianus* as a plea to be allowed to add to Cicero's pagan vocabulary, as so many scholars believed that no word not used by Cicero could be acceptable. For the rationalists of the eighteenth century he had still another appeal; his unfinished *Republic* is the earliest expression of the concept of natural law. Orators like Burke (and in our own day Churchill) and prose stylists like Gibbon have all found a model in his expressive periods, and the French republican philosophers like Mirabeau admired him as a constructive statesman and a champion of human rights. The continuity of Greek thinking through Rome and western civilization could hardly have been maintained if Cicero had not transmitted it → [50].

Cincinnatus, Lucius Quinctius

A genuine figure of history of the time when Rome was establishing her position among the Italian tribes, Cincinnatus was 'called from his plough' in 458 B.C. to take reinforcements to the Roman army besieged in the Apennines by the Aequi. He was elected dictator, won his victory, resigned his office, and returned to his small farm near the Tiber within sixteen days. The story is told in Livy, book 3, and Cincinnatus is often quoted by the poets as an example of old-fashioned Roman virtue. Similar stories are told of the simplicity and incorruptibility of Gaius Fabricius and Curius Dentatus, both admired by Cato.

Circe

In Homer she is the daughter of the Sun, a goddess and sorceress living on the island of Aeaea with her wild beasts, who, it is implied but never said, are the victims of her skill with herbs and potions. She changes Odysseus's men into pigs, and he resists her spells only by means of the herb 'moly' given him by Hermes. He forces her to restore his men and then lives with her for a year, after which she gives him advice about his visit to the Underworld and his return home. In post-Homeric legend she has two sons by Odysseus, and in Apollonius Rhodius's *Argonautica* she receives Jason and Medea on their way back from Colchis. Circe's island was later identified with the promontory of Circeii on the Campanian cost of Italy and she was worshipped there in the form of Feronia, goddess of wild beasts. A sorceress's cave is still shown there on the slopes of Monte Circeo, and the woods have wild boars and pigs. Until the Pontine marshes were drained the region was dangerously malarial, and it has been suggested that Circe's drugs refer to the hallucinations of severe malaria. Milton makes his wizard Comus the son of Circe and Bacchus.

Claudian (Claudius Claudianus)
(*c.* A.D. 370–*c.* 404)
Claudian was an Alexandrian Greek but lived at the Roman imperial court from about 395; nothing is heard of him after 404. This was a time of continuous pressure from the tribes across the frontiers, when the Visigoths under ALARIC were held in check as a buffer against the Huns by the great general STILICHO, born a Vandal, but a loyal servant to the young Emperor Honorius. Gibbon often quotes Claudian in chapter 29 of the *Decline and Fall*, rather unfairly dubbing him 'the servile poet of Stilicho'. A good deal of his poetry is in the form of panegyrics of Stilicho and Honorius, but he also wrote a marriage-song for Honorius and Stilicho's daughter Maria and a *Rape of Proserpine*, both of which bear comparison with the Silver Latin poets for their descriptive passages. Claudian was honoured by the Emperor and senate in a bronze statue, of which the inscription is now in Naples. He is one of the pillars in Chaucer's description of the *House of Fame* along with other famous poets of the classical period.

Claudius (Tiberius Claudius Nero Germanicus, Roman Emperor
A.D. 41–54)
He was the younger brother of GERMANICUS and was hailed as emperor by the army in Rome after the murder of his nephew Gaius (Caligula), though he had held no office of distinction under Augustus and Tiberius. Claudius had a limp and a stammer which made him an object of ridicule, and he may have been spastic, so that he has generally been misrepresented in tradition. But he was a scholar and historian, and both the imperial enactments preserved in inscriptions and his speeches quoted by Tacitus show him as an administrator of firmness and acumen. He was thought to have been poisoned by his wife, the younger AGRIPPINA, and the palace intrigues surrounding him are well described by Robert Graves in his two novels. Like the other emperors he was deified after his death, and this was satirized by Seneca in his *Apocolocyntosis* ('Pumpkinification').

Cleopatra (*c.* 70–30 B.C.)
Daughter of the Macedonian King Ptolemy Auletes of Egypt and joint

heir to the throne with her brother, she was made queen by Julius Caesar in 48. She became his mistress, and her son Caesarion claimed him for a father. She came to Rome, but returned to Alexandria after Caesar's death. Then she was Antony's mistress, though he left her for four years for a political marriage with Octavian's sister. He returned to her when he broke with Octavian, but at the battle of Actium the Egyptian fleet was routed and his troops would not fight. Antony killed himself, and when her attempts to negotiate with Octavian failed, she committed suicide by means of an asp, a small poisonous snake sacred to the Egyptian sun-god. The Roman imperial propagandists hated and feared Cleopatra as a dangerous Oriental influence (there is something of her in Virgil's Dido), though Horace at least respected her courage. She was undoubtedly an astute and ambitious woman, as G. B. Shaw recognized in his *Caesar and Cleopatra*, and as E. M. Forster put so well in *Alexandria*:

> She did not differ in character from the other able and unscrupulous queens of her race, but she had one source of power that they denied themselves – the power of the courtesan – and she exploited it professionally. Though passionate she was not the slave of passion, still less of sentimentality. Her safety, and the safety of Egypt were her care; the clumsy and amorous Romans, who menaced both, were her natural prey.

Plutarch's *Life of Antony* suggested to Shakespeare his *Antony and Cleopatra*, where the emphasis is on love and passion on a heroic scale, as it is in Dryden's *All for Love*, and Cleopatra has always been treated in the grand manner, whether in Cagnacci's painting of her death, or the great canvases by Tiepolo of her with Antony [8], in Handel's *Julius Caesar*, or as the soloist in Berlioz's dramatic aria *La Mort de Cléopâtre*. One of the best tributes to her is in J.-M. de Heredia's sonnet in *Les Trophées*:

> *... Et sur elle courbé, l'ardent Impérator*
> *Vit dans ses larges yeux étoilés de points d'or*
> *Toute une mer immense où fuyaient des galères.*

Clodia

Mistress of the Roman poet Catullus (who wrote of her as Lesbia) and after him of CAELIUS. Her morals were attacked by Cicero in his speech *Pro Caelio*, and she was the subject of constant gossip in Rome.

Clodius, Publius

Her brother, a member of the distinguished Claudius family, himself notorious for sacrilege, bribery and hostility to Cicero, whom he forced into exile for a year after the execution of CATILINE. His gang-warfare against the rival gang of Milo shows the state of uncontrolled lawlessness in Rome at the time, and makes the general relief at Augustus's one-man rule more understandable. He was murdered by Milo, and in the demonstrations which followed the senate-house was burnt down. Cicero's speech on behalf of Milo is an attack on Clodius and his type.

Clytemnestra
Daughter of Tyndareus and LEDA, sister of Helen, wife of Agamemnon king of Mycenae. During his absence in the Trojan War she took his cousin Aegisthus for a lover and on his return they murdered him along with his Trojan captive Cassandra. For this she was killed by her son Orestes. Homer charitably makes her a weak woman led astray, but from the Greek dramatists onwards she has been a forceful character with a double motive for revenge – jealousy of Agamemnon's infidelity, grief and fury at the sacrifice of her daughter IPHIGENIA. This is how she also appears in Richard Strauss's opera *Elektra* (based on von Hofmannsthal's play).

Codrus
The last king of Athens, worshipped as a hero because he had disguised himself and provoked the Dorian invaders to kill him in order to circumvent the Delphic oracle, which had told him that the Dorians would be successful if his life was spared. It has been suggested that this myth is a rationalization of the end of the early period of rule by kings in Athens; but another version said that Codrus was succeeded by his son Medon, from whom Solon and Pisistratus claimed descent.

Colossus of Rhodes
A bronze statue of the sun-god Helios or Apollo, one of the Seven Wonders of the World, cast by a sculptor of Rhodes to stand at the entrance to the harbour and said by the elder Pliny to be seventy cubits (over 100 feet) high. It stood for about fifty years and was destroyed by earthquake in 224 B.C.

Constantine the Great (Flavius Valerius Constantinus, Roman Emperor A.D. 306–37)
The son of Constantius Chlorus who died at York and his wife or concubine Helena, who was believed to be British and was afterwards canonized as the discoverer of the true Cross. Constantine defeated his rival Maxentius in 312 in a battle at the Milvian Bridge (the Ponte Molle). This is commemorated by the Arch of Constantine near the Colosseum in Rome. It was before this battle that Constantine was said to have had a vision of the Cross. He reigned as sole emperor from 323 and transferred the capital of the Empire to Byzantium, renaming it Constantinople. His title was well deserved, for what he achieved in reforming the army and the monetary system, for his integrity as an administrator, and for his edict of toleration to both pagans and Christians (the Edict of Milan) and his work for unity in the Christian Church, though he himself was baptized on his deathbed. Gibbon, however, believed that 'boundless ambition' was the motive behind all he did, and that Christianity was a disastrous influence within the Empire. Constantine founded the church of St Peter in Rome, and is appropriately honoured in an equestrian statue by Bernini on the Scala Regia of the Vatican. Two Roman statues of himself and his son have stood on the balustrade of the Piazza del Campidoglio since 1653. Scenes from his life were painted by Raphael in the Sala di Constantino

in the Vatican, and Rubens made twelve designs for Gobelin tapestries.

The 'Donation of Constantine', a document purporting to donate Rome and its territories to the popes, was a medieval forgery intended to justify the temporal powers of the papacy, and was proved so from its style and anachronisms by the Renaissance scholar Lorenzo Valla.

Corinna

A Greek poetess of Tanagra in Boeotia, traditionally a rival and critic of Pindar. Only fragments of her poems on local myths survive, all in later versions of the mid second century A.D., and some critics have thought she should be dated to the fourth rather than the sixth century B.C. Her name was given by Ovid to his mistress in the *Amores*.

Coriolanus, Cnaeus (or Gaius) Marcius

Roman general who captured the Volscian town of Corioli, but failed to be elected consul in 491 because of his contempt for the *plebs*. In his anger he led a Volscian army against Rome and was persuaded to turn back only by the entreaties of his mother Veturia and wife Volumnia. He then returned to the Volscians and either lived to old age in exile or, in another version, was assassinated. Both Livy and Plutarch regard this as history, but it is probably legend. Shakespeare follows Plutarch in calling the mother Volumnia and wife Virgilia. Coriolanus was admired for his Roman virtues by Poussin, who painted him with the pleading women (perhaps with an earlier painting by Signorelli in mind), and the Austrian neoclassical dramatist von Collin wrote the play for which Beethoven's *Coriolan* is the overture.

Cornelia

'The mother of the Gracchi', daughter of Scipio Africanus, and the model Roman matron, she is known through Plutarch's *Lives* of her sons, the social reformers Tiberius and Gaius Gracchus. She retired to Misenum after their deaths (in 133 and 123 B.C.) and her home remained a centre of culture. Plutarch tells the well-known story of how when a visitor asked to see her jewels she brought out the boys with the words 'These are my jewels.'

Cornelius Nepos (*c.* 99–*c.* 24 B.C.)

Roman historian and biographer, and friend of Cicero. Twenty-five of his *Lives of Famous Men* survive, and make dull reading, but his admitted purpose was to point a moral.

Coronis

A Thessalian princess who was already pregnant by Apollo when she fell in love with an Arcadian youth. Apollo was told of this by a crow (though Pindar says that he knew it through his omniscience) and sent Artemis to kill Coronis. The unborn child was snatched from her and given to Chiron the centaur to rear: it was ASCLEPIUS. The crow has been black ever since – a notion common in folklore. This is the theme of Pindar's third Pythian Ode, and is also told by Ovid, through whom it is known to Chaucer who makes it the subject of the *Manciple's Tale*. There the central figure is the crow.

Corydon

A conventional Arcadian shepherd's name which has gained significance from its use by Virgil in his second *Eclogue*. There the shepherd Corydon laments his love for 'faithless Alexis', and so Corydon has become a symbol for homosexual love. The name is indeed the title of a Platonic dialogue of justification by André Gide.

Crassus, Marcus Licinius (*c.* 112–53 B.C.)

The third member of the First Triumvirate with Caesar and Pompey, useful to them because of his great wealth, for which he was given the surname Dives (rich). He set out to campaign in the East hoping to win power and prestige and be equal to the other two, and invaded Mesopotamia, but he was defeated and killed at Carrhae. His armies were completely routed and their standards captured, and the disaster was long considered a particular disgrace to the Roman army.

Creon

A name meaning 'ruler' or 'prince' which was given to more than one subsidiary character in Greek legend; e.g. the brother of Jocasta and successor to Oedipus at Thebes, whose son Haemon was to have married Antigone, and the king of Corinth who features in several stories about Jason and Medea.

Creusa

The feminine form of 'Creon'. The best-known of the rather dim women given that name is the wife of Aeneas in the *Aeneid*. Virgil sees nothing odd in making Aeneas escape from the flames of Troy carrying his old father on his shoulders and holding his son by the hand, leaving Creusa to follow behind as best she can; his priorities demand it. No one notices she is missing until they are well away from Troy, and though Aeneas returns and searches for her, he meets only her ghost which bids him go on to fulfil his destiny.

Croesus

The last king of Lydia, in the mid sixth century B.C., who was overthrown by CYRUS THE ELDER of Persia. His wealth was proverbial, and he was regarded as a model of piety because of the rich offerings he gave to Apollo at Delphi, mostly of solid gold. However, the oracle double-crossed him when it said that if he fought the Persians he would bring down a mighty empire; only after the event was it clear to Croesus that the empire was his own. Book I of Herodotus describes his conversations with SOLON and with Cyrus, and his escape from death when he called on Solon's name as a sacrificial pyre was lit, so that he was pardoned and became the friend and adviser of Cyrus. Later legend said that Apollo rescued him and carried him off to live happily in the land of the HYPERBOREANS.

Cupid

The Roman god of love, identified with the Greek EROS, and the lover of PSYCHE. For the Romans he was mainly the playful winged putto who is the Hellenistic Eros rather than the tormenting daimon of earlier times, though he was also a symbol of the life after death promised by the Mysteries. This accounts for the common use of cupids on ancient sarcophagi where they are sometimes playing with satyrs' masks (they were copied in a series of paintings of putti by Poussin). From the sarcophagi they came into the Christian churches as decorative winged cherubs, and there are even instances of medieval thinkers who identified Cupid with the angel of the Annunciation. More often, however, Cupid is a symbol of carnal love, and his ardour is indicated by a torch; he stands defeated, with torch inverted, on a relief on the west façade of the cathedral at Modena.

With the development of the ideal of courtly and romantic love Cupid with his bow and arrows is heavily symbolic of the power of love, he is often blindfolded to show how his victims are chosen at random, and like his mistress Venus, he can be cruel and is to be feared. Chaucer makes this clear in the *Knight's Tale*, and in *Troilus and Criseyde*, where Cupid hears Troilus boast of his independence, takes out his bow, and 'sodeynely he hitte him atte fulle'. From Elizabethan times onward this is softened into a convention and elaborated in conceits, as in John Lyly's lyric:

Cupid and my Campaspe played
At cards for kisses – Cupid paid:
He stakes his quiver, bow and arrows,
His mother's doves, and teams of sparrows . . .
At last he set her both his eyes,
She won, and Cupid blind did rise.
O Love! has she done this to thee?
What shall, alas, become of me?

The symbol becomes a commonplace, to linger on in popular verse ('Miss Buss and Miss Beale Cupid's darts never feel . . .').

From the Renaissance onwards Cupid was constantly painted, sometimes with Venus and Vulcan, his parents in legend, as in two pictures by Tintoretto, more often with Venus. There are famous paintings by Correggio, Bronzino, Titian, Poussin, Velazquez and Reynolds, as well as one by Lucas Cranach, and by Rembrandt in one of his rare classical subjects.

Curetes

A half-divine people in central Crete who feature in legends of the birth of Zeus. They protected him from KRONOS by clattering their weapons so that his cries were not heard, and brought him up with the help of AMALTHEA. In later times they were conflated with the Corybantes who were also half-divine, and were traditional attendants on the goddess Cybele. All of them then become part of the Dionysiac ritual. As early as the fifth century B.C. the Greeks used the 'Corybantic ritual' of song and dance in the treatment of certain mental disorders.

Curtius, Marcus

The hero of a Roman myth invented to explain the existence of a deep pit or dried-up pool in the Roman forum known as the 'Lacus Curtius'. The story was that a chasm opened miraculously, and could only close if Rome's greatest treasure were thrown in, whereupon a brave young knight mounted his horse fully armed and leapt in, sacrificing himself for his country. The tale was popular in classical times, and was commemorated on a sculptural relief now in the Capitoline Museum. There were several late Italian pictures painted of the scene. The best is perhaps that of Panini, in Cambridge, where the Colosseum and Trajan's Column appear in the background with a fine disregard for the traditional date of Curtius in the mid fourth century B.C.

Cybele

The great mother-goddess of Phrygia, where she was represented by a sacred stone, and worshipped along with her youthful lover ATTIS in ecstatic rites and ceremonies of purification, which included a ritual bath in the blood of a sacrificed bull. Her cult spread to Greece by the fifth century B.C. and was traditionally brought to Rome in 204, though it was not until the reign of Claudius that Roman citizens were allowed to serve as her priests, and the oriental eunuchs who served her cult were always found distasteful. There is a detached account of her worship in book 2 of Lucretius, and an impressionistic one in Catullus's *Attis*. In classical art she was represented wearing a crown of towers, carrying a libation dish and tambourine, and flanked by lions, as she was also mistress of wild nature. The left half of Mantegna's *Triumph of Scipio* shows the arrival of her cult image in Rome and its reception by members of the Scipio family, as described by Livy. There is also a statue of the goddess by Rodin, simply as a woman of great presence and power.

Cyclops, Cyclopes

In Homer they are a race of one-eyed giants who live without laws or government in a distant country, traditionally identified later with Sicily. Book 9 of the *Odyssey* describes the adventures of Odysseus in the cave of POLYPHEMUS. Hesiod follows a different tradition and has three Cyclopes who make thunderbolts for Zeus and are skilled craftsmen who work in the forge of Hephaestus (Vulcan). This is how they appear in Hellenistic poetry, and in post-Renaissance paintings like Tintoretto's *Vulcan and the Cyclopes*. The Greeks also credited them with making the walls found in pre-Greek cities; the walls of Tiryns, for example, are 'cyclopean' and are Mycenean work of the thirteenth century B.C.

Cymbeline (Cunobellinus)

An early king of Britain, father of CARACTACUS, who was popular in medieval legend. Shakespeare's play takes its setting from Holinshed's *Chronicles*, though the plot is adapted from Boccaccio.

Cynthia

(i) A name given to Artemis or Diana, from Mount Cynthus in Delos where the goddess was born. In English pastoral poetry this can be used for Elizabeth I, the virgin queen, who is referred to in Ben Jonson's *Cynthia's Revels* and as 'Cynthia the Ladie of the Sea' in Spenser's *Colin Clouts Come Home Againe*.

(ii) The name given by the Roman poet Propertius to his mistress Hostia, who inspired his most striking personal poems: *Cynthia prima fuit, Cynthia finis erit.*

Cyrus the Elder (559–529 B.C.)
The founder of the Persian empire, who extended his conquests to Lydia (see CROESUS), Babylonia, Assyria, Syria and Palestine, where in most places he was welcomed as a liberator, and by the Greeks was looked upon as a model ruler. Xenophon's *Cyropaedia* is an idealized account of his education. He is the 'Cyrus the King' of the Old Testament, who orders the rebuilding of the Temple in Jerusalem in *Ezra.*

Cyrus the Younger (*c.* 430–401 B.C.)
The younger son of Darius II of Persia, who held high command in Asia Minor during the Peloponnesian War. After his brother became emperor as Artaxerxes II, Cyrus led an army against him but was killed at Cunaxa, near Babylon, in 401. The march of the 10,000 Greek mercenaries back to the Black Sea is described in his *Anabasis* by XENOPHON, who was among them.

Daedalus (Greek 'artful')
Legendary inventor, craftsman and artist, said to have migrated from Athens to Crete, where he made the labyrinth to house the Minotaur and the hollow cow for Pasiphaë; then when Minos detained him he contrived wings of feathers and wax for himself and his son ICARUS. Icarus was drowned, but Daedalus flew successfully to Cumae on the Bay of Naples and thence to Sicily, where he was credited with making many marvels, including a golden honeycomb for the temple of Aphrodite on Mount Eryx. The Greeks saw evidence of his work in any remarkable archaic statue or building, and his name became synonymous with uncanny skill and ingenuity. At a later date Trimalchio names his ingenious chef Daedalus in the *Satyricon* of PETRONIUS. 'Daedal' and 'daedalian' are still usable English adjectives. James Joyce chose the name Stephen Dedalus for his youthful self longing to spread his wings outside Dublin; *A Portrait of the Artist as a Young Man* ends with an appeal to Daedalus: 'Old father, old artificer, stand me now and ever in good stead.' Daedalus is the searching artist and spokesman of Michael Ayrton's novel, *The Maze-maker.*

Damocles
A member of the court of Dionysius I, tyrant of Syracuse. According to Cicero, Dionysius invited him to eat a splendid dinner with a sword suspended by a hair over his head, to illustrate the tyrant's life of luxury at the cost of insecurity. 'A sword of Damocles' became proverbial.

Damon and Pythias
A pair of friends often cited for their devotion. Damon was in fact a philosopher of Syracuse who stood bail for his friend (who was really called Phintias) when he was sentenced to death by the reigning tyrant. He was saved from execution when Pythias/Phintias returned, reprieved, at the last minute.

Danaë
The daughter of Acrisius, king of Argos, imprisoned by her father in a bronze

tower because an oracle said that a son of hers would kill him. (Acrisius was in fact eventually killed accidentally by Perseus when throwing a discus.) There she was visited by Zeus in the form of a shower of gold and gave birth to Perseus. Acrisius put her and the baby out to sea in a box, but they were rescued by fishermen off the island of Seriphos and protected by its King Polydectes. Perseus was afterwards sent off to fetch the Gorgon's head and Polydectes pestered Danaë with unwelcome attentions. Perseus turned him to stone on his return and took his mother back to Argos. The nature of Zeus's visitation was a popular story throughout antiquity, and there are fragments of a beautiful lyric by Simonides. In Terence's *Eunuch* there is a description of a picture of it which was erotic in intent, and this profoundly shocked St Augustine. It was also one of the most popular themes for Renaissance painters, some of whom at any rate could see in Danaë a symbol of the transfiguring effect of divine love. There are four versions by Titian as well as those of Correggio [51] and Tintoretto, one of Rembrandt's rare nudes, and another painting of his where Mercury is giving Danaë reassurance. *Die Liebe der Danaë* is a late opera by Richard Strauss.

Danaïds, Danaus

The legends about them are oriental or Egyptian but known in Greece at an early time. Danaus was the son of Belus (the Greek form of Ba'al or Bel of the Old Testament) and had fifty daughters, while his brother Aegyptus had fifty sons and wanted to arrange a mass marriage. Danaus objected to this, and took his daughters from Egypt to Argos where they settled and he became king. The sons of Aegyptus followed, and Danaus agreed to the marriage, but made his daughters promise to kill their husbands on their wedding night. Only one, Hypermestra, spared her husband Lynceus. Later legends made the Danaïds eternally punished in Hades by having to collect water in leaking vessels. Their story is told in one of Pindar's most famous odes, the ninth Pythian. The Danaïds are the chorus and collective heroine of Aeschylus' *Suppliants*, the first and only surviving play of a Danaïd trilogy.

Daphne ('bay' or 'laurel')

A Greek mountain-nymph who was pursued by Apollo, and in answer to her prayer for help was changed by Mother Earth into a bay or laurel tree. (There was a famous sanctuary of Apollo in Hellenistic times in a forest of bay trees at Daphne, near Antioch, where the original tree was shown to visitors, including Pausanias.) To console himself Apollo made himself a laurel crown. This was the prize for the victor at the Pythian Games in honour of Apollo, and has been a symbol of victory since antiquity. It was worn by Julius Caesar, by Virgil as described by Dante, and the memory lingers on in the word 'baccalaureate'. Daphne's metamorphosis was well known in the Middle Ages from Ovid's account; she is referred to by Chaucer in the *Knight's Tale*, though her name is corrupted to Dana. She could be interpreted as a soul who is menaced by a demon and escapes through the power of prayer, and for Petrarch she was especially significant because as a laurel she could stand for his Laura. Petrarch also took great pride in the laurel crown he received on the Capitol in Rome for his poetry. The tradition of Daphne in art goes back at least as far as an ivory panel of the late fifth century A.D. in Ravenna and possibly to a Pompeian fresco, and there are many paintings of her with Apollo; the best known are those of Giorgione, Pollaiuolo and Poussin (his last painting). Above all, there is Bernini's superb statue-group in Rome [52], which Cardinal Barberini hoped to make more acceptable to the Church by adding a Latin couplet to the base pointing the moral that the pursuit of appearances can only end in disillusion.

Daphnis

A Sicilian shepherd in pastoral poetry who was said to have invented the genre, and to have been blinded by the Muses and died for love; his story is told by Theocritus and he appears in Virgil's *Eclogues* and later pastoral verse.

Daphnis and Chloe is the title of an idyllic pastoral romance ascribed to Longus and doubtfully dated to the mid third century A.D. The innocent lovers inspired Saint-Pierre's novel *Paul et Virginie*, and Ravel wrote music for a ballet *Daphnis et Chloé* based on Longus.

Darius

The name of three kings of Persia, the most famous of whom was Darius I, husband of Atossa and father of Xerxes, who reigned from 521 to 486 B.C. He crossed the Bosporus twice with his army, once to invade Scythia, and again to invade Greece as a reprisal for the help given by the mainland Greeks to the Greek cities in Asia Minor who had risen against their Persian overlords. These events and his defeat when the Athenian general Miltiades led the Greeks at the battle of Marathon in 490 B.C. are described in the histories of Herodotus, and the Greek victory is the subject of *The Persians* by Aeschylus. There are famous inscriptions and sculptured reliefs at Behistun describing the exploits of Darius, and a huge mixing-bowl of the late fourth century B.C. shows him in council before his expedition to Greece. Darius III was the king who was overthrown by ALEXANDER THE GREAT.

Decius Mus

Several early Roman generals bore this name, and one led the army which was defeated by PYRRHUS at Asculum, but the most famous is the hero of the Samnite Wars of the fourth century B.C. Livy in book 8 of his history tells the popular story that Decius Mus dreamed that one army would have to sacrifice its leader, the other its entire force. He therefore dedicated himself to the gods of the Underworld and charged the enemy alone, to meet his death. Rubens left six oil paintings of the cartoons he designed for Brussels tapestries on this story, his most 'Roman' work, and especially interesting because he knew it only from his reading of Livy and had no pictorial tradition to draw on.

Deianira

Daughter of Oeneus of Calydon, sister of Meleager and wife of Heracles. Heracles asked the centaur NESSUS to carry her over a swollen river. He assaulted her and was shot by Heracles. As he died he gave Deianira his blood-soaked shirt telling her it was a love-charm. Some years later Heracles fell in love with Iole, and Deianira sent him the shirt as a gift. Its poisons were released when he put it on, and he flung himself on a burning pyre to end his agony. Deianira then killed herself. This is the plot of Sophocles' *Women of Trachis*. The story was known later from Ovid, and the *Rape of Deianira* was painted by Pollaiuolo and by Veronese. It is also the title of a marble relief by Michelangelo, though this shows Heracles, who is fighting among figures who are not certainly centaurs.

Deidamia

The daughter of the king on the island of Scyros, who fell in love with Achilles when he was hidden there, disguised as a girl, and bore him a son, NEOPTOLEMUS or Pyrrhus. This is a post-Homeric legend but known to the Athenian dramatists, and from the version by the Roman poet Statius it was used as a theme for opera in the seventeenth and eighteenth centuries. Handel's last opera was *Deidamia*, which is still occasionally revived.

Delia, Delius

(i) Epithets of Artemis and Apollo because they were born on the island of Delos.

(ii) The name used in his poems by TIBULLUS to denote the woman he loved. Her real name is said to have been Plania.

Delphic Oracle

The most important oracle in Greece, presided over by Apollo who established himself and his Olympian divinity by killing a guardian serpent, a chthonic deity called the PYTHON. This is described in the Homeric *Hymn to Apollo*, the first mention of the oracle. Oracles were given through a young priestess, the Pythia, in a state of ecstasy, and were translated by the priests in charge. They were well-known for their ambiguity (→ CROESUS). Nor were the priests incorruptible; Delphi discouraged resistance to Persia, and supported Sparta against Athens, and Philip of Macedon against Greece. Its period of greatest influence was at the time of Greek colonization overseas, when its advice on a patron and site for a new city was always asked. It was regularly consulted on points of religious cult by communities and on personal problems by individuals. It encouraged Rome to hold out against Hannibal, was looted by Sulla and visited by Nero, but though Hadrian tried to revive its prestige, it gradually declined as Christianity advanced and astrology became popular as a rival form of prophecy. Pausanias (book 10) describes vividly how it was attacked by the invading Gauls under Brennus in 279 B.C. They were met by a combination of the Greek army, earthquake, thunderstorm, snow, rockfalls sent by Apollo and blind terror induced by Pan, and not surprisingly were routed.

The temples were probably destroyed in A.D. 396 by Alaric and the Goths.

The oracle which was traditionally said to have been given to an emissary of the Emperor JULIAN is more likely to be a later forgery by Christians wishing to denigrate the Apostate's memory, and yet they are three lines which still evoke the haunting desolation of Delphi:

Go, tell the king – the carven hall is felled,
Apollo has no cell, prophetic bay
nor talking spring; the cadenced well is stilled.

Translated by Peter Jay

This was the epigraph chosen by Swinburne for his *Hymn to Proserpine*. A similar ambivalence reappears in the Nativity Hymn of Milton (who was almost the last person to conflate Delphi and Delos into Delphos, as medieval writers did):

The oracles are dumb
No voice or hideous hum
Runs through the arched roof in
words deceiving.
Apollo from his shrine
Can no more divine,
With hollow shriek the steep
of Delphos leaving.
No nightly trance or breathed spell
Inspires the pale-eyed priest from
the prophetic cell.

Delphi was believed to be the centre of the earth, and a sacred navel-stone (omphalos) of an early date has been found there as well as the marble copy seen by Pausanias. Its site and ruins are described at length by Pausanias, and are among the most impressive in Greece. The buildings include the treasuries of the different cities who dedicated offerings, the theatre, stadium, and the Temple of Apollo, rebuilt in the fourth century B.C. on sixth-century foundations, with the famous maxims 'Know thyself' and 'Nothing too much' engraved on its façade, traditionally said to have originated in a visit of the Seven Sages to Delphi. There are also remains of the *lesche* or club-house, which Pausanias saw when it still had its magnificent paintings by Polygnotus of scenes from the Underworld and the Trojan War.

Demeter

The Greek corn-goddess, with whom the Roman Ceres was identified. She was also a mother-goddess, mother of Persephone, who is also Kore ('the maiden'). Her search for her daughter, carried off to the Underworld, is first described in the Homeric *Hymn to Demeter*. It took her to Eleusis, where she found Persephone, and in gratitude gave an ear of corn to the king's young son Triptolemus, with instructions to take it round the world. This is shown on a famous fifth-century votive relief from Eleusis. Demeter became associated with the pre-Hellenic Great Mysteries and the ritual which celebrated the death and rebirth of the corn and also the mystic rebirth of the celebrants through the purification of death. She was widely worshipped elsewhere, especially in Arcadia, Sicily and Cnidos. The seated statue known as the Demeter of Cnidos in the British Museum dates from the fourth century B.C. and has a compelling power even in its broken state. There are also seated figures of Demeter and Persephone among the Elgin Marbles.

Democritus (*c.* 460–*c.* 370 B.C.)
Greek philosopher of Abdera in Thrace, none of whose works survive, though they covered a wide scientific field. In ethics he taught the pursuit of enlightened self-interest and influenced EPICURUS and the later materialists, but he is chiefly remembered for his development of the atomic theory which he learned from his teacher Leucippus. He held that everything was due to the chance collision and aggregation of immeasurable, indivisible and homogeneous particles, and that other worlds were continuously generated by spontaneous movement in the universe. He was popularly known as the 'laughing philosopher', and Juvenal speaks of him as perpetually amused by the follies of man.

Demogorgon
It has been rightly remarked that 'Demogorgon is a grammatical error, become god'. Plato in both the *Republic* and *Timaeus* writes of Demiurgos, the divine Creator of the world, and this may be what the scholar Lactantius (third century A.D.) intended to write as a note on a reference in the *Thebaid* of Statius to 'the most high whom it is unlawful to know'. Instead he wrote 'Demogorgon', and the name was taken by Boccaccio in his *Genealogy of the Gods* to refer to a primeval god whom he conceived as the parent of all the other ancient gods. Demogorgon then appears in Marlowe's *Dr Faustus*, in Spenser and in Milton; and in Shelley's *Prometheus Unbound* as an eternal divine principle which will oust the gods of false theology.

Demosthenes (384–322 B.C.)
Athenian orator and statesman, generally considered to be the greatest of Greek orators for his political sincerity and his mastery of prose style. The popular story that he overcame a speech impediment by declaiming on the seashore against the noise of the waves with a mouth full of pebbles is doubtless apocryphal. He won his reputation for speeches in private legal suits, and many of these survive. Then he started on his political career by constantly attacking the growing power of Philip of Macedon which he saw as a menace not only to Athens but to the liberty of all the Greek city-states. His *Olynthiacs* and *Philippics* are directed against Philip, and his most famous speech *On the Crown* (*De corona*) ostensibly defends one Ctesiphon who had been charged by Aeschines with illegally offering Demosthenes a golden crown, but is really a justification of his own political policy and an attack on those who would have preferred peace with Macedon. 'Philippics' as a title for speeches of invective was adopted by Cicero for his own speeches against Mark Antony after the death of Caesar.

Deucalion
The Noah of Greek mythology, son of Prometheus, who told him to build an ark or small boat so that he could escape with his wife Pyrrha when Zeus covered the earth with a flood. After

the waters subsided he was told by divine command to throw his mother's bones over his shoulder. He and Pyrrha threw stones from Mother Earth which became human beings and repopulated the land. Deucalion was the father of Hellen, the eponymous ancestor of the Greek race: the Greeks always spoke of themselves as Hellenes and their country as Hellas.

Diana

An indigenous Italian goddess, associated with wooded places, women and childbirth, and with the moon, through her identification with ARTEMIS. Her most ancient cult-centre was in a grove at Aricia, on the shore of the volcanic Lake Nemi which was known as Diana's Mirror.

... The still glassy lake that sleeps
  Beneath Aricia's trees,
Those trees in whose dim shadow
  The ghastly priest doth reign,
The priest that slew the slayer
  And shall himself be slain.

Macaulay, *Lays of Ancient Rome*

There the priest, called the *rex*, had to be a runaway slave who must murder his predecessor (→ GOLDEN BOUGH). She also had an ancient temple on the Aventine hill, said to have been founded by King Servius Tullius. Her functions are all referred to in Catullus's *Hymn to Diana* and were all known from antiquity onwards; e.g. for Ben Jonson she is not only 'Queen and huntress, chaste and fair' but 'Goddess excellently bright'. Artemis/Diana brought normal death from natural causes to women, as Apollo did to men, but both could be cruel; for Diana's victims see ACTAEON, CALLISTO, MELEAGER and NIOBE. These are listed in a description of her temple paintings in Chaucer's *Knight's Tale*. She appears with them in many Italian paintings, and also with Apollo or her companions; there are unusual versions of these subjects by the elder Cranach and Vermeer.

Dictys

A legendary Cretan said to have accompanied Idomeneus to the Trojan War and to have kept a diary of events. This was supposedly buried in a tomb near Knossos and found in the reign of Nero. A Latin prose version along with one of another imaginary hero of the war, Dares the Phrygian, was widely used by medieval writers on the Troy saga.

Dido

Daughter of a king of Tyre and originally called Elissa, she escaped after the murder of her husband Sychaeus and sailed with a few followers to Libya, where she founded Carthage. Local early legend said that she burnt herself on a funeral pyre to escape marriage with a native king, Iarbas. The Roman version of her story brought Aeneas to Carthage, but Virgil's treatment of it in books 1 and 4 of the *Aeneid* is his own; Dido seeks death for unrequited love for him. Aeneas abandons her in obedience to divine command to resume his role as the founder of Rome, and this was acceptable to Roman sentiment though not to later romanticists. Dido's love and death then make her a sympathetic heroine, in Chaucer's *Legend of Good Women*, in Marlowe's *Tragedy of*

Dido, in Purcell's opera *Dido and Aeneas*, and in part 2 of Berlioz's opera *Les Troyens*.

Diocletian (Gaius Aurelius Valerius Diocletianus, Roman Emperor A.D. 284–305)

In 305 Diocletian abdicated and retired to live until his death in 313 in his immense palace on the Dalmatian coast at Aspalathos, where its remains enclose the modern town of Split. They were visited and drawn by Robert Adam who published his designs in 1764. These designs had great influence on the architecture and interior decoration of Adam and his school. Diocletian carried out widespread reforms in the Empire, in coinage and taxation, in the army, and in his division of the imperial power between two emperors of East and West, each with a Caesar as his assistant and possible successor. His reputation has suffered chiefly from his systematic persecution of the Christians. The Church of Santa Maria degli Angeli in Rome was converted by Michelangelo out of the central hall of the Baths of Diocletian.

Diogenes (*c.* 400–*c.* 325 B.C.)

Greek philosopher from Sinope on the Black Sea, who lived in Athens in extreme poverty and asceticism and taught that man should live by satisfying his natural needs in the easiest practical way, ignoring conventions. He was therefore nicknamed Kyon (Greek 'dog', the type of shamelessness), and his followers were called Cynics. Many colourful tales were told of his eccentricities; he lived in a 'barrel', a large storage jar; he rolled this up and down the streets when everyone else was busy preparing for war with Philip of Macedon, in order, he said, to be busy too; he was seen carrying a lantern by daylight, trying to find an honest man. When visited by Alexander the Great who asked if he could do anything for him, Diogenes is said to have asked Alexander to get out of his light. To Alexander's credit he is said to have remarked that if he were not Alexander he would like to be Diogenes. Diogenes' teaching was largely negative, though in its dislike of humbug it was modelled on that of Socrates, and it was later modified and incorporated in Stoic philosophy.

Diomedes

Hero of Argos and son of Tydeus. In the *Iliad*, where his disciplined courage is perhaps intended to contrast with the waywardness of Achilles, he plays a leading part. He wounds both Ares and Aphrodite, leads an attack on Troy in the absence of Achilles, and raids the Trojan camp with Odysseus (the theme of Euripides' *Rhesus*). In post-Homeric legend he helps Odysseus to bring PHILOCTETES from Lemnos and also to murder Palamedes and to steal the Palladium, the sacred image of Athene on which the fortunes of Troy depended. He is the 'Diomed' in Chaucer and in Shakespeare who wins Cressida from Troilus, and both poets stress his haughty masculine competence. Dante puts him with Odysseus/Ulysses in the consuming flames which are the punishment for the 'counsellors of fraud' in the Eighth Circle of Hell. But he is seen again as a hero in the painting *Venus Wounded by Diomedes* by Ingres.

Dion (*c.* 408–354 B.C.)
A relative of Dionysius I of Syracuse and, under Plato's influence, an opponent of tyranny. He tried to instil Plato's view into the young Dionysius II, failed, and was exiled in 366. He stayed in Greece for ten years, and then returned with an army and occupied Syracuse. His attempts to impose a Platonic aristocracy made him unpopular and he was murdered.

Dionysius I (*c.* 430–367 B.C.)
Tyrant of Syracuse who was responsible for the fortifications of the city and the building of the fortress of Euryalus, the extensive ruins of which can still be seen. The so-called 'Ear of Dionysius' is a stone-quarry with a narrow aperture at the top; local legend supposed that Dionysius listened through it to prisoners talking inside. He aimed at expelling the Carthaginians from Sicily and at extending his power over the Greek cities of Sicily and southern Italy, but without lasting success. He also had cultural aspirations and competed unsuccessfully in Greece with poems, though he won a prize for a tragedy.

Dionysius II
The son, who was tyrant from 367 until his expulsion in 343, though he was kept out of Syracuse by Dion and his successors between 356 and 346. Plato and Dion had hoped to make a philosopher-king out of him, and he had cultivated interests, but his character was too weak to respond to Plato's teaching. His story is told in Plato's *Letters* 7–8, and the whole vexed situation in Syracuse is the subject of Mary Renault's novel *The Mask of Apollo*.

Dionysus (Roman **Bacchus**)
Greek or pre-Greek god, associated with wine, with the release of mass emotion, and with a fertility cult celebrated in Mysteries of great secrecy. He was generally said to be the son of ZEUS and SEMELE, and was snatched by Zeus from her dead body and taken to Mount Nysa, in India, where he was brought up by the nymphs and taught the use of the vine by Silenus and the satyrs, and also of ivy, which is a mild intoxicant when chewed, and a symbol of everlasting life. Carrying his thyrsus, an ivy-entwined magic staff, he led his followers, the maenads or bacchants, across Asia and eventually reached Greece. His triumphal progress was a popular subject in art; e.g. a mosaic of the second century B.C. shows him riding a panther (cf. Titian's *Bacchus and Ariadne*, where he is driving panthers harnessed to his chariot). Another legend (told in the Homeric *Hymn to Dionysus*) describes his crossing the sea by boat and making vineleaves spring from the mast: this too is illustrated in a famous black-figure vase of the sixth century B.C. by Exekias, the Athenian vase-painter [25]. He was accepted by Apollo at Delphi, and his cult continued there in less frenzied form, while in Athens the dramatists produced their plays as part of the spring festival of the Great Dionysia. The release of powerful irrational impulses through controlled

ritual was considered a necessary catharsis, or purge, as Aristotle makes clear in his analysis of the effect of tragedy (in his *Poetics*). After that can come relaxation and relief, and this is perhaps what is captured in the reclining Dionysus of the Elgin Marbles. But the unleashed communal ecstasy, particularly among women, was not forgotten. It could culminate in the ritual killing of animals and even of human victims; this is illustrated by the killing of PENTHEUS in the *Bacchae* of Euripides. In the course of the fifth century Dionysus became a god of the dead and of immortality: see ARIADNE. In Rome, despite the attempts of the early republicans to prevent the cult reaching Italy, the mysteries of Dionysus were a closely guarded secret cult. The frieze in the Villa dei Misteri at Pompeii shows an initiation ceremony, flagellation, and mystic marriage of a novice with the god.

The term 'Dionysian' is generally used to express the sensual and irrational in nature, and was contrasted by Nietzsche in his earlier aesthetic works with the 'Apollonian' principle – the creative and passionate *v.* the critical and rational – so that he could speak of tragedy as the result of the subordination of Dionysus to Apollo. But as he developed his special view of the 'will to power' he tended to make Dionysus synonymous with his superman, and spoke of his hero Goethe as 'Dionysian man'.

Dirce

In Theban legend, the wife of Lycus and persecutor of ANTIOPE, whose sons avenged her by tying Dirce to the horns of a bull so that she was dragged to her death. This is illustrated by the famous statue of *c.* 100 B.C. known as the Farnese Bull, in the National Museum at Naples.

Dis

The Greek god of the Underworld, better known as Pluto. In Dante's *Inferno* Virgil uses this classical name for Satan, and the lower regions of Hell are enclosed in the walled city of Dis. → PERSEPHONE.

Discobolos

This statue of a discus-thrower by Myron, a Greek sculptor of the fifth century B.C., survives only in copies, two of which are in the Terme Museum, Rome. Even in these imperfect reproductions it is clear that the original was a masterpiece of arrested action.

Dodona

The oracle of Zeus at Dodona in north-western Greece was said to be the most ancient known to the Greeks. It was centred on an oak tree, and its messages were delivered through the rustling (or markings) of the leaves, the cooing of pigeons nesting there, the murmuring of the brook near by, and the bronze gongs clashed by the priestesses who were called 'pigeons'. Homer in *Iliad* 16 calls the priests the 'Selloi' and describes them as primitive, 'with unwashed feet, sleeping on the ground' (to maintain contact with Mother Earth?). All oracles were originally chthonic and pre-Greek, and Zeus took over in Dodona as Apollo did at Delphi. Dodona's prestige was eclipsed by Delphi, and it had recently ceased to be consulted at the time of Strabo in the early first century A.D., but it probably flourished locally much later.

Domitian (Titus Flavius Domitianus, Roman Emperor A.D. 81–96)

An intelligent despot, who has been generally misunderstood because of the hostility of contemporary writers (Juvenal, Tacitus, Suetonius and the younger Pliny) who saw in him only the ruthless terrorist of the later years of his reign which ended in his murder. He aimed at strengthening the existing frontiers, especially on the Rhine, and exercised strict control over the administration of the provinces and collection of taxes, but he was determined to break any remaining powers of opposition in the Senate and did so by confiscations of property and executions, becoming increasingly suspicious and embittered. Some Christians were victims of the reign of terror, as were the doctrinaire opponents known as the 'Stoic opposition', but there is no evidence of the widespread persecution attributed to him by later Christian apologists.

Dorians

The last of the northern invaders of Greece, coming at intervals from *c.* 1200 B.C. and firmly established by 1000. They are thought to have been Greeks of a lower cultural level, bringing little with them but the iron slashing sword to replace the bronze thrusting one. They destroyed the Mycenean civilization and plunged Greece into a dark age, though when their sense of form was blended with the art of Ionia it produced the splendid geometric pottery of Corinth and Attica. In most places they fused with the local populace, but in Sparta and Crete they remained the ruling class with the indigenous people as serfs. The Doric dialect was spoken in the Peloponnese and the Doric colonies of Sicily and southern Italy, and it was traditionally used for choral odes and pastoral poetry. The Doric order in architecture is the earliest and simplest form of a slightly tapering rounded pillar supporting a plain square slab beneath the lintel – as, for example, in the sixth-century temples in the Doric colony of Paestum (Pesto in Italian Campania).

Draco

According to ancient tradition an Athenian lawgiver who drew up a code of law in 621 B.C. with fixed rules of procedure and penalties. The latter were so harsh that they were repealed or modified by Solon, and a 'Draconian law' became synonymous with severity.

Dying Gladiator or **Gaul**

This famous statue [18] in the Capitoline Museum, Rome, is in fact a dying Galatian, and is a Roman copy of one of the statues from the monument set up in Pergamum by King Attalus I to commemorate his victory in about 230 B.C. over the Galatians, a Celtic people settled in central Asia Minor. It was of this statue that Byron in *Childe*

Harold's Pilgrimage used the phrase 'butchered to make a Roman holiday'.

Echo

A nymph deprived of normal speech by Hera so that she could only repeat the words of others. She fell in love with NARCISSUS, pined away when he was not interested, and only her voice was left. This is the version told by Ovid (*Metamorphoses* 3) and is a good example of an 'aetiological myth', i.e. one that has arisen out of an attempt to explain some phenomenon.

Egeria

An Italian goddess or nymph connected with water, worshipped in conjunction with Diana, and generally said by the Romans to have advised an early king, Numa Pompilius, especially on religious matters. She is mentioned in Plutarch's life of Numa and by Livy, who says they met in a sacred grove outside Rome – an assignation which amused Juvenal, but for Byron (*Childe Harold's Pilgrimage*, canto IV) was a symbol of the human heart's search for an ideal love.

Eileithyia

The goddess presiding over childbirth, associated by the Greeks with Artemis, and identified by the Romans with Juno Lucina.

Elagabalus (Roman Emperor A.D. 218–22)

His name (sometimes in the form Heliogabalus) was taken from the local sun-god worshipped in Emesa, on the river Orontes in Syria, whose priest he was. His grandmother was Syrian, the sister of Julia Domna, wife of the Emperor SEPTIMIUS SEVERUS, and his mother claimed that he was the son of the Emperor Caracalla. They organized his proclamation as emperor and brought him to Rome as a boy of fifteen, bringing the cult-stone (a meteorite) of his god. There he instituted rituals of fantastic perversion which outdid anything known in the capital before. He left state affairs to his mother and grandmother and devoted the rest of his short life to extravagance and depravity. After complicated intrigues he was murdered. He is the subject of the historical novel *Family Favourites* by Alfred Duggan.

Electra

The daughter of Agamemnon and Clytemnestra, not mentioned in Homer and first named by Stesichorus. For the Greek tragedians she is one of the central figures in the drama of murder and revenge. Aeschylus, Sophocles and Euripides all represent her as fanatically hostile to her mother and the driving force behind her brother Orestes; in Euripides' *Electra* especially she is obsessed with her hatred, her feelings for her father, and then by guilt and remorse. Freud gave the name 'Electra complex' to a woman's fixation on her father accompanied by jealousy of her mother (the counterpart of the Oedipus complex), and Electra's character has been the subject of psychological treatment in the opera *Elektra* by von Hofmannsthal and Richard Strauss, in O'Neill's *Mourning Becomes Electra*, and in the film *Electra* by Cacoyannis.

Elgin Marbles

These marbles were removed from the ruins of the Parthenon at Athens by the seventh Earl of Elgin in 1801–3 when he was ambassador to Turkey, and after long haggling they were bought by the British Museum in 1816, for about half what Lord Elgin gave for them and for far less than the French would have given. Their reception in England is described in the autobiography of the painter B. R. Haydon, the friend of Keats, and Keats himself drew inspiration from them for his *Ode on a Grecian Urn*, *Endymion*, and *Hyperion*. They are now well displayed in a special room in the museum, and consist of portions of the frieze, metopes and figures from the east and west pediments; they are the best surviving examples of the work of PHIDIAS and were made between 467 and 432 B.C. It seems certain that Lord Elgin saved them from destruction by exposure and the selling-off of fragments by the Turks, and that if he had not bought them they would have gone to France, but philhellenes have asked for them to be returned to Greece ever since Byron's attack on Lord Elgin for removing 'the last poor plunder from a bleeding land'.

Elpenor

In the *Odyssey*, one of Odysseus' crew, said to be young, weak and foolish, who fell off the roof of Circe's palace in his sleep and broke his neck. His ghost met Odysseus in the Underworld and begged for cremation and a barrow with his oar on top. This episode is adapted by Virgil in *Aeneid* 6; → PALINURUS. Elpenor is one of the central figures in the sequence of poems, *Myth-history* (Mithistorema) by George Seferis, where he is 'sympathetic, sentimental, mediocre, wasted . . . He symbolizes those to whom we refer in daily conversation with the expression "the poor devil".' Elpenor reappears with Circe in Seferis's later sequence *Thrush*.

Elysium

Like Homer, the Greeks in general believed that the dead lived a dreary life in the Underworld, but the different concept of the Elysian Fields as an abode for the blessed, singled out by the gods for eternal happiness, is mentioned both by Homer and by Hesiod and may be a survival from pre-Greek religion. Elysium was situated in the Islands of the Blessed in some remote part of the earth, though in the literary tradition it was moved to the Underworld to conform with Homer as far as possible. There Aeneas meets his father Anchises in *Aeneid* 6. The idea was also absorbed into the promise of an after-life provided by the various mystery-cults, and the name survives in the Alyscamps at Arles, the celebrated Roman and later Christian burial ground. The Champs Elysées in Paris, laid out in the seventeenth century and redesigned in 1815, are of course named after the Elysian Fields.

Empedocles (*c.* 493–*c.* 433 B.C.)

Greek philosopher of Acragas in Sicily, teaching that reality is compounded of four elements, fire, air, earth and water, which continually mingle and separate under the influence of love and strife. He was also interested in medicine and was an active democrat in politics, and like PYTHAGORAS he taught transmigration of souls and vegetarianism. Empedocles acquired legendary fame, some of it self-created; he claimed he was an incarnate god and that his pupils could raise the dead. Of the many stories told of his death the most colourful is that he leapt into the crater of Etna. This inspired Matthew Arnold's poem *Empedocles on Etna* and Hölderlin's *Death of Empedocles.*

Endymion

Either a legendary king of Elis and founder of the festival at Olympia, or a shepherd in Caria, but in either case, a beautiful young man with whom the moon fell in love while he was sleeping on Mount Latmos. She made him sleep everlastingly so that she could look at his beauty for ever. This is late legend with romantic attraction; 'the moon sleeps with Endymion' later becomes a literary commonplace. In the Middle Ages it was also thought by some to signify a mystic union with God through the moon, and Keats's first long poem *Endymion* develops the theme as an allegory of the poet's search for ideal beauty.

Ennius, Quintus (239–169 B.C.)

The 'father of Roman poetry' was born in Calabria near Brindisi, an area of Greek influence, so that he knew both Greek and Latin. He came to Rome, soon became the friend of the cultivated Romans of the time, and wrote a great number of plays and poems as well as his *Annals* – an epic poem on Roman history in eighteen books, of which about 550 lines survive. In this he adapted the quantitive Greek hexameter to accentual Latin and set the pattern for Latin verse; he had great influence on Lucretius and Virgil. Ennius is said to have believed in reincarnation and thought himself a reincarnated Homer.

Eos

The Greek goddess of the dawn, the Roman Aurora. In Homer she is yellow-robed and rosy-fingered and drives her chariot across the sky each morning, a tradition which continued in art and literature; among the Elgin Marbles is the sculptured head of one of her horses. There are also many legends of the beautiful young men she carried off to be her lovers: see CEPHALUS, ORION, and TITHONUS, by whom she had a son, Memnon. It has been suggested that such legends are a euphemism for death, life being at its lowest ebb at dawn.

Epaminondas (died 362 B.C.)

The hero of fourth-century Thebes, whose courage and nobility of character were universally admired. He liberated Thebes from Spartan rule in 379 and unified Boeotia, and in 371 led the Boeotian army which defeated the invading Spartans at the battle of Leuctra by the new tactics he devised. He then invaded the Peloponnese, helped the Arcadians to form an independent Arcadian League, and established the independence of Messenia. He even challenged Athenian supremacy at sea, took a fleet as far as Byzantium, but was recalled to support the Arcadians against Sparta, and died fighting in the battle of Mantinea. Thebes never regained her short-lived powers, nor did Sparta resume her hegemony in Greece. Epaminondas was supported by his fellow-Theban Pelopidas, leader of the famous Sacred Band, a picked company of 300 Thebans who lived and fought as 150 pairs of lovers.

Epictetus (*c.* A.D. 55–135)
Stoic philosopher of Phrygia, a freed slave teaching in Rome and subsequently in Nicopolis in Epirus, where he had a large circle of pupils. These included the historian Arrian, who published notes on his lectures which had great influence on the Stoic Emperor Marcus Aurelius. Epictetus had a deeply religious faith in the divine principle of the Stoics and taught that absolute trust in providence and indifference to the external world was the only way to achieve happiness.

Epicurus (341–271 B.C.)
Greek philosopher and founder of the Epicurean system of philosophy. He came to Athens from Samos and set up a school, known as the Garden, where the organized teaching rivalled that of the Academy of Plato. Women and slaves were admitted as pupils. The basis of his teaching was the atomic theory of DEMOCRITUS, and in ethics he developed the theory that, though the gods exist, they are unconcerned with the affairs of men, so that men need neither placate nor fear them and are consequently free to pursue their natural aim of happiness and tranquillity. Such freedom from pain and anxiety can be won only by renunciation of worldly aims. The best exposition of his views is in the *De rerum natura* of the Roman poet LUCRETIUS. Epicureanism was very popular in the ancient world and was defended by its adherents against attacks by both Stoics and Christians, but it could easily be misunderstood by the unenlightened as a selfish pursuit of pleasure and material benefits. It was also naturally admired by rationalists of the eighteenth century, and happiness as a right to be pursued is written into the American Declaration of Independence.

Erechtheus
In classical times he was believed to be an early king of Athens and was often confused or identified with the equally legendary king Erichthonius; both were sons of earth, associated with snakes, and reared by Athene, and must have been chthonic deities who were superseded by the Olympians (cf. APOLLO and PYTHON.) Erechtheus was worshipped with Athene on the Acropolis at Athens, and the cult was already known to Homer. The temple known as the Erechtheum dates from the late fifth century and is thought to be on the site of the old royal palace; it contains a snake-pit and a Mycenean cistern and the reputed tomb of Cecrops, but its characteristic feature outside is the famous south-west porch, supported by caryatids. One is a copy, the original being in the British Museum along with one Ionic column. The whole porch was closely copied in the church of St Pancras, London.

Erinyes

The Greek spirits of vengeance, or Furies, often known by the euphemistic name of Eumenides ('kindly ones'). They avenge wrongs done to kindred, particularly murder within a family, and so can be thought of as personified pangs of conscience or remorse among those who have broken a taboo. ALCMAEON and ORESTES, who both murder their mothers, are driven mad by the Erinyes. Tradition says that when represented as the chorus in Aeschylus's *Eumenides* their appearance made women in the audience faint or miscarry.

Eros

The Greek god of Love, the Roman CUPID, generally said to be the son of Aphrodite. The lyric poets and tragedians stress his omnipotence and cruelty to those who are considered his victims, though at the same time he can be young and beautiful, and in Sappho he is 'bitter-sweet'. In Hellenistic literature he appears with PSYCHE and also becomes more playful, while in art he is often a winged putto and can be multiplied; friezes of Erotes at play are common in Pompeii and in later Roman art. There are Erotes/Cupids in scenes of fishing and harvesting grapes in the famous mosaics from the great fourth-century imperial villa at Piazza Armerina, Sicily. He carries a bow and arrows at least from the time of Euripides, and it is in this form that he is about to 'bury his shaft' in the centre of the Eros fountain in Piccadilly Circus, as a memorial to the nineteenth-century philanthropist, Lord Shaftesbury.

Eteocles

The elder (twin?) son of Oedipus and Jocasta, brother of Polynices and Antigone. After their father cursed his sons and departed into exile from Thebes, the brothers agreed to reign alternate years, but Eteocles refused to give up the throne at the end of his year. This precipitated the action known from early Theban saga as the Seven against Thebes. Polynices and six chieftains led an army against the city, but in the battle all of the Seven but Adrastus were killed, and the two brothers killed each other. This is the situation at the opening of Sophocles' *Antigone*. The war is also the subject of Aeschylus's *Seven against Thebes* and Euripides' *Suppliants* and *Phoenician Women*; such plays are all derived from the lost saga-cycle *Thebais* which Aristotle ranked next to the *Iliad* and *Odyssey*. The rivalry of the brothers is also the subject of the epic *Thebaid* by the Roman poet Statius, and later of *La Thébaïde*, which was Racine's first play.

Etna

The highest volcano in Europe, over 10,000 feet high, on the east side of Sicily between Catania and Taormina. The fertility of its lower slopes and its periodic eruptions made a great impression on both Greeks and Romans; there was an important cult of Demeter/Ceres there, and it was believed that one of the giants, Enceladus or Typhon, was buried underneath and struggling to get out. In one version, Zeus had hurled Etna on top of Typhon in the war with the GIANTS.

Euclid
The famous Greek mathematician, living about 300 B.C. at the court of Ptolemy I in Alexandria, and best known for his *Elements of Geometry*. This was translated into Arabic, Hebrew and Latin and all the major European languages, and was the universal textbook on the subject until quite recent times. Ptolemy is said to have complained about its length and difficulty; to which Euclid replied that there could be a Royal Road in Egypt but not to geometry.

Euhemerus
The Greek author of the *Sacred Scripture*, a fantasy travel novel written about 300 B.C. in which he developed the theory that the Greek gods were deified kings and conquerors. He was probably influenced by the exploits of Alexander the Great. In the Latin translation of Ennius this had a certain influence on the Romans, and later became a weapon in the hands of Christian apologists to discredit the pagan gods by showing that they were no more than human in their vices and weaknesses. Euhemerism was especially popular in the Middle Ages, when the gods were thought of as forerunners of civilization and were linked with biblical kings and prophets.

Eumaeus
In the *Odyssey*, the faithful swineherd of Odysseus who entertained his master in his hut without recognizing him, and then helped him to destroy the suitors of Penelope. In book 15 he tells his story: he was of royal birth on a distant island, given by his nursemaid to Phoenician slave-dealers, and then sold to Odysseus' father Laertes. This is one of the several 'travellers' tales' told in agreeable circumstantial detail and incorporated in the *Odyssey*.

Euripides (*c.* 480–406 B.C.)
The latest of the three great Athenian tragic dramatists, nineteen of whose ninety-two plays survive. Within the traditional framework of Attic drama Euripides was an innovator, often making the chorus a commentator rather than an integrated participant in the plot, and creating characters who discuss their human problems in contemporary language; he was deeply interested in feminine psychology (→ MEDEA, PHAEDRA), to a degree which shocked his contemporaries. He was also much criticized in his lifetime for destroying the dignity of tragedy, for his rationalism and for alleged obscenity, and was brilliantly parodied in Aristophanes' *Frogs*. In 408, annoyed at his lack of success in Athens, he left for Thessaly and then Macedon, where he wrote *The Bacchae*, and died at the court of King Archelaus. After his death he was the most popular of the dramatists, and his plays were frequently performed. In his logical working-out of a situation and love of debate he has been called Shavian, as he is too perhaps in his championship of women and the underprivileged, and in his belief in democracy and hatred of the horrors of war. He also wrote lyric poetry of great beauty in his choral odes, and for Aristotle he was the most 'tragic' of poets. Milton refers to the tradition in Plutarch that the Spartans

spared Athens from destruction in 404 B.C. because they heard part of the chorus of *Electra* sung (quoted under PINDAR).

Europa

The daughter of a legendary king of Tyre and sister of Cadmus, who was carried away by Zeus in the form of a bull to Crete, where she bore him three sons, Minos, Rhadamanthys and Sarpedon. She was identified with a Cretan goddess and worshipped on the island, and her story may well be a Greek interpretation of the bull-leaping and bull-riding ritual found there; see the MINOTAUR. In late legend the bull became the constellation Taurus (bull). Europa appears seated on her bull in a metope of the mid sixth century from the Siphnian treasury at Delphi, and in one a century later from one of the temples at Selinus in Sicily, and she was a popular subject for later painters. Ovid's description of the scene where the friendly white bull allows the girl to garland his horns and then venture on to his back is closely followed by Titian, whose bull is endearingly benign; there are also famous versions by Rubens, copying Titian, two by Veronese, by Rembrandt (one of his rare classical pictures) and a landscape with Europa by Claude Lorraine.

Eurydice

The name of several mythological women, the most important being a nymph or dryad who was the wife of ORPHEUS. She was bitten by a snake and died; Virgil alone (in *Georgic* 4) follows a tradition that she was trying to escape from the bee-keeper ARISTAEUS when this happened. Orpheus went down to the Underworld in search of her, and charmed by his music Pluto and Persephone, so that one or both of them agreed that Eurydice should return with him. Like many famous legends of antiquity, there were variants; in the commonest one, Orpheus was told he must not look at her on the upward journey, but he could not resist turning round, and lost her for ever. This was transmitted by Virgil and Ovid, by Seneca in his *Hercules Furens* and by Statius. But it was also said that Orpheus was told he could have her only for a day, and then Hermes (in his capacity as guide to the dead) fetched her back again. This is probably the meaning of the many copies of a large relief [2] which in its original form is thought to be a panel from the sides of the altar of the Twelve Olympians in the market-place of Athens, and is dated to the late fifth century B.C. There Eurydice appears between Orpheus and Hermes (who is not mentioned by Ovid and Virgil). (See Introduction p. 20.)

Plato gives the story an ironic twist in Phaedrus's speech in the *Symposium*, where Orpheus is contrasted with Alcestis; he lacks the courage to die for love, enters Hades alive and is only given a phantom to bring back, and his death at the hands of the maenad women is a punishment for his cowardice.

Much more significant is the interpretation of the legend by the Christian poet of late antiquity, Boethius, in his *Consolation of Philosophy*, book 3. There

Orpheus loses Eurydice as an illustration of Lady Philosophy's teaching that once the soul has turned to God there must be no looking back to sensuous pleasures. 'By turning the fate of Orpheus to another purpose, Boethius breathed into the creaking machinery of literary antiquity a new life which would carry it through the Middle Ages and the Renaissance.

Consider this story before you,
turn your mind to higher things.
If you escape the flesh but
even once look back to that hell,
you will be lost.'*

Through Ovid and Virgil the story continued to be well known, and in the medieval *Sir Orfeo* it is transformed into a ballad of courtly love in which the devoted husband wins back his lady Heurodis from the king of Fairyland. With the Renaissance came Politian's *Orfeo*, the earliest Italian drama on a classical theme. Sung to a lute accompaniment it was the forerunner of many operas, of which the best known today are Monteverdi's *Orfeo* and Gluck's *Orfeo ed Eurydice*, the latter ending happily with Eurydice restored by the gods' forgiveness. Much later came Offenbach's burlesque *Orphée aux enfers*.

The myth is treated symbolically and given a twentieth-century setting in Jean Anouilh's play *Eurydice*, in Marcel Camus's film *Black Orpheus* (*Orfeu Negro*) played by Negro actors in Rio de Janeiro, and in two surrealist plays, both filmed, by Cocteau.

Q. Fabius (Maximus Verrucosus) Cunctator (? 275–203 B.C.)
Roman general and statesman, known as the Delayer or the Shield of Rome. During the Second Punic War he was appointed dictator in Rome after the victory of Hannibal at Lake Trasimene in 217 B.C., and won his derogatory nickname by his policy of avoiding open battle with the Carthaginians. When the Roman army was totally defeated at Cannae the following year his delaying tactics had to be continued until the morale of the people improved. Then their merits were recognized; as Ennius said, *unus homo nobis cunctando restituit rem* (one man by his delaying restored the situation for us). He continued to campaign successfully in Italy but opposed the more imaginative strategy of Scipio and the invasion of northern Africa, and died in 203, before the end of the war. 'Fabianism' as a policy of cautious advance is named after him.

Fasces (Latin 'bundles')
The elm or birch rods bound together by a red thong and officially carried by the lictors attendant on a Roman consul to signify his magisterial authority. Outside Rome an axe was added to show that he had the power to execute as well as to flog. Through the Italian word '*fascio*' the Italian Fascist party took its name from them, with the Roman fasces as its symbol.

Fate
From the concept of an impersonal destiny, which in Homer seems both to implement the will of Zeus and yet be

* Harold Isbell, *The Last Poets of Imperial Rome*, Penguin Books, 1971.

stronger than the gods, there develops a trio of goddesses (*Moirai* in Greek, *Parcae* in Latin) who are first named by Hesiod and said to be the daughters of Zeus and Themis (Righteousness), though Plato makes them the daughters of Ananke (Necessity). They are Lachesis who assigns man's lot at birth, Clotho who spins the thread of life, and Atropos 'who cannot be turned' from cutting it at the moment of death. They sing the marriage song of PELEUS and Thetis in Catullus's poem. Milton in *Lycidas* intensifies the image of Atropos by calling her 'the blind Fury with th' abhorred shears'.

Faunus

An Italian god, associated with herdsmen and shepherds, woods and pastures, and identified with Pan. His name is then used for goat-legged half-human woodland creatures similar to Greek satyrs though usually more gentle. Fauns are later among the followers of Bacchus and the inhabitants of ARCADIA, and one of the most touchingly farouche fauns is the one in Piero di Cosimo's picture of the *Death of Procris* in the National Gallery, London [27].

Faustina

The elder Faustina was the wife of the Roman Emperor Antoninus Pius and aunt of the Emperor Marcus Aurelius, whom her daughter, the younger Faustina, married. Both women were said to be faithless and immoral, but there is no evidence to prove this. The younger Faustina went with Marcus on his northern campaigns, and it seems from his *Meditations* that he genuinely loved her.

Felix, Marcus Antoninus

A freed slave in the service of the imperial family, the brother of Pallas, financial secretary to the Emperor Claudius. He was procurator of Judaea from A.D. 52–*c.* 60, when he was recalled and succeeded by Porcius Festus. He tried unsuccessfully to suppress Jewish unrest and is denounced for his cruelty by both Tacitus and Josephus. He was the judge of St Paul (Acts xxiv) and kept him in prison for two years, hoping for money for his release.

Festus, Porcius

He succeeded Felix as procurator of Judaea and allowed the Jews to reopen their case against St Paul. He found Paul innocent but accepted his appeal to Caesar and accordingly sent him to Rome (Acts xxv–vi). He died after a short time in office.

Flora

Italian goddess of flowers and spring, not given a temple in Rome until the mid third century B.C., but afterwards worshipped there and at her April festival (*Ludi Florales*) where, according to Ovid's *Fasti*, there were scenes of drunken gaiety. Ovid also tells the legend that the earth-nymph Chloris was pursued by Zephyr and changed into Flora with flowers coming from her breath and spreading over the countryside. These details are closely followed in Botticelli's *Primavera* [5] where Zephyr is at the right of the picture, and Chloris is fading from his grasp to merge into the radiant Flora. She is a natural subject for painters, including Titian, and Poussin in two classic scenes of the *Triumph of Flora* and the *Kingdom of Flora.* Rembrandt also painted several touching portraits of his young wife Saskia as Flora—pregnant, crowned with flowers, and holding a flowered staff.

François Vase

This splendid early mixing bowl [26] was made *c.* 570 B.C., six feet in circumference and about two feet high, and painted in black-figure style by Clitias, in six strips showing mythological scenes which include the funeral games for Patroclus, the wedding of Peleus and Thetis, and the Calydonian Boar-hunt. It was named after Alessandro François who found it in 1864 in an Etruscan grave at Chiusi, and is now in the Archaeological Museum, Florence.

Frontinus, Sextus Julius (*c.* A.D. 30–104)

Roman soldier and administrator, governor of Britain and curator of the water-supply of Rome. He wrote a number of technical treatises, on military science, on land-surveying, on stratagems in war, and on the aqueducts of Rome; the two latter works survive, and the one on aqueducts is of great interest. Frontinus described the history of the water-supply, the technical details of construction and the administrative organization; in his day a staff of 700 was responsible for over 270 miles of aqueducts. The lost manuscript of *De aquis* was found in Monte Cassino library in 1429 and was used as a manual of instruction by the engineers who restored the old aqueducts and constructed new ones for the redevelopment of Rome.

Fronto, Marcus Cornelius (*c.* A.D. 100–166)

A famous orator of his day, though none of his speeches survives. He was also tutor to the future Emperor Marcus Aurelius, and a collection of his letters to his pupil was discovered in 1815. These give a good picture of the daily life of the period and the friendly relations between the two, though they do not often rise above small-talk. They also illustrate Fronto's expressed wish to get away from the standard Latin of Cicero and the rhetoric of Seneca.

Fulvia

An ambitious woman of character, who married, as her third husband, Mark Antony, and who was active in the political disputes between him and Octavian. In Shakespeare's *Antony and Cleopatra* she is dismissed by Cleopatra as 'shrill-tongued Fulvia', but when news of her death reaches Antony he pays her passing tribute: 'There's a great spirit gone!' She was attacked by Cicero in his speeches against Antony and is said to have insisted on his execution.

Galatea

(i) A Greek sea-nymph, in love with the Sicilian shepherd ACIS and pursued by the Cyclops Polyphemus. To escape him she dived into the sea off the coast of Sicily and turned Acis into a river. The story was a favourite one in pastoral poetry and is told by Theocritus and mentioned by Virgil, but it was best known from Ovid. It provided painters with a splendid subject for compositions with sea-horses, dolphins, cupids, nereids and tritons, and there are famous versions of the *Triumph of Galatea* by Raphael, Carracci and Poussin. Galatea also appears with Acis and Polyphemus in the Fontaine des Médicis in the Luxembourg Gardens, Paris.

(ii) The name of the statue of a beautiful woman which came to life in answer to the prayers of the sculptor PYGMALION.

Galba (Servius Sulpicius Galba, Roman Emperor A.D. 68–January 69)
A member of an old patrician family, Galba had a distinguished military career and was governor of eastern Spain from 60 until the revolt of Julius Vindex, governor of western Gaul, against Nero in 68. He was invited to succeed the murdered emperor, and quickly made himself unpopular by his parsimony and limited outlook. By mid January 69 the army under OTHO mutinied and killed him. He is summed up for all time in an epigram by Tacitus: *omnium consensu capax imperii nisi imperasset* (by common consent he had the makings of a ruler – had he never ruled).

Galen (*c.* A.D. 129–99)
The famous physician and anatomist from Pergamum who practised in Rome and was the friend and attendant doctor of the Emperor Marcus Aurelius. Many of Galen's medical writings survived to influence medicine and anatomy right through the Middle Ages and indeed until much later. His knowledge of the functions of the spinal cord was not fully appreciated until the nineteenth century, and his investigations by dissection of bones and muscles have provided names which are still in use.

Gallus, Gaius Cornelius (*c.* 69–26 B.C.)
Politician and poet, native of Forum Julii (Fréjus) and friend of Catullus; like him, one of the *neoterici*, or 'new poets' who modelled their work on the Alexandrian love lyrics. He was one of Octavian's supporters, and was appointed as first imperial prefect of Egypt. There he fell into disgrace (perhaps for indiscreet ambition), was recalled and committed suicide. He was also a friend of Virgil who wrote of him in his tenth *Eclogue*, and, according to uncertain tradition, had to rewrite the later part of the fourth *Georgic* after Gallus's disgrace. Nothing of his poems survives, and we would give much to read them.

Ganymede(s)
A Trojan prince, mentioned in Homer as the son of King Tros, who was carried off to be cup-bearer to Zeus in exchange for some marvellous horses, or, in post-Homeric epic, a golden vine. On a red-figure mixing-bowl of the early fifth century B.C. a bearded Zeus with his sceptre is on one side, and on the other a beautiful Ganymede holding a hoop and a cock in his outstretched hand, a favourite gift from men to the boys they loved. In a later, more popular version of the legend he was carried off by an eagle sent by Zeus, or by Zeus in the form of an eagle, because he desired the boy. This is how Ganymede

appears in a fine painted terracotta of the fifth century at Olympia, and in Roman copies of Greek original statues. Aristophanes parodies the myth in his *Peace*, in which the hero flies up to heaven on the back of a large dung-beetle. Plato makes use of it in *Phaedrus* to account for Socrates' feelings for his pupils. The erotic interpretation appealed to Hellenistic poets and artists, as it did to Roman; the Latin version of his name is the derivation of the word 'catamite'.

Right through the Middle Ages he typified homosexuality, and the pros and cons of the two types of love are argued in a light-hearted Latin poem, *The debate between Helen and Ganymede*. It was the neoplatonist allegorists of the Renaissance who read into the myth something more spiritual and found a symbol in it of the soul's ascent to the absolute, and there were even theologians who could compare the ascending Christ with Ganymede. Similarly Goethe's Ganymed aspires to the ethereal embrace of the all-loving Father. But he remained in the flesh for the artists, for Cellini who added head, limbs and eagle to an antique torso, for Correggio and for Rubens. Only Rembrandt with characteristic humanity painted him in the grip of the eagle as a terrified struggling child.

Ge or **Gaea**
The Earth, personified as the daughter of Chaos and the wife of Heaven (Uranus) by whom she was mother of the Titans and Cyclopes; by the blood from his castration (→ KRONOS) mother of the Giants and the Furies; by Tartarus (Hell) she was also mother of Typhon. Her cult was basic throughout Greece, but in most places superseded by later gods – e.g. she originally delivered the oracle at Delphi until the serpent Python, a creature of the earth, was killed by Apollo. The Roman earth goddess Tellus was identified with her; she appears as a symbol of peace and prosperity on the Altar of Peace set up by Augustus in Rome.

Gellius, Aulus (*c.* A.D. 130–*c.* 180)
Roman lawyer and man of letters, the author of *Attic Nights*, a compendium in twenty books of anecdotes and discussions on a wide range of topics, the material for which he assembled during winter nights in Athens. They contain extracts from lost works by earlier authors, provided themes for later writers, and were praised by St Augustine and by Erasmus.

Georgics
Virgil's didactic poem on agriculture, in four books dealing with crops, fruit trees and vines, cattle and horses, and bee-keeping. Virgil himself says it is based on Hesiod's *Works and Days*, but the tone is individual, combining practical advice with Virgil's deep love of the Italian countryside and its farmers and his perceptive sympathy with all living creatures. John Dryden translated it and thought it 'the best poem of the best poet', but its influence on poetry was slight until the publication of James Thomson's *Seasons*, which in its turn influenced the poet John Clare and lesser poets of rural life.

Germanicus Julius Caesar
(15 B.C.–A.D. 19)
The nephew and adopted son of the Emperor Tiberius, husband of Agrippina the elder, and father of the future Emperor Caligula and of Nero's mother, the younger Agrippina. He was a successful army commander in Germany until Tiberius recalled him – Tacitus says because he was jealous of Germanicus's popularity. He was then given command in the East, and travelled out via Egypt in order to look at the antiquities there, especially the pyramids and the statue of MEMNON. He died in Antioch, convinced that he had been poisoned by Cnaeus Piso, the governor of Syria. (Poussin painted *The Death of Germanicus* as his first mature work.) Tacitus pays high tribute to his charm and abilities; people compared him with Alexander the Great in looks, age, potentiality, and mysterious death, which was popularly said to be due to black magic practised by Piso.

Geryon
A three-bodied giant, living in the extreme west (in late legend this was said to be Spain), whose marvellous cattle Heracles had to steal and drive back to Greece as his Tenth Labour (→ CACUS). Dante in *Inferno* 17–18 makes Geryon the symbol of Fraud and guardian of the Eighth Circle of Hell; it is he who carries Dante and Virgil down to the region of lowest Hell.

Giants (Gigantes)
In post-Homeric legend they are the sons of Heaven and Earth (Uranus and Ge), of great size and strength, and rebelled against the Olympian gods. In one version they were led by Ephialtes and Otus and piled Mount Pelion on Mount Ossa in an attempt to reach the heavens. They were defeated only when Zeus called in the help of Heracles, and were traditionally said to be buried beneath mountains and volcanoes (→ ETNA) or suffering punishments sent by Zeus; e.g. Odysseus sees Tityus in the Underworld stretched out over nine acres with a pair of vultures pecking at his liver. The battle was an obvious theme for sculptured groups, of which those that form the frieze of the Siphnian treasury at Delphi and those on the Hellenistic altar of Pergamum are the best known. The Palazzo del Te in Mantua contains a fresco by Giulio Romano depicting the fall of the giants.

Glaucus
The name of several Greek mythological figures, in particular (i) a fisherman of Boeotia who pursued Scylla and was changed into a god of the sea after eating a magic herb; he tells his tale in Keats's *Endymion*; (ii) the father of Bellerophon of Corinth, who fed his mares on human flesh and was killed and eaten by them; (iii) his great-grandson from Lycia who appears in the *Iliad* fighting on the Trojan side, and in book 6 tells Diomedes the story of Bellerophon and then exchanges armour with him when they find their grandfathers were bound by ties of hospitality – a poor bargain for Glaucus who got a bronze set in exchange for gold.

Golden Age
The concept of four ages of man, golden, silver, bronze and iron, is first developed in Hesiod's *Works and Days*; immediately before the Iron Age he adds a heroic age – that of the Homeric heroes and other figures of saga. His own life of toil and hardship in troubled times was that of the iron age. Life in the Golden Age was peaceful and idyllic (see also ARCADIA) with Kronos or Saturn as the ideal king. Horace, Virgil in the *Georgics* and Ovid in *Metamorphoses* 1, all look back to an idealized Golden Age, and indeed throughout classical literature runs the nostalgia for a happier past and pessimism about a worsening future. Hopes of a change for the better are expressed in terms of a return to the Golden Age, as Virgil does in his 'MESSIANIC ECLOGUE', following a prophecy of cyclic change in the Sibylline books; just as Shelley in *Hellas* was to write that

The world's great age begins anew
The golden years return . . .

Golden Bough
In *Aeneid* 6 Aeneas is told by the Cumaean Sybil that before he can enter the Underworld he must find and break off a golden bough as a gift for Proserpine. Virgil compares this with mistletoe, which was sacred to the Druids, and in the Mysteries boughs were carried by the initiates who went through a symbolic death and rebirth. The bough was also associated with the cult of DIANA at Aricia, near Rome, where it had to be broken off a sacred tree by a runaway slave who would then kill the priest and take his place. The legend is given by the fourth century grammarian Servius in his commentary on Virgil. This ritual killing of a sacred priest-king can be paralleled in other societies, and that is why the anthropologist Sir James Frazer gave the title of *The Golden Bough* to his twelve-volume work on primitive religions and societies, published from 1890 to 1915. J. M. W. Turner painted two large pictures of *Aeneas and the Sibyl* and *The Golden Bough*.

Gordian Knot
Gordius, a legendary peasant whose son MIDAS rose to be king of Phrygia, was said to have dedicated his chariot or ox-cart to Zeus with the yoke tied to the pole in a special knot. Anyone who discovered how to undo it was to become lord of all Asia. Alexander the Great saw this at Gordium, and simply solved the problem by cutting the knot with his sword. The story was often told in antiquity and 'cutting the Gordian knot' became proverbial for finding a way out of a difficulty. 'The Gordian Knot Untied' is a suite of incidental music by Purcell to an unknown play.

Gorgo(n) or **Medusa**
One of three monstrous sisters in early Greek mythology, collectively called the Gorgons, living in the far west. Medusa had the power to turn into stone anyone who looked at her. She was eventually killed by PERSEUS and her head was cut off; it was then represented on the aegis or cloak of Zeus and Athene from Homer onwards. A

gorgon is a very popular subject in archaic art, especially on the black-figured vases of Corinth, where it is shown as a winged female with snakes for hair and boar's tusks for teeth. The central figure of the pediment of the Artemis temple of the early sixth century B.C. at Corfu is a gorgon, and the head often appears in grotesque form on Hellenistic engraved gems and cameos [31.7]. But Pindar follows another tradition in calling the Gorgons beautiful, and this reappears in Hellenistic representations of a dying maiden, Gorgo. In *Inferno* 9, when Dante's heart begins to fail him on his journey through Hell, the Furies threaten him with Medusa – a symbol of despair which turns the heart to stone.

Vasari in his *Life* of Leonardo da Vinci describes how as a boy he wished to paint a Medusa on a peasant's shield, and regardless of the stench assembled a variety of dead animals and snakes into a composite monster which he copied in the painting, with staggering effect on his father; an episode in which Walter Pater saw the fascination of corruption. In modern Greek folklore gorgons are the double-tailed mermaids which haunt the Aegean (→ ALEXANDER).

Graces (Charites or **Gratiae)**

The three Graces, daughters of Zeus, are first named by Hesiod, Aglaia, Euphrosyne and Thalia, and personify beauty, charm and grace, and also favour and gratitude. They are often attendant on Aphrodite, as they are in Horace's famous Odes on the return of spring (1.4 and 4.7), and like the HORAE they are a common feature of classical literature of all periods. Pausanias says they were originally clothed, but their nude figures in an interlaced group were popular with sculptors and painters from Hellenistic times; there are several Graeco-Roman statue groups as well as the famous wall-painting from Pompeii. When they occasionally appear in medieval illustrations they are naturally clothed [44] and teach the moral that a benefit conferred is twice repaid; but from the fifteenth century onwards they are the medium through which pagan beauty could be shown, and were symbolically associated with giving and receiving thanks, or with pleasure, chastity and beauty. Their nakedness was to indicate that they were free from deceit. They were painted by Botticelli in his *Primavera* [5], by Raphael, Correggio, Tintoretto and Rubens; the Tate Gallery in London has a group in classic style by Maillol, and they reappear in Picasso's late drawings [11].

Graiai or **Graeae**

These are the three sisters of the Gorgons in early mythology, grey-haired from birth, sharing one eye and one tooth between them. They feature mostly in the legends about Perseus, who stole the eye in order to force them to tell him where to find the Gorgons.

Greek (or **Palatine**) **Anthology**

A collection of fifteen books of short epigrams, compiled by a tenth-century Byzantine scholar Cephalas, which incorporates earlier collections such as the *Garland* of Meleager. The manuscript was found in the library of the Elector Palatine at Heidelberg. It ranges from the sixth century B.C. to Cephalas's own day, and though some of the verses are trivial there are also many of the loveliest of Greek short poems, and the whole is a remarkable tribute to the continuity of Greek style and epigrammatic genre. For examples, see DELPHIC ORACLE, HERACLITUS, MUMMIUS ACHAICUS.

Gyges (*c.* 685–657 B.C.)
According to Herodotus, a Lydian shepherd who murdered the king of Lydia, married his widow and usurped the throne, though this may be later invention to account for the takeover by the dynasty he founded. Gyges tried to extend his power over the Greek cities of the Ionian coast, sent offerings to Delphi, and introduced a system of coinage. In *Republic* 2 Plato used the legend that he won his position by means of a magic ring of invisibility to illustrate the view that men are never honest when they need not fear the consequences, and 'Gyges' ring' became proverbial.

Hades
One of the three sons of Kronos, brother of Zeus and Poseidon, also called Dis or Pluto, husband of Persephone and ruler of the Underworld. In Greek mythology the dead are said to go 'to the house of Hades'. No favours were expected from him and no temples dedicated. Later the name was transferred to his kingdom, the gloomy sunless region to which the souls of the dead were taken across the river Styx.

Hadrian (Publius Aelius Hadrianus, Roman Emperor A.D. 117–38)
Hadrian came from a distinguished Roman family in Spain, and was adopted by his relative and predecessor, the Emperor Trajan. He abandoned Trajan's policy of expanding the Eastern Empire and aimed at securing the frontier defences. 'Hadrian's Wall' from Newcastle to Carlisle is one of these, though it was originally designed not as a defensive wall but as a cordon sanitaire between the area of Britain intended for intensive Romanization and the less tractable tribal north. He also worked to secure economic prosperity at home, was a patron of the arts and founder of the Athenaeum in Rome, and wrote poetry himself. For the great love of his life, see ANTINOUS. He was buried in the tomb he had designed for himself, the present Castel Sant' Angelo, which was finished by his successor Antoninus Pius and crowned with a statue of Hadrian. The last emperor to be buried there was Caracalla in 217. It was then used as a fortress against the Goths in the fifth century, and by later factions and popes; Clement VII was besieged there by the French in 1527. At Tivoli are the extensive remains of Hadrian's famous villa, and in Athens are the ruins of his library and of the great Temple of Olympian Zeus which he completed.

Hannibal (247–183/2 B.C.)
The son of Hamilcar Barca, the great Carthaginian general of the First Punic War between Rome and Carthage, Hannibal took command in the second war in 221 B.C. He marched from Spain

and crossed the Alps with a large army, won decisive victories in battles at Lake Trasimene and Cannae (→ FABIUS CUNCTATOR), and then remained sixteen years campaigning in Italy and living off the land until ordered to return to Africa and defend Carthage against SCIPIO AFRICANUS. He was defeated at the Battle of Zama. He then worked for the reorganization of Carthage, but was forced by Roman pressure to take refuge in Syria and then Bithynia, where he committed suicide to avoid capture by the Romans. Hannibal has always been considered one of the world's greatest soldiers in tactics as in strategy, and his feat of bringing a whole army over the Alps is still discussed. It also inspired paintings by Poussin and Turner. For the Romans Hannibal was almost a legend, much as 'Boney' was to nineteenth-century England. We know from Juvenal that his exploits were stock subjects for debate in the schools of rhetoric, and *Hannibal ad portas* ('Hannibal is at the gates') was a rallying cry in times of danger.

Harpies (Greek 'snatchers')
Originally wind-spirits, the harpies appear in Homer only as carrying people off to their death, but in later legend they are winged monsters who snatch away people or their food. Apollonius Rhodius describes how the Argonauts rescued Phineus, the blind seer of Thrace, from their attacks, in return for which he helped them on their journey, and Virgil in *Aeneid* 3 describes them as birds with women's faces. This is how they appear in ancient art, notably on the fifth-century Harpy-tomb from Xanthus in Lycia; and they reappear in Dante's *Inferno* perpetually mutilating the suicides who have turned into trees.

Hebe
The personification of the Greek word for youth, and then said to be the daughter of Zeus and Hera; a minor deity, and from Homer onwards the server of nectar to the Olympian gods. She is sometimes a wife of Heracles after his apotheosis.

Hecate
A primitive pre-Greek goddess of the Underworld, who was afterwards associated with Artemis, worshipped at crossroads as a statue with three heads or three bodies, and connected with sorcery and black magic. Her name is invoked by the sorceress Medea in Euripides' play, and again in Theocritus's incantatory *Idyll* 2, as a love-charm, and this is how she traditionally appears occasionally in post-classical times. In Shakespeare's *Macbeth*, for example, she makes two brief appearances to direct the three witches. There is also a remarkable picture of her by Blake.

Hector
The eldest son of King Priam of Troy and Hecuba, and the Trojan hero of the *Iliad*. He is the husband of ANDROMACHE and father of Astyanax. He leads the Trojans in battle, fights Ajax in single combat, and kills Patroclus. In revenge he is killed by Achilles, who then drags his mutilated body behind his chariot round the walls of Troy and back to the Greek ships. Finally the old

king comes to beg for his son's body, and Hector's funeral is the closing episode of the *Iliad.* Later poets add nothing to his legend, though Pausanias says that his bones were fetched from Troy by the Thebans and buried in Thebes, where he had a hero-cult. Hector's chivalrous nature had a particular appeal for medieval writers on the Tale of Troy, and he is naturally one of the Nine Worthies, as in *Love's Labour's Lost.* His cruel death in *Troilus and Cressida* is the last bitter episode in the play: 'Hector is dead; there is no more to say.'

Hecuba (Greek **Hecabe**)
The wife of King Priam of Troy, and mother of many of his children, including Hector, Paris, Cassandra and Polyxena. She plays no special part in the *Iliad*, but the Greek tragedians, particularly Euripides, saw the dramatic possibilities in her survival after the sack of Troy and the death of Priam and most of her children. In *The Trojan Women* she leads the women who are taken captive; in *Hecabe* she has to witness the sacrifice of Polyxena and finds the body of her murdered son Polydorus. Later legend says that she was driven mad by her sufferings and turned into a bitch at her death. Hecuba is the 'mobled queen' of the First Player's impassioned speech in *Hamlet* and Hamlet's retort:

What's Hecuba to him or he to Hecuba
That he should weep for her?

Helen
Helen is generally remembered for her beauty, but there are many conflicting legends about her which cannot really be reconciled. She was said to be the daughter of ZEUS and LEDA, sister of the twins Castor and Pollux and half-sister of Clytemnestra; she was certainly hatched from the famous egg, though there is disagreement on which of the other three was also and which was fathered by King Tyndareus of Aetolia. Pausanias says that fragments of the egg were preserved at Sparta, and Helen was worshipped there along with her brothers. It seems likely that she was originally a pre-Greek goddess in Laconia associated with birds and trees, for Pausanias also refers to a peculiar tale that she was hanged from a tree, and in Rhodes there was a cult of Tree-Helen. The same association appears in Theocritus's marriage hymn for Menelaus and Helen (*Idyll* 18). None of this has really any part in the literary tradition, which starts with Homer. There Helen is entirely humanized as the wife of Menelaus of Sparta, seduced by Paris and carried off to Troy, and thus the cause of the long Trojan War. (She is, of course, the most beautiful of all women promised to him at the JUDGEMENT OF PARIS.) In the *Iliad* she is tenderly treated and given to self-reproach; her beauty is never described but there is a touching episode in book 3 where the old men of Troy agree that it was worth fighting a war to keep her in Troy. In the *Odyssey* she is reconciled with Menelaus and domesticated as a hospitable housewife. Later legends said that she was abducted by Theseus before her marriage and rescued by her brothers, and that at her death she was carried off to live eternally with

Achilles on a 'white island' in the Black Sea; and a moralizing note comes in with the suggestion that she was not the daughter of Leda but of NEMESIS.

Most of the non-Homeric details are local legend and folklore, but there is a remarkable variant from the poet STESICHORUS, who wrote that it was only a phantom which went to Troy and the real Helen was left in Egypt. This is referred to by Herodotus and by Plato (in *Phaedrus*) and is followed by Euripides in his *Helen*. It reappears in the von Hofmannsthal/Strauss opera *Die Ägyptische Helena* and in George Seferis's poem *Helen*:

... so much suffering, so much life,
joined the abyss
all for an empty tunic, all for a Helen.

In his *Orestes* and *Trojan Women* Euripides keeps to the traditional view, and is as hostile to Helen as Aeschylus is in *Agamemnon*. This is the general Greek attitude to Helen for the disaster she caused. Rhetoricians like Gorgias and Isocrates could plead at length on her behalf, but these are really examples of exercises in encomia. The Romans – Virgil, Ovid, Seneca – when they mention Helen take a critical moral view of her weaknesses. And as one would expect, she is among the lustful in the swirling storm of Dante's Second Circle:

Elena vedi, per cui tanto reo
Tempo si volse ...

(Look at Helen, on whose account so long a time of evil unrolled.)

Helen came into the Faust legend through the Gnostic mysticism of late antiquity which linked her with the magician Simon Magus. Marlowe had seen in the German Faust-book how she was conjured up, and so she makes her unforgettable brief appearance in his *Doctor Faustus*: hers is 'the face which launched a thousand ships'. For Goethe she was a symbol of all he idealized in Hellenism. In part 2 of *Faust* she is allegorized as the sublime beauty of the Greek ideal which Goethe hoped to marry to German medieval romanticism through his poetry. The whole of act 3 is modelled on Euripidean drama, set in Arcadia, with Helen married to Faust and mother of his short-lived son, Euphorion, a Byronic hero.

Shakespeare's Troilus naturally puts up a romantic defence of the

Grecian queen whose youth and freshness
Wrinkles Apollo's, and makes stale the
  morning

but by the end of this harsh play one is more likely to agree with Hector that 'she is not worth what she doth cost/The holding'. Yet it is her beauty and beauty's short life which haunts English verse, from Nashe's

Brightness falls from the air
Queens have died young and fair
Dust hath closed Helen's eye...

down to Yeats, for whom Leda was such a powerful symbol and Helen often a tormented reference to Maud Gonne ('Was there another Troy for her to burn?'). We are taken back to Ronsard, and the *Sonnets pour Hélène* written for his last love, Hélène de Surgères:

Nom malheur des Troyens, sujet de mon souci,
Ma sage Pénélope et mon Hélène aussi
Qui d'un soin amoureux tout le cœur m'enveloppe . . .

There is little of Helen in art. She appears occasionally on a red-figure vase in conventional style, and must have been painted in many lost frescoes of the Troy saga. In an enchanting little picture in the National Gallery [30] listed as a *Rape of Helen* by a follower of Fra Angelico, she is a fair-haired girl perched happily on her lover's shoulders, and she is a statuesque neoclassical woman in a painting by David. The predominantly literary tradition has given no real scope for modern psychological interpretation, and so, for the most part, she has remained as a symbol for lovers and poets.

Helenus

Son of Priam, gifted with prophetic powers, and in post-Homeric legend captured by the Greeks. He foretells the fall of Troy if PHILOCTETES is brought from Lemnos with the bow and arrows of Heracles. He was also said to have been given to Pyrrhus as a captive, along with Andromache, whom he married.

Helios

A Greek sun-god, a Titan not an Olympian, worshipped particularly in Rhodes, and generally thought of as driving his chariot east to west across the sky; in later legend identified with HYPERION or Apollo. He is the father of PHAETHON. The Greeks were concerned with the question of how he got back to the east every morning, and in one version of his legend he floats round on the stream of Ocean in a large cup, which Heracles borrows on his way to the HESPERIDES. Plato gives him new significance in the *Laws* when he plans for his ideal state a joint cult of Apollo with Helios, Apollo to supply the masses with the archaic ritual they expect, Helios to provide a rational form of worship for the enlightened few.

Hellas, Hellenes, Hellenistic

Homer speaks of the Greeks as Achaeans or Panhellenes, but Greeks of the classical period called their country Hellas and themselves Hellenes, with an eponymous ancestor Hellen, said to be a son of Deucalion. In modern terms, Hellenic Greece refers to the historic period between the first Olympiad of 776 B.C., from which dates were calculated, to the death of Alexander the Great in 323 B.C. Hellenistic refers to the more extended influence of Greek power and culture eastwards after Alexander's conquests for the next two centuries until Greece became absorbed into the expanding power of Rome. The Romans took the name 'Greeks' from the Graians or Graii, an obscure tribe of north-west Greece.

Hephaestus (Roman **Vulcan**)

The god of fire and a metal-smith, son of Zeus and Hera, said to have been flung from heaven in one of their quarrels and lamed by falling on to the volcanic island of Lemnos:

. . . from morn
To noon he fell, from noon to dewy eve,
A summer's day, and with the setting sun

Dropped from the zenith, like a falling
star
On Lemnos, th'Aegean isle.
Paradise Lost 1.742–6

He was also said to have a forge below Mount Etna. He was brought back to Olympus by Dionysus to act as attendant on the gods, a theme which is often illustrated on early Greek vases, e.g. the FRANÇOIS VASE. In the *Iliad* he makes marvellous objects like Agamemnon's sceptre and Achilles' armour, but is also a comic figure limping among the gods. In the *Odyssey* the minstrel at the court of Alcinous tells the story of Hephaestus's marriage to Aphrodite and how he traps her in a net when she is making love with Ares, a delightfully told episode which moralists from early times have thought unworthy of Homer. Hesiod makes him the creator of Pandora, the first woman, or of mankind in general; cf. PROMETHEUS. Later writers, including Virgil, say that he was helped in his forge by the Cyclopes (→ VULCAN). Following this tradition there are several well-known post-Renaissance paintings of Vulcan's forge, including one by Tintoretto and one by Velazquez, one of his rare classical scenes. The Doric temple of the mid fifth century above the Athenian agora which is commonly called the Theseum is really a Hephaesteum or temple of Hephaestus.

Hera (Roman **Juno**)
An early pre-Hellenic goddess, associated with women and marriage, whose name means no more than 'lady', Hera was absorbed into the Olympian pantheon by being made the wife of Zeus – and also his sister, as both were children of Kronos. Accounts of her quarrels with Zeus may well preserve the memory of a time when the two cults had to be reconciled; she is generally shown as violently jealous of his many love-affairs and cruel to her rivals: see, e.g., ALCMENE, IO, SEMELE. In Homer she is hostile to Troy, and in Virgil (as Juno) hostile to Trojan Aeneas, because she was a loser in the JUDGEMENT OF PARIS, but in the Argonaut legend she is Jason's guide and support. Hera was originally worshipped especially at Argos, but her cult spread over Greece, and a Heraeum, or temple of Hera, can be found in many towns. There are examples in the earliest temple at Olympia, in the third temple at Paestum (Pesto) in south Italy dating from the fifth century, and an earlier one nearby at Sele. See also POLYCLITUS.

Heracles (Roman **Hercules**)
The most popular of all Greek heroes, who was worshipped all over Greece, particularly in the Argolid and southern Greece. The man behind the wealth of legend may have been a lord of Tiryns in Mycenean times who was in the service of the king of Argos. Heracles was said to be the son of Zeus and Alcmene, wife of Amphitryon, though as a putative grandson of Amphitryon's father he is often called Alcides. He showed his potentiality while a baby by strangling two snakes which Hera had sent to kill him in his cradle. All his famous exploits derive from his strength and courage, the most famous being his Twelve Labours which he had to per-

form for King Eurystheus of Argos as an act of expiation after he had killed his own children in a fit of madness sent by Hera (the theme of Euripides' *Hercules Furens*). These were (i) the killing of the Nemean Lion, which had an invulnerable pelt. Heracles strangled it with his bare hands and flayed it. Most representations in classical art show him wearing the skin, and there is a fine romantic picture of the struggle by Delacroix. (ii) The HYDRA of Lerna. (iii) The Hind of Ceryneia, golden-horned and dedicated to Artemis, which he hunted for a year and succeeded in carrying off alive. (iv) The Boar of Mount Erymanthus, a gigantic beast which Heracles carried back alive to Mycenae on his shoulders. (v) The cleaning of the stables of AUGEAS. (vi) The Stymphalian Birds. (vii) The killing of a fire-breathing Cretan bull at the request of King Minos. (viii) The capture of the man-eating mares of the savage King Diomedes of Thrace; Heracles stunned him with his club and fed him to his own mares, then harnessed them and drove them back to be dedicated to Hera. (ix) The Girdle of Hippolyte (→ AMAZONS). (x) The cattle of GERYON. (xi) The descent to Tartarus to capture CERBERUS. (xii) The golden apples of the HESPERIDES. The two mountains on opposite sides of the western entrance to the Mediterranean through which Heracles sailed in some versions in the floating cup of HELIOS were known in antiquity as the Pillars of Heracles/Hercules. Most of these feats are elaborations on the theme of a struggle with and conquest of death, which in its simplest form is told by Homer in *Iliad* 5, how Heracles met and overcame Hades at the gates of Hell.

There were many other legends told about him. He joined in the Argonaut expedition, but when Hylas, the boy he loved, was pulled down into a pool by the nymphs at Cios in Mysia, Heracles stayed behind to look for him; this suggests that he was not in the original Argo saga, and a ritual search for the lost boy went on into late classical times, as a local cult. When he was returning with the girdle of Hippolyte he rescued Hesione and sacked Troy (→ LAOMEDON). Apollo once refused him purification, so he made off with the sacred tripod at Delphi – a popular subject for archaic vases, and also shown among the sculptures from the Siphnian treasury at Delphi. Apollo gave in, and told him to serve a Lydian queen, Omphale. He did so in woman's clothes, a bizarre episode which lent itself to satire and which later moralists could use as an instance of a strong man enslaved by a woman. He went down to the Underworld again to rescue ALCESTIS, and in Euripides' play makes his first appearance as a rowdy drunkard. (We have Eliot's word for it that this episode accounts for the behaviour of the unknown guest in *The Cocktail Party*.) He overcame ANTAEUS. For his marriage and death, see DEIANIRA, NESSUS. He was taken up from his funeral pyre on Mount Oeta and became a god, with Hebe for his wife. All these episodes feature on vase-paintings and in sculpture – the Twelve Labours are the subject of the metopes on the temple of Zeus at Olympia, and there is a fine statue of the early fifth century of Heracles drawing a bow, from the east pediment of the temple of Aphaia at Aegina. They also feature in the Hellenistic-Roman paintings from Pompeii.

As Hercules he was particularly popular at Rome as a defender against evil, and the Stoic philosophers idealized him for his endurance and courage and his services to men. In the Middle Ages he was well known through Ovid and Boethius, and his deeds and death are briefly but fairly accurately described by Chaucer in the *Monk's Tale*, where 'Hercules the sovereyn conquerour' is listed with famous men such as Adam, Samson and Alexander. The Burgundian royal house traced their descent from his supposed marriage with a princess Alise on his way back from Spain, and as time went on he was closely linked with Christian saints. The façade of the Colleoni chapel at Bergamo and the Campanile at Florence both have reliefs of Hercules' labours as well as Old Testament scenes, and this practice goes back to the fourth-century paintings in some of the catacombs of Rome. On the pulpit in Pisa Cathedral Nicola Pisano transformed a nude Hercules into an image of Christian fortitude, [29] and one of Ronsard's most famous *Hymnes* was *Hercule Chrétien*. It was not difficult to find Christian symbolism in a life of dedication and a death which led to immortality.

The legend known as 'The Choice of Hercules' is first told in Xenophon's *Memoirs of Socrates* as originating from the sophist Prodicus, a contemporary of Socrates. Before Heracles began his Labours he was confronted by two beautiful women, one of whom offered him a life of ease and pleasure and the other a life of duty and labour for mankind. This does not seem to have ever been depicted in classical art and it was ignored in the Middle Ages, although there are two references to Hercules' choice in Cicero's *On Duties*; it would not have been thought possible for any Christian to have the right to choose the direction of his life. But Petrarch knew it from Cicero, and it was he who wrote of Hercules going alone to think over his decision 'at a parting of the ways'. This provided an alternative title, and there were several Italian and German operas of the eighteenth century called *Hercules at the Crossroads*, as well as a cantata by Bach. There are also several paintings on *The Choice of Hercules* which show him as a conventional nude male between the two women offering him pleasure and duty, including examples by Carracci, Veronese and Poussin.

The Farnese Hercules, found in 1540 in the Baths of Caracalla, Rome, and now in the Museo Nazionale, Naples, shows the hero leaning on a club after his labours. It is the work of the Athenian sculptor Glycon (first century B.C.) and is probably a copy of an original of the late fourth century by Lysippus.

Heraclitus

(i) of Ephesus, a philosopher and scientist of about 500 B.C., who taught that everything originated in fire and was in a state of flux. He was famous for his cryptic statements and his attacks on

Greek religious practices, such as burial rites, cults of images, and belief in dreams.

(ii) of Halicarnassus, a poet and friend of the poet CALLIMACHUS, whose poem on his death still appears in verse anthologies in the rhymed doggerel of W. J. Cory, a Victorian master at Eton ('They told me, Heraclitus, they told me you were dead . . .'). His poems were known as 'nightingales'.

You are dead then, Heraclitus, so they say,
And I shed tears, remembering the times
We talked and watched the sun sink, you and I.
Somewhere long since you crumbled into dust,
Only your nightingales are left to sing;
Death who takes all shall not lay hands on them.

Hermae (Herms)

Square pillars, supporting busts of the god Hermes and given male genitals, which stood at the crossroads in Greek cities as protective guardians from the early fifth century onwards. Their mutilation in 415 B.C. was an unexplained act of sacrilege, attributed to Alcibiades, and an ill omen for the doomed expedition of the Athenian fleet to break Spartan power in Sicily. By Roman times herms were popular as decorative features of wall-paintings and as garden ornaments, and the form is no longer phallic nor confined to Hermes. There is a famous series in the gardens at Versailles designed by Poussin which includes Pan, Faunus, Hercules, Flora, Pomona and Venus. His models were a group of ancient herms once in the Villa Ludovisi in Rome; six are now in the Museo delle Terme. A herm is also the centrepiece of one of Poussin's Bacchanal paintings [7].

Hermaphroditus

According to Ovid, the son of Hermes and Aphrodite who refused the advances of the nymph Salmacis; the gods then answered her prayer that their bodies could be joined into one. This is an 'aetiological myth' devised to account for the existence of bisexual persons: cf. ECHO. Roman copies of Greek statues of sensuously reclining hermaphrodites are not uncommon both in Italy and in English stately homes, where presumably they had been brought home by travellers making the grand tour.

Hermes (Roman **Mercury**)

Originally a phallic god occupying a stone set up by a roadside (→ HERMAE), Hermes was accepted as the son of Zeus and Maia, daughter of Atlas, and considered an Arcadian. The Homeric *Hymn to Hermes* describes his childish tricks and ingenuity; he stole Apollo's cattle, invented the lyre by stringing a tortoiseshell with cow-gut, and presented it to Apollo. In return for this Zeus made him his messenger and gave him the broad-brimmed hat and winged sandals in which he is usually shown, as well as his *caduceus* or herald's staff, with its traditional white ribbons (in later representations these appear as entwined serpents). In the *Odyssey* it is Hermes who takes Zeus's instructions to

Odysseus to leave Calypso's island (just as Mercury is sent to recall Aeneas from Dido), and in his capacity as guide to the dead he takes the suitors down to the Underworld in book 24. He is also escort to EURYDICE. From his primitive association with roads he is patron of all wayfarers – traders, travellers and thieves. One of the few possibly original statues of PRAXITELES is a naked Hermes carrying the infant Dionysus, presumably at Zeus's command. For post-classical references, see MERCURY.

Hero

A priestess of Aphrodite at Sestos whose lover Leander used to swim the Hellespont from Abydos to visit her, until a storm put out the light she guided him with and he was drowned. The story is probably Alexandrian, but in extant literature is told by Virgil in *Georgic* 3 and by Ovid. It has inspired many poets since, notably the late fifth-century epic poet Musaeus and, via Ovid, Marlowe in his *Hero and Leander*. Keats wrote one of his less successful sonnets on Leander's death, and A. E. Housman characteristically saw the lovers' happiness overcast by thoughts of

The sea he swam from earth to earth
  And he must swim again.

There is a fine stormy *Hero and Leander* by Rubens, and another by Turner in the National Gallery, London.

Herod the Great (*c.* 73–4 B.C.)

King of Judaea by Roman nomination from about 40 B.C., Herod was an able administrator, but unpopular with the Jews for his policy of Hellenization, and eventually alienated Augustus by his brutal murders of his family at the end of his reign. He is the 'Herod the King' of Matthew ii who orders the Massacre of the Innocents, i.e. all the male children in Bethlehem, in order to destroy the newly born Christ, though there is no actual evidence to confirm this widespread legend. He is the swaggering tyrant of medieval Christian plays, and the words first used in *Hamlet*, 'to out-Herod Herod', have become proverbial.

Herodes Atticus (Herod of Athens, A.D. 101–77)

A native of Marathon, a famous sophist and man of letters whose *Life* was sympathetically written by Philostratus. He was a cultivated patron of the arts and a generous benefactor to Athens and other Greek cities. He built the Athenian Odeum (Music-hall) on the south slope of the Acropolis as a memorial to his wife, added the stone terraces to the Stadium at Delphi, and gave a swimming bath to the town of Thermopylae. Pausanias describes a gold and ivory statue group he dedicated in the temple at Corinth, and he was certainly enormously wealthy; Philostratus adds that he was disappointed when his plans for financing a canal through the isthmus of Corinth came to nothing.

Herodotus (*c.* 484–*c.* 420 B.C.)

Greek historian of Halicarnassus in Asia Minor, 'the father of history'. He moved to Samos and then to Athens, travelled widely in Egypt, eastern Europe and Asia, and died at Thurii in southern Italy. He was the first to write a major work in prose, and the first to arrange his material systematically and assess his sources critically, in order to create a nine-book history of the wars between Greece and Persia. These he saw as a conflict between the ideals of Europe and of Asia. He incorporated his observations made on his travels into digressions on anthropology and geography, and devoted a whole book to Egypt. It was these colourful episodes which made his fellow-Greeks attack him as 'the father of lies' (→ ARIMASPI and HYPERBOREANS). He was quite free from racial prejudice, and his appreciation of the vagaries of human nature and perceptive interest in personalities make him one of the most readable of writers.

Heroes

The cult of heroes was widespread in ancient Greece and had its beginnings in the late eighth century when the Homeric poems became generally known in their final form. Local personalities then became identified with the legendary figures who had fought in the Theban and Trojan wars of the Heroic age, Heracles, Perseus and Theseus being among the most famous. Sometimes rites were performed at the tombs of historical persons; the Spartan general Brasidas, for example, was given heroic honours after his death in battle. Heroes were believed to help the living in return for sacrifices and rites performed at their tombs. The term 'heroic poetry' means epic poetry, and 'heroic verse' is that in which literary epics have been commonly written: in English the rhymed heroic couplet, in French the twelve-syllable Alexandrine.

Hero(n) of Alexandria

A mathematician, hydraulic engineer and scientist of unknown date (probably first century B.C.), whose discoveries ranged from steam-engines, siphons and surveying instruments to a form of penny-in-the-slot machine and ingenious devices to work 'temple miracles'. These are all known from the surviving parts of his written works.

Hesiod

The earliest known Greek poet after Homer, probably living around 700 B.C., at Ascra in Boeotia where he worked a smallholding on the slopes of Mount Helicon; there, he tells us, the Muses visited him when he was watching his sheep and gave him the gift of song. His father had been an immigrant from Ionia, and he was involved in a lawsuit with his brother Perses about the property; this is evident from the autobiographic details of *Works and Days*, addressed to Perses, in which practical details of peasant farming, personal grudges, pithy humour and proverbial lore are blended to make a remarkable poem. It includes the myths of PANDORA and the GOLDEN AGE. In the *Theogony* he attempts a systematic account of the genealogy of the gods and the events leading to the kingship of Olympian Zeus: → KRONOS, PROMETHEUS, TITANS. This provides a basis for much later mythology.

Fragments of a *Shield of Heracles* and *Catalogue of Famous Women* attributed to him are spurious. The didactic part of Virgil's *Georgics* was modelled on the *Works and Days*, and there are verbal borrowings from Hesiod's Greek, but this is the least important part of Virgil's achievement.

Hesperides
The 'daughters of the evening' who guarded a tree of golden apples in a garden at the world's end in the far west, helped by a dragon. Heracles had to gather these for his twelfth labour, and did so with the help of ATLAS. They are certainly associated with the setting sun and the evening star, and an apple is a love-symbol in most folklore, but they and their exact whereabouts are never certainly defined. In art they can be confused with the Three Graces; in Raphael's painting of the Graces, each is holding an apple. Robert Herrick called his book of Arcadian lyrics *Hesperides* because they were written when he was rector of a parish in the west of England, Dean Prior in Devon.

Hesperus
The evening star, the Greek form of the Latin *vesper*, evening, to which Sappho addresses one of her most eloquent lyrics. We have only a mutilated scrap of this, preserved by chance in a Renaissance treatise on etymology. It may have been part of a marriage hymn:

Evening star, bringing back all that the
bright dawn scattered,
You bring the sheep, bring the goat,
You bring home the child to its mother.

Hippias and Hipparchus
Sons of the Athenian 'tyrant' PISISTRATUS. The elder, Hippias, ruled Athens from 527 B.C. until 510 when he was expelled for his oppressive government by King Cleomenes of Sparta. Hipparchus, who like his father was a patron of art and literature, was murdered in 514 by ARISTOGITON.

Hippocl(e)ides
Athenian nobleman of the sixth century B.C., the chosen suitor for the daughter of Clisthenes, tyrant of Sicyon, and well remembered from the story told by Herodotus (6.128) in which Hippoclides danced at the betrothal feast with such abandon that he ended by standing on his head on a table waving his legs in the air. When told by his prospective father-in-law that he had 'danced away his marriage' he answered that he couldn't care less, and according to Herodotus the expression 'Hippoclides doesn't care' became proverbial in Greece.

Hippocrates of Cos (*c.* 469–399 B.C.)
The famous Greek physician, 'the father of medicine', whose teaching school was established at the shrine of Asclepius at Cos, though he himself taught in all parts of Greece. He is said to have been the first to separate medicine from history and from superstition, and to make scientific observations on causes of disease. It is unlikely that any of the extant writings of the Hippocratic school are written by him, but most show marks of his teaching. They cover all the known branches of medicine and surgery, with first-hand

reports on cases and epidemics for the teaching of clinical theory. The methods of diet and treatment prescribed have been said to be not unlike those of an intelligent if conservative general practitioner of about 1800. The Hippocratic Oath stating the ethics of the school was taken by qualifying physicians in England until the present century.

Hippolytus

The son of Theseus king of Athens and Hippolyte, queen of the Amazons. In most versions of his legend he was dedicated to chastity and service to the virgin goddess Artemis. His stepmother PHAEDRA fell in love with him, and when he repulsed her, accused him of assault. Theseus then prayed to his divine father Poseidon to kill Hippolytus as he drove from Athens to Troezen along the coast. Poseidon sent a sea-monster which terrified the horses; Hippolytus was flung from his chariot and dragged to death. The dramatic intensity of this legend produced one of Euripides' greatest plays (a second one has not survived), and then Seneca's *Phaedra*, and after him, Racine's *Phèdre*. In the Roman version of the legend, told by Ovid in the *Fasti* and *Metamorphoses*, Hippolytus was restored to life by Artemis/Diana and carried off to her sacred grove in Aricia under the name of Virbius (→ GOLDEN BOUGH). It was an element in the cult there that no horses were allowed in the grove. According to Pausanias the Greeks continued to worship him and lament his death at Troezen. Hippolytus was painted among the wall-decorations of Pompeii, and one might expect that Ovid at least would have suggested his fatal drive as a subject to painters in the High Renaissance or later romantic styles, but he seems to have been ignored. *Hippolyte et Aricie* is Rameau's first opera, and has a happy ending with Hippolytus restored to life, to suit eighteenth-century taste.

Homer

The Greeks believed that the *Iliad* and the *Odyssey* were composed by Homer, and seven Greek cities claimed to be the birthplace of the blind poet, but nothing is known of his life or date, nor can it be proved that both epics were put together by a single person at the same time. Both incorporate a good deal of earlier legend or 'travellers' tales' and also descriptions handed down from the Mycenean age, but the firm grasp of plot and consistency of character rule out the idea that they were evolving oral poems, at any rate from the time of Pisistratus when the text was well established. It seems likely that about 700 B.C. someone in Ionia made the *Iliad* out of the wealth of material dealing with the Troy saga: the action covers only a few weeks, but the whole previous span of the war is subtly suggested by reference to what has gone before. The *Odyssey* may well have been created by the same person at a rather later date. The relationships there are more sophisticated, and the psychology of the main characters less 'heroic' and more subtle, and there is more knowledge of the orientalized civilizations of the eastern Mediterranean. In general it seems more inventive and less traditional, but its connection with the

Iliad is close, and it seems to be intended as a sequel. Alexander the Great was never without his copy of the *Iliad*, which he kept in a gold casket taken from the spoils of the Persian king Darius.

From the sixth century B.C. the 'Sons of Homer' existed as a guild with the right to give public recitals of Homer, and in the 'Homeric Hymns' there are several preludes to such recitations, addressed to various gods and of varying date. (→ APOLLO, DEMETER, DIONYSUS, HERMES for the more important of these poems.)

In his *Poetics* Aristotle gives his highest praise to Homer as an epic poet, and Homer has had more influence on western literature than any other writer. He leads the '*quattro grand'ombre*' whom Dante and Virgil meet in Limbo (*Inferno* 4); he is '*un être pareil aux dieux*' for Montaigne; he features in many post-Renaissance paintings in the grand style, notably in Raphael's *Parnassus* and *The Apotheosis of Homer* by Ingres. Translations of Homer have naturally reflected their age, from the Elizabethan Chapman which inspired Keats, through the elegance of Pope's *Iliad* (which Johnson thought 'a poetical wonder' that 'no age nor nation can pretend to equal', but which Bentley dismissed as 'a pretty poem, but you must not call it Homer'), and the melodious biblical prose of Butcher and Lang down to the more recent plain prose of T. E. Lawrence and E. V. Rieu. There are modern verse translations by Edward Fitzgerald, Richmond Lattimore and Christopher Logue. The problems of the Homeric translator were set out in Matthew Arnold's famous essay *On Translating Homer*.

A Homeric simile is one in which, once the point of comparison is made, the image is expanded to make it complete within itself. Homer is the creator of such similes and uses them with subtle emotional effect, particularly in the *Iliad* where they can heighten tension or relieve it momentarily by introducing a glimpse of domestic life in an epic of war. Zeus, for example, weighs the issue between the two armies like a poor woman weighing wool on a balance which she must spin for a livelihood; Achilles compares Patroclus when he weeps with a small girl running by her mother's side, tugging at her skirt and crying until she is picked up. The massed armies of the Greeks are compared with a forest fire, swans or cranes gathering for migration, and flies buzzing round the full milk-pails in a cowshed – a wonderfully vivid image on which Pope remarked, 'The lowness of this image, in comparison with those which precede it, will naturally shock a modern critic, and would scarce be forgiven in a poet of these times. The utmost a translator can do is to heighten the expression, so as to render the disparity less observable; which is endeavoured here, and in other places.' But he does better with the birds:

Not less their number than th'embody'd cranes,
Or milk-white swans in Asius' watry plains,
That o'er the windings of Caÿster's springs,
Stretch their long necks, and clap their rustling wings,

Now tow'r aloft, and course in airy
rounds;
Now light with noise; with noise the
field resounds.

Virgil's mastery of the extended simile is complete, and this is how he creates an atmosphere of foreboding for Aeneas's entry into the Underworld (Dryden's translation):

Obscure they went through dreary
shades, that led
Along the waste dominions of the dead.
Thus wander travellers in woods by
night,
By the moon's doubtful and malignant
light,
When Jove in dusky clouds involves the
skies,
And the faint crescent shoots by fits
before their eyes.

Virgil's simile of the souls waiting to be ferried by Charon is one of birds seeking warmer climes at the first chill of winter and of falling leaves, and the latter (which is itself an echo of Homer) is repeated in canto 3 of Dante's *Inferno*, where the waiting spirits are like leaves which the parent branch watches falling one by one until it sees them all scattered on the ground:

Come d'autunno si levan le foglie
l'una appresso dell' altra, infin ch'il ramo
vede alla terra tutte le sue spoglie . . .

These too are Milton's fallen angels:

Thick as autumnal leaves that strow the
brooks
In Vallombrosa, where th'Etrurian
shades
High over-arched embower . . .

In Milton's case, the simile gives his Hell a firm reality, and is often his bridge with the pagan world he never ceased to love. There are splendid Homeric similes in Spenser, in Keats's Miltonic *Hyperion*, and in Coleridge's *Ancient Mariner*, where the fantastic scene suddenly becomes an experience common to most of us at some time:

Like one, that on a lonesome road
Doth walk in fear and dread,
And having once turned round walks on
And turns no more his head;
Because he knows, a frightful fiend
Doth close behind him tread.

Horace (Quintus Horatius Flaccus, 65–8 B.C.)

Roman poet, born the son of an Italian freedman in Apulia, and educated in Rome and Athens. He fought for Brutus at Philippi and returned home penniless; then he took to writing poetry, became friendly with Virgil and his circle, and came under the patronage of MAECENAS. All his known work survives – verse epistles, satires (informal miscellanies), an *Art of Poetry*, odes and epodes – and in these his personality comes through as one of the most likeable of men, tolerant, humorous, observant and a lover of the good things of life. At the same time, he is the Roman poet who shows most understanding of the Dionysiac ecstasy (*Odes* 2.19; 3.25). In his *Odes* especially his skill in matching Latin to Greek lyric measures, his delicate irony and subtle choice of words, all contribute to what was called his *curiosa felicitas*, and made him a school classic only a century after his death.

Horace was Ronsard's favourite poet, and it is in Ronsard's short *Odes* that Horace lives again, not only in the conscious imitations like *A la fontaine Bellerie* which is an early transformation into French of Horace's *Odes* 3.13 (*The Bandusian Spring*), but still more in such famous lyrics as '*Mignonne, allons voir si la rose*'. In England he has inspired more translations and imitations than any other classical writer, though his deliberate imitators like Robert Herrick have sometimes read his philosophy of life at a superficial level and left it at 'Gather ye rosebuds while ye may'. But Ben Jonson is a true Horatian, and Andrew Marvell's *An Horatian Ode upon Cromwell's Return from Ireland* and William Collins's *Ode to Evening* resemble his more serious odes in both form and content. In the eighteenth century he was especially popular for his urbanity and philosophy of moderation (the ideal of the 'Golden Mean'). Pope's *Imitations of Horace* and his *Essay on Man* and *Epistle to Burlington* are very much in the Horatian spirit. And the only classical poem that A. E. Housman translated and admitted to finding deeply moving was Horace's *Odes* 4.7, ('*Diffugere nives*'), on the intimations of mortality that return with each spring. The latest poet to acknowledge his debt to the humour and irony of Horace was Louis MacNeice, in his sequence of poems *Memoranda to Horace*:

Though elderly poets profess to be
  inveterate
Dionysians, despising Apollonians,
  I find it, Flaccus, more modest
To attempt, like you, an appetitive
  decorum...

Horae

'The Hours' were originally the Greek goddesses of the seasons and were three in number (perhaps indicating the growth, flowering and ripening of vegetation), sometimes identified with the Graces, and rarely shown except in attendance on other gods. They first appear on the FRANÇOIS VASE. In Hellenistic times they become four, and are common in paintings and mosaics as the seasons of the year, with suitable attributes. This is how they appear in Renaissance art; e.g. the four statues on the rebuilt S. Trinità bridge in Florence. Three of them encircle the goddess Luna in an important painting by Tintoretto.

Horatii

Three brothers of this family are the heroes of a famous episode in Roman history (or historic legend), which is told in detail in the first book of Livy's history, and is dated in the mid seventh century when Tullus Hostilius was the traditional third king of Rome. During his reign Alba Longa, an ancient Latin city on the site of Castelgandolfo, was destroyed and its people mostly transferred to Rome. In the course of the fighting the three Horatii volunteered to meet three champions from the Alban side in a sword battle. Two Horatii were killed but the third killed the three Curiatii on the Alban side. As he returned in triumph to Rome he met his sister, who had been engaged to marry one of the Curiatii, weeping for his death. Horatius stabbed her to death, and was tried for the murder by Tullus. He was eventually acquitted after ceremonies of expiation. He is the hero of Corneille's tragedy *Horace*, and the three brothers are commemorated in *The Oath of the Horatii*, the first of David's great classical pictures, in which the single-minded determination of the men is symbolic of the purpose behind the French Revolution.

Horatius Cocles ('one-eyed')
From the same family in the sixth century came the Roman who traditionally held the Etruscans at bay on the wooden Sublician bridge into Rome until it was cut down behind him and he swam across the Tiber to safety. The story is told as early history by Livy, but is more probably invention to glorify the heroic ideal of the founders of Rome or to account for a primitive one-eyed statue which stood near the bridge in historic times. This Horatius is the hero of the best known of Macaulay's *Lays of Ancient Rome*, and of a painting by Géricault.

Hyacinthus
A pre-Hellenic god worshipped at Amyclae in Laconia, and at Sparta where he had a three-day festival, the Hyacinthia. Pausanias saw a statue of him which was bearded, and not in the usual tradition that he was a beautiful boy whom Apollo loved and accidentally killed by a discus which was diverted to hit him by the jealous ZEPHYRUS. From his blood sprang flowers marked with Apollo's cries of grief, '*AI AI*', which have been identified with the hyacinth, iris or gladiolus. This romantic story arose as an explanation of the fact that in classical times the cult of Hyacinthus had been taken over by Apollo. It is told by Ovid in *Metamorphoses* 10, and in 13.397 ff. he ends his account of the death of AJAX by saying that the flowers henceforth bore both the cry of distress and the name of Ajax (Greek *ΑΙΑΣ*). One of Cellini's statue-groups is of Apollo and Hyacinthus.

Hydra
The many-headed monster living by Lake Lerna in the Peloponnese which Heracles had to destroy as his second labour [31.5], the difficulty being that as one head was cut off, two others grew. (A 'hydra-headed' problem presents new difficulties as fast as one is solved.) Heracles eventually succeeded, and dipped his arrows in the hydra's blood to make them poisonous. There are many representations of his struggle in antiquity, and Heracles provided Renaissance artists with fine examples of the nude in action. Though Pollaiuolo's great series of the Labours for the Medici palace is lost, his smaller painting of Heracles struggling with the Hydra is in the Uffizi, Florence.

Hymen, Hymenaeus
It was the custom at Greek weddings to call 'Hymen O Hymenaeus!', as we know from the marriage songs of Alcman, Sappho and Theocritus, and the poems of Catullus. Hymenaeus means a wedding-song, and from this evolved the idea of a deity, Hymen, who presided over weddings and who is sometimes represented as the tutelary god wearing a wreath (as in the

ALDOBRANDINI WEDDING) or as a boy carrying a torch.

Hyperboreans
A legendary race of Apollo-worshippers living in perpetual sunshine and plenty 'at the back of the North Wind' or 'beyond the mountains'; Apollo was supposed to leave Delphi to spend the winter months with them. Herodotus locates them in southern Russia on the borders of the ARIMASPI and near the Cimmerians of the Black Sea, whom Homer knows only as living in a land shrouded in mist. Herodotus (4.33) says that they sent offerings wrapped in wheat-straw to Apollo of Delos via the Adriatic, but did not come themselves. Some people have seen the truth behind the legend as the amber trade route to the Baltic (for which, see PHAETHON), others the rich corn-lands of the steppes. Herodotus also mentions their priest of Apollo, Abaris, who was reputed to travel around the world on a golden arrow and never needed to eat; cf. Aristeas, priest of the ARIMASPI.

Hyperion
One of the Titans, a sun-god and father of the Dawn, the Sun and the Moon (Eos, Helios and Selene), according to Hesiod. In *Odyssey* 12 he keeps his sacred cattle on an island which has been tentatively identified with eastern Sicily, on the fertile pastures below Taormina (the city's name was associated with cattle from the time of its Greek foundation), and is identified with Helios. In Keats's unfinished poem *Hyperion* he is the last of the Titans who is about to be deposed by the young Olympian sun-god, Apollo. *Hyperion* is also the title of the long philosophic novel by the German romantic poet Hölderlin, his major work on his ideal Greece: the Byronic hero fails to liberate Greece from the Turks but finds his spiritual home as a hermit in Greece in communion with the ancient spirits of nature.

Hypnos
The Greek god of Sleep, son of Night and brother of Death (Thanatos), generally thought of as a winged boy who touches the foreheads of the weary or pours a soporific from a horn. In Homer he and Thanatos carry dead warriors from the battlefield (→ SARPEDON), and he is depicted on the Chest of Cypselus (→ PERIANDER) and in Hellenistic art. 'Death and his brother Sleep' are a later poetic convention. See also MORPHEUS.

Icarus
The son of DAEDALUS who made him wings of feathers and wax so that they could both escape from Crete. Icarus disobeyed instructions, flew too near the sun, the wax melted and he was drowned. Daedalus buried his body on the island afterwards called Icaria, and the part of the Aegean round it was known as the Icarian Sea. The story is best known from Ovid, *Metamorphoses* 8, where he says that some fisherman or shepherd leaning on his staff or peasant bent over his plough would wonder at their flight. All these details are reproduced in the foreground of Pieter Breughel's *The Fall of Icarus*, though his peasants appear indifferent to

the boy disappearing into the sea. There is also a sketch by Rubens from the series on Ovid planned for Philip IV of Spain, a moving statue by Rodin of the fallen boy, and many bronzes of Icarus in flight and fallen among the work of Michael Ayrton [33]. The story of Icarus has been interpreted in many ways, but always with the symbol of soaring aspirations. For the eighteenth-century French poet Philippe Destouches he was '*un esprit glorieux*':

Le ciel fut son désir, la mer sa sépulture:
Est-il plus beau dessein ou plus riche tombeau?

In Goethe's *Faust* Euphorion (Byron) falls symbolically to premature death (→→ HELEN). André Gide in *Thésée* sees him as '*l'image de l'inquiétude humaine*,' destroyed by the truth he seeks.

Ictinus

Greek architect, about whom little is known except that he was the architect of the Parthenon at Athens, on which he worked from 448 to 437 B.C., along with a fellow-architect Callicrates and the sculptor Phidias. He also rebuilt and enlarged the Hall of the Mysteries at Eleusis, and it is probable though not certain that he designed the Temple of Apollo at Bassae. He is also said to have been commissioned by Pericles to design the Odeum or Music-hall in the agora of Athens, of which only foundations can be traced.

Idomeneus

In the *Iliad* he is a king of Crete, and leader of the Cretan allies of the Greeks, a rather older man who is distinguished in battle. The fourth-century commentator on Virgil, Servius, seems to be the only authority for the additional tale, possibly a piece of Cretan folklore, that on his return he vowed to sacrifice to Poseidon the first thing he met if his ship could be saved from a storm. This was his own son. He was then expelled by the Cretans in expiation. Mozart's early opera *Idomeneo* seems to have a purely invented plot, though it is set in Crete at the homecoming of Idomeneus. The chief characters are his son, Idamante, and a captive Trojan princess, Ilia.

Io

A priestess of Hera at Argos, loved by Zeus and changed into a heifer to protect her from Hera's jealousy. Hera is not deceived, sets ARGUS to watch Io, and then drives her on by a gadfly to wander around Europe and Egypt, where she is restored by Zeus and becomes an ancestor of DANAUS. Io visits PROMETHEUS and describes her tribulations in Aeschylus's play, and her story is also told by Ovid. She was probably a primitive moon-goddess, who would be represented with horns from which her legend developed. She can be seen with Argus on the faded frescoes of the House of Livia on the Palatine, Rome, and was painted with Zeus by Correggio.

Ion, Ionians

The eponymous ancestor of the Ionians, the son of Creusa, daughter of ERECHTHEUS, and either her husband Xuthus or the god Apollo. He was taken by

Hermes to serve in the temple of Apollo at Delphi; Euripides' controversial play *Ion* turns on his search for his identity and contains sharp criticism of the officially worshipped Olympian gods. It is the basis of Eliot's play *The Confidential Clerk.*

Ionia was the central coastal area of Asia Minor in historic times, and tradition said that it was colonized by refugees from the mainland at the time of the Dorian invasions. Herodotus rightly says that Athens' claim to be their mother-city cannot be confirmed, but it is possible that Attica was by-passed by invaders coming in from the north-west and that Athens organized the emigrations. From before 700 B.C. the Ionians were far advanced in the arts; Homer was generally said to be Ionian, and his poems are written in Ionic dialect. The early philosophers and scientists were all Ionian (→ THALES, PYTHAGORAS) and laid the foundations of Greek rationalism.

Iphigenia

In origin possibly a local goddess identified with Artemis, but in classical mythology the daughter of Agamemnon and Clytemnestra. She was summoned to Aulis when the Greek fleet was waiting to set sail for Troy to be sacrificed to Artemis, who was sending contrary winds – why Artemis demanded this is never made clear. In the version referred to in Aeschylus's *Agamemnon* she is killed, and her death adds to Clytemnestra's motive for killing her husband. Euripides followed another tradition in which Artemis carried her off at the crucial moment; this can be assumed from his last, unfinished *Iphigenia in Aulis.* In his *Iphigenia in Tauris* she is a priestess of Artemis among the Taurians (in the Crimea) and officiates at the local rite of sacrificing to Artemis any stranger who is captured. Her brother Orestes and his friend Pylades are brought to her, there is a classic recognition scene, and a dramatic escape. More than one Greek temple later claimed to possess the image of the goddess she carried away with her. Both plays were followed by Gluck in his operas *Iphigénie en Aulide* and *Iphigénie en Tauride.* Racine explored Agamemnon's appalling dilemma in his *Iphigénie*; Goethe created an idealized heroine in his *Iphigenie auf Tauris.*

Iris

The Greek goddess of the rainbow and messenger of the gods, perhaps because a rainbow seems to link sky and earth. Homer assigns her to Zeus, but she generally serves Hera/Juno, and seems to have had no specific myths attached to her. There are two statues of Iris among the Elgin Marbles.

Isaeus (*c.* 420–350 B.C.)

Attic orator, traditionally a pupil of Isocrates and teacher of Demosthenes, an expert on cases of inheritance. Fifty speeches of his are known, and from the eleven which survive it is clear that he was an expert advocate.

Isis

An Egyptian goddess, wife of Osiris and mother of Horus, Isis in Hellenistic times became one of the most important deities in the Mediterranean world, and her cult spread throughout the Roman empire. Its special features were its Egyptian professional priests, initiation ceremonies, processions, dances and music to arouse religious fervour; these are described in the *Golden Ass* by APULEIUS. The best preserved of the temples of Isis is at Pompeii, in which bodies of priests clutching cult objects were found, and also a fresco painting of a young priest. Some details of the ritual of fire and water have lingered on in the ceremonies of Freemasonry and in the lovers' ordeals in Mozart's *Magic Flute*.

Isocrates (436–338 B.C.)
Athenian orator, famous for his forensic speeches and still more for the political views he expressed in his teaching and his political pamphlets, notably his *Panegyricus* and *Philip*. He hoped to put an end to city factions by preaching an enlightened monarchy, and worked for panhellenic unity against the threat of Persian expansion. But the Greek states could never be persuaded to unite in a common cause, nor could Philip of Macedon's ambitions be reconciled with Isocrates' teaching. Traditionally he killed himself after the Greek defeat by Philip at Chaeronea:

. . . as that dishonest victory
At Chaeronea, fatal to liberty,
Killed with report that old man
eloquent.
Milton, *To the Lady Margaret Ley.*

Itys, Itylus
King Tereus of Thrace married Procne, daughter of King Pandion of Athens, and then either pretended she was dead or invited her sister Philomela to visit them and raped her. The horrific consequences of this act are generally agreed on, though details vary. In one version he hides Procne and cuts out her tongue, in another it is Philomela he mutilates. Whichever sister it was told the other by means of a message woven into a piece of tapestry, and in revenge the two killed Itys, the son of Procne and Tereus, and served up his flesh as a meal to his father. Tereus pursued them, but the gods intervened and he was changed into a hoopoe (a royal, crested bird). Both sisters also became birds, in most versions Procne a nightingale and Philomela a swallow. Pausanias tells the tale with reference to the town of Daulis in Phocis, where he says no swallows would nest and no nightingales sing. Ovid in *Metamorphoses* 6 lingers on the gruesome details and makes Philomela the nightingale. This becomes the generally accepted version: 'Philomel with melody' is a common image in poetry. Lavinia's mutilation in Shakespeare's *Titus Andronicus* is often compared with that of Philomela, and in act IV, i she is seen looking through a copy of the *Metamorphoses* to find 'the tragic tale of Philomel', cf. Imogen in *Cymbeline* II, ii. The nightingale is also a recurrent image in T. S. Eliot's *The Waste Land*:

The change of Philomel, by the
barbarous king
So rudely forced; yet there the
nightingale
Filled all the desert with inviolable voice
And still she cried, and still the world
pursues,
'Jug, Jug' to dirty ears.

The legend is further confused by association with that of Itylus, son of King Zethus of Thebes and Aëdon (which name in Greek means 'nightingale'). Aëdon accidentally killed her own child when she intended to kill one of Niobe's sons, and was changed by Zeus into a nightingale whose song forever laments her dead son. This is the simile for Penelope's grief in *Odyssey* 19.518 ff. Swinburne makes things no easier by calling a poem *Itylus* which clearly refers to Itys, as the nightingale reproaches her sister the swallow for forgetting the death of her first-begotten, and

The woven web which was plain to follow,
The small slain body, the flowerlike face.

Ixion

A king of the Lapiths and according to Pindar the first man to murder a blood relative; later mythographers make the victim his father-in-law. He was purified by Zeus but then tried to rape Hera. He was deceived by a cloud made in her image, on which he begat the father of the Centaurs, and then fixed to a revolving wheel on which he suffered eternal punishment in hell for his sins. He, Sisyphus and Tantalus were well known in the Middle Ages from Ovid's *Metamorphoses*, and exemplified three of the major sins punished in Hell: Lewdness or Sensuality, Pride and Avarice.

Janus

A Roman god with no Greek equivalent, his name derived from the word for gate or barbican (*ianua*). He is always represented with a head facing both ways, perhaps suggesting the need for a cautious look in all directions before action, and this is commonly stamped on Roman republican coins. He then became associated with beginnings, and in the reform of the calendar by Julius Caesar, his month of January became the first of the year. The temple of Janus stood in the Roman forum and had double gates; these were symbolically closed in times of peace and left open in war.

Jason

Son of Aeson king of Iolcos in Thessaly. His uncle Pelias usurped the throne, and Jason was brought up by the centaur Chiron. He returned to claim his heritage and arrived with one sandal, having lost the other crossing a torrent. Pelias recognized in this that he was the stranger who an oracle had foretold would kill him. He therefore challenged Jason to fetch the Golden Fleece and rid him of the curse of PHRIXUS. Jason assembled a number of heroes for the expedition; see ARGONAUTS. Later legends added to their numbers, as families liked to claim descent from an Argonaut. HERACLES was said to have joined them after he had killed the Erymanthian boar, but stayed at Cios to look for Hylas. Their many adventures included a long stay on the island of Lemnos, where the women and their queen, Hypsipele, had murdered their husbands and were only too eager to welcome a party of men. This episode is probably based on a recollection of a primitive community ruled by priestesses. They rescued Phineus from the HARPIES and sailed through the Clashing Rocks (Symplegades) which guarded the entrance to the Bosporus, by first sending a dove through and then checking them by means of Orpheus's music. (In Homer's account these rocks are described as 'wandering' and are not localized. They have been rationalized as ice-floes in the Black Sea from the Russian rivers.) At Colchis (the Crimea) Jason carried out the task set by King Aeëtes of yoking a pair of fire-breathing bulls and sowing dragon's teeth (cf. CADMUS) with the help of the witch-princess MEDEA. By her sorcery he also took the Golden Fleece from its guardian dragon and sailed off with her. All interest in his legend then shifts to her; in Euripides' *Medea* Jason is presented as a weak-willed selfish man, and in Apollonius's *Voyage of the Argo* he is a colourless character. The manner of his death is briefly foretold by Euripides but elaborated by later mythographers; after wandering around Greece he returned to Corinth and was killed by a piece of the *Argo* dropping off on to his head – a suitable act of retributive justice for the moralists.

Jocasta

In Theban legend, the wife of King Laius of Thebes, mother of OEDIPUS and afterwards his wife. She hanged herself when the truth of their incestuous relationship was known. In *Odyssey* II she is called Epicaste, and Odysseus sees her shade in the Underworld. Homer makes it plain that she acted in ignorance, and Sophocles implies this too. In Euripides' *Phoenician Women* she dies only after the death of her sons. She is given a more complex personality by the post-Freudian dramatists Cocteau and Gide.

Josephus (born A.D. 37–8, date of death unknown)

Jewish historian, writing in Greek, and governor of Galilee at the time of the Jewish revolt against Nero. He was captured by the Romans but granted his life, and after the fall of Jerusalem in 70 settled in Rome and became a Roman citizen. There he wrote his *Jewish Antiquities* and the *Jewish War*. The latter ends with a moving and dramatic account of the siege and capture of the fortress of Masada, and Josephus's facts have now been confirmed by recent excavations.

Judgement of Paris

This is an early story, though not mentioned in Homer, of the kind which is common in folklore, where everything turns on a choice of alternatives, and is intended to account for the start of the Trojan War. Why it should be attached to Paris, son of Priam of Troy, is never clear. At the wedding of PELEUS and Thetis, Eris (Strife) threw down an apple marked 'for the most beautiful'. Paris, who was living as a shepherd on the slopes of Mount Ida, was asked to decide between the goddesses Hera, Athene and Aphrodite, who offered him respectively empire, military glory and the most beautiful woman in the world (Helen). He chose HELEN. Hence the Trojan War in which the rejected Hera and Athene supported the Greeks.

The story was depicted as early as the seventh century B.C. on an ivory comb from Sparta, and appears on vase-paintings. Later writers such as Lucian added embellishments (the apple becomes magic and golden), and from Ovid's detailed account in his *Heroides* it was known in the Middle Ages as well as in garbled form from the *Tale of Troy*. The scene with Paris and the goddesses appealed to later painters as widely different as Cranach, Rubens [37] and Watteau, and was the subject of the first mythological painting of Claude. It develops a high moral tone in Tennyson's poem on OENONE.

Julian (Flavius Claudius Julianus, Roman Emperor A.D. 361–63)
In Christian tradition he is generally known as 'the Apostate' because of his renunciation of the Christian faith and attempts to restore the pagan gods and suppress the Church. Though his work *Against the Christians* was destroyed after his death, many of his letters and satirical writings survive, and his reign saw the issue of several allegorizing treatments of pagan myths which were to be important for the Middle Ages. There seems to be no historical foundation for the story that he was stabbed by a Christian and died saying '*Vicisti Galilaee*' – which Swinburne expanded into the refrain 'Thou hast conquered, O pale Galilean'. The paradox of Julian's puritanical form of neo-paganism, which made him no more popular with pagans than with Christians, was one of Cavafy's special interests. There is a good picture of him and his times in Gore Vidal's recent novel *Julian*. See also DELPHIC ORACLE.

Julius Caesar, Gaius (*c.* 100–44 B.C.)
Roman patrician, general and statesman, and sole dictator in Rome after his defeat of his rival POMPEY; in all respects he is one of the most striking figures of the ancient world. He was an accomplished orator and a master of prose style; his commentaries on his conquest of Gaul and his account of the Civil War with Pompey are the best examples we have of unadorned narrative in Latin. He was also a great womanizer, with Cleopatra among his many mistresses, and immensely popular with his troops. Suetonius in his *Twelve Caesars* gives a highly coloured account of his personal life. He was never liked by younger men like Catullus nor conservative democrats like Cicero. His murder by BRUTUS and the conspirators on the fateful Ides of March is the subject of Shakespeare's play, following Plutarch's *Life* in North's translation. Among modern biographies and reconstructions of his life are those by John Buchan, Michael Grant, and Rex Warner in his novels (*The Young Caesar* and *Imperial Caesar*). He was said to have been delivered at birth by what has since been called a Caesarian operation, and the deafness in the left ear and attacks of giddiness mentioned by Plutarch (and after him Shakespeare) were due more probably to Ménière's disease than to epilepsy. Every beginner in Latin knows that he conquered Gaul, and afterwards landed in Britain, but if he really said *Veni, vidi, vici* ('I

came, I saw, I conquered') it is more likely to have been after his victory over the Pompeian supporters at the Battle of Zela. 'Caesar' became an official title of all the Roman emperors, and lingered on in titles like 'Kaiser' and 'Tsar'. There are several Roman portrait busts of Caesar which are considered authentic and show a face which is both austere and melancholy. The best known, in the British Museum, confirms what Suetonius says, that he combed his thinning hair forward. He was also said to wear his laurel wreath on all occasions to conceal his baldness. Mantegna was inspired by the literary tradition of Caesar to paint his *Triumphs of Caesar*, which have been much copied and engraved. Nine of the vast canvases were purchased by Charles I of England and survive, though much restored, and it was probably these which impressed Rubens so much that he painted a Triumph himself.

Juno

An early Italian goddess originally associated with women and childbirth and later identified with HERA.

Jupiter

Originally the Italian sky-god, connected with rain, storms and thunder, and later identified with the Olympian Father of the gods, ZEUS. The temple of Jupiter Optimus Maximus (Best and Highest) on the Capitol at Rome was the centre of the state cult, which was traditionally said to have been introduced by the Etruscan kings, and linked with that of Juno and Minerva; the *flamen Dialis*, the priest of Jupiter, was the chief priest of the fifteen *flamines*, each assigned to the cult of a god. To this temple came generals in their triumphal processions, to lay their spoils on the altar of Jupiter.

In his *Autobiography* Gibbon describes how he 'conceived the idea of a work which has amused and exercised near twenty years of my life':

> It was at Rome, on the 15th of October, 1764, as I sat musing amidst the ruins of the Capitol, while the barefooted friars were singing vespers in the Temple of Jupiter, that the idea of writing the decline and fall of the city first started to my mind.

Gibbon would hear the Franciscans in the church of Aracoeli, though this stands on the Arx, or citadel of early Rome; the temple stood on an adjacent spur. There are also remains of temples to Jupiter in his capacity of *Stator* (Founder), *Tonans* (Thunderer) and *Ultor* (Avenger).

Justinian (Roman Emperor in the East, A.D. 527–65)

While he held Persian and Balkan invaders back from encroaching on the territory of the Eastern Empire, Justinian largely recovered the Western Empire through his general BELISARIUS. He was responsible for the codification of Roman law (the *Digest*, *Institutes* and *Novellae*). He built on the grand scale the church of St Sophia in Constantinople, and as part of his ecclesiastical policy he closed the Greek schools of philosophy, including the Academy which had been teaching since its foundation by Plato. The history of his times is known from the historian PROCOPIUS, and there are contemporary portraits of him and the Empress Theodora in the magnificent processional series of mosaics in the church of San Vitale at Ravenna. Justinian appears in canto 6 of Dante's *Paradiso* and surveys the progress of Roman history; Dante must have seen the mosaics and been impressed by Justinian's majesty during his own years of exile in Ravenna.

Juvenal (Decimus Junius Juvenalis, *c.* A.D. 60–*c.* 130)

Roman poet, whose sixteen satires are a bitter commentary on the immorality and social injustice of contemporary Rome. Almost nothing is known of his life except what he mentions in his poems, though an inscription (now lost) said that he came from Aquinum (Aquino) in central Italy. He seems to have been exiled for a time, possibly to Egypt about which he shows some first-hand knowledge, but otherwise lived in poverty in Rome, until the Emperor Hadrian, it is said, gave him a small country property. Juvenal has had more influence on western satirists than any other ancient writer, from Sebastian Brant in his *Ship of Fools* through Boileau, Dryden, Pope in the *Dunciad*, and Byron right down to the sharp criticism of contemporary *mores* we find in Eliot, or Ezra Pound in the *Cantos*. One of the best known of his many eighteenth-century imitators is Dr Johnson, whose *London* and *Vanity of Human Wishes* are modelled on *Satires* 3 and 10 of Juvenal, though the author most resembling him in temperament is Swift, who surely possessed the true *saeva indignatio*. It was Juvenal's sincerity, his deep concern with the corruption he saw around him, and his regrets for the simpler values of the past which made him the favourite poet of the painter Rubens. Over the portico of Rubens's house in Antwerp were lines 356–60 of *Satire* 10:

> ... then ask
> For a sound mind in a sound body, a valiant heart
> Without fear of death, that reckons longevity
> The least among Nature's gifts, that's strong to endure
> All kinds of toil ...

At the same time Juvenal had no use for the worn-out conventions of the classical gods and heroes, and seizes every chance to mock at them:

> Must I stick to the usual round
> Of Hercules' labours, what Diomede did, the bellowing
> Of that thingummy in the Labyrinth, or the tale of the flying
> Carpenter, and how his son went splash in the sea?
>
> (*Satire* 1. 52–5)*

In this he speaks for most of the sophisticated Romans of his day.

Kronos (Cronos)

One of the Titans of mythology, the youngest son of Heaven (Uranus) and Earth (Ge), who castrated his father in order to gain his throne, married his

* Peter Green, *Juvenal: the Sixteen Satires*, Penguin Books, 1967.

sister Rhea, and swallowed all his children as they were born with the exception of Zeus, who was smuggled away to Crete and a stone substituted (→ AMALTHEA, CURETES). These extraordinary tales first appear in Hesiod and are certainly pre-Greek; later mythographers idealized Kronos as the king of a GOLDEN AGE in a distant past.

Laestrygones

A race of cannibal giants who in *Odyssey* 10 sink all but one of Odysseus's twelve ships. Homer describes their summer night as so short that shepherds taking out their flocks in the morning meet those returning at sunset, which is evidently a reminiscence of some traveller in the far north, but tradition generally located them in eastern Sicily or at Formiae in central Italy. Recently Ernle Bradford (*Ulysses Found*) has claimed that Bonifacio in southern Corsica best answers Homer's description of the harbour. The land of the Laestrygones is one of the eight 'Landscapes from the Odyssey', a famous series of Roman wall-paintings which were found in a Roman house in 1848 during excavations on the Esquiline hill; they are now in the Vatican library.

Laocoön

In post-Homeric epic he was a Trojan prince and priest of Apollo who tried to stop the Trojans from opening their gates to the WOODEN HORSE. He was then killed with his two sons by serpents which came from the sea, sent either by Apollo or by Athene as patron of the Greeks. His story is dramatically told by Virgil *Aeneid* 2, but Laocoön is best remembered from the group of statues [34] carved in Rhodes about 25 B.C. and brought to Rome by the Emperor Titus in A.D. 69, where it was highly praised by the elder Pliny. It was found and recognized from his description in the ruins of the Baths of Titus in 1506 and bought by Pope Julius II for the Vatican Museum, where it is now. The *Laocoön* is essentially a baroque work, technically marvellous for its tension, and was much admired by Michelangelo, Bernini and Rubens. It also had a peculiar fascination for Titian, who caricatured it in his 'Monkey Laocoön'. It is rather surprising then to find that in the dispute between the German neoclassical critics Lessing and Winckelmann, Lessing gave the title *Laokoön* to his essay analysing the different media of poetry and the fine arts because he admired the statue group for what he saw as its classical restraint.

Laodamia

The wife of Protesilaus, the first Greek to be killed immediately on landing at Troy. Homer says no more than that he left his wife mourning and his house unfinished, but a later romantic story is told, mainly by Latin poets: by Catullus, by Virgil, who puts her among unhappy lovers in the Underworld, and by Ovid in his *Heroides*; from Ovid she is known to Chaucer as a faithful lover. She was granted her prayer to have the shade of her husband restored to her for three hours, after which she killed herself since she could not bear to be parted from it. Wordsworth altered his poem *Laodamia* thirty years after it was first written, in order to make Protesilaus administer an austere rebuke to Laodamia for her 'rebellious passion', which conflicted with the duty demanded of her by the gods.

Laomedon

King of Troy, father of Priam, famous for his treachery. He refused payment to Apollo and Poseidon when they helped to build the walls of Troy, so in revenge they sent a sea-monster which would have devoured his daughter Hesione if she had not been rescued by Heracles. Laomedon then refused to hand over the famous horses he had promised (the ones given by Zeus in exchange for Ganymede), so Heracles sacked the city and killed all his sons except Priam.

Lapithae, Lapiths

A primitive mountain tribe in Thessaly, related to the centaurs through common descent from IXION. They are chiefly famous for their battle with the drunken centaurs at the marriage of Hippodamia with their king, PIRITHOUS. This features in the metopes of the Parthenon, in the frieze of the temple of Apollo at Bassae and in the sculptures from the west pediment of the temple of Zeus at Olympia. The story was subsequently well known from the detailed account in Ovid, but there are few representations of it; the best known are a sculptured relief by Michelangelo and a strange, disturbing battle-scene by Piero di Cosimo [22].

Lares

In Roman mythology these are the spirits of the dead, worshipped at crossroads and in the home as guardian deities; the *lares familiares* have their shrine in each home and are generally associated with the Penates who were guardians of the household stores.

Lars Porsen(n)a

A legendary Etruscan chieftain (*lars* means 'overlord') who was said by Livy to have been invited by the exiled King Tarquinius Superbus to besiege Rome. It seems likely that he was no more than a personification of Etruscan domination over Rome in the sixth century B.C. → HORATIUS COCLES and SCAEVOLA.

Latinus

The eponymous king of the Latini in Italy, said by Hesiod to be the son of Odysseus and Circe, and by Virgil to be the son of Faunus. In the legend followed by Livy and Virgil he is unwilling to allow the Trojans and Aeneas to land in Italy, but then agrees that Aeneas shall marry his daughter Lavinia. He then has to fight with Aeneas against Turnus, prince of the neighbouring Rutuli to whom he had previously promised Lavinia. In Livy's account he is killed in the fighting and Aeneas becomes king of the Latini; in the *Aeneid* he survives to be wholly reconciled and celebrate the marriage which is to link the two peoples.

Leda

An Aetolian princess, wife of Tyndareus, king of Sparta, the mother of

Clytemnestra, Helen, Castor and Polydeuces (the Dioscuri). Most versions of her legend say that she was loved by Zeus in the form of a swan and gave birth to an egg from which were hatched Helen and Polydeuces, while Castor and Clytemnestra were fathered by Tyndareus, but one variant makes Helen the daughter of NEMESIS, who deposited the egg with Leda to incubate and bring up Helen as her own child. This is known to Sappho, but it is elaborated only by later moralists. Homer disregards the swan's egg entirely: Leda is mentioned only as the mother of the Dioscuri and is among the women seen by Odysseus in the Underworld. And on the famous jar from Vulci in Etruria, painted by the sixth-century Athenian Exekias, the scene of 'the Dioscuri at home' is purely domestic; Leda and Tyndareus are with their two handsome sons, horses and a dog.

But the swan's visitation has been a powerful image down the ages. It was a popular decorative motif in antiquity, particularly on Roman sarcophagi, and it was from an antique relief of Leda that Michelangelo took the form of his painting, which is now lost. From copies and from a statue by his pupil Ammanati we know that it closely resembled his figure of Night in the Medici Chapel, Florence. The result is singularly joyless. The painting by Leonardo is also lost, but there are copies, including a sketch by Raphael, and his own sketches, which show that he saw Leda as a symbol of fertility – she herself is a radiant figure, and everything around her is breaking into life; flowers and grasses are in bloom, and the babies are bursting out of two eggs (Concord indicated by the Twins, Strife by Helen and Clytemnestra). There is also a beautifully sensuous Leda by Tintoretto, and one by Correggio, where Leda is bathing with other women and a swan leaves its fellows to single her out. The Neoplatonists who believed in life-through-death and in love as a means of obtaining union with the absolute could see in Leda a symbol of this; cf. Ariadne, Psyche. And of all Zeus's many forms, none is more evocative of majesty than the swan.

Whiles the proud Bird, ruffing his
  fethers wyde
And brushing his faire brest, did her
  invade,
She slept: yet twixt her eyelids closely
  spyde
How towards her he rusht, and smiled
  at his pryde.

The Faerie Queene III.11.32

Rilke, in his *Leda*, also concentrates on the god's assumption of new power, whereas most poets have thought more of Leda's response.

Swans are a recurrent image in English poetry, but there is no poet who made so urgent a symbol out of Leda as W. B. Yeats. He was well aware of the neoplatonist interpretation of the myth, and at the same time always conscious that 'Love and War came from the eggs of Leda'; see, especially, his *Lullaby* and *Leda and the Swan*, where the last couplet has been taken to refer to the divine power and wisdom of the Heavenly Twins:

A shudder in the loins engenders there
The broken wall, the burning roof and
  tower
And Agamemnon dead.
                    Being so caught up,
So mastered by the brute blood of the
  air,
Did she put on his knowledge with
  his power
Before the indifferent beak could let
  her drop?

Leonidas
King of Sparta who in 480 B.C. held the pass of Thermopylae for two days against the invading Persian army under XERXES. When outflanked he held on with 300 companions to cover the retreat of the Greek fleet and died fighting. They were commemorated in a famous couplet by SIMONIDES. Leonidas's heroism was a subject likely to appeal to the neoclassicist painter David, who painted a *Leonidas at Thermopylae*.

Lepidus, Marcus Aemilius
The third member of the triumvirate with Antony and Octavian, who took the side of Octavian when the break came; this is the minor role he plays in Shakespeare's *Antony and Cleopatra*. He is the central figure in Alfred Duggan's novel *Three's Company*.

Lethe
In Greek it means only 'forgetfulness', and the conception of it as one of the six rivers of the Underworld is a late development which is generally accepted by the Latin authors. Virgil in *Aeneid* 6 connects it with what he says there about reincarnation; the souls gather on its shores to drink and forget before they can be born again. Ovid mentions it as a river flowing round the Cave of Sleep in a famous passage in *Metamorphoses* 11, where its murmuring induces drowsiness; this is closely imitated by Chaucer in the *Book of the Duchess* and by Spenser in his description of Morpheus in *The Faerie Queene* (I.1.39–41). Dante develops the Virgilian concept, and his Lethe flows down bearing with it the memory of sin from Purgatory to the place of sin, which is Hell (*Inferno* 14). In later poets Lethe is an accepted symbol for forgetting.

Leto (Roman **Latona**)
A Titaness, mentioned by Homer and Hesiod as the mother by Zeus of Apollo and Artemis, and in the Homeric *Hymn to Apollo* as having given birth to them on the island of Delos. She had a cult in several places, particularly in Lycia, but this legend accounted for the fact that in historic times Delos was even more closely associated with Apollo than Delphi. She was said to have wandered there in labour which was prolonged because of jealous Hera's refusal to let Eileithyia help her. Later mythology added the details that she was forbidden to give birth on land, and Poseidon helped her to the island which was permitted because it floated and was washed by the waves. Among the many ruined shrines and temples still to be seen are those of the great sanctuary of Apollo and the lions which line the processional way. Leto destroyed the children of NIOBE.

Leucippus
A king of Messenia whose daughters Hilaera and Phoebe were carried off by

Castor and Pollux. Their brothers Idas and Lynceus fought to rescue them and Castor was killed, but Pollux was allowed to stand proxy for him in the Underworld on alternate days. The story is told in Pindar's *Nemean Ode* 10, though he refers only to a cattle raid. Rubens found a subject for a splendid baroque picture in *The Rape of the Daughters of Leucippus* [6].

Leucothea ('White goddess')
A sea-goddess whose name perhaps refers to white foam. She was originally Ino, daughter of Cadmus, wife of Athamas and the typical jealous stepmother of all folklore (→ PHRIXUS). She was also said to have helped Zeus to save the infant Dionysus at the death of SEMELE, in revenge for which Hera sent her mad so that she leapt into the sea and became Leucothea. Her son became Palaemon, a minor sea-deity, remembered by Milton in his invocation to Sabrina in *Comus*:

By Leucothea's lovely hands
And her son who rules the strands . . .

In *Odyssey* 5 Leucothea rises from the sea in the form of a sea-mew when Odysseus's raft breaks up, and she gives him her veil to tie round his waist, so that he manages to swim through the stormy sea to the island of Phaeacia.

Lichas
The herald of Heracles, who in Sophocles' *Women of Trachis* brings from DEIANIRA the poisoned shirt of Nessus for Heracles to wear when he is about to offer sacrifice to Zeus after his capture of the town of Oechalia in northern Greece. Heracles in his agony then took Lichas by the ankle, swung him round three times and hurled him into the Euboean Sea, where, according to Ovid, he turned into a rock of human shape called after him.

As when Alcides, from Oechalia
  crowned
With conquest, felt th'envenomed robe,
  and tore
Through pain up by the roots
  Thessalian pines,
And Lichas from the top of Oeta threw
Into th' Euboic sea.
Paradise Lost, 2.542–6

Hercules' flinging Lichas to his death is the subject of a famous vigorous statue-group by Canova, of which the story is told that in 1799 some of his contemporaries interpreted it as Monarchy cast down and destroyed; to which Canova retorted that Lichas could equally well represent 'licentious liberty'.

Livia (58 B.C.–A.D. 29)
The wife of the Emperor Augustus, and mother of Tiberius by her first husband, Tiberius Claudius Nero. She was given the titles Julia Augusta by Augustus's will and was an active influence on Tiberius until her death. She was a woman of great intelligence and character; Robert Graves in *I, Claudius* describes the unfounded rumours of personal ambition and intrigue which surrounded her. The House of Livia, on the Palatine hill, is famous for its mural paintings in early style, though the mythological scenes depicted are not easy to distinguish.

Livy (Titus Livius, 59 B.C.–A.D. 17)
Roman historian, born at Patavium (Padua) but living in Rome, where he devoted his whole life to literature, especially to his History 'from the foundation of Rome' (*ab urbe condita*) to his own times. Of its 142 books only thirty-five and a few fragments survive, and cover the early history and legend up to the end of the fourth century B.C., the Second Punic War against Hannibal, and the wars with Macedonia up to 166 B.C. Livy became famous in his own day (the tale was told of a Spaniard who came from Cadiz simply to look at him), and only ASINIUS POLLIO criticized him for what he called *patavinitas*, a provincialism which might be a certain ignorance of practical matters and naïveté in handling his sources. His great gifts were his historical imagination, his power to re-create a great scene, his sense of Rome's historic past and his firm moral values; his expressed purpose in writing was to show the lessons to be learnt from history. He was admired throughout the Middle Ages, and for Dante he was '*Livio che non erra*' (Livy who does not err). One of Machiavelli's early works was a commentary on the first ten books, as a medium for working out the laws of political cause and effect. Livy was also one of the best-loved authors of Montaigne.

Longinus
(i) The unknown author credited with a Greek treatise *On the Sublime* which is thought to have been written in the mid first century A.D. This is one of the few outstanding pieces of critical writing in antiquity, an analysis of what makes for excellence in writing, under such headings as noble conceptions, passionate feeling, proper use of figures of speech and words, and grasp of structure, and is illustrated by quotations from a wide range of Greek authors whose works 'Longinus' obviously knew at first hand.

(ii) The Longinus known to history was a Greek rhetorician, teacher of Porphyry at Athens, and later minister to ZENOBIA, queen of Palmyra.

Lotus-Eaters
In the *Odyssey*, a fabulous people who lived on lotus-fruit which induced forgetfulness and made its eater lose any desire to return to his own country. They were known to Herodotus as living in western Libya, and their land may have been the island of Djerba. Their climate was probably more seductive than their fruit, if it was indeed the sort of sour plum (*cordia myxa*) described in Pliny's *Natural History*. The lotus-eaters gave Tennyson a subject for one of his best-known poems.

Lucan (Marcus Annaeus Lucanus, A.D. 39–65)
Roman epic poet, born in Spain, nephew of the philosopher SENECA, whose Stoic beliefs he shared. He was forced to commit suicide after being involved in the conspiracy of Piso against Nero. His only extant work is his ten-book epic on the Civil War between Caesar and Pompey, known as the *Pharsalia*. This was probably planned as twelve books culminating in the death of Caesar, who, for Lucan, is the

tyrant villain, while Pompey is inspired by his republican spirit to be its hero. The epic is a masterpiece of rhetorical style, over-elaborate at times, but full of a young man's powerful imagination. It was admired by Dante, who groups Lucan with Homer, Horace and Ovid as the four great poets who greet him in Limbo (*Inferno* 4), and by Marlowe, who translated the first book. Lucan was also one of the authors read and quoted by Montaigne. As a youthful martyr to the cause of republican liberty, Lucan appealed to Shelley in his own youth, and *Pharsalia* is even quoted in an early letter of Shelley's as 'a poem of wonderful genius transcending Shakespeare'.

Lucian (*c.* A.D. 120–*c.* 180)
Greek writer, born at Samosata on the Euphrates in Syria, and widely travelled as a public lecturer; he was also known to have studied philosophy in Athens and he wrote in good Attic Greek. Lucian was a witty satirist, and from his knowledge of the Platonic Dialogue, the Old and New Comedy (e.g. Aristophanes and Menander) and the satires of MENIPPUS, he created a form (which has been known since as the Lucianic Dialogue) in which to poke fun at the follies and superstitions of his day. Several of these dialogues deal with variations on the theme of death and popular notions of an after-life, and he also sharply criticized Christian fanatics and religious impostors in a way which many Christian apologists misunderstood but which was appreciated by more imaginative scholars like Erasmus and Thomas More. Erasmus translated a good deal of Lucian, and owed something to him both in his *Praise of Folly* and his own conversational dialogues, the *Colloquies*. Lucian's reputation as a blasphemer naturally appealed to Shelley and his friends; both W. S. Landor's *Imaginary Conversations* and T. L. Peacock's satirical novels stem from the dialogues. Lucian also wrote a famous *True History* as a parody on improbable travel-stories and, as he is known to have been the favourite Greek author of Rabelais, he may have been a model for *Gargantua* and *Pantagruel*, as he certainly is for More's *Utopia* and Swift's *Gulliver's Travels*.

Lucretia
The wife of Tarquinius Collatinus, who was raped by Sextus, son of Tarquinius Superbus; after confessing her shame to her husband she stabbed herself. This led to the rising headed by JUNIUS BRUTUS and the expulsion of the TARQUINS. Lucretia and her story are probably legendary, though they are told by Livy as history, and also by Ovid in his *Fasti*.

From these two sources she was well known to Chaucer, who not only puts her into the *Legend of Good Women* but says that

The grete Austyn hath gret compassioun
Of this Lucresse that starf in Rome toun

– a reference to St Augustine's *City of God*. When Brutus takes an oath by her spirit to drive out the Tarquins, Chaucer interprets this in Christian terms as meaning that 'she was holden there/A seynt' (saint). Shakespeare's longest early poem is *The Rape of Lucrece*, on which

Benjamin Britten's opera *The Rape of Lucretia* is based. Lucretia was also a favourite subject for the painters; Botticelli, Filippino Lippi, Titian, Tintoretto and Veronese all painted her death, and she was also painted by the German Lucas Cranach. *Brutus Swearing to Avenge Lucretia's Death* is a heroic picture by the neoclassicist Gavin Hamilton.

Lucretius (Titus Lucretius Carus, *c.* 95–*c.* 55 B.C.)
Roman Epicurean philosopher and poet, whose only work was *De rerum natura* ('On the Nature of the Universe') written in six books and probably not completed; it is dedicated to the senator Gaius Memmius (whom Catullus accompanied to Bithynia). Lucretius's expressed intention was to explain the world in the physical terms of Epicurus and so to free men from their superstitious belief in the gods and their fears of death and the unknown. Lucretius is a very great poet, who combines a passionate concern for his purpose with a real feeling for nature and a delicate sympathy for all living things, all of which he tries to express in what he called the poverty of his native tongue; so that he can almost be felt to be struggling to carve out something monumental from unworked stone. He has vivid descriptions of natural phenomena, epidemics (including the plague at Athens), earthquakes and eruptions, and it is thought that Piero di Cosimo's painting, *The Forest Fire*, is taken from Lucretius's account in book 5. →→ VULCAN. Tennyson's poem on his suicide comes from a statement by St Jerome which cannot be confirmed, and in fact nothing at all is known of his life.

Lucullus, Lucius Licinius
(*c.* 117–55 B.C.)
Roman senator and general serving under the dictator Sulla and then campaigning successfully against MITHRIDATES, king of Pontus, until he was replaced by Pompey. Lucullus then devoted himself to gracious living, as he had amassed great wealth, and his name became synonymous with sybaritic luxury. It is still possible to use 'Lucullan' as an epithet, usually of good food. The famous Gardens of Lucullus in Rome, on the slopes of the Quirinal and Pincian hills, became the property of the emperors.

Ludovisi Throne
A famous relief of Ionian origin, dating from the early fifth century B.C., which shows Aphrodite rising from the sea (→ ANADYOMENE) between two attendants, flanked by two nude girl flute players [35]. It is in the Terme museum in Rome, and forms part of the collection made in the seventeenth century by Cardinal Ludovisi. Originally it was probably the front and sides of an altar. It was seen and admired by Rilke, and probably inspired the sculptural imagery of his poem *The Birth of Venus*.

Lycurgus
(i) A mythical king of Thrace who opposed Dionysus, was blinded and driven mad. (ii) The founder of the constitution and military regime of

Sparta, first mentioned by Herodotus and given a *Life* by Plutarch, but as many of these institutions did not exist before the sixth century B.C. and are likely to have evolved over a long period, Lycurgus was probably wholly invented. He was said to have been inspired by the oracle at Delphi, and was worshipped as a god in Sparta.

Lysander
The Spartan admiral who finally defeated the Athenians in the Peloponnesian War at the battle of Aegospotami in 405 B.C. and helped to bring about the collapse of Athenian democracy. His arrogance and high-handedness then lost him the confidence of his own people and his policies were reversed, though Pausanias says that he was honoured as a hero at his tomb in Boeotia. He is known from Xenophon's histories and from Plutarch's *Life*, and his association with Alexander, Heracles and Hector 'and such great names as these' in the seventeenth-century marching song, *The British Grenadiers*, is at first surprising; but in an early version Lysander is more suitably paired with his Athenian opponent Conon.

Lysias (*c.* 459–*c.* 380 B.C.)
Attic orator, the son of Cephalus from Syracuse, a wealthy 'metic' or resident alien in Athens, whose home in the Piraeus is the setting for Plato's *Republic*; Lysias and his brother are present at the discussion. He escaped into exile under the THIRTY TYRANTS and returned to impeach one of them in his speech *Against Eratosthenes*, which gives us an all too familiar picture of the violence and confusion which follow a political coup. Lysias was famous for his well-arranged subject-matter and plain, clear style, and 800 speeches were known in antiquity. Of these twenty-three survive intact, along with many fragments, and cover a wide range of criminal prosecutions, both public and private.

Macrobius, Ambrosius
Roman grammarian and philosopher of about A.D. 400, of whom nothing is known except that he was of high rank and probably pagan. His known works are the *Saturnalia*, a compilation in the form of table-talk modelled on the *Attic Nights* of GELLIUS, which contains valuable comments on Virgil, and his commentary, preserved with the text, on SCIPIO'S DREAM, which was known and widely read throughout the Middle Ages. Chaucer appears to think that Macrobius wrote the *Dream* himself: he refers in the *Nun's Priest's Tale* to 'Macrobius that writ the avisioun/In Affrike of the worthy Cipioun'.

Boswell, in his account of Johnson's arrival at Oxford at the age of nineteen, says that 'He sat silent until upon something which occurred in the course of conversation he suddenly struck in and quoted Macrobius, and thus he gave the first impression of that more extensive reading in which he had indulged himself.' Even so, Pembroke College elected him only as a commoner.

Maecenas, Gaius (*c.* 70–8 B.C.)
Roman diplomat and personal friend of the Emperor Augustus, to whom he

bequeathed his house and gardens on the Esquiline hill. He was never a senator, but a man of wealth and prestige who dabbled in poetry and was celebrated as a patron of literature and the arts, particularly for his encouragement of the poets Virgil, Propertius and Horace, to whom he gave his small farm in the Sabine hills. Horace refers to him with affection and gratitude in several of his *Odes*. His name is still synonymous with generous patronage of the arts.

Maia

Homer and Hesiod refer to her as one of the Pleiades, daughter of Atlas and mother by Zeus of Hermes; in Roman mythology she is a nature goddess who gives her name to the month, and the two become identified (as in Keats's *Ode to Maia*).

Manes

The Roman name for the spirits of the dead who were thought of as having gained a sort of collective divinity as the *Di Manes* (the old Latin adjective *manus* means 'good') and needing propitiatory ceremonies at the grave. *Dis Manibus sacrum* was inscribed on Roman tombstones with the name of the dead person in the genitive, or more commonly the abbreviation D.M. The word is also used by Roman poets for the gods of the Underworld or the realm of the dead in general, much as English poets loosely use the word 'shades'.

Manilius, Marcus

(early first century A.D.)

Roman poet, the author of the *Astronomica*, a long didactic poem on astronomy and astrology, which is generally thought to be virtually unreadable, but the poet and Latinist A. E. Housman devoted nearly thirty years to a five-volume edition of the text, a monument of critical scholarship. The withering sarcasm of Housman's comments on his fellow-scholars provide a good deal of what he himself called 'low enjoyment'.

Manlius Capitolinus, Marcus

Roman consul and hero of a well-known legend (told in detail as history in Livy, book 5) in which he was awakened by the cackling of the sacred geese kept on the Capitol, and so was able to rally the guards and repel the Gauls from their attack in 387 B.C. From references in Ennius and elsewhere it seems certain that the invading Gauls did occupy the Capitol for a while, and this is either a face-saving story or one devised to explain why one branch of the Manlius family had that surname.

Manlius Torquatus, Titus

Another hero of early Rome who was said to have killed a gigantic Gaul in 361 B.C. and taken the gold neck-torque from his body (again, an explanation of a surname). He also exemplified Roman *pietas* in saving his father from prosecution, and a stern sense of justice in sentencing his own son to death (cf. LUCIUS BRUTUS). Consequently he features in accounts of Rome's glorious past, such as the survey given to Aeneas by his father's shade in *Aeneid* 6. The name continued in the Manlius family; a descendant who was a contemporary of Catullus is celebrated by him in a marriage hymn.

Marcellus

The name of a family distinguished for their public services to Rome from the time of the Punic Wars to the third century A.D. One of them married Octavia, sister of the Emperor Augustus; their son Marcus Claudius Marcellus was born in 42 B.C. and recognized as the probable heir to his uncle. He married Augustus's daughter Julia in 25 and died of illness in 23 at the popular sea-resort of Baiae – the subject of a poem by Propertius (3.18). Marcellus was commemorated by Augustus in the Theatre of Marcellus in Rome, a good deal of which still stands, and was the first person to be buried in the Mausoleum of Augustus, a ruin which was freed from superstructures only in 1938. In *Aeneid* 6 Anchises ends his forecast of Rome's history with a description of the Marcellus who was one of the great generals against Hannibal and known as 'the sword of Rome', and of a young man whose name Aeneas asks. He is told that it is the ill-fated Marcellus, whose name has become a symbol for promise unfulfilled. The story is told by the grammarian Donatus (fourth century A.D.) that when Octavia heard the passage read she fainted. *Virgil Reading the Aeneid to Octavia and Livia* is the subject of a painting by Ingres.

Marcus Aurelius Antoninus
(Roman Emperor A.D. 161–80)

Adopted as his successor by the Emperor Antoninus Pius from an aristocratic family settled in Spain, Marcus had been carefully educated (→ FRONTO) and devoted himself to the Stoic philosophy as taught by EPICTETUS. He was the author of what are always called his *Meditations*, though he named them simply 'To himself', which he wrote in Greek in his various army-camps as he struggled to preserve his empire against the disasters of his reign – invasions on the Danube front, war with Parthia, internal rebellion and plague. This is one of the most personal and moving works of ancient literature. The portrait busts also show him as a deeply thoughtful and lonely man. The Piazza Colonna in Rome is called after the Column of Marcus Aurelius, which was set up to commemorate his victories on the Danube (though it has been topped by a statue of St Paul since the seventeenth century); and on the site of the Capitol (Piazza del Campidoglio) stands his magnificent equestrian statue, one of the very few large-scale bronzes to escape the melting-pot. It was preserved because, when it stood by the Lateran church, it was thought to be of the Christian Emperor Constantine, and was moved in 1538 when Michelangelo redesigned the Capitol. It influenced many later statues, notably that of Gattamelata by Donatello in Padua, the first large bronze monument to be cast since Roman times.

Marius, Gaius (157–86 B.C.)

A provincial Italian who made his way by his abilities, Marius defeated the African king Jugurtha in the campaigns described by SALLUST, and also the Celtic tribes threatening north Italy. He reorganized the Roman army on a semi-professional basis, and was active in the so-called Social War against the allied Italian peoples (Latin *socii*). Marius was repeatedly consul, and at one stage in his career was extremely popular. He allied himself with the extreme democrats in Rome and so became the rival of the dictator SULLA. This led to the first of the civil wars between military leaders which ended in the collapse of the Roman Republic. It was a period of history which evidently interested the Greek historian Plutarch, whose *Life* of Marius is full of dramatic detail. It includes the account of Marius's hiding in the Pontine marshes and later escaping from Sulla to Libya, where he was forbidden to land by the governor. His answer to the messenger was 'Tell your master that you have seen Gaius Marius sitting as a fugitive among the ruins of Carthage.'

Mars

The Italian war-god, who in early mythology is also concerned with agriculture; later he was almost completely identified with the Greek ARES. His love for Venus was early established as a subject for artists, and their courtship is shown in an early fresco still in Pompeii. This took on new significance for the Renaissance painters from the later legend that Harmony was born of the union between Love and Strife; hence such pictures as the Botticelli *Venus and Mars*, where his helmet and arms have become playthings for her cupids. There are similar paintings by Piero di Cosimo, Tintoretto, Veronese and Poussin, and *Mars Disarmed by Venus* was the last picture painted by David. Mars was the patron god of the city of Florence, but according to popular legend, when the citizens were converted to Christianity they replaced his temple with a church of St John the Baptist (the present Battistero) and hid his statue in a tower in the Arno. After the town was burnt by the Goth Totila, the broken image was set up on the Ponte Vecchio, where it stood for a long time; or else, according to superstition, Florence could never be rebuilt. Dante refers to this fiction, though he confuses Totila with Attila, and adds that the city's notorious civil troubles were sent by Mars for its faithless treatment of him (*Inferno* 13; *Paradiso* 16). Mars is appropriately linked with Neptune in Venice, in the pair of huge statues at the head of the stairs in the Doges' Palace, the most famous of Jacopo Sansovino's statues.

Marsyas

A flute-player in Phrygia, sometimes called a SILENUS, as representing primitive nature, who took up the flute, which Athene had created and discarded, and presumed to challenge Apollo to a contest to be judged by the Muses. Apollo won, and had Marsyas tied to a tree and flayed alive. Ovid adds that all the woodland gods and animals wept for him and their tears became the river Meander. This is perhaps the cruellest of the many instances of the intolerance of the Olympians towards anyone who challenged their superiority. There was a famous statue-group of Athene and Marsyas by the fifth-century Greek sculptor Myron, known to us from Roman copies, and one of the finest examples of the third-century art of Pergamum is a bearded Marsyas stretched out and bound to await his fate [46]. This formed part of a group of which several copies were known in the Renaissance, when the story of Marsyas gained in significance. For the early Christian moralists he represented no more than vain pride suitably punished, but Apollo's victory later became a symbol of divine harmony triumphing over earthly passions, of light and reason over primitive darkness. Raphael painted Apollo and Marsyas in his series on Apollo in the Vatican, so did Tintoretto, and Titian in his *Flaying of Marsyas.*

The neoplatonist philosophers would also know that in Plato's *Symposium* Socrates was called a Marsyas and a Silenus, and in the *Republic* the flute was spoken of as rousing the dark Dionysian passions, by contrast with Apollo's lyre. It could then be said that Marsyas must suffer initiation into the mysteries of the god and be flayed to find his true inner being. Dante uses the same image in his invocation to Apollo in *Paradiso* I. But the most moving and sympathetic treatment of Marsyas is in the painting by Perugino [36] in the Louvre, where the cool self-confidence of the Olympian emphasizes the simple innocence of the frail figure concentrating on his flute. This is his only listed painting on a classical subject.

Martial (Marcus Valerius Martialis, *c.* A.D. 40–*c.* 104)

Roman poet, writer of epigrams and short poems which range from a sophisticated obscenity to a lyric delicacy or pungent satire. He came from Spain, and retired there after thirty-five years in Roman society, during which his observant eye missed nothing, so that he is now a source of information on contemporary life. His economy of expression, wit and sheer expertise have always delighted, and one of his imitators was Goethe in his *Roman Elegies.* There are also echoes of Martial in the epigrams of Pound's early *Lustra.*

Masinissa

Prince of eastern Numidia, in exile at the time of the Second Punic War, who brought his cavalry to join Scipio Africanus and helped him to defeat the Carthaginians at the battle of Zama. See also SOPHONISBA. He was restored to his kingdom and remained a loyal ally of Rome. The Third Punic War broke out when the Romans intervened on his side after he had provoked the Carthaginians to attack him. He died in 149 B.C. The younger Scipio who recounts SCIPIO'S DREAM gives it a setting in Masinissa's home just before his death as an old man.

Mausolus

Ruler of Caria 377–353 B.C., formally on behalf of Persia, but virtually independent. His expansionist policy led to conflict with Athens and her loss of influence in Rhodes and Cos. His widow, Artemisia, erected the white marble Mausoleum, over 130 feet high, which became one of the Seven Wonders of the ancient world. It collapsed in an earthquake before the fifteenth century, but the site was excavated in the mid nineteenth century and large portions of the frieze, showing the battle of Greeks and Amazons, are in the British Museum. These are the works of the sculptor Scopas, who is famous for his ability to express movement and emotion. Two huge statues with them are usually identified as Mausolus and Artemisia.

Medea

The daughter of Aeëtes, king of Colchis, and generally said to be a priestess of Hecate and a witch. She helped JASON to win the Golden Fleece and returned with him to Iolcos, where she rejuvenated his father Aeson by boiling him with magic herbs. She then encouraged the daughters of his brother Pelias to try to do the same to their father and saw to it that they killed him. This is a variant legend, illustrating her unmotivated wickedness. Jason and Medea fled to Corinth, where he abandoned her for the king's daughter, Glauce or Creusa. Medea destroyed the girl and her father by means of a poisoned robe and diadem, killed her two children, and escaped in a dragon-drawn chariot first to Athens and then to Asia. Pausanias saw the children's tomb at Corinth and discusses the legends about her. Homer does not mention her and Pindar says nothing of her evil nature, but the three great dramatists all wrote plays about her, of which Euripides' *Medea* survives. Here she is a passionate character, tragically aware of the impulses which rule her, and a feminist. Seneca's play emphasizes her witchcraft and savagery; it was the model for Corneille's *Médée*. The story is more romantically treated by APOLLONIUS RHODIUS and in Ovid's *Heroides* and *Metamorphoses*, and it was from Ovid's account that she features both in Gower's *Confessio amantis* and Chaucer's *Legend of Good Women.* Prospero's invocation in *The Tempest* ('Ye elves of hills, brooks . . .') is directly imitated from Golding's translation of Medea's speech in *Metamorphoses* 7. There is a sort of barbaric splendour about Medea as the heroine both of Cherubini's opera and of Jean Anouilh's *Médée*, where the death she chooses is the centre of the short play. The latest treatment of the theme is that of Pasolini in his film, with Maria Callas in the part for which she is famous in the opera.

Meleager

(i) The son of Oeneus, king of Calydon and Althaea, about whom two main legends are told. In *Iliad* 9 he is spoken of as a hero of the past who was persuaded to defend his city and also killed the CALYDONIAN BOAR. In later legend (repeated in Ovid's account) there is an element of popular folktale. Meleager's life was guaranteed by the Fates as long as a firebrand was not burnt. His mother kept this safely until he quarrelled with her brothers after the boar-hunt and killed them. She then threw it into the fire in revenge and Meleager died. Meleager had given the boar's head or skin to ATALANTA, and in some versions had married her. He was also said to be one of the Argonauts.

(ii) Greek poet (*c.* 140–*c.* 70 B.C.) and compiler of the *Garland*, an anthology of short epigrammatic poems and lyrics ranging from those of Archilochus to his own day. It was the basis of the GREEK ANTHOLOGY.

Memnon
The son of Eos (the dawn) and Tithonus, king of Ethiopia. In post-Homeric epic he fought on the Trojan side and was killed by Achilles. A famous cup of about 500 B.C. painted by the Athenian vase-painter Douris shows Eos holding his body. In Egyptian Thebes he was said to have survived the Trojan War and ruled in Ethiopia for five generations. He was identified with one of two seated statues commemorating the Pharaoh Amenophis; this was partially broken by an earthquake about 26 B.C., and then became famous for the musical note, like a breaking lyre-string, which it gave out at sunrise. It was a great attraction for travellers in Roman times, and ceased only when the Emperor Septimius Severus tried to repair it at the end of the second century A.D., and presumably blocked the air-passages which had been affected by change of temperature at dawn. Pausanias mentions birds called Memnonides which gathered annually at his tomb: apparently migrating swifts.

Menander (341–290 B.C.)
The most distinguished author of Greek New Comedy, known to have written over a hundred plays, of which, to date, only one is virtually complete. This is the *Dyscolus* or *Bad-Tempered Man* which was recovered from an Egyptian papyrus as recently as 1958. Since then more substantial fragments have been found (the most important being *The Girl from Samos*), all confirming Menander's skill in drawing humorous or romantic characters and making inventive use of a limited range of plots with stock scenes of disguise and recognition. Through his Roman imitators, Plautus and Terence, he had great influence on the European comedy of manners.

Menelaus
Younger brother of Agamemnon, king of Sparta and husband of Helen; in neither Homeric poem is he a particularly heroic character though he is one of the leaders of the Trojan War and describes his adventures on his return voyage in *Odyssey* 4. In cult and in literature he is always associated with HELEN, and he was worshipped at a shrine of Therapne near Sparta. Theocritus's *Idyll* 18 is a marriage-song for Menelaus and Helen.

Menippus
A slave from Sinope on the Black Sea, living in the first half of the third century B.C., who bought his freedom and came to Thebes where he studied to become a Cynic philosopher. He was the originator of the Menippean Satire, in mixed prose and verse, which influenced PETRONIUS and LUCIAN.

Mentor
The friend and adviser of Odysseus, who is too old to go to Troy and stays behind in Ithaca. Athene takes his form in the *Odyssey* when she accompanies Telemachus on his search for his father. Hence the use of the name for a trusted counsellor.

Mercury
The Roman equivalent of HERMES, who is apparently introduced and given

this name to mark his patronage of merchants and traders; not a native Italian god. He replaces Hermes in Roman accounts of his legends (→ BAUCIS) and has the same attributes of winged hat, shoes and caduceus. As the influence of astrology developed in the Middle Ages Mercury grew in importance; people under the influence of his planet were blessed with a 'mercurial' temperament, lively, inquiring and ingenious. His quickness of movement accounts for the name of the substance mercury, which is sometimes known as quicksilver. Medieval illustrations sometimes show him as a scholar or musician, and for the Renaissance philosophers he was of great importance as a symbol of man's aspiring intellect, the mediator between the human mind and the divine wisdom. He was also the leader of the GRACES as he is in Botticelli's *Primavera* [5] (for which see Introduction p. 27), and in a painting by Tintoretto. Mercury is one of the four figures made by Jacopo Sansovino for the loggetta of St Mark's, Venice, where he has his usual attributes but retains a medieval stiffness. His most famous representation, copied for many fountain-figures, is that of the delicately poised and upward pointing figure in bronze by Giovanni da Bologna in Florence.

Messalina, the Elder

The wife of the Emperor Claudius, mother of Octavia and Britannicus, who was notorious for her profligacy and rightly attacked by Tacitus in his *Annals*. She was put to death for plotting against Claudius after she had gone through a form of marriage with her lover Gaius Silius. See AGRIPPINA.

Messalina, the Younger

The third wife of the Emperor Nero, a woman of personality who continued to hold a high position in Roman society after his death.

'Messianic Eclogue'

This is the fourth of Virgil's ten *Eclogues* or pastoral poems, in which he foretells the birth of a child who will bring peace to the world and a return of the Golden Age. It is uncertain whether this refers to an expected child of Octavian (Augustus) and Scribonia, or of Antony and Octavia, or whether it is wholly imaginary. The imagery recalls that of the prophet Isaiah, and it was largely on the strength of this prophecy that Virgil was thought to be a forerunner of Christianity and a white magician in the Middle Ages. St Augustine for one believed that Virgil was referring to the birth of Jesus, and Dante made him his guide in the *Divine Comedy* as a symbol of inspired wisdom. Two lines of the prophecy are almost literally translated in *Purgatorio* 22. See also SIBYL.

Midas

A king of Phrygia about whom various late legends are told. He had wonderful rose-gardens, in which he once entertained Silenus, who had been left behind drunk by Dionysus's rout, and told Midas marvellous stories of ATLANTIS. When Midas sent him back to Dionysus the god granted Midas's wish that everything he touched should turn to gold.

He soon wanted to be rid of this gift and was then told to bathe in the river Pactolus, whose sands have been golden ever since. Midas also voted against Apollo in a music contest between him and Pan, so in revenge Apollo changed his ears to ass-ears. Only his barber knew the secret, and when he felt he could not keep it he dug a hole and whispered the news into the earth. Unfortunately some reeds sprang up, and when rustled by the breeze they repeated what the barber had said. The main details are all told by Ovid in *Metamorphoses* XI, and may well have suggested the ass's head of Bottom in *A Midsummer Night's Dream*. A drunken Silenus in a garden was a popular subject for paintings, and Poussin has two versions of Midas bathing in the river.

Milon

A famous Greek athlete of the late sixth century B.C. from Croton in south Italy, who was said to have won the wrestling match six times at the Olympic and six times at the Pythian games, and on one occasion to have carried a heifer to the stadium, killed and eaten it in a day. He died eaten by wolves when he was caught in the cleft of a tree he had split open with his bare hands.

Minerva

The Roman goddess of wisdom and the arts, identified with the Greek ATHENE and so also a goddess of war, her worship ousting that of Mars. In post-classical times she is identified much more with prudence and wisdom, though she is still generally shown wearing a helmet, as she does in Mantegna's *Triumph of Wisdom over Vice* where she is routing Venus and her attendant vices. Similarly she supports Diana in Perugino's *Combat of Love and Chastity*.

Minos

An early king of Crete, son of Zeus and Europa, husband of PASIPHAË, about whom there are conflicting legends. Both Homer and Thucydides refer to the tradition of his vast sea-power. Knossos in Crete was said to be his capital city, and since the excavations by Sir Arthur Evans at the palace there, the Bronze Age culture centred in Crete in 1600–1400 B.C. has been called Minoan. Homer also calls him a nine-year king and friend of Zeus, and Plato says that he retired every ninth year to 'the cave of Zeus' to renew his friendship. This suggests identification with the young male god of Crete, whose name and honours the Achaean conquerors usurped. His just administration made him one of the three judges of the Underworld with Aeacus and Rhadamanthys, and this is an accepted myth in the Roman poets. Dante also made him judge in Hell, assigning souls to their proper circle for punishment (*Inferno* 5), and Rodin's famous statue of the Thinker, which was intended to sit above his Gates of Hell, has sometimes been called Minos. On the other hand, in the Attic tradition he makes war on Megara (→ NISUS), and on Athens, and it is he who exacts the annual tribute from Athens after the death of his son Androgeus (→ THESEUS). He also imprisoned DAEDALUS and was said to have been killed when pursuing him to Sicily.

Minotaur

The offspring of a bull sent from the sea by Poseidon and PASIPHAË, wife of Minos, a monstrous creature half man, half bull. Daedalus was said to have made the labyrinth in which to hide it [31.8]. In fact this maze of passages with its pre-Hellenic name is connected with the rite of the *labrys*, the Cretan double-headed axe which features on many of the Minoan frescoes still to be seen, along with 'horns of consecration' and scenes of acrobatic bull-leaping which were also ritual. These may have given rise to the legends of the Athenian boys and girls sent out as annual tribute to Minos, and the killing of the minotaur by the Athenian national hero, Theseus. They have recently been well told in L. Cottrell's *The Bull of Minos* and Mary Renault's novel *The King Must Die*. The minotaur ('*l'infamia di Creti*') (the infamy of Crete) guards the Seventh Circle in Dante's Hell, as a symbol of the brutality and perversion punished there. In a very different way it inspired Picasso's fifteen plates in his *Vollard Suite* of 1930–37 [12], his own creative interpretation of the Minotaur as man's animal nature freed from the restrictions of his analytical intellect. Some ten years later André Gide's *Thésée* appeared with its vivid impressionistic picture of the languors of the Minoan court, a labyrinth of intoxicating pleasure, and a Minotaur of animal beauty and erotic fascination, which recalls the young Tunisian Negroes and their uninhibited charms which for Gide were an escape into paganism. Michael Ayrton has described himself as preoccupied for over twenty years by the labyrinth as a symbol of doubt and perplexity and by the Minotaur struggling to escape from his animal form. At Arkville, New York State, he has designed a vast stone maze around the monumental bronze figures of the Minotaur and Daedalus with Icarus [32].

Minyae, Minyans

A prehistoric people living in parts of Boeotia and Thessaly, associated with the legend of the ARGONAUTS. Their legendary ancestor was Minyas, whose 'treasury' was known at Orchomenus in Pausanias's time. This is in fact a Mycenean beehive tomb; see also ATREUS. 'Grey Minyan' pottery dating from about 2000 B.C. is so called because it was first found at Orchomenus, but it has no connection with the Minyans. The Argonaut story is partly taken from a lost epic *Minyas*.

Misenus

The trumpeter of Aeneas who was drowned by a TRITON and buried on the northern headland of the Bay of Naples (see *Aeneid* 6), which was then called Misenum and is still called Capo Miseno. From the time of AGRIPPA it was the chief station for the Roman fleet. The Elder Pliny was in command there at the time of the eruption of Vesuvius.

Mithras

An Indo-Iranian god whose cult came to Rome in the late Republic and spread throughout the Empire, especially among the army, as it was confined to men. The ritual was secret, carried out in caves or artificially constructed underground chambers, and included seven ceremonies of progressive initiation. Mithras is always depicted with a bull, which he captured and sacrificed; he seems to have undergone a trial of strength with the sun-god and then become identified with the sun. Through his eastern origins he is linked with astrology, but he was seen as a saviour who offered rebirth into an immortal life, and consequently was the one really serious competitor against Christian teaching in the Empire. Altars to Mithras have been found in several places in England where there were garrisons, notably on Hadrian's Wall; and in London a large temple of the mid second century A.D. was found in the City after the bomb-damage of the Second World War. The first reference to the cult in Roman literature is in book I of the *Thebaid* of STATIUS, but the Greeks knew of the worship of Mithras in Persia at least from the time of Herodotus, and the name Mithridates was common. Mithras with a bull appears on the capital of a column in the cloisters in Monreale, Sicily; it has been suggested that it symbolized the ritual slaughter practised by the Jews which the Christian sacraments had replaced.

Mithridates
Several kings of Pontus bore this name, the most famous being Mithridates VI, 'the Great' (120–63 B.C.), against whom the Romans fought three wars before he was finally defeated by Pompey. It was commonly said that he immunized himself against poison by taking repeated small doses; a detail which A. E. Housman characteristically used in a poem as an illustration of his philosophy that life demands that we should 'train for ill and not for good'. He appears to be the Mithridates who gives his name to *Mitridate Re di Ponto*, the opera written by Mozart at the age of fourteen.

Morpheus
In Homer (and Virgil, following Homer) dreams and visions simply pass through the 'Gates of Sleep', one of ivory for dreams which are false, one of horn for dreams which are true. The personification of Morpheus as one of the sons of the god of sleep (HYPNOS), and himself as the god who sends dreams and visions of human forms, is best known from Ovid's famous description of the Cave of Sleep in *Metamorphoses* II, from which Sleep sends Morpheus to ALCYONE in the form of her drowned husband. Morpheus who gathers the sleeping into his arms is then a commonplace of poetry. →→ LETHE.

Moschus
Greek pastoral poet from Syracuse, writing about 150 B.C. *The Lament for Bion*, which is traditionally said to be one of his few surviving poems, is wrongly attributed, as Bion lived a generation later, and the *Europa and the Bull* may not be his either; this tells not only the story of EUROPA in engaging detail but incorporates other myths in the description of the decorations on her flower-basket, a typical Alexandrian conceit.

Mummius Achaicus, Lucius
(died *c.* 141 B.C.)
The Roman general who finally brought Greece under Roman rule. He dissolved the Achaean League of resistance, and sacked and destroyed the splendid city of Corinth, shipping all its movable treasures to Italy. The city's epitaph was written by a contemporary poet and is one of the best short poems in the *Greek Anthology* (9.151). Corinth was refounded in 44 B.C. as the capital of the Roman province of Achaea.

Where is your fabled Doric beauty, the
  fringe
of your towers, Corinth, your ancient
  properties,
the temples of gods and men's homes,
the women of the city of Sisyphus
and your onetime countless inhabitants?

There is no trace of you left.
War crushed and gorged it all.
We who remain, the Nereids, daughters
  of Ocean, we alone are unravished –
as kingfishers, sole tenants of your
  affliction.
Antipater of Sidon, translated by Peter Jay.

Muses
Following Hesiod's account in his *Theogony*, there is general agreement in antiquity that the Muses were nine in number, the daughters of Zeus and Mnemosyne ('memory'). They were born in Pieria at the foot of Mount Olympus, and Mount Helicon in Boeotia was also sacred to them; that is where they gave Hesiod his knowledge and gift of song. Sometimes such a gift was at a cost; Demodocus at the court of ALCINOUS in the *Odyssey* had been blinded by a Muse and then given something better, the gift of song, because she loved him. Thamyris is mentioned in the *Iliad* as a musician of Thrace who challenged the Muses to a contest; for his presumption he was blinded and his power of song removed. The Muses also judged the contest between Apollo and MARSYAS. Hesiod also names them, but their specialities were not distinguished until later, Roman times. Each one then presides over one of the arts or sciences: Calliope (heroic epic), Clio (history), Euterpe (flutes and music), Terpsichore (lyric poetry and dancing), Erato (hymns), Melpomene (tragedy), Thalia (comedy), Polyhymnia (mime), Urania (astronomy). (These attributions can vary.) As embodiments of the highest intellectual and artistic benefits to man, they are naturally presided over by Apollo (as they are in Raphael's great painting of Parnassus) and they are common in poetry and art of all periods. Plato and Aristotle considered that in their teaching they cultivated the Muses, and a Museum originally meant a 'place of the Muses'; the famous Museum of Alexandria, founded by the Ptolemies in the third century B.C. housed a great library and was a centre of scholarship and research.

Plato speaks of 'possession by the Muses' as a form of 'divine madness' necessary for poets, and this concept of an inspired poet as a man apart has had a long history; 'the poet's eye in a fine frenzy rolling' is still with us, though a practical critic like Horace (*Art of Poetry* 295 ff.) is quick to point out that eccentricity (which in his day meant an aversion to the barber and the public baths) does not make a poet.

Narcissus

In a late Greek legend Narcissus was a beautiful boy, the son of a nymph, who fell in love with his own reflection in a pool. He took no notice of ECHO, who died for love of him; eventually he too pined away and died, and was changed into the flower (though the Greek narcissus is not certainly identified; cf. Hyacinthus). Pausanias saw the spring and pool of Narcissus on Mount Helicon, and roundly declared that the story was nonsense. He preferred a local variant that Narcissus had been in love with his twin sister who died, and looked at his reflection to remind himself of her. Narcissus and Echo are well known from Ovid, and were used in the Middle Ages to point the moral of the fate that awaits vanity, but it was the pathos of his end which touched painters as different as Caravaggio, Tintoretto, Claude and Turner, and particularly Poussin, who painted Narcissus with Echo and more than one version of the dead boy. Cellini's statue [38] shows him sitting on the edge of his pool and was for a long time in the Boboli Gardens, Florence. Milton too could use the imagery of Ovid to describe Eve seeing her own beauty in a pool in Eden (*Paradise Lost* 4.449 ff.) and convey her innocence. As a psychological term, narcissism means a self-fixation.

Nausicaa

In the *Odyssey*, the daughter of Alcinous, king of Phaeacia, the heroine of a particularly human and charming episode. She has done the family washing in the river-mouth and is playing ball with her maids when Odysseus appears after his shipwreck. She receives him with dignity, when her maids run from his nakedness, gives him food and clothing, and takes him home to her father; and rather sadly sees him sent on his way home to his wife. Samuel Butler argued that she was the real authoress of the *Odyssey*, a notion which has had some support from Robert Graves.

Nemesis

In mythology a minor goddess or nymph who was worshipped at Rhamnus in Attica; and in one version of the birth of Helen she laid the egg which was hatched by LEDA. In Boeotia she also had a cult under the name of Nemesis Adrasteia ('unescapable'). It is not clear how this is connected, if at all, with the more general concept of Nemesis as the personification of retribution, especially the indignation of the gods when men show signs of *hubris*, or presumption. There were devices to avert Nemesis, common to many branches of folklore: for example, spitting. The word is still used for an act of retributive justice. Dürer's strange picture of Nemesis as a winged female treading the clouds above a rural landscape is heavily symbolic, and owes more to Renaissance allegory than to any classical allusion.

Neoptolemus (Pyrrhus)

The son of ACHILLES and DEIDAMIA. Homer says he was sent for after his father's death, was present at the sack of Troy, and was one of the Greeks who entered the city in the Wooden Horse. He returned home safely and married Menelaus's daughter, Hermione. In later legend he goes to fetch PHILOCTETES; and he brings away ANDROMACHE as part of his booty, and incurs the anger of the gods by killing King Priam at the altar of Zeus; he is also given the alternative name Pyrrhus. This is the version followed by Virgil in *Aeneid* 2. In revenge the gods prevented his homecoming, and he was said either to have been killed in a brawl with the priests at Delphi, or to have travelled north to the territory of the Molossi in Epirus. In historic times the Molossi claimed descent from his son by Andromache, Molossus, and his name was borne by the historic PYRRHUS.

Neptune (Neptunus)

The Italian god of water, later identified with the Greek god of the sea, Poseidon, and given the same attributes of a trident and a shell-shaped chariot drawn by sea-horses. He had a festival in Rome in August, and his cult was widespread, though the great Doric 'Temple of Neptune' at Paestum (Pesto in Campania) is now known to be a temple of Hera. He is common as a decorative feature of mosaics and reliefs; there is a good example dated *c.* A.D. 200, a marble relief of ships in the harbour of Ostia with Neptune and his trident in the centre. In post-classical times Neptune was a popular figure in medieval pageantry, something of which has lingered on in the curious ritual performed on ships crossing the equator. He was also a natural subject for the splendid Renaissance and baroque fountains of Italy. Perhaps the most famous of these are the Neptune fountain by Giovanni da Bologna in Bologna, another by Ammanati in the Piazza della Signoria, Florence, and Bernini's Trevi fountain in Rome, though there are noble Neptunes in fountains in the Piazza Navona and Piazza del Popolo. He reclines holding his trident and facing a nymph who represents earth on the celebrated gold salt-cellar which Cellini made for François I and which is now in Vienna, and Bernini's *Neptune and Triton* is one of the most splendid acquisitions of the Victoria and Albert Museum, London [39].

Nereus, Nereids

A primitive sea-god, known to Homer and Hesiod, and said to be endowed with wisdom and the gift of prophecy. He is the father of fifty or even a hundred daughters, the Nereids, the most famous of whom are Amphitrite, wife of Poseidon, and Thetis, mother of Achilles. He appears as a benign old man on early vases, and is shown on the François Vase bringing gifts for the wedding of THETIS with PELEUS. The Nereids with their floating, flowing forms and draperies were ideal subjects for decorative art from the fourth century onwards. The Nereid Monument of Xanthus in Lycia takes the form of a small Ionic temple on a high base, called after the figures of Nereids between its columns. They feature in the Hellenistic mosaics at Olynthus, in Pompeian wall-paintings, and on the famous Mildenhall Dish of the fourth century A.D., a masterpiece of embossed silver with marine scenes in its centre [3]. Nereids were also commonly carved on the sides of Roman sarcophagi, as symbolizing the passage of the soul into another element; these were well known in later times, as they were often taken over for use in Christian churches. Scenes such as the birth of Eve on the doors of Orvieto Cathedral or on Ghiberti's bronze doors of the Baptistery in Florence have been traced to the influence of the Nereid rhythmic form.

Nero (Nero Claudius Caesar, Roman Emperor A.D. 54–68)

The last of the Julio-Claudian line, Nero owed his position largely to the intrigues of his mother AGRIPPINA. He was tutored by the philosopher SENECA, and his enthusiasm for art, music and the stage seems to have been genuine. His philhellenism certainly shocked Roman puritans. But his vanity and jealous fears drove him to persecution and murder, even to matricide; see also OCTAVIA, POPPAEA. He alienated his subjects, and when the armies of the Rhine provinces revolted, Nero committed suicide, with the words *Qualis artifex pereo* ('What an artist dies in me'). Rumour also said when the great fire of 64 destroyed half Rome that Nero had started it himself and tried to fix the blame on the Christians, though the story that he 'fiddled while Rome burned' is certainly apocryphal. Nero's colourful personality led to rumours that he had not really died, and more than one 'false Nero' is mentioned by the historian Tacitus as being seen in the eastern provinces. His *Life* by Suetonius is full of scandalous personal detail which makes it hard to assess him fairly. After the Fire of Rome Nero built his famous Golden House (*domus aurea*) on an extravagant scale in a royal park overlooking an ornamental lake, later filled in and covered by the Colosseum; in its forecourt stood a huge statue of himself as the sun-god. Parts of this were excavated in Renaissance times to give a glimpse of its paintings on walls and ceilings in classical architectural style, with panels showing mythological scenes, and had considerable influence on architects and painters in Italy. See also VESPASIAN.

Nerva (Marcus Cocceius Nerva, Roman Emperor A.D. 96–8)

On the murder of Domitian, Nerva was elected emperor by the senate for his aristocratic and conservative background and impeccable character. He was already in his sixties, and lacked both administrative experience and the necessary authority over the army. He therefore adopted Trajan as his official successor to give him support. His short reign was marked by a return to more humanitarian administration and the beginning of a system of poor relief for needy citizens.

Nessus

The centaur who assaulted DEIANIRA and was killed by Heracles; the blood which soaked his garment was later to kill Heracles, and a 'shirt of Nessus' became proverbial for a fatal gift. Nessus is with the centaurs in the Seventh Circle of Dante's Hell (cf. the MINOTAUR) and is told by Chiron to guide the way to the ford over the river Phlegethon and carry Dante across.

Nestor

Homer identifies Nestor as King of Pylos in the western Peloponnese. In the *Iliad* he is old and respected, full of advice and reminiscences, and the father of ANTILOCHUS. In the *Odyssey* he is back in his palace and entertains Telemachus. He seldom appears in post-Homeric literature. Three places were called Pylos in historic times, and the grave which Pausanias saw as Nestor's was not at the one now thought to be Nestor's city. There a huge Mycenean palace has been excavated and numbers of clay tablets found, inscribed with the Linear B script. The 'Cup of Nestor' in Athens, a Mycenean vase of beaten gold with winged doves on its two handles, is so called because it is a less elaborate example of the type of great gold cup described in *Iliad* 11, which Nestor had brought with him from Pylos.

Nicias (*c.* 470–413 B.C.)

Athenian politician and general, responsible for the armistice between Athens and Sparta half-way through the Peloponnesian War (the Peace of Nicias) and then, against his better judgement, one of the leaders of the ill-fated Athenian expedition to Sicily. After defeat in the naval battle in the harbour of Syracuse Nicias tried to lead his troops into the interior, but they were cut off and captured. Nicias was executed and the survivors died painfully in the quarries of Syracuse. He was admired for his moderation and honesty by Thucydides and by Plutarch, though his ill-health and lack of confidence contributed largely to the failure of the enterprise.

Niobe

The daughter of Tantalus, king of Sipylus in Lydia, and wife of Amphion, king of Thebes, by whom she had an equal number of sons and daughters – six of each, according to Homer, nine or ten in other versions, and seven in Ovid's account. She boasted that she was superior to LETO, who had only two children, Apollo and Artemis; Leto then sent her divine pair to kill all the children of Niobe, and in some versions, her husband too. Niobe wept for nine days and nights, and then the Olympians buried the bodies and Niobe was turned into a great stone, still dripping tears, on Mount Sipylus. This was near the birthplace of Pausanias, who had seen the crag but judged it a natural formation. Niobe's story is told as common knowledge in *Iliad* 24 by Achilles to Priam to indicate that even grief such as hers and Priam's must pause for rest and food. It is a good example of the NEMESIS which follows hubris. Niobe weeping and the Niobids, or children of Niobe, were popular subjects for Hellenistic sculptors, and there are many extant Roman copies. Michelangelo's unfinished *Captives* owe something to them, and their death was also the subject of a classical painting by David. Niobe has remained a symbol of grief; Byron, for instance, spoke of the Italy of his day as 'the Niobe of Nations'.

Nisus

(i) A king of Megara whose life along with the fortunes of his realm depended on a lock of his hair, which was red. (There are many variants on this theme, the best known being that of the biblical hero, Samson.) This was cut off by his daughter, Scylla, for love of King Minos of Crete, who was besieging Megara. Nisus was turned into a sea-eagle, Scylla into a bird called a ciris. The legend is told in a poem (*Ciris*) wrongly attributed to Virgil, and by Ovid in the *Metamorphoses*.

(ii) A young Trojan prince who was killed in a raid on the Latin camp along with his close friend, Euryalus, in a tragic episode described in *Aeneid* 9.

Numa Pompilius

The second king of Rome, successor to Romulus, who is semi-mythical but traditionally the founder of the Roman religious system and the calendar. He was believed to have been guided by the Italian goddess EGERIA. His reforms are described by Plutarch and by Livy in the first book of his history of Rome.

Nymphs

Spirits of nature in Greek mythology, often worshipped in caves or woods (dryads or hamadryads) or by springs (naiads), and always represented as beautiful young girls. Their cult was widespread and continued into Roman times; the earliest mention is in Homer, when Odysseus is brought back to Ithaca and left sleeping in a cave of the nymphs or naiads, to whom he offers thanks on waking. Sometimes they are called daughters of Zeus and can inspire men with prophetic power, or they are attendants of Hermes or Pan and join the followers of Dionysus. From their associations with wild nature they can be as hurtful to mortals as the fairies of any folklore; they blind Daphnis, drown Hylas, destroy Hermaphroditus. They are often the victims of the passions of gods or men; Daphne, Echo and Eurydice are all nymphs. From Homer onwards they frequently appear in art and literature, and in the Arcadia of romance they are traditionally linked with shepherds. They are so common as secondary figures in post-Renaissance paintings that it is difficult to particularize, but one of the most famous nymphs is the bronze *Nymph of Fontainebleau* made by Cellini for François I as a lunette for the gateway of the palace, now in the Louvre, Paris. A 'sleeping nymph' is also common from Hellenistic times onwards, and there is a particularly attractive one by a fountain by Lucas Cranach [28].

A Nymphaeum was a Hellenistic contribution to fountain architecture, and was originally a city fountain which was not connected with any temple and dedicated only to water-nymphs. Nymphaea were then built into wealthy homes, and there are examples from Herculaneum and Pompeii which are richly decorated with statues and mosaics. There is a sixteenth-century example in the Villa Giulia, Rome, and they were popular in the eighteenth-century 'grottoes' of English houses.

Oceanus

In early mythology Oceanus is much more an element than a personality; in

Homer he is the river which encircles the whole world and in which the sun and stars rise and set, and is depicted on the shield made for Achilles by Hephaestus as the rim running round it. Hesiod makes him the son of Uranus and Ge (sky and earth) and through his wife, Tethys, he is the father of the sea and the river gods. He is never fully personalized, as Poseidon and Neptune are, and he appears as a character only in Aeschylus's *Prometheus Bound*, preaching submission to the lawful authority of Zeus. The geographers rationalized him into the ocean in the usual sense, but in Roman times he was often represented as a bearded god on sarcophagi. He is the 'Marforio' of the Piazza del Campidoglio and appears on a huge mosaic of the second century A.D. from Carthage, now in the British Museum.

Octavia

(i) The sister of Octavian (Augustus), wife of Mark Antony, and mother by a former husband of the young MARCELLUS. Antony divorced her in 32 B.C., thus finally severing his relations with the future emperor. Octavia was generally admired for her loyalty and devotion, though Shakespeare's Enobarbus describes her in contrast with Cleopatra as 'of a holy, cold and still conversation'. She appears briefly in the play, and plays a larger part in Dryden's *All for Love*.

(ii) The daughter of the Emperor Claudius and Messalina, married to Nero in A.D. 53, and divorced by him in 62 so that he could marry POPPAEA. She was banished first to Campania and then to the island of Pandateria where she was executed on a false charge of treason. She is the heroine of the Latin tragedy *Octavia* which deals with the events of 62, the only extant Latin play on a contemporary subject. It is usually printed with Seneca's tragedies, though it is certainly not by him.

Odysseus (Roman **Ulixes** or **Ulysses**)

There are three main interpretations of this complex character of mythology, two ancient and one medieval, all of which have had later influence. The Homeric Odysseus is the son of Laertes, king of Ithaca (modern Leucadia), husband of Penelope and father of Telemachus, one of the heroes of the Trojan War. In the *Iliad* he is sensible, enterprising and courageous. He is chosen with Ajax and Phoenix to take Agamemnon's offer of reconciliation to Achilles; he and Diomedes carry out the night raid on the Trojan camp (→ RHESUS); he wins the foot race in the funeral games of Patroclus. He is the hero of the *Odyssey*, that skilful amalgam of epic and folktale, where he is the 'man of many devices', resourceful in crisis, eager for new experiences, but at heart loyal to his wife. Homer says explicitly that he was unable to resist Calypso and Circe because they are goddesses; from Nausicaa, who is clearly attracted to him, he politely withdraws. His thoughts are firmly fixed on his homecoming, and he is reunited with Penelope after an absence of twenty years and all his adventures and tribulations; see AEOLUS, LAESTRYGONIANS, CYCLOPES, SCYLLA, SIRENS. He has a reputation for cunning, but he does nothing seriously deceitful, unlike his biblical counterpart, Jacob; and though he enjoys telling a tall story, he generally lies out of necessity, never with malice. This heroic concept of Odysseus is reflected in later treatments like the character in Shakespeare's *Troilus and Cressida*, in Monteverdi's opera *Il ritorno d'Ulisse in patria*, in scenes from the *Odyssey* painted by Piero di Cosimo, and in the series of baroque tapestries designed by Jordaens. He is also a symbol of safe return, as he is in du Bellay's famous sonnet ('*Heureux qui, comme Ulysse, a fait un beau voyage* ...').

In non-Homeric epic fragments he begins to show signs of being a rascal, and the Greek dramatists mistrusted his versatility and blackened his character. In the extant plays he is magnanimous only in Sophocles' *Ajax*. He is the diplomat chosen to persuade PHILOCTETES, and proves to be a lying scoundrel who tries to corrupt the young Neoptolemus. He is callously cruel to Euripides' HECUBA and refuses to spare the life of her daughter Polyxena. In fifth-century Athens his image as a 'sacker of cities' was unpopular, and he exhibited the worst qualities of the unscrupulous among the sophists. For the Romans he was probably associated with the quick-witted Levantine Greeks whom they instinctively disliked, and even the Homeric Odysseus showed a marked lack of the sterner virtues they admired. In Virgil's account of the fall of Troy, Odysseus is presented as the man who had no scruples about stealing the PALLADIUM, and the traitor SINON tells a plausible tale of how Palamedes had been executed on a charge of treason invented by Odysseus/Ulysses. The epic writers Dares and DICTYS, who set out to rival Homer, showed him in the same light, and their influence on the western view of Ulysses lasted throughout the Middle Ages, especially as the British believed themselves descended from the mythical Trojan BRUTUS. He is an unprincipled rogue in the *Tale of Troy*, and in *Confessio amantis* Gower makes him out a magician, taught by Calypso and Circe. The Oxford Dictionary under the rare epithet 'ulyssean' gives 'resembling Ulysses in craft or deceit'. This on the whole is the predominant view of him taken by the modern French writers who emphasize his chameleon-like character: in Giono's *Naissance de l'Odyssée* he is an old ruffian who invents most of his adventures to account for his years spent with other women; he is adept at 'making the worse appear the better reason' in Giraudoux's *La guerre de Troie n'aura pas lieu*; and a cynical perverter of the truth in Gide's *Philoctète*.

The third aspect of Odysseus/Ulysses is foreshadowed in the curious prophecy of TIRESIAS given to him in *Odyssey* II, in the Underworld. He will return to Ithaca, but must set out again on his travels, carrying an oar, until he reaches a people who eat unsalted food, know nothing of boats and take the oar for a winnowing-fan. He must set up the oar as a monument, offer appeasing sacrifices to Poseidon, and then return home, where death from the sea will come upon him in old age. The suggestion of further travels was taken up in a lost epic, the *Telegony*, but the idea of

Ulysses as the perpetual wanderer starts with Dante. In *Inferno* 26 Ulysses and Diomedes are found among the Counsellors of Fraud, consumed by the twin flame (→ STATIUS). Ulysses is perhaps also punished for his curiosity about forbidden things, for which Dante feels a paradoxical admiration. In a passage of wonderful poetry Dante offers what seems to be entirely his own interpretation of Ulysses' end, though he may have known of the voyages of the Celtic saints like St Brendan. Ulysses and a few companions sail out beyond the Pillars of Hercules to 'gain experience of the world and of human worth and vice'; he tells his men

fatti non foste a viver come bruti
ma per seguir virtute e conoscenza.

(You were not made to live like brutes, but to follow virtue and knowledge.) On they sail, until they have a vision of Mount Purgatory; then the storm breaks and the ship goes down. This, of course, is the Ulysses of one of Tennyson's greatest poems, and it leads to the conception of Ulysses as the wanderer in search of knowledge and the seeker for the truth of his own identity which reappears in the poetry of Cavafy and Seferis, and in the Epilogue of Dallapiccola's opera *Ulysses*. It is the inspiration of the vast *Odyssey* of Nikos Kazantzakis, which carries on from where Homer leaves off. Odysseus travels all over the world as king, soldier, lover and pilgrim, always meeting with failure; he tries to found a world-city in Africa, he ends in Antarctica (symbolic of his isolation) in his search for self-knowledge:

Then flesh dissolved, glances congealed,
 the heart's pulse stopped,
and the great mind leapt to the peak of
 its holy freedom,
fluttered with empty wings, then
 upright through the air
soared high and freed itself from its
 last cage, its freedom.
All things like frail mist scattered till
 but one brave cry
for a brief moment hung in the calm
 benighted waters:
'Forward, my lads, sail on, for Death's
 breeze blows in a fair wind!'
(Translated by Kimon Friar)

Kazantzakis's Odysseus is a rejector of life and ends in a negation which perhaps speaks for our times, but some fifteen years earlier James Joyce's *Ulysses* had appeared with a hero who is cast in the Homeric mould. Leopold Bloom as a Jew may be detached from his fellows to some extent, but he is a character of warm and positive vitality who embraces life, and his journey through Dublin on that memorable 16 June 1904 is homewards. Joyce comes at the end of a line which started with PETRONIUS, whose *Satyricon* follows the same Odyssey pattern, and nearly every character and image in his novel is derived from Homer's epic. At an obvious level, for example, the brothel is Circe's cave, and Bella Cohen is Circe; the restaurant which disgusts Mr Bloom represents the cannibal Laestrygonians; the Citizen who hurls the biscuit tin is Polyphemus; and of course Molly Bloom is Penelope, and Stephen Dedalus, with whom Bloom comes to feel spiritual kinship, stands for Telemachus and the son he wants. But the analogy goes much deeper than this, and no novel has been so much discussed; nor is anything in the future likely to influence our interpretation of Odysseus to the extent that *Ulysses* does.

Oedipus ('Swollen-foot')
In the *Odyssey* Oedipus is mentioned as the son of Laius, king of Thebes, who had the misfortune, through ignorance, to marry his mother; when the truth came out, she hanged herself, but he continued to reign in Thebes; see JOCASTA. The *Iliad* adds briefly that he was eventually killed in battle and buried with military honours. There is no mention of an oracle. It was doubtless the lost epic *Thebais* which was the source for the later concept of Oedipus as a polluted outcast, burdened with his guilt, and also for the working out of the curse on the House of Labdacus. Laius had been warned by Apollo's oracle that the son born to Jocasta would kill him. The baby was therefore exposed on Mount Cithaeron, with its ankles pierced by a long pin, but was rescued by a shepherd from Corinth who took him to his king, Polybus. Oedipus was brought up in Corinth as son and heir to Polybus. He was taunted for resembling neither of his parents and went to Delphi for reassurance. The oracle told him he would kill his father and marry his mother, so he decided not to return to Corinth. He travelled alone towards Thebes, met Laius at a narrow crossroads, and killed him. He went on to Thebes, rid the people of the SPHINX [9]; was acclaimed king and married Laius's widow, his mother. Their four children were ANTIGONE, Ismene, ETEOCLES and Polynices. Some years later, Thebes suffered from a plague which the oracle said could only be removed if the murderer of Laius was driven out of the country. This is the point at which Sophocles' *King Oedipus* begins. By his resolute investigations Oedipus finds out the truth, blinds himself in horror, and is led into exile by Antigone. He reaches Colonus in Attica after years of wandering, is given sanctuary by Theseus of Athens, and mysteriously disappears in a sacred grove – the theme of Sophocles' *Oedipus at Colonus*, a play which had great influence on Shelley and W. B. Yeats, and is the basis of Eliot's last verse drama, *The Elder Statesman*. His curse on his sons for trying to force him back to Thebes is worked out in the duel between them and the fate of Antigone.

Sophocles' *King Oedipus* was the model for Seneca's tragedy, which in its turn inspired Corneille, but the fascination of the myth for recent writers is largely due to Freud's interpretation. He gave the name 'Oedipus complex' to the repressed hostility of the boy-child towards his father as a rival for the affection of his mother, which can result in a mother-fixation in later life. Cocteau's *The Infernal Machine*, and his Latin *Oedipus-Rex* (the libretto for the 'opera oratorio' by Stravinsky), the free adaptation of Seneca's play by the poet Ted Hughes, and Pasolini's film *Oedipus Rex* are only some of the variants on the theme. The most individual interpretation is that of Gide, in his play *Oedipe*, and in Oedipus's meeting with Theseus in *Thésée*. The incest is of secondary interest, and Oedipus is a symbol of man' s ambition to be independent of accepted gods and tradition (for which Tiresias and Creon speak). Yet it is only when blinded that he sees that there may be riddles for which Man has not the answer.

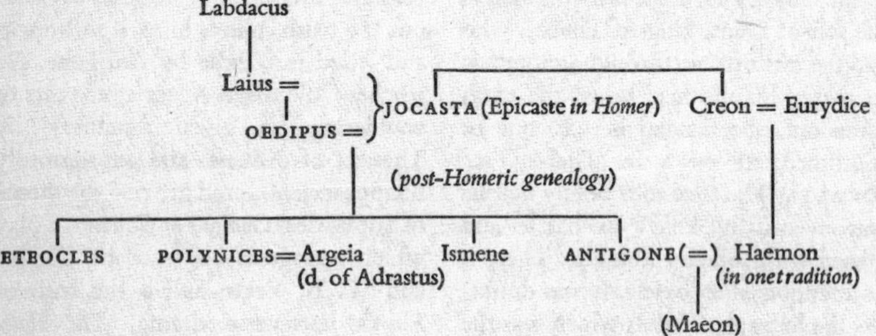

Oenone

A nymph of Mount Ida who was deserted by her lover PARIS for Helen. She was bitterly jealous and refused to help him when he was fatally wounded in the Trojan War. Then she killed herself in remorse. This is a late legend in Greece which inspired one of Ovid's *Heroides*, and which also seems to have captured Victorian imagination. Oenone is best remembered from Tennyson's *Oenone*, and her story is also told by William Morris in *The Earthly Paradise*.

Olympus

The highest mountain in Greece, on the borders of Macedonia and Thessaly, which in mythology was believed to reach the sky and to be the home of the gods. The Olympian gods (sometimes called the Twelve Olympians) are the main deities introduced by the northern invaders (→ DORIANS) in a patriarchal system which replaced the old pre-Greek chthonic gods; e.g. ERECHTHEUS and PYTHON.

Orbilius, Lucius

A teacher and grammarian in Augustan Rome whose best-known pupil was the poet Horace. He is remembered chiefly as a flogger (*plagosus*) from Horace's *Epistles*, but is also known to have written satire on contemporary society.

Orestes

The son of Agamemnon and Clytemnestra, Orestes is generally agreed to have killed his mother's lover Aegisthus in revenge for his killing of AGAMEMNON. Homer does not say that he also killed his mother, but implies it. He gives no details, simply saying that Aegisthus reigned for seven years in Argos until Orestes returned from exile in Athens and performed a praiseworthy act of vengeance. The version followed by the three dramatists was probably taken from the lost *Oresteia* of STESICHORUS. Orestes is smuggled out of the country by his sister Electra and brought up by the king of Phocis, whose son, Pylades, becomes his close companion. In Aeschylus's trilogy the emphasis is on the working out of the curse on the House of Pelops, and on Orestes' feelings of guilt and remorse and his being haunted by the ERINYES, or Furies. Pursued by them he flees to Delphi and is told to return to Athens, where he is tried and absolved by the homicide court of the Areopagus. Pausanias saw an altar there which Orestes was said to have set up in gratitude for his acquittal, and in Aeschylus the goddess Athene appears on the stage to calm the Furies and settle them in a shrine with the beneficent title of Eumenides; thus Olympian justice triumphed over the old chthonic deities of blood-guilt and vengeance. In Sophocles and Euripides the Furies do not appear, and are the imagined phantoms of his conscience; the interest moves to the contrasted characters of Orestes and Electra. Euripides also follows the variant that Orestes could only be freed from his self-torment if he brought to Greece the statue of Artemis from the country of the Tauri; see IPHIGENIA. There was a cult of this statue in Attica; but it was shown to Pausanias in Sparta. He also saw the tomb where Orestes' bones lay after they had been brought to Sparta in the mid sixth century at the bidding of an oracle. Both dramatists make Orestes a weak character dominated by ELECTRA, and this is how he appears in modern versions of the drama.

Orpheus

The greatest singer and musician conceived by the Greeks, son of the Muse Calliope by either a king of Thrace or Apollo; said to be the founder of the mystic cult of Orphism. Apollo gave him a lute with which he was able to charm wild beasts and make rocks and trees move. He sailed with the Argonauts and was able to help them, by his music, through the Clashing Rocks and past the Sirens. On his return he married EURYDICE. When he descended to Hades to recover her after her death he could charm Cerberus and make the damned forget their tortures, and so moved Dis and Persephone that they allowed her to leave. Then when he lost her he wandered about Thrace singing of his love until he was torn to pieces by women, either Thracians who were infuriated by jealousy of Eurydice, or by maenad followers of Dionysus because he failed to honour the god; the latter version was the subject of a lost play by Aeschylus. In later legend the Muses collected and buried his fragments, but his head, still singing, and his lyre floated out to sea to Lesbos, the seat of lyric music, where they were dedicated to Apollo: a subject symbolic of the artist's immortality for the French painters Moreau and Redon.

What could the Muse herself that
  Orpheus bore,
The Muse herself, for her enchanting son,
Whom universal nature did lament,
When, by the rout that made the
  hideous roar,
His gory visage down the stream was
  sent,
Down the swift Hebrus to the Lesbian
  shore?

Milton: *Lycidas*

Orphism adopted him as its founder as early as the seventh century B.C., and there were many poems and oracles purporting to be by him, though the *Orphic Hymns* date from later, Roman times. Gold leaves found in tombs in south Italy dating from the Hellenistic age contain verses which were to be spoken by initiates on entry into the Underworld, which in Orphic teaching was thought of as a place of punishment leading to the soul's purification. The idea that the soul could find freedom only by separation from the body is also found in Plato and in Virgil. Orpheus with his lute and Orpheus's love for Eurydice are themes for poets and musicians of all periods. To the examples listed under the name of Eurydice can be added the *Elégies* of the French romantic poet André Chénier, the poems of the French Parnassians, and Rilke's *Sonnets to Orpheus*, where the recurrent image is that of the poet who communicates what is silent and unites what is divided. Perhaps the most evocative of all poems on the theme is Rilke's *Orpheus, Eurydice, Hermes.*

Otho, Marcus Salvius

He succeeded Galba as Roman emperor for a few months in A.D. 69, 'the year of the four emperors', until his army was defeated near Cremona by the legions of the Rhine under Vitellius. Tacitus, Suetonius and Plutarch all describe him as dissolute and incompetent.

Ovid (Publius Ovidius Naso
43 B.C.–A.D. 17/18)

Roman poet and one of the leading figures in Roman society until he was banished by Augustus in A.D. 8 to Tomis (Costanza), a frontier town on the Black Sea inhabited by a mixed Greek and native people and subject to raids from the Scythian tribes beyond the Danube. There he continued to write his *Elegies* (*Tristia*) and his *Letters from Exile* (*Epistulae ex Ponto*), always hoping for the recall which never came. Exactly why he was exiled is not known, but Ovid says himself that the reasons were a poem and an 'error'. The poem was the witty and sophisticated *Art of Love* (*Ars amatoria*) which led to Ovid's works being banned from the public libraries of Rome, and the blunder which he never disclosed was probably connected with some scandal involving the emperor's daughter Julia, who was also banished. In *Tristia* 2 Ovid significantly compares his fate with Actaeon's:

Actaeon saw Diana's nakedness
By chance; his hounds devoured him
none the less.

Ovid was a prolific writer of polished and lucid verse and can often achieve a delicacy of description which lights up a scene and makes it memorable. He was genuinely sensitive to beauty in nature and has a sense of colour and visual form which is rare in the ancient world. This is one reason why he has been so popular with painters, who have often copied his details exactly; e.g., EUROPA or DAPHNE. Delacroix in his painting of *Ovid among the Scythians* also brings in the fact mentioned in the *Tristia* that they drink mares' milk.

As well as the notorious *Ars amatoria*, Ovid wrote a *Remedium amoris* on how to end a love-affair, a series of short love-poems (*Amores*), and the *Heroides*, verse letters from the women of myth or history to their absent lovers and husbands. The *Fasti* was planned as a poetical calendar of the Roman year, but only the first six months were finished before Ovid left Rome. Some early work and a tragedy, *Medea*, are lost, some poems are doubtfully attributed to him, but the work which brought him immediate fame was the *Metamorphoses*, in fifteen books, a sort of encyclopedia of over 200 legends involving changes of shape, all woven into a continuous narrative poem of great variety. No other classical work has had such influence on European artists. There are innumerable pictures on individual subjects as well as tapestries on mythological scenes from the fifteenth century onwards, and several series by the great painters. There are the scenes in the panels on the borders of the bronze doors of St Peter's, Rome, the decorations in the palaces of Fontainebleau and Sans Souci, a series of 112 subjects which Rubens designed for Philip IV of Spain, a splendid series of drawings by Poussin now in Windsor Castle, and thirty illustrations for the *Metamorphoses* by Picasso published in 1931.

The same book is known to have been favourite reading in their youth for people as widely different as Chaucer, Montaigne, Wordsworth and Goethe. Chaucer says in *The House of Fame* that he had his own copy, and that 'Venus clerke, Ovyde' is his inspiration both here and in the *Legend of Good Women*, which draws largely from the *Heroides*. Ovid is one of the four great poets in Dante who greet Virgil and Dante on their entry into Hell. He also acquired great reputation in the Middle Ages in his native town of Sulmo (Salmona in the Abruzzi) as a wizard, and tales of the magical powers of 'Uiddie' survive in local folklore. For the writers of the Renaissance it was certain that 'Ovidius Naso was the man'. The first printed Ovid dates from 1471, and William Golding's English translation was published in 1567 and had immediate influence on Marlowe, Spenser and Shakespeare (→ HERO; ADONIS; MEDEA; PYRAMUS).

But for those who felt the need to interpret Ovid's pagan legends symbolically, an even greater influence was the anonymous French poem of the early fourteenth century called *Ovide moralisé*, along with a Latin prose treatise with similar intent written in 1342 by Petrarch's friend Pierre Bersuire. Here everything was interpreted as Christian parable; Ceres, for example, is the Church seeking to recover the souls of the faithful (Proserpina) by the light of the Gospel, her torch. (Compare the interpretation of *The Song of Songs* by the editors of the Authorized Version of the Bible.) Such ingenuity was mocked by Rabelais in his preface to *Gargantua* when he roundly declared that Homer was no more concerned with allegory than 'Ovid in the *Metamorphoses* could have been thinking of the Gospel Sacraments'. But *Ovide moralisé* continued to be studied, and with it Boccaccio's *On the Genealogy of the Gods*, where the symbolism was more moral than scriptural; see e.g. the interpretation put on legends of PERSEUS, HERACLES and LEDA. Some of the humanist philosophers could also see confirmation in the *Metamorphoses* for their belief in metempsychosis, and particularly where the characters changed into plants and flowers they could be taken as symbols of life-through-death (→ ARIADNE, PSYCHE).

Ovid continued to be admired in the eighteenth century, but more for his virtuosity as writer of verse, especially at a time when the English heroic couplet was used to match the Latin elegiac. He had a special appeal for the Augustan poets, and was more translated in their style than at any time since. As long as Latin verse-writing was part of a gentleman's education, Ovid was the obvious model, but his amoral views cannot have appealed to Victorian educational reformers. As Greek myths became increasingly important for their psychological and anthropological interest, Ovid's treatment has come to seem second-hand and superficial. But his vitality is not extinguished, and few poets have exceeded him in dislike of pretentiousness, in sensuous awareness, and the gift of carrying learning lightly.

Palinurus

In *Aeneid* 5 he is the helmsman of Aeneas who guides the ship past Scylla and Charybdis and through the storm after the Trojans have left Carthage, but is tempted by the god of sleep to close his eyes while steering from Africa to Italy and falls into the sea, taking the tiller and part of the stern with him. He is cast ashore and murdered by local tribesmen. He tells his story in *Aeneid* 6, when his spirit begs Aeneas to take him across the Styx so that he may find rest, but is sternly refused by the Sibyl because he has had no proper burial. She does, however, promise him that he shall have a shrine which will bear his name (Capo Palinuro in Lucania); cf. ELPENOR, MISENUS. 'Palinurus' was the pseudonym taken by the critic Cyril Connolly for his book of self-analysis, *The Unquiet Grave*. He sees in Palinurus a weariness with Aeneas' mission, a will-to-fail and a death-wish, and suggests that Virgil's inborn melancholy makes him identify himself with Palinurus who represents the introspective artist, while Aeneas stands for Augustus and the will to succeed.

Palladium

A legendary statue of Pallas Athene said to have been sent down from heaven by Zeus to Dardanus, the founder of Troy, to ensure the city's protection. In post-Homeric legends of Troy it was stolen by Diomedes and Odysseus, the version followed by Virgil in *Aeneid* 2. In another legend Aeneas rescued it from the flames of Troy and brought it to Rome, where it saved the city on several occasions in its early history. Other cities also claimed to possess it, and probably all such sacred talismans came to be known as 'palladia'.

Pallas

A title of the goddess Athene, of unknown derivation, often used in post-classical times as a synonym for the goddess – as in Botticelli's *Pallas and the Centaur*.

Pan

An Arcadian god, son of Hermes, patron of shepherds and herdsmen, who appears early in literature in the Homeric *Hymns* and in Pindar, and is generally represented as having goat's horns, ears and legs (though he has horns only in the Pompeian wall-painting of Pan playing to the nymphs). The 'Pan painter' of red-figure vases is named after a famous scene of Pan pursuing a shepherd.

He was a fertility god, and amorous towards both sexes; perhaps the best-known story of his loves is that of SYRINX, the nymph who escaped by being turned into a bed of reeds from which Pan made the Pan-pipes which are associated with him and are said still to be played by shepherds. He also tried to woo Selene by the gift of a fine sheep's fleece. Pan could be dangerous, especially if disturbed in the heat of noonday, when he could stampede flocks, give nightmares, and induce irrational 'panic' terror in men. One of the most evocative accounts of this is in E. M. Forster's *Story of a Panic*. Pan gave help to the Athenians against the Persians, and according to Herodotus, book 6, he was seen on the mountain track by the runner PHEIDIPPIDES, who was hurrying to ask help from Sparta before the battle of Marathon. After their victory the Athenians dedicated to Pan the cave-shrine still to be seen on the north slopes of the acropolis.

Pan became the patron of pastoral poets from classical times onwards, as the god of wild nature in an idealized Arcadia; this is how he appears in Shelley's *Hymn to Pan* and in Keats's *Endymion*. He was also curiously attractive to Christian writers. Plutarch has a story (dated to the reign of the Emperor Tiberius) of passengers on a boat who heard a mysterious voice on the island of Paxi, south of Corfu, calling to the god Thamus that 'Great Pan is dead'. This was likely to have been a misinterpretation of the Greek epithet *pammegas* (all-great) applied to Thamuz, a Syrian Adonis, but astrologers could not explain it and Christians took it to refer to the death and resurrection of Christ, which meant the death of the pagan gods. Some humanist philosophers could even associate Pan's divine *furor* with the non-rational state of the soul which made it receptive to knowledge of the divine, and Rabelais actually identified Pan with the Good Shepherd, 'for all that we are . . . all that we hope is him' ('all' in Greek is *pan*). Thus the primitive half-human half-animal god comes to be a symbol of the word incarnate. It has also been suggested that the reason why Pan appears with Venus and Cupid in so many Renaissance and later paintings is because the well-known 'love conquers all' is strained to mean 'love conquers Pan'. By far the most disturbing painting of Pan is in reproductions of Luca Signorelli's *The Realm of Pan* [40] (the original was destroyed in the last war), with the nymphs, a mysterious youth with pipes, and the brooding, shaggy god.

Panathenaea
The Athenian summer festival on the birthday of Athene, consisting of games, sacrifices, and, above all, a procession along the Sacred Way up to the Parthenon to present the goddess with a new robe or *peplum*. This is the subject of the temple frieze, most of which is among the ELGIN MARBLES.

Pandarus
A Trojan archer mentioned in the *Iliad* but with no reference to the part he plays in Chaucer's *Troilus and Criseyde* or in Shakespeare's play. Chaucer's source is the *Filostrato* of Boccaccio, which tells the same story, though Pandarus there is a young cousin introduced from the Troilus episodes in the medieval *Roman de Troie*. In Chaucer and Shakespeare he is Cressida's uncle and the go-between for the lovers; hence the continued use of the word 'pandar' for a procurer.

Pandora ('all gifts')
According to Hesiod, Pandora was the first woman and was created by Zeus to punish man after PROMETHEUS had created and helped the human race. She came with a box or storage-jar in which all evils and diseases were stored, and when Prometheus's guileless brother Epimetheus married her and opened the box, all these escaped, leaving only hope at the bottom to be some alleviation of the troubles let loose upon the world. 'Pandora's box' became proverbial. This sounds like common folklore (compare the part played by Eve in the book of Genesis), though Pandora was probably originally a pre-Greek earth-goddess and her name meant 'giving all'. The story is retold by Charles Kingsley in *The Water-Babies* with a surprising moral slant: Epimetheus is represented as the honest hard-working man (unlike his suspiciously clever brother) who will be able to surmount his troubles with the aid of his wife and his experience gained from life.

Paris
One of the sons of Priam, known as Alexandros in Homer, where he is held to be responsible for the Trojan War because of his abduction of Helen from Menelaus. He is a rather uxorious and unheroic figure, though not critically spoken of. In the duel he fights with Menelaus he has to be rescued by Aphrodite. Later legend introduced the JUDGEMENT OF PARIS and his abandonment of OENONE, his killing of Achilles, and death by an arrow from Philoctetes, but neither in antiquity nor in later references to him does he develop a real personality.

Parnassus
A mountain in the Pindus range, north-east of Delphi, which was traditionally sacred to Apollo and the Muses. Consequently 'Montparnasse' was the name given to the low hill on the left bank of the Seine where the university and the cultural centre of Paris was sited. The 'Parnassian School' of poetry refers to the group of nineteenth-century French poets led by Leconte de Lisle and J.-M. de Heredia, whose reaction against the materialism of the industrial age and the extravagances of the early

romantics made them seek the dignity and restraint and the perfection of form which they saw in classical antiquity. There, they believed, was the true noble ideal, the cult of 'art for art's sake'. In painting, the Parnassian ideal is seen early in A. R. Mengs (whose most famous painting is a *Parnassus*), then in David and his pupil Ingres, and finally in the French symbolists of the nineteenth century, especially Gustave Moreau in his many paintings on classical subjects. Of the many earlier paintings of Parnassus with Apollo and the Muses the most famous are those by Raphael, in the Vatican, by Mantegna and by Poussin, while the National Gallery, London, possesses a series of frescoes by Domenichino from the 'Parnassus room' in the Aldobrandini Villa at Frascati, which show scenes from the legends of Apollo taken from Ovid's *Metamorphoses*.

Parthenope
A nymph or siren whose body was said to have been washed up at the site of Neapolis (Naples), a Greek city founded *c.* 600 B.C., though there is no evidence that it ever was called after Parthenope. Nevertheless she gave her name to the short-lived Parthenopaean Republic of Naples set up by the French in 1799.

Parthenos ('virgin')
A title of Athene, as a virgin goddess. The Parthenon on the Athenian acropolis was rebuilt under PERICLES after the Persians had destroyed the earlier temple, and was dedicated to Athena Parthenos. Its architects were CALLICRATES and ICTINUS. For its sculptures, → ELGIN MARBLES and PHIDIAS.

Pasiphaë
The daughter of Helios, the sun-god, wife of Minos, king of CRETE. She fell in love with the bull which Poseidon had sent to the island for sacrifice, and with the help of Daedalus, who made her a hollow cow to get inside, she was mated with the bull and gave birth to the MINOTAUR. She was also the mother by Minos of Ariadne and Phaedra, and of Androgeus, who was killed by the Athenians when they were jealous of his success in the Panathenaeic games. In revenge Minos made war on Aegeus of Athens and was pacified only by the annual tribute of Athenian boys and girls for the Minotaur. →→ THESEUS.

Patroclus
In the *Iliad*, the friend and attendant of Achilles, and a slightly older man. Homer nowhere says that their relationship was homosexual, though their devotion, like that of David and Jonathan, does seem to be 'passing the love of women'. Shakespeare's Achilles in *Troilus and Cressida* also suggests a feminine type. For his death, → ACHILLES.

Pausanias
Greek traveller and writer, born near Mount Sipylus near Smyrna, who flourished *c.* A.D. 150, and wrote his unique *Guide to Greece* in ten books on the topography, antiquities, legends and history of the places he visited. This

was intended as a guide-book for travellers, to tell them what was most worth seeing; Pausanias was the Baedeker of his times. He still is an invaluable guide to Greece today, both for what can still be seen and for what he saw but has now disappeared, and to Pausanias we owe descriptions of many Greek statues and paintings in Athens and Delphi, of which no other account exists; → POLYGNOTUS. He is also an informed observer of local religious cults and a critical commentator on myths and their variants.

Pegasus

In post-Homeric legend, the winged horse of BELLEROPHON, born of the blood of Medusa when she was killed by Perseus. He was said to have been caught by Bellerophon when he was drinking at the spring of Pirene, which is still to be seen in the ruins of Old Corinth, and a 'Pegasus Untamed' was the symbol for the city on the magnificent coins of Corinth [31.3]. Pegasus was beloved by the Muses for creating the spring Hippocrene on Mount Helicon by a stamp of his magic hoof. With Bellerophon he is a popular subject for Greek vases, either fighting the Amazons or killing the Chimaera. Pegasus later became a symbol for immortality and for flights of imagination, and provided Keats with a good phrase in which to damn the pretensions of the heroic couplet; of the eighteenth-century Augustan poets he wrote

They sway'd about upon a rocking-horse
And called it Pegasus.

Peleus

The son of Aeacus, king of Aegina, Peleus is generally associated with Thessaly (late mythographers provide various reasons, usually saying that he left home after some killing in order to be purified). He takes part in heroic episodes like the Calydonian Boar-hunt, the battle between the Lapiths and Centaurs, and the voyage of the Argonauts. He is best remembered for his marriage to the nereid THETIS by whom he became the father of Achilles. The story is as old as Homer and retold by Pindar and Aeschylus; and it is the subject of Catullus's long poem (64) *Peleus and Thetis*, which is a brilliant adaptation of the Alexandrian literary *epyllion*, a poem dealing with a selected epic theme. There Peleus first sees Thetis with her sisters when he is returning home on the Argo, and their wedding is described in vivid pictorial terms, with digressions such as the tale of Bacchus and Ariadne, which is embroidered on their bedspread. All the gods and goddesses come bringing gifts, with the exception of Eris, or Discord, who arrives uninvited and throws down the fateful apple which leads to the JUDGEMENT OF PARIS. The marriage-song too is sung by the Fates who spin their thread and foretell the fate of Achilles. This is a deeply felt poem beneath its sophistication, and it has been said that it expresses more fully than any comparable poem the nostalgia Romans felt for a Golden Age when the gods could still move among men.

Pelops

The son of Tantalus, king of Lydia, and founder of the Pelopid family after whom the Peloponnesus is named. For his bizarre experiences in childhood, → TANTALUS. Pelops was given a golden chariot and a team of immortal horses by Poseidon, enabling him, according to some versions of his legend, to drive across the Aegean in search of a wife. He competed for Hippodamia in a chariot race at Olympia against her father, Oenomaus, king of Pisa and Elis, which he won by bribing the charioteer Myrtilus to remove the pins from Oenomaus's wheels. He then drowned Myrtilus instead of paying him, and so his entire house was cursed. (→ Tree of the House of Pelops.) Pelops drove on to the stream of Ocean in the far west and was purified, and then returned to marry Hippodamia and reign as king of Elis, where he won respect for his wealth and wise administration. He tried to appease the ghost of Myrtilus by paying him heroic honours; Pausanias saw both the shrine of Myrtilus and the sanctuary of Pelops at Elis, and his chariot race against Oenomaus was depicted on the east pediment of the Temple of Zeus at Olympia. It also appears on Etruscan sarcophagi, perhaps from a common source in Asia Minor. His spear, which was also his royal sceptre, the work of Hephaestus and gift of Zeus, descended to Atreus and then to Agamemnon, who carries it to the assembly of the Greeks in *Iliad* 2. The curse on the house is renewed under ATREUS and is not finally worked out until the purification of Orestes.

Penelope

The Homeric Penelope is the faithful wife of Odysseus and mother of Telemachus, and her epithet in the *Odyssey* is usually 'wise' or 'prudent'. Left to manage affairs in Ithaca, she is beset by the local nobles who press her to remarry. She staves them off at first by saying that she must finish weaving a shroud for her father-in-law Laertes; this she unravels every night, but after three years she is betrayed by one of

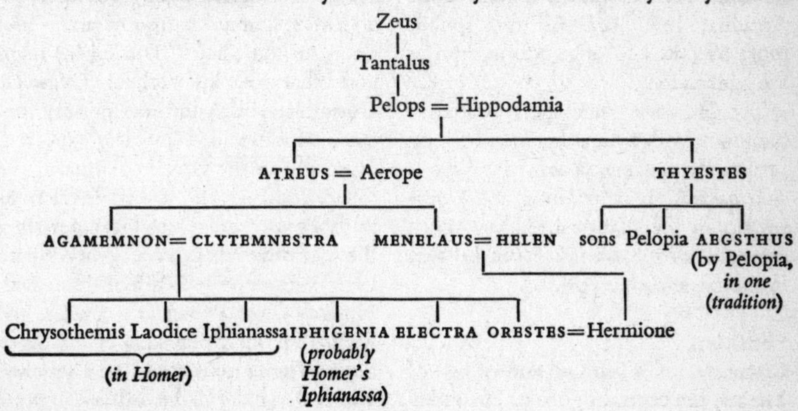

her maids and obliged to finish it. Eventually when Odysseus has been away twenty years and Telemachus has gone in search of him, she is prompted by Athene to offer herself to any of the suitors who can string the great bow of Odysseus and shoot through a row of double-headed axes. By now Odysseus is in the hall, disguised as a beggar; he takes up the bow and kills off the suitors. He and his wife are then re-united in a scene of subtle delicacy and insight. Outside Homer she appears only as a symbol of fidelity, apart from legends associated with her cult in the Peloponnese which make her adulterous and cannot be reconciled with the Homeric Penelope (cf. HELEN). Pausanias refers to the legend that she was the daughter of Icarius of Sparta, and as he was said to be the brother of Tyndareus, that makes her the putative first cousin of Helen and the Dioscuri. She was worshipped in eastern Arcadia, where she was supposed to have died, and connected there with birds, some sort of duck; Herodotus also refers to the belief that she was the mother of the Arcadian god, Pan. All this sounds more like the cult of a local nymph of the same name.

The Homeric Penelope is seated at her loom, with a cat at her feet, looking up at a Renaissance young man who is Telemachus, in a painting by Pintoricchio in the National Gallery, London; the sirens and Circe can be seen in the background [48].

Pentheus

Grandson of Cadmus and king of Thebes, the central figure of Euripides' *Bacchae*. He refuses to allow the god Dionysus into the city, he is persuaded by the god in disguise to go up to the mountains to watch the orgies, and there he is killed and torn to pieces by the Theban women in their frenzy, led by his own mother Agave. She returns carrying his head, still in a state of blind ecstasy, and only when questioned by her old father, Cadmus, does she realize the enormity of what her *furor* has led her to do. Pentheus is one of Euripides' most subtly drawn characters, and his is a much more complex case than that of a mortal who pits himself against a god and meets his just deserts. He is both violent and puritanical, refusing to listen to the god when he first comes in peaceful form, because he fears to relax his self-control; yet he is drawn by fascinated curiosity to put on women's dress to spy on the bacchants. Only at the moment of his terrible death does he come to self-knowledge.

Periander

Ruler of Corinth *c.* 625–585 B.C. (→ TYRANTS), and a patron of artists and poets such as ARION. During his reign and that of his father, Cypselus, Corinthian black-figured pottery became famous and was widely exported, especially to the Greek colonies in the West. Periander also had trade relations with Egypt, and Herodotus describes the Corinth of his day as a city where both commerce and culture flourished. Plutarch chose Periander's court as the setting for his *Symposium of the Seven Sages*. The famous 'chest of Cypselus' which Periander dedicated at Olympia was seen and described in detail by Pausanias in book 5 of his *Guide to Greece*. It was decorated on each side with gold and ivory reliefs of mythological scenes and with inscriptions in archaic 'cattle-turning' (*boustrophedon*) style, i.e. alternately left-right and right-left.

Pericles

Athenian general and statesman who controlled affairs in Athens from about 460 B.C. until his death in the plague in 429. He was therefore responsible for Athenian policy in the early part of the Peloponnesian War against Sparta, and for the conversion of the League of Delos, which had been intended as a combination of equal allies against the possibility of a renewed attack from Persia, into an Athenian empire. As a right-wing democrat, in marked contrast with the extreme democrats like Cleon who succeeded him, he had many enemies but was much admired by Thucydides, and his views on an idealized Athens are expressed in the famous Funeral Speech in book 2 of Thucydides' *History*. His *Life* was also written by Plutarch and paired with that of the Roman FABIUS CUNCTATOR.

Pericles was responsible for the magnificent buildings on the acropolis and known to be friendly with the sculptor Phidias, with Sophocles and the rationalist philosopher ANAXAGORAS. → ASPASIA.

Persephone (Roman **Proserpina**)

A pre-Greek goddess, also called Kore ('maiden') who was afterwards said to be the daughter of Zeus and DEMETER. The story of her being carried off by Hades or Dis (Pluto) and then forced to spend half the year underground clearly refers to the germination of seeds and their rebirth each spring. With Demeter she was associated with the secret Mysteries of Eleusis. Later legends add that she was obliged to compromise with Dis because although she had refused food from him, she had bitten into a pomegranate and swallowed seven of its seeds. As queen of the Underworld she was there to receive Orpheus on his search for Eurydice. Of the many places associated with Demeter which claimed to be the scene of Persephone's abduction, one is unforgettable from Milton's simile in *Paradise Lost* 4.268–71; this is central Sicily in

> that fair field
> Of Enna, where Proserpin gathering
> flowers
> Herself a fairer flower, by gloomy Dis
> Was gathered . . .

A famous Roman wall-fresco from Stabiae of a girl with flowers is sometimes said to be Proserpina. Her story was known to the Middle Ages from Ovid, and given new significance by *Ovide moralisé*; and when Dante wants to describe Matilda, the lady in the meadow in the *Purgatorio*, he does so by comparison with Proserpina. She sometimes appears in manuscript illustrations either sitting stiffly with her husband, the three-headed Cerberus at their feet, or as a medieval country-girl by a roadside, about to be hauled into a primitive wagon. She and Demeter and Pluto also appear on Roman sarcophagi; the one in Aachen Cathedral is said to have been the original coffin of Charlemagne. She features in paintings by Turner and Rembrandt, and in statue-groups with Pluto by Bernini, Giovanni da Bologna and François Girardon, whose *Rape of Proserpine* is in the gardens of Versailles. In later literature she is a symbol of death, with special appeal for Swinburne; two of his better poems are *Hymn to Proserpine* and *The Garden of Proserpine*: 'For there is no god found stronger than death; and death is a sleep.'

Perseus

The son of Zeus and DANAË, famous for his rescue of Andromeda and his killing of the GORGON MEDUSA. For this task he is helped by Athene and Hermes who give him a sickle, a bag, a helmet of darkness to make him invisible, winged shoes and a shield in which to reflect the Gorgon. He has to visit the GRAEAE and there is a large element of fairy-tale in his exploits. Perseus is depicted with his various attributes from early times, notably on black-figure vases and on a metope in the temple at Selinus, Sicily, which dates from the mid sixth century B.C. There are two paintings of him with Andromeda among the wall-paintings in Pompeii [17], the larger one thought to be a direct copy of a Greek original by a contemporary of Praxiteles. Later allegorists could see in Perseus the conquest of sin and ascent to virtue, with Andromeda as a soul saved, or his killing of Medusa could even be a symbol of Christ triumphing over the Prince of evil. He and Andromeda were often painted; there are examples by Titian, Veronese, Rubens and Delacroix, while Cellini's bronze Perseus holding up the severed head is one of the most famous statues in Florence. He also inspired a series of pictures by the English pre-Raphaelite painter, Burne-Jones.

Persius Flaccus, Aulus (A.D. 34–62)

Roman satirist, friend of the poet LUCAN and a member of the group of Stoics who were pledged to oppose the principle of one-man rule by an emperor who was not a Stoic philosopher-king. His work was influenced by Lucilius and Horace, but his style is idiosyncratic and often cryptic, going even beyond that of Propertius in esoteric literary allusions. He is said to have written slowly and with difficulty, and only six of his satires are extant. He was often quoted and copied in the Middle Ages and Renaissance, admired by John Donne and translated by Dryden.

Pervigilium Veneris ('The Vigil of Venus')

Both author and date of this unique Latin poem are unknown, but it is probably late third century A.D. It is set in Sicily, on the eve of the spring festival of Venus Genetrix, and describes the new surge of life in plants and all living creatures, ending on a personal *cri du cœur* from the poet whose spring awakening does not come. Its trochaic metre and assonance foreshadow later accentual Latin poetry, and each stanza ends with the haunting refrain *Cras amet qui nunquam amavit quique amavit cras amet* ('He shall love tomorrow who never has loved, and the lover shall love tomorrow').

Petronius Arbiter, Gaius *or* Titus
(*fl.* first century A.D.)
Roman satirist, author of the *Satyricon*, a satire on the sterility and corruption of Roman society in the form of a vast picaresque novel, of which only fragments of books 15 and 16 survive. These deal with the adventures of two disreputable young men, Encolpius and Ascyltos, and the boy Giton, who plays the others off against each other, as they travel through the low haunts of Campania and south Italy. The whole was probably intended as a parody on the wanderings of Odysseus, for Encolpius, the narrator, is cursed with sexual inadequacy through being pursued by the wrath of PRIAPUS. The longest episode is that of the famous Dinner with Trimalchio, a multi-millionaire freedman of pretentious vulgarity, and there are also long rhetorical poems (intended perhaps as parodies of Lucan) on the Civil War of Caesar and Pompey, and the Fall of Troy. Even in its fragmentary state the *Satyricon* is bursting with vitality and panache, and its gaps are tantalizing. Petronius also tells us more about Roman common speech and slang than anyone except the much earlier dramatist Plautus. The story of the Widow of Ephesus told in one of the episodes has been popular ever since; it is the subject of Christopher Fry's *A Phoenix too Frequent*. The *Satyricon* has recently been successfully adapted for a film by Federico Fellini.

Petronius also wrote lyric poetry, some of which has survived, and he is generally identified with the 'Arbiter of Taste' at Nero's court, who was accused of being implicated in the conspiracy of Piso in 66 and committed suicide. His personality is succinctly described by Tacitus in *Annals* 16.

Phaedra
Daughter of Minos, king of Crete, and Pasiphaë; sister of Ariadne, young wife of Theseus of Athens, and stepmother of HIPPOLYTUS, whom she loved and drove to his death when he rejected her. Phaedra then hanged herself. Euripides' *Hippolytus* is the only surviving Greek tragedy on the subject of this ancient myth, which is similar to that of BELLEROPHON and the biblical Joseph and Potiphar's wife; all may have a common Egyptian or Near-Eastern source. Pausanias saw the tombs of both Phaedra and Hippolytus in Troezen. Seneca's tragedy *Phaedra* probably drew something from Ovid's *Heroides* (where there is a passionate letter from Phaedra to Hippolytus). Racine says in his introduction to *Phèdre* that he owes his conception of Phaedra's character to Euripides. This is the last play on a classical subject which he wrote before his conversion to Jansenism; this perhaps accounts for the obsession with guilt and predestination which pervades the play.

Phaethon
An early legendary figure who asked permission of his father HELIOS to drive the horses of the sun for a day. He proved quite unable to control them and would have set the world on fire if Zeus had not killed him with his thunderbolt. Phaethon traditionally fell from the chariot into the river Eridanus

(the Po) and his sisters mourned him until they turned into trees (either alders or the poplars of the Lombardy plain), while their tears became the fossilised resin which is amber. Amber had been imported and carved in the Mediterranean region since Mycenean times, and as it all came from the Baltic, this points to a trade route along the rivers of Europe ending at the head of the Adriatic. (There is also some evidence that the original Argo story was concerned not with a voyage to Colchis in the Black Sea but with trade with the 'land of Aeëtes' in the Adriatic region.) Phaethon provides a classic example of hubris followed by nemesis, and was the subject of a (lost) play by Euripides. His story is told in full by Ovid in *Metamorphoses* 2, whence the pictorial description of the Sun on his throne surrounded by the Seasons and the Hours who harness the horses is closely copied in a painting by Poussin. Phaethon has given his name to a light fast-moving open carriage (a phaeton) drawn by a pair of horses, common in scenes by such painters as George Stubbs.

Phalaris

A sixth-century tyrant of Acragas (Agrigento) in Sicily who was notorious for his cruelty, his speciality being to roast his victims alive in a hollow bronze bull. The great English classical scholar of the eighteenth century, Richard Bentley, first established his reputation by his *Dissertation* in which he exposed the so-called *Letters of Phalaris* as a forgery of the second century A.D.

Phaon

There is no historical evidence for the existence of the handsome young boatman from Lesbos for whom Sappho had a hopeless passion in middle age. But the tradition is old, and romantics like Ovid in his *Heroides* and Peter Green in *The Laughter of Aphrodite* have thought him dramatically appropriate as a reason for Sappho's reputed death by suicide by leaping off the cliff in the island of Leucas. He appears with Sappho in a painting by David.

Ph(e)idias (*c.* 490–*c.* 415 B.C.)

Athenian sculptor, famous for his work in bronze and in ivory and gold, and also for the marble statues of the Parthenon (the Elgin Marbles), the only surviving originals which are known either to have been carved by him or by sculptors to his designs. There are small copies to show us what the gold and ivory Athena Parthenos was like, and the 'Strangford shield' in the British Museum is a Roman marble copy of her shield with a gorgon's head in the centre. Nothing is left (except a tiny representation on coins of Elis) to give any idea of the splendour of the great Zeus at Olympia which Pausanias saw. This was removed to Constantinople and was destroyed in a palace fire in A.D. 475. But Phidias's workshop has been found at Olympia, and his drinking-cup inscribed with his name. There is no copy of his thirty-foot bronze statue of Athena Promachos ('champion') which stood on the acropolis near the Propylaea, but the bronze Athene he made for the island of Lemnos is known from a copy, a beautiful head in Bologna and a body in Dresden. Phidias is known to have been banished from Athens about 432 by political enemies of Pericles, and probably died in exile.

Pheidippides (or in some MSS. of Herodotus, **Philippides**)
The Greek runner who was sent from Athens to Sparta to ask for help against the Persians just before the battle of Marathon in 490 B.C. (The Spartans were busy celebrating a religious festival and this was refused.) He covered the distance of 150 miles in two days, and on his way back met the god Pan who promised aid. His feat has given the name to the 'marathon race' of the Olympic Games, or to any long-distance foot-race.

Philip
Several kings of Macedon bore this name, the most famous being Philip II who ruled from 359 to 336 B.C., the father of Alexander the Great. He made Macedon a major power and created a highly trained professional army, and his sphere of influence extended as he skilfully exploited the dissensions between the Greek city-states. DEMOSTHENES saw him as a menace to democratic liberty, ISOCRATES as a potential leader of a Greece united against Persia. Philip forced the issue at the Battle of Chaeronea in 338 and gave the Greeks a federal constitution with himself as leader, but he was assassinated before he could lead a combined army against Persia. The famous Lion of Chaeronea still marks the tomb of the Greeks killed at their defeat in the battle. He founded the town of Philippi in Macedonia, the site of the battle in which Brutus and Cassius were defeated by Antony and Octavian in 42 B.C.

Philip V allied himself with Hannibal against the Romans and was defeated at the Battle of Cynoscephalae in 197 B.C. The Romans then restored freedom to the Greek cities, i.e. nominal independence from Macedonian interference.

Philoctetes
One of the Greek leaders in the Trojan War, of whom Homer says that he had to be left behind on the island of Lemnos suffering from a snake-bite but eventually recovered and returned home. Non-Homeric legend said that Odysseus heard that Troy could not be taken unless he was fetched from Lemnos, and went with Diomedes to get him. The three tragedians wrote plays about him, but only Sophocles' *Philoctetes* survives. In it Odysseus takes the young NEOPTOLEMUS with him, and much of the play turns on the contrast between the honesty of the boy, the unscrupulous wiliness of Odysseus, and the embitterment of Philoctetes who knows that he is wanted only for the bow and arrows of Heracles which had been given to him for lighting Heracles' funeral pyre on Mount Oeta. It takes the divine intervention of Heracles to overcome his reluctance.

Philomela
The daughter of Pandion, King of Athens, who became the nightingale; for her complex story, see ITYS.

Philon of Alexandria
(*c.* 30 B.C.–A.D. 45)
The head of the Jewish community in Alexandria, generally known as Philo Judaeus. He headed a deputation to the Emperor Caligula to ask for exemption for his people from the duty of worshipping the emperor, a privilege finally granted by Claudius. A pamphlet describing this mission is extant, and also several of his philosophical writings which interpret Jewish doctrine in terms of Greek philosophy and develop the idea of an all-pervading mind or spirit. These were to have marked influence on both early Christian writers and the Neoplatonists, especially PLOTINUS.

Philopappus (C. Julius Antiochus Epiphanes Philopappus)
Syrian prince, grandson of Antiochus IV, the last king of the north Syrian kingdom of Commagene, who was an Athenian citizen, and Roman consul in A.D. 109. He was a generous benefactor to the city, and was granted a splendid sepulchral monument, built between 114 and 116 on the hill now called after him, though it had originally been the Hill of the Muses and had a shrine to the Muses. The marble monument has a frieze and statues of Philopappus himself and of his royal ancestors, and every visitor to Athens climbs the hill for the sake of the view.

Phlegethon ('blazing')
One of the rivers of the Underworld. In Plato's *Phaedo* it is called Pyriphlegethon, 'river of fire', into which the souls of those who have committed acts of violence against their kin are thrown until they can obtain forgiveness for their sins. In Dante it is the third great river of Hell with Acheron and Styx, and sinners who shed blood are plunged for ever in this river of boiling blood flowing all round the Seventh Circle.

Phocion
An Athenian general and statesman of the fourth century B.C., a supporter of the peace policy of AESCHINES. He was chosen by Plutarch for one of his *Lives* because of his stern sense of duty and stoic character. Phocion had a special appeal for Poussin, who believed that the artist's life should be detached from popular interests, and painted several landscapes to illustrate Phocion's heroic life and death in the hands of an irresponsible populace.

Phoebe ('bright')
In early Greek legend she was the daughter of Heaven and Earth and the mother of LETO. She was later identified with Artemis or Diana and her name is often used among poets to refer to the moon.

Phoenix ('red')
(i) In the *Iliad*, a prince brought up by Peleus as a companion and tutor for his son Achilles. He tries to reconcile Achilles with Agamemnon in *Iliad* 9 and tells how he came to live with Peleus; he also tells the story of MELEAGER.
(ii) The eponymous ancestor of the Phoenicians, about whom nothing is told except that he was a brother of

Cadmus and Europa. In early Greek myths the 'Red Men' usually mean the Minoan Cretans, who would be darker-skinned than the northern Hellenes; though Homer knows of the Semitic Phoenicians as traders, and Cadmus was said to have introduced their alphabet into Greece.

(iii) A fabulous bird of Egypt, described by Herodotus, which died on a funeral pyre every 500 years and rose again miraculously. A phoenix rising from the flames became a symbol of death and resurrection both for believers in the mystery cults and in Christianity. *The Bird Phoenix*, an elegiac poem attributed to Lactantius, who was a Christian professor of rhetoric under the Emperor Diocletian and an important writer on the early persecutions, treats the bird as a symbol for the resurrection of Christ, and Milton introduces it into the last semichorus of *Samson Agonistes*:

So Virtue, given for lost,
Depressed and overthrown, as seemed,
Like that self-begotten bird
In the Arabian woods embost,
That no second knows nor third,
And lay erewhile a holocaust,
From out her ashy womb now teemed,
Revives, reflourishes, then vigorous most
When most inactive deemed;
And though her body die, her fame survives,
A secular bird, ages of lives.

The phoenix was also a favourite device of Queen Elizabeth I who saw her reign as the rebirth of an earlier Golden Age.

Phrixus and Helle

In early Greek legends they are brother and sister, children of Athamas, king of Aeolia, and victims of their stepmother Ino's jealousy. They were about to be sacrificed (in some primitive fertility rite) but escaped on the back of a golden ram sent by Hermes or Zeus. Helle fell off into the sea which was afterwards called the Hellespont, but Phrixus reached Colchis on the Black Sea and sacrificed the ram to Zeus. Later legends say that it became the constellation Aries (Latin 'ram'). Its Golden Fleece was famous in the next generation when it was sought by JASON and the ARGONAUTS.

Phryne

A celebrated Greek courtesan of the fourth century B.C., said to have been the model for the Aphrodite of Cnidos by Praxiteles and the painting of Aphrodite Anadyomene by Apelles.

Pilate (Pontius Pilatus)

Roman governor of Judaea A.D. 26–36, who sentenced Jesus Christ to death by crucifixion, the normal punishment for non-Romans found guilty of sedition. The episode is mentioned briefly in Tacitus's *Annals* 15, but the main authority is the four Gospels. Pilate held a relatively minor post in the imperial administration and nothing else is known of him. A great deal of spurious information circulated in later times, including a forged report on the trial supposedly sent to the Emperor Tiberius.

Pindar (518–438 B.C.)

Greek lyric poet, born in Boeotia and educated in Athens, an aristocrat by birth and also by temperament. His works were known in antiquity to be collected into seventeen volumes and to cover every kind of lyric. Of these, apart from fragments, only four books of Epinician Odes survive; these are choral songs composed in honour of victors in the athletic games – a traditional genre which Pindar was to transform. For him the details of victory meant much less than the glory which comes to man only as a gift from the gods and confers on him a kind of immortality, raising him to the level of the great heroes of mythology. The odes are often cast in the form of thanksgiving and praise, and are infused with deep religious feeling. The Greeks considered him their greatest poet, and among the Romans he was particularly admired by Horace, who believed that his own odes could never reach such heights. Milton refers in a sonnet to the tradition that Alexander spared Pindar's house when he destroyed Thebes, linking it with a similar tradition about the fame of Euripides:

Lift not thy spear against the Muses' bower:
  The great Emathian conqueror bid spare
  The house of Pindarus, when temple and tower
Went to the ground; and the repeated air
  Of sad Electra's poet had the power
  To save th'Athenian walls from ruin bare.
(*When the Assault was Intended to the City*)

A Pindaric ode has come to mean one which has something of Pindar's soaring imagination and free range of themes. In style, structure and imagery the great imitator of Pindar was Ronsard in his early *Odes*, and in England the first truly Pindaric ode is Milton's *On the Morning of Christ's Nativity*. Dryden's *Alexander's Feast* and *Ode for St Cecilia's Day*, Gray's *Progress of Poesy*, Shelley's *Ode to Naples*, Wordsworth's *Ode on the Intimations of Immortality*, Hopkins's *Wreck of the Deutschland* are only a few of the poems for which Pindar's vigour and freedom of movement have been an inspiration.

Pirithous

King of the LAPITHS in Homer, mentioned as fighting the CENTAURS at his wedding with Hippodamia, and in later legends generally associated with his close friend THESEUS, king of Athens. He then plays a part in the early abduction of Helen and the battle with the Amazons, and went down into Hades with Theseus in an attempt to carry off Persephone. Pluto forestalled this, and in most versions Theseus escapes, and Pirithous is left to suffer the torments of hell, but in some accounts both had to stay until they were rescued by Heracles.

P(e)isistratus

'Tyrant' of Athens 561–527 B.C., a benevolent despot under whom the city developed culturally and economically and the farmers of Attica prospered. Attic black-figured pottery began to be exported all over the Greek world and Attic coinage went with it. The Greek historians say that it was he who instituted the dramatic contests at the Dionysia, and arranged for a definitive written text of Homer's poems. He retained the constitution of SOLON, kept on reasonably good terms with the nobility, and prepared the way for the more democratic reforms of his successors.

Pittacus (*c.* 650–570 B.C.)
Ruler of Mytilene, a moderate democratic reformer like his contemporary SOLON and afterwards considered one of the Seven Sages of Greece. He was the political opponent of the poet ALCAEUS.

Plato (*c.* 429–347 B.C.)
Athenian philosopher, pupil of Socrates, teacher of Aristotle, nearly all of whose known works survive. These are the *Apology* in vindication of Socrates, twenty-five dialogues in most of which Socrates takes part, and letters not all of which are genuine, describing his intervention in the politics of Sicily (see DION and DIONYSIUS). The earlier dialogues present Socrates and his teaching that Virtue is Knowledge: that we cannot be good until we know what we mean by 'good', and equally, that full understanding of the Good ensures that our conduct will be good. From this Plato develops his theory of Forms or Ideas, in which abstract concepts have an unchanging reality beyond that of the world of the senses, and the Supreme Form is that of the Good. The ten books of the *Republic* set out a complete system for an ideal society in which Guardians ('philosopher-kings'), who have the education and capacity to know the archetypal forms of Justice and the Good, rule in the interests of the majority, who have only a limited perception of the shadows of reality which form the ordinary world. Plato's metaphysical views were deeply influenced by the Pythagoreans of western Greece whom he met on his travels. To them he owes his use of dreams and visions and the stress he lays on dedication for his Guardians. Through the myth of Er, for example, in *Republic* 10, he describes the joys of after-life in mystical terms.

In the olive-grove of Academus outside Athens, Plato founded his Academy where his teaching methods were followed. Reinforced by neo-Platonism from Alexandria in the third century A.D., this teaching continued until the Academy was closed by Justinian in A.D. 529. Plato's aim was partly political; he wished to train statesmen, and in Sicily he tried to realize his ideal of the philosopher-king. When he failed, he wrote the *Laws* as a much more practical blueprint for a city-state, organized to the last detail. Only in recent years have his political views been seriously questioned. The Republic with its rigid caste-system, military training, communism of property and censorship of the arts is too much of a totalitarian state, and has been condemned as such in books like R. H. S. Crossman's *Plato Today*.

Plato's moral philosophy had great effect on Roman thinkers, particularly Cicero, and his influence on the western world has been immense ever since his works were translated into Latin in the late fifteenth century by the Florentine Marsilio Ficino. A Platonic Academy flourished in Florence under the patronage of Lorenzo dei Medici, and the Renaissance Neoplatonists were able to reconcile Plato's account of the divine origin of the cosmos with Christian theology (→ TIMAEUS). In nineteenth-century England, with the revival of Greek studies, he was particularly important in very different ways. The British public schools admired him for his education of an élite through gymnastics and the cultural arts. Walter Pater, pupil of the great Platonist Benjamin Jowett, saw in him the artist and mystic, and wrote *Plato and Platonism* in revolt against materialism. Nietzsche, on the other hand, consistently attacked Plato in his philosophic works as a dangerous falsifier of reality and a 'symptom of decay'.

Plautus, Titus Maccius
(*c.* 254–184 B.C.)
Roman comic dramatist, twenty-one of whose plays survive. These are all imitations of Greek New Comedy (→ MENANDER), but at the same time are genuine re-creations for the Roman public, written with great comic gusto and expertise in dialogue and word-play. They also tell us practically all we know about current speech of the time. Plautus was virtually unknown in the Middle Ages because of his difficulty, but he was widely translated in the Renaissance and a popular influence. Shakespeare used the plot of *The Brothers Menaechmus* in *The Comedy of Errors*, and Molière's Harpagon in *L'Avare* is taken from Euclio in *The Pot of Gold*. Molière also wrote his own AMPHITRYON, and the type-character of a boastful soldier in Restoration comedy goes back to Plautus's *Miles gloriosus*.

Pleiades
Homer mentions both the Pleiades and Orion as constellations and, as both of them rise in May and set in November, they were associated with rain and stormy weather. Later mythographers made the seven Pleiades the daughters of Atlas, and Orion a famous giant and hunter, son of Eos, the dawn; he had pursued them until they were all translated to the sky. A group of seven poets in Alexandria (including Aratus and Theocritus) in the third century B.C. called themselves the Pleiad, and the name was taken over by La Pléiade of sixteenth-century France. Seven poets grouped round Ronsard and du Bellay aimed at breaking with medieval tradition and writing in French, so that the language could be developed to treat the same classical themes that had hitherto been confined to Greek or Latin.

Pliny the Elder (Gaius Plinius Secundus, A.D. 23–79)
Roman administrator and encyclopedic writer who died in the eruption of Vesuvius which destroyed Herculaneum and Pompeii. Of his vast output only his *Natural History* in thirty-seven books survives. In this he claimed to record 20,000 facts which were worth noting, either from his own observations or from a great range of Roman and non-Roman authors. It was considered an important scientific authority in the Middle Ages, and is indeed a mine of heterogeneous and often valuable information for those

who are not put off by Pliny's crabbed Latin style. It was widely translated, and known in English from the translation of Philemon Holland in 1601.

Pliny the Younger (Gaius Plinius Caecilius Secundus, A.D. 61/2–112/13)
Nephew and adopted son of Pliny the Elder, senator and distinguished advocate, and friend of Tacitus, Suetonius and the poet Martial. He selected and published his personal letters in nine books, giving first-hand information on himself and his times, seen from the angle of an able and cultivated public servant; and also a long and elaborate *Panegyric* of thanks to the Emperor Trajan for his consulship. A tenth book of letters, published posthumously, contains his official correspondence with Trajan while he held an administrative post as the Emperor's representative in Bithynia-Pontus. This book contains the celebrated exchange of letters on the problems raised by the provincial Christian communities.

Both Pliny and his uncle were natives of Comum and held large estates there, and are suitably honoured by fifteenth-century statues outside Como Cathedral showing them as Renaissance scholars (the Elder looking surprisingly like Harpo Marx). Throughout the Middle Ages they were believed to be one person until a Veronese scholar in the early fourteenth century established that they were two.

Plotinus (A.D. 205–70)
Neoplatonist Greek philosopher, teaching first in Alexandria and then in Rome. His works were collected by his pupil PORPHYRY and arranged in six groups of nine books (the *Enneads*). In these he combined Plato's philosophy with ideas taken from Oriental mysticism, and developed the doctrine of the One all-pervading spirit with which the philosopher can hope to be united in a state of ecstasy only after a life of asceticism and contemplation. His views were known to St Augustine through whom they influenced Christian thinking, and were especially important for the Renaissance humanists.

Plutarch (A.D. *c.* 46–*c.* 126)
Greek essayist and biographer, born at Chaeronea in Boeotia and later resident in Rome, or in his home town where he was active as a teacher and in civic affairs. A great deal of his large output of essays on matters of scientific, literary or ethical interest survives, including his *Moralia* ('moral essays') which were early translated by Jacques Amyot into French and Philemon Holland into English, and make entertaining reading; and his famous *Parallel Lives* in which twenty-three pairs of Greek and Roman soldiers and statesmen are compared; there are also some single *Lives*, and some losses, notably the *Life of Scipio Africanus*. In Amyot's French translation these became favourite reading for Montaigne, who often refers to Plutarch in his own essays. Sir Thomas North's translation was Shakespeare's source for *Coriolanus*, *Julius Caesar*, *Antony and Cleopatra*, and *Timon of Athens*.

Plutus
Greek god of wealth, originally associated with agricultural prosperity, and

in Hesiod the son of Demeter and the Titan Iasios. Later he is a figure of popular legend and depicted as blind because his gifts were indiscriminately or unsuitably bestowed. Aristophanes plays on this in his comedy *Plutus* in which the honest hero gets the god's sight restored at the temple of Asclepius, after which riches go only to the deserving. Dante's 'Pluto' who guards the avaricious and the spendthrifts in the Fifth Circle of Hell is Plutus in the Italian form, not the god of the underworld Pluto/Dis.

Polybius (*c.* 200–after 118 B.C.)
Greek statesman and historian, active in the Achaean League against the Romans, and after the Greek defeat in the Battle of Pydna in 168, brought to Rome as a political hostage. There he became the friend of SCIPIO AEMILIANUS and accompanied him to Spain and North Africa. He was also well travelled in Italy and Greece, and so had access to first-hand information for his *Universal History*. This covers events in Roman history from 220 B.C. and the start of the Second Punic War to the destruction of Carthage and Corinth in 146–5. Only the first five books survive intact, but the substantial fragments of the later books contain his analysis of the Roman constitution and theory of historiography. For the war with Hannibal he is an important alternative source to Livy.

Polyclitus
Greek sculptor of the second half of the fifth century B.C., a younger contemporary of Phidias, working in the Peloponnese and specializing in bronze statues of the Olympic victors. None of his originals survives, but there are many Hellenistic and Roman marble copies, notably of his *Diadumenos* (an athlete crowning himself) and *Doryphoros* (spear-bearer), in which the well-marked formal structure of the muscles on the torso became the prototype of many Renaissance bronze figures. His most famous work, a colossal ivory and gold statue of a seated Hera for the Heraeum of Argos, is described by Pausanias and thought by Strabo and others to rival the Olympian Zeus of PHIDIAS. It survives only on the coins of Argos.

Polycrates
'Tyrant' of Samos in the mid sixth century B.C., who established Samos as a naval power, encouraged the building of public works (temples, harbour and an aqueduct), and was a patron of the arts (→ ANACREON). His career is described in book 3 of Herodotus's *History*, along with the legend that he was advised to ward off the disaster (nemesis) which must one day overtake his prosperity by throwing away his most precious possession. He threw his favourite ring into the sea, but it was soon returned to him in the belly of a fish – a tale which is common in folklore everywhere. The ring was said by the Elder Pliny to have been preserved in the Temple of Concord, Rome· not a very likely story.

Polygnotus
The first named Greek painter on a large scale, working in the mid fifth

century B.C. None of his work survives, but his famous series of mural paintings in the 'Painted Stoa' of Athens, and the *lesche* (clubhouse) at Delphi, which showed the Sack of Troy and scenes in the Underworld, are described in detail by Pausanias. The elder Pliny writes admiringly of his figure-grouping and composition, and of his painting of thin drapery and facial expression.

Polyphemus

One of the CYCLOPES who captures Odysseus and his men in the *Odyssey*, shuts them up in his cave, and eats two of them every evening until they escape by blinding him in his one eye and slipping out with the sheep and goats next morning. He is the son of Poseidon, and in answer to his cry for help, Poseidon delays Odysseus's return home. The blinding of Polyphemus is shown in a famous painting on an early seventh-century amphora from Eleusis and was a popular subject for later vases. He is also a comic character in Euripides' satyr-play, *Cyclops*. Polyphemus's home was described by Homer as being on the mainland opposite an uninhabited island full of goats, and this has been identified with one of the Aegadian islands off the west coast of Sicily (Greek *aigos* means 'goat'). But ancient tradition (followed by Virgil) placed him in eastern Sicily, where there are the seven Scogli de' Ciclopi, the rocks which the blinded Polyphemus hurled after the boat of Odysseus as he escaped. They are not far from the mouth of the river ACIS, and it was here that local legend made Polyphemus the rejected lover of the nymph GALATEA. This too is the coastline which has inspired some splendid landscape paintings, notably one by Poussin and *Ulysses Deriding Polyphemus* by Turner.

Polyxena

The daughter of Priam and Hecuba, not mentioned in Homer, but in post-Homeric legend sacrificed to the shade of Achilles by his son, Neoptolemus, as the Greeks are about to sail from Troy. This is the theme of Euripides' tragedy *Hecabe*; see HECUBA. Polyxena is known to have been a popular subject in early lyric poetry.

Pomona

An Italian goddess of *poma*, i.e. tree-fruits such as apples, who was given a priest of minor rank by the Romans and had a sacred precinct outside Rome but no known festival. What we know of her comes from Varro, and from the story told by Ovid in *Metamorphoses* 14 where her connection with Vertumnus seems to be his own invention or derived from lost sources. Vertumnus was possibly Etruscan in origin, a god of changing seasons (Latin *vertere* means 'change'), and especially of the ripening fruits of autumn; he had the power to change his shape and became associated with money-changing. From a poem by Propertius in which Vertumnus is the speaker (4.2) and a reference in Horace's epistle of farewell to his 'little book' (1.20) it is certain that his statue stood in the *Vicus Tuscus*, which was called after him as an Etruscan and was a busy street full of shops and brothels. Ovid says that he fell in love with Pomona and used to follow her around disguised as a harvester, a herdsman or a vine-dresser, and in the form of an old woman begged her to have pity on him, but succeeded only when he reverted to his true shape. Pomona and Vertumnus then appear together in masques celebrating Ceres and the harvest, in occasional frescoes and paintings, and in garden statues, among which those by Poussin at Versailles are the best known. See HERMAE.

Pompey the Great (Cnaeus Pompeius Magnus, 106–48 B.C.)
Roman general who first distinguished himself fighting against Marius on the side of SULLA, then put down a slave rebellion, cleared the Mediterranean of pirates, and ended the war with MITHRIDATES of Pontus. He married Julia, the daughter of Julius Caesar, and was a member of the First Triumvirate with Caesar and Crassus. During Caesar's absence in Gaul he ruled Rome as sole consul, but after Julia's death the increasing rivalry between the two led to open rupture in 49. Pompey led the aristocratic and conservative party and was (reluctantly) followed in his policy by Cicero; after Pompey had taken his army to Greece and was defeated at the battle of Pharsalus, Cicero supported Caesar. Pompey escaped to Egypt where he was murdered on landing. He is sympathetically treated in the *Pharsalia* of LUCAN, though Lucan does not wholly succeed in making a tragic hero out of him. The many extant portrait busts show a face which looks weak and irresolute. The outline of the Theatre of Pompey can be traced in Rome, and next to it was the Porticus of Pompey and the assembly-hall in which Caesar was murdered at a meeting of the Senate:

Even at the base of Pompey's statua
Which all the while ran blood, great
Caesar fell.

According to Suetonius, the hall was never used again. A colossal statue and detached head found in the sixteenth century near the theatre was long thought to be that of Pompey, but the head is obviously from another body and the figure holding a globe topped by a Victory-symbol is now thought to be a Hercules. Pompey 'surnam'd the Big' is not usually among the medieval Nine Worthies, but he appears as one of four in *Love's Labour's Lost.*

Pompeius, Sextus
The younger son of Pompey, who held out against the forces of Caesar after his father's death and occupied Sicily as a naval base. He played off Antony against Octavian in 40 B.C. and was given command of Sicily, Sardinia and Achaea by the Treaty of Misenum (as in *Antony and Cleopatra*, II). He was later accused of breaking the treaty, and was eventually defeated at sea and executed.

Poppaea Sabina
The mistress of the Emperor Nero in A.D. 58, and then his wife from 62 until her death three years later. Josephus says that she was interested in Judaism, though not herself a Jew. Tacitus in the *Annals* says she was twice married before and describes her as a woman of

bad character who influenced Nero to murder his mother and to divorce his wife Octavia for sterility, but this is not confirmed. Monteverdi's last opera, *L'Incoronazione di Poppaea*, deals with the circumstances of her marriage to Nero and takes its plot from the Senecan tragedy, OCTAVIA.

Porcia

The daughter of Cato of Utica and wife of Caesar's murderer, the republican BRUTUS. As 'Portia' she is the 'true and honourable wife' who appears in Shakespeare's *Julius Caesar*.

Porphyry (A.D. 232–*c.* 305)

Greek scholar and philosopher of Tyre, pupil of LONGINUS and of PLOTINUS at Rome, whose philosophic works he edited. He wrote extensive commentaries on the Greek philosophers and on the problems of Homeric scholarship; his *Isagoge*, which was an introduction to the *Categories* of Aristotle, became the standard textbook of logic in the Middle Ages in the Latin version of Boethius. His treatise against the Christians was condemned to be burnt in 448 but fragments survive to illustrate his critical method.

Portland Vase

A celebrated vase of dark blue glass, $9\frac{3}{4}$ inches high, with a cameo-style relief showing scenes from the wedding of Peleus and Thetis [41]. It was probably made in Rome by Alexandrian craftsmen in the reign of Augustus, and the first mention of it is in the seventeenth century when it was in the Barberini Palace. It was later bought by Sir William Hamilton and then sold to the Duke of Portland, who lent it to Josiah Wedgwood to reproduce its style in his famous pottery. It was on loan to the British Museum when in 1845 it was smashed into more than two hundred pieces by a demonstrating student from Trinity College, Dublin; but it was skilfully repaired and finally bought by the museum in 1945. A similar cameo-style vase was found at Pompeii and is now in Naples.

Poseidon

The Greek god of earthquakes and later of the sea, who is worshipped with horses: see the opening chorus of Aristophanes' *Knights*. These are originally chthonic, not sea-horses; compare the horses of Hades and the worship of the earth-goddess Demeter in Arcadia with a horse's head. Poseidon was also said to be the father of the horse Pegasus by Medusa, and of the giant ANTAEUS by Ge. In Olympian mythology he is one of the three sons of Kronos, with Zeus and Hades, and has the sea for his domain. He is particularly important for Athens as he was the father of the Athenian hero Theseus, and he competed with Athene for ownership of Attica, offering the horse; this had to take second place to her offer of the olive. In the Homeric poems Poseidon is the enemy of the Trojans because he was cheated when he built the walls of Troy for LAOMEDON, and he sets out to delay the homecoming of Odysseus after his son Polyphemus is blinded. His contest with Athene features on the west pediment of the Parthenon, and there are also several fine ancient statues of Poseidon, notably the great bronze of the fifth century B.C. where he stands about to hurl his trident, and a statue from Melos of about 200 B.C. The marble temple of Poseidon on the promontory of Sunium in Attica, which dates from the late fifth century B.C., is as much a landmark to travellers today as it was to Pausanias, though he thought it was a temple of Athene. From Roman times onwards Poseidon's functions as a sea-god were taken over by NEPTUNE.

Posidonius (*c.* 135–50 B.C.)
Greek historian and philosopher from Syria, who taught Cicero at Rhodes where he was head of the Stoic school. His *Histories* were planned as a continuation of Polybius, but few fragments of their fifty-two books remain. As a personality and a teacher he had great influence in the development of Stoic philosophy. He admitted some of the passions, provided that they were properly controlled by reason, and he identified the Roman Empire with the Stoic brotherhood of man, since it was intended to cover all the peoples of the world. He also taught that the Empire was a reflection of the divinely ordered cosmos to which statesmen and philosophers could belong when they had fulfilled their tasks on earth. This is a view taken over by Cicero and expounded in SCIPIO'S DREAM.

Praxiteles
Athenian sculptor of the mid fourth century B.C., much admired and imitated throughout antiquity. Many of his marble statues are known through copies; for example, the APHRODITE of Cnidos described by Lucian and the elder Pliny, the Aphrodite of Arles [45], and Apollo the lizard-slayer (*Sauroctonus*). The famous Hermes carrying the infant Dionysus at Olympia is probably the original one seen by Pausanias. It is possible though not certain that he worked on the Mausoleum (→ MAUSOLUS).

Priam
The last king of Troy, son of Laomedon, husband of Hecabe, father of many sons and daughters (fifty of each in Homer) by his wife or concubines. In the *Iliad* he is already old and worn by suffering in the war, but he is unfailingly gentle to Helen, and goes to the Greek camp to ask Achilles for the body of Hector in one of the most moving episodes in the poem. In later legend he is killed at the altar of Zeus by NEOPTOLEMUS; see Virgil, *Aeneid* 2, and the Player's Speech in *Hamlet*. His name became a symbol for one who has suffered extremes of fortune, and he features in several of the cycles of paintings on Homeric themes from the walls of houses in Pompeii.

Priapus
A fertility god of the Hellespont region whose cult spread to Greece and Alexandria in the third century B.C. and afterwards to Italy, but never seems to have been taken very seriously. Priapus was treated with affectionate disrespect as a sort of scarecrow with a red-painted face and a phallus, set up as a god of gardens to ward off thieves. Donkeys were his sacrificial animal, as being an embodiment of lust. Horace, Tibullus

and Martial all wrote lightheartedly about him, and there is also a collection of eighty-five *priapeia*, short Latin poems of unknown authorship and varying obscenity. In Petronius' *Satyricon* the hero, Encolpius, is pursued by the wrath of Priapus and made sexually incapable in many of his encounters. In Poussin's large *Dance in Honour of Priapus* he appears as a conventional HERM.

Procopius (*c.* A.D. 500–after 562)
Byzantine historian and secretary to BELISARIUS, whom he accompanied on his campaigns. He returned to be prefect of Constantinople. Procopius is our main source for the reign of Justinian through his eight-book *History* and his description of the buildings and treasures of art of the city, and also in his very remarkable *Secret History*. He must have written this alongside his official one but shown it to no one because of its violent attacks on the policy of Justinian, and its scurrilous (and often well-founded) comments on the morals of the Empress Theodora.

Procrustes
A legendary robber of Attica, owner of a bed on which his victims had to fit, either by being hammered out and stretched, or by having their limbs lopped off. He was killed by Theseus. 'Procrustean' as an epithet still means the forcible subordination of individual differences to a system.

Prometheus ('foreseeing')
A Titan of early Greek legend of whom two main stories are told by Hesiod. (i) He created man out of clay and taught him the arts, then gave him fire, which Zeus took away; but Prometheus stole a spark in the pith of a stem of fennel. Zeus then sent PANDORA to punish mankind. On his travels in Phocis, Pausanias was shown a huge clay-coloured stone which the local people claimed smelt of human flesh and was left over from the creation.

(ii) Prometheus himself was punished by Zeus by being chained to a rock on Mount Caucasus with an eagle continuously pecking at his liver. This is the subject of Aeschylus' *Prometheus Bound*; Prometheus is punished both for the theft of fire and for refusing to reveal the secret that Thetis is destined to bear a son who will be greater than his father. He is the champion of man against the new Olympian authority, and the play is the first of a trilogy in which the freeing of Prometheus by Heracles followed in a lost play. Shelley develops this theme in his poetic drama *Prometheus Unbound*; Prometheus's knowledge would bring freedom and a reign of love instead of hate and oppression.

As the suffering creator of man and as the independent thinker and champion of freedom, Prometheus has had an appeal for widely different people. The early Fathers of the Christian Church saw his sufferings as symbolic of the Passion, and Tertullian could even write of Christ as *verus Prometheus*, the true Prometheus. For Byron as for Shelley he stood for the fight for freedom, while Goethe in his poem (well known from its settings by Schubert and Hugo Wolf) emphasized his sympathy with suffering humanity. He also inspired Beethoven's music for the ballet *The Creatures of Prometheus*, a symphonic poem by Liszt, and Scriabin's *Poem of Fire*. André Gide in his early *Le Prométhée mal enchainé* gives a characteristic ironic slant in his modernized version: Prometheus takes a masochistic delight in his tormenting eagle, as a symbol of man's self-destructive aspirations. The latest interpretation is that of Robert Lowell in his 'imitation' of Aeschylus.

Prometheus was painted by Piero di Cosimo in his last two paintings as the creator of man and the giver of fire, with his punishment awaiting him; civilization, like the Tree of Knowledge, brings evil with good. He was also painted by Titian, and by Michelangelo in a design for a pendentive in the Sistine Chapel. The most compelling scenes of his torments are by Rubens and Jordaens.

Propertius, Sextus (*c.* 50–*c.* 16 B.C.)
Roman elegiac poet from Assisi, living and writing in Rome, four books of whose poetry survive. These are unique in ancient literature. Propertius writes with passionate intensity when he traces the stormy course of his love for CYNTHIA, and he has rare insight into the psychology of lovers, particularly women. His imagery and allusive use of the old myths can be very difficult, but no more so than in poets such as Eliot and Pound, and he has a wonderful visual imagination, for which he finds expression in Latin which is stretched to the far limits of meaning. His moods shift quickly in a single poem, and he has a haunting sense of the inevitability of death, as well as a ready feeling for the ridiculous. In his later, less personal poems he claimed to be the Roman CALLIMACHUS, in the sense that he refused to write long epics; but he can be very like the Alexandrians in his recondite allusions. He is probably read more today than at any time since his own, at any rate in Ezra Pound's *Homage to Sextus Propertius*, which may gloss over his difficulty but brings out his ironic and 'modern' qualities, and in its own way is unique as a supreme example of 'creative translation'.

Protagoras (*c.* 485–*c.* 415 B.C.)
Greek sophist from Abdera in Thrace, a professional teacher in Athens of 'virtue' (*arete*), meaning efficiency in conduct of life, for which he was attacked by Socrates in the Platonic dialogue called after him. He was an agnostic, and believed that knowledge could not go beyond the subjectivity of human opinion. 'Man is the measure of all things' sums up his doctrine. He was condemned at Athens in 416 for 'impiety' and said to have been drowned in a shipwreck.

Proteus
A minor sea-god, shepherd of the flocks of sea-creatures, endowed by Poseidon with the gift of prophecy and also the power to change his shape until firmly held. (Hence the epithet 'protean', meaning variable or versatile.) He was said to live in a sea-cave on the island of Pharos off the Nile Delta, and was consulted by Menelaus in the *Odyssey* and by ARISTAEUS in Virgil's fourth *Georgic*.

Prudentius (Aurelius Prudentius Clemens, A.D. 348–? 410)

Christian Latin poet from Spain whose most famous surviving works are his *Cathemerinon*, a collection of hymns for daily use, and his *Psychomachia* ('battle of the soul'), an allegory of man's spiritual struggle set in epic form, which was well known in the Middle Ages.

Psyche ('soul')

In Homer the souls of the dead appear in the Underworld looking as they did in life, and it was under the influence of Orphism that the soul was conceived by poets and philosophers as being materially different from the body. In funeral art it was often depicted as a bird and later as a butterfly. Plato's famous version in *Phaedrus*, of the chariot of souls driven by Eros, presupposes a close connection between the soul and love, but the personification of Psyche as a girl visited at night by her lover Eros/Cupid has all of the characteristics of a fairy-tale, and is first told by APULEIUS in *The Golden Ass*. She is forbidden to look at him, but cannot resist holding a lamp over him to do so. The god is waked by a drop of hot oil, disappears, and Psyche has to search the world for him until Zeus takes pity on the lovers and reunites them. This has often been taken as an allegory of the soul's journey through life, or as a mystic union with the divine after suffering and death. Keats in his *Ode to Psyche* sees her more simply:

> O latest-born and loveliest vision far
> Of all Olympus' faded hierarchy.

Psyche's story was popular in Hellenistic poetry and art, and a marble group (*Invention of the Kiss*) is known from many Roman copies. The House of Amor (Cupid) and Psyche at Ostia also has a statue group dating from the fourth century A.D. For the Renaissance humanists, the symbolic interpretation was most important; the Loggia di Psyche in the Farnese Palace, Rome, is decorated with scenes from the story painted by Raphael. There is also a famous statue group by Canova [42], and one in a very different style by Rodin.

Ptolemy (Claudius Ptolemaeus, *fl.* A.D. 127–48)

Greek geographer of Alexandria, who also wrote on mathematics, music and astronomy, but who is most famous for his *Geography* and atlas in eight books. This was a standard work for a long time, as being the best of the ancient geographical studies; its errors are largely due to his miscalculation of the earth's circumference and reliance on sailors' reports rather than on astronomical calculation. It was superseded only in the sixteenth century when Copernicus established that the universe was centred not on the world but on the sun.

Pygmalion

A king or a sculptor of Cyprus in late legend, who made an ivory statue of a woman and fell in love with it. In answer to his prayers, Aphrodite breathed life into it, so that it became a woman, and mother of his son Paphos. At some point in the telling, the statue was given the name of

Galatea. The story was known from Ovid's *Metamorphoses*, and is recalled in the final scene of the living statue in Shakespeare's *The Winter's Tale*. It was lightly treated in a one-act opera by Rameau, which provoked a more idealistic interpretation from Rousseau; for him and for the German romantic poets, Pygmalion was a symbol of the romantic lover who could create his ideal beauty through the intensity of his desire, and this view continues into William Morris's *The Earthly Paradise*. G. B. Shaw turned Pygmalion into an expert in phonetics and Galatea into the cockney Eliza Doolittle who gains her independence through his education. This has now been vulgarized into the musical *My Fair Lady*.

Pyramus and **Thisbe**

Their story is told only by Ovid in *Metamorphoses* 4, where he says he heard it from the East. The setting is Babylon. The lovers are forbidden to meet, but talk through a chink in a wall, and arrange to meet by the tomb of Ninus. Thisbe arrives first and has to run from a lion, thereby dropping her veil. Pyramus finds this, and thinking her dead, stabs himself. She returns and kills herself with his sword, ever since which the mulberry tree near by has borne blood-red fruit. This is of course 'the most lamentable' comedy played by Bottom the weaver and his friends in *A Midsummer Night's Dream*, but it was also known in a medieval French version and was told by Chaucer in his *Legend of Good Women* and by Gower in *Confessio amantis*. There is a particularly delightful illustration to a French thirteenth-century manuscript with the lovers in medieval dress, Gothic script on 'Ninny's tomb', and accurately drawn mulberry leaves and berries [43]. Poussin also painted a *Pyramus and Thisbe*, in which everything is subordinated to the magnificent stormy landscape.

Pyrrhus

(i) The alternative name of the hero NEOPTOLEMUS.

(ii) King of Epirus (319–272 B.C.) in north-west Greece, an adventurer of great courage and enterprise who claimed descent from Neoptolemus. He carried on a series of campaigns against Macedonia, and was then called in to help the Greek cities of south Italy and Sicily against the expanding power of Rome. In 279 he defeated the Romans at Asculum in Apulia, but with such heavy losses in his own army that a 'pyrrhic victory' became proverbial for one gained at too great a cost. He was forced to leave Italy in 275 and returned to Greece, where he died in street fighting in Argos. Plutarch's *Life* of Pyrrhus was known to Poussin who painted the episode in chapter 2 (the crossing of a swollen river) in *The Saving of the Infant Pyrrhus*. A statue head with a Macedonian helmet and an oak garland found at Herculaneum is generally thought to represent Pyrrhus.

Pythagoras (*fl. c.* 530 B.C.)

Greek philosopher and mathematician who emigrated from Samos to Croton in south Italy, where he became the leader of a disciplined ascetic community of both men and women, and was locally identified with Hyperborean Apollo (→ ARIMASPI and HYPERBOREANS). He was a strict vegetarian, teaching that souls transmigrated between animal and man in a process of purification through reincarnation, and this was to have great influence on Plato and EMPEDOCLES. He also determined the principal intervals of the musical scale and taught that the heavenly bodies were divided by regular intervals according to the laws of harmony; this is the doctrine of the 'music of the spheres' (→ SCIPIO'S DREAM). Pythagoras left nothing in writing (the theorem in geometry which bears his name was set out by Euclid), and it is difficult to sort out fact from the legend which grew up around him, especially as the Pythagoreans' way of life had much in common with mystery-cult. There is good information in Aristotle and Plato and, rather surprisingly, in the last book of Ovid's *Metamorphoses* Pythagoras expounds his doctrine of transmigration to Numa Pompilius, who, if he was really successor to Romulus, is traditionally dated to about 150 years before Pythagoras's known date. → [50].

Pythia, Python

The priestess of Apollo at Delphi who delivered the oracles was called the Pythia and took her title from the Python, a dragon or snake which lived near the site of the oracle and was killed by Apollo. The bronze column in the form of a three-headed snake (originally supporting a gold tripod) described by Herodotus and Pausanias was removed by Constantine, and can still be seen on the site of the old hippodrome, in front of the Blue Mosque at Istanbul. The legend represents the victory of the Olympian god over the earlier chthonic deity; this was celebrated every four years in the Pythian games and competitions in music, drama and recitation. It is first told in the Homeric *Hymn to Pythian Apollo*. See also APOLLO; DELPHIC ORACLE.

Quintilian (Marcus Fabius Quintilianus, *c.* A.D. 35–*c.* 100)

Roman rhetorician and teacher from Spain, appointed first Professor of Rhetoric at Rome by the Emperor Vespasian. Tacitus and the younger Pliny were among his pupils, and he was admired by Juvenal. His speeches are lost, but his most important work has survived complete. This is the *Institutio Oratoria* (Education of an Orator) in ten books; following Cato's dictum that an orator must be a 'good man skilled in speaking', this covers the whole range of education, moral, literary and rhetorical. Some of it is rather technical and arid, but Quintilian is a valuable guide to what was considered good prose style in his own and in earlier days, and book 10 consists of a comparative survey of Greek and Latin literature. He was read by most of the Renaissance scholars after the discovery of a complete manuscript of the *Institutio* in 1416.

Quintus Smyrnaeus (*fl. c.* A.D. 400)

Greek epic poet from Smyrna, the author of the *Posthomerica* written in a pastiche of Homeric Greek, a long epic poem which recounts events from the end of the *Iliad* to the beginning of the *Odyssey* – for example, the arrival of the Amazons, the death of Achilles, and the Sack of Troy. For these, like Virgil, he drew on the (lost) sagas of the Epic Cycle, the *Little Iliad*, *Aethiopis* and *Sack of Ilium*.

Rape of the Sabines

A dramatic episode described in the first book of Livy, in which the Romans, led by Romulus, invite neighbouring tribes to celebrate a festival in the newly founded city, traditionally in the Circus Maximus, so that at a given signal the young men can carry off the native girls. This leads to war with the Sabines and eventual reconciliation and intermarriage after the mothers of the girls intervene. The tale is clearly a fiction designed to explain the gradual infiltration of early settlers into the indigenous peoples of Italy, but Livy's account and Ovid's in the *Fasti* are the source of some spirited interpretations in the post-Renaissance period, notably in the famous statue-group by Giovanni da Bologna, two paintings by Poussin, and a splendid Rubens which William Hazlitt described as 'plump florid viragos struggling with bearded ruffians'. David also painted the scene of the mothers' intervening to prevent further bloodshed, a picture which despite the purity of his intentions brought him the nickname of '*Raphael des sansculottes*'.

Regulus, Marcus Atilius

Roman consul and general of the third century B.C., remembered for his heroism in the wars with Carthage. He was taken prisoner with his army in 255 and later sent to Rome on parole to arrange an exchange of prisoners and to negotiate peace terms. He firmly advised the senate to refuse the terms offered and insisted on returning to Carthage to certain torture and death.

Well witting what the torturer's art
  Design'd him, with like unconcern
The press of kin he push'd apart
  And crowds encumbering his return,
As though, some tedious business o'er
  Of clients' court, his journey lay
Towards Venafrum's grassy floor,
  Or Sparta-built Tarentum's bay.

Horace, *Odes* 3.5, translated by J. Conington.

This famous ode is the centre of one of Rudyard Kipling's most successful schoolboy stories: 'Regulus' in *A Diversity of Creatures*. Regulus and his sense of honour were also used by Cicero as an illustration in his *On Duties*, book 3, and he became a national hero. Unfortunately there is only doubtful evidence for the episode and it has been suggested that it was invented by his family to paint the Carthaginians as torturers after his wife had tortured some Carthaginian prisoners-of-war. An alternative version said that he starved himself to death in a Carthaginian prison after his voluntary return.

Rhadamanthys

Son of Zeus and Europa, brother of Minos of Crete, and mentioned from Homer onwards with him and Aeacus as one of the judges of the dead in the Underworld.

Rhesus

In *Iliad* 10 a king of Thrace and ally of Priam, who is killed by Odysseus and Diomedes in a night raid on his camp, when his magnificent white horses are stolen. In the Greek tragedy *Rhesus* he is said not to die but to live on as a demi-god, and the horses, like those of Achilles, may originally have been divine; the scholiast commentators on both Homer and Virgil say that they had to be captured before they could taste Trojan grass and water, or else Troy could never fall. Euripides is known to have written a *Rhesus*, but it is doubtful whether this play is his.

Romulus and **Remus**

Romulus is the legendary founder of Rome, his name being a back-formation from the city's. The story of the twins is well known from Livy and from Plutarch's *Life* of Romulus. Their mother was Rhea Silvia, daughter of Numitor, king of Alba Longa, whose brother had deposed him and compelled Rhea Silvia to become a VESTAL VIRGIN. She claimed that Mars was their father, though Livy is sceptical about this. Her uncle imprisoned her and threw the babies into the Tiber. They were found by a shepherd (Faustulus) with a wolf suckling them; he took them home and his wife reared them [4]. They returned when grown men to restore Numitor and to found a city of their own on the site of Rome. In a quarrel over seniority, Remus was killed and Romulus became king. He took in fugitives for his citizens, found them wives (→ RAPE OF THE SABINES), and after reigning forty years mysteriously vanished in a whirlwind in the Campus Martius. He was then identified with the Sabine god, Quirinus, who was worshipped on the Quirinal Hill. This tale is also told by Ovid in the *Fasti*. The *Lapis Niger*, a square of black marble still in the Roman forum, was believed to cover the tomb of Romulus; a ritual law inscribed in early Latin was found below it. The wolf appears on early Roman coins, and the famous bronze she-wolf now in the Capitoline Museum, Rome, was traditionally set up on the Capitol in 296 B.C., though it is in fact very much older and may well be Etruscan work. It was known to Cicero, and in later times preserved in the Lateran Palace. The twins are not earlier than the sixteenth century. Also in the Capitoline Museum is an engaging Rubens of the wolf feeding the rosy babies.

Romulus Augustulus

The last of the Roman emperors of the West was also ROMULUS, though he was the son of one of Attila's officers, and Rome, by then, was plundered and half-derelict; as Gibbon says, 'the appellations of the two great founders, of the city and of the monarchy, were thus strangely united in the last of their successors . . . but the first was corrupted into Momyllus by the Greeks, and the second has been changed by the Latins into the contemptible diminutive Augustulus'. He was deposed by a German mercenary soldier, Odoacer, in A.D. 476, who spared the life of 'this inoffensive youth' and pensioned him off in the splendid Villa of Lucullus in

Campania. From then on the Emperor of the East reigned alone in Constantinople.

Roscius Gallus, Quintus
A famous Roman actor, distinguished in both comedy and tragedy, mentioned by Cicero as being rich and popular and having the dictator Sulla as patron. He died in 62 B.C., and his name immediately became synonymous with fine acting, as it was in later times. 'The young Roscius', who features in the dramatic criticism of Hazlitt and Charles Lamb, was the child actor William Betty, born in 1791 and appearing on the London stage in 1804.

Rubico(n)
A river flowing from the eastern Apennines into the Adriatic, which in the days of the Roman Republic was the boundary between Italy and Gaul. By law a general could not enter Roman territory at the head of his army, so that when Caesar crossed the Rubicon in 49 B.C. it was tantamount to a declaration of war on Pompey. The river is not certainly identified among several sited north of Rimini, but is probably the river Uso. Suetonius says that Caesar saw a vision of a superhuman figure which beckoned him across, and gives him the words *alea iacta est* ('the die is cast'). Lucan in his *Pharsalia* amplifies this vision into a woman personifying his distracted country. 'Crossing the Rubicon' is proverbial for an irrevocable decision:

This is no river of the dead or Lethe,
Tonight we sleep
On the banks of the Rubicon – the die
is cast;
There will be time to audit
The accounts later, there will be
sunlight later
And the equation will come out at last.
Louis MacNeice (*Autumn Journal*, 1939)

Sallust (Gaius Sallustius Crispus, 86–34 B.C.)
Roman politician and historian, anti-senatorial in his views, and a supporter of Caesar in the Civil War. He was later governor of Numidia where he became immensely rich at the expense of the provincials. He does not appear to have been brought to trial, but retired from public life to his famous Gardens of Sallust, where he wrote several historical works. Of these only two survive, the *Conspiracy of* CATILINE and *The War against Jugurtha*, the king of Numidia on whom the Romans had made war from 111 to 105 B.C. These monographs are Sallust's original contribution to historiography; they are written in a terse, epigrammatic style which is modelled on Thucydides and was to influence Tacitus.

Salmoneus
Son of Aeolus and brother of Sisyphus, Salmoneus was a king of Elis who presumed to imitate the thunder and lightning of Zeus, so that he was punished by being struck by a thunderbolt and cast into Tartarus. He is often quoted by classical writers as a typical instance of NEMESIS following on hubris.

Sappho (born *c.* 612 B.C.)
Greek lyric poet of Mytilene in Lesbos, contemporary of ALCAEUS, and the

centre of a group of young women and girls dedicated to the cult of Aphrodite. Sappho's expressed affection for them is the origin of the word Lesbianism. Very little is known of her life, and her love for PHAON and her suicide are not confirmed. She is said to have leapt off a cliff into the sea on the island of Leucas, but such leaping in an ecstatic state is known to have featured in the local festival of Apollo. The fragments of her seven books of poetry, written in Aeolic dialect and in a variety of metres including the 'Sapphic', copied by Horace, consist of hymns to the gods, marriage-songs and love-poems, written with an intensity and directness which makes her one of the great poets of all time. → → HESPERUS.

Sarpedon

In the *Iliad* he is an ally of the Trojans and a prince of Lycia leading his own troops, who is killed by Patroclus and mourned by his father Zeus, then carried off to Lycia by Sleep and Death (*Iliad* 16). There was a hero-cult of him in Lycia of great antiquity, and later mythographers said he was a son of Zeus and Europa and uncle of GLAUCUS, making him live three generations to fit the chronology. This is more likely to be a conflation of two Lycian heroes with the same name.

Saturn

An early Italian god of agriculture (*satus* means 'sown') afterwards identified with KRONOS. He was then husband of Rhea and father of Jupiter. His temple in Rome was traditionally consecrated in 497 B.C., and housed the State Treasury; eight columns from the building stand in the Forum. His festival, the *Saturnalia*, was celebrated on 17 December and succeeding days with annual jollification; slaves were allowed liberties, presents were exchanged, candles lit and a Lord of Misrule appointed. These festivities were transferred to New Year's Day in the fourth century A.D., to become part of the traditional domestic celebrations of Christmas. In the classical Roman poets, Saturn's rule on earth was identified with a GOLDEN AGE, and this becomes one of the conventions of later poetry. In Keats's *Hyperion* he is the 'poor lost king' of the Titans who has to yield to the Olympian gods.

Satyrs

In early mythology satyrs are half-bestial spirits of woods and hills, mischievous and amorous, and they appear chasing nymphs or revelling with Dionysus at drinking-parties, on vases from the sixth century onwards, often with horses' tails. The satyr play which traditionally followed each trilogy of tragedies at the drama festivals had horse-tailed satyrs for a chorus; the *Cyclops* attributed to Euripides is the nearest we have to a complete play of this kind. Praxiteles is known to have made several statues of satyrs, known now from copies, of which a satyr pouring wine is famous; these are nearer to the rustic satyrs of Hellenistic Arcadia. The Romans associated satyrs with Pan and Faunus and gave them the goats' legs and horns with which they commonly appear in post-Renaissance paintings; in Titian's *Bacchus and Ariadne*

[20], for instance, in Rubens's *Nymphs and Satyrs*, and in many paintings by Poussin. They can even be small and childish, as they are in Botticelli's *Venus and Mars*, and in Michelangelo's *Bacchus*. By then they are conventionally grouped with Arcadian shepherds and nymphs and their more sinister aspect is forgotten. Only the mischievous hobgoblins of Greek folklore, the 'kallikantzaroi', combine some of the old characteristics of satyrs with those of CENTAURS.

Scaevola, Gaius Mucius

The legendary ancestor of the Mucius family in Rome who was given his surname (meaning 'Left-handed') because he went to the camp of LARS PORSENNA and laid his right hand on a burning altar to show his fortitude, and thereby convince the Etruscans that there were numbers of Romans like him who were prepared to kill the Etruscan leader. This is a typical legend of the heroic early Romans, told as an edifying example by Livy and painted by Mantegna and Tiepolo. The Scaevola family produced several distinguished jurists, the last one legal adviser to the Emperor Marcus Aurelius.

Scipio Africanus Major, Publius Cornelius (236–184 B.C.)

One of the greatest members of a great Roman family, Scipio is the hero of the Second Punic War against Hannibal, whom he defeated at the battle of Zama in 202 B.C.; he was then given the suffix Africanus. Scipio's mastery of tactics and strategy has been admired right up to the present day. When Hannibal was established in Italy for so many years after the Roman defeat at Cannae, Scipio first took the offensive in Spain and captured it from the Carthaginians, then carried the war into Greece against Philip V of Macedon, who was supporting Hannibal, and finally landed in Africa in spite of opposition from the Senate. He led a devoted army for over ten years, flouted conventions of dress and manners, and built up a mystique round himself of receiving divine guidance. The Romans saw in him the spiritual descendant of Alexander the Great. In civil life he was less happy, and after being twice consul was accused of bribery by his political enemies and died in retirement. One of Seneca's most likeable *Moral Letters* (86) describes the simplicity of his country home near Naples.

Livy is the main source of his life, and his admiration made Scipio a medieval and Renaissance hero. Petrarch wrote a long Latin epic on him entitled *Africa*, which incidentally was a treasure-house of mythological lore for the fourteenth century, as its third canto was devoted to descriptions of the Olympian gods which decorated the imagined home of the king of Numidia. He was mentioned many times by Dante, who knew all about the career of *Scipion di gloria reda* ('Scipio, heir to glory'), and many times too by Montaigne in his essays. A set of tapestries on his fame was designed for the palace of Fontainebleau by Giulio Romano and was much admired by Poussin, who also painted a picture on the popular theme of the *Continence of Scipio*. This refers to an episode in Livy, book 26: Scipio was offered a beautiful captive for his slave but nobly refused and restored her to the young man she was pledged to marry. Mantegna's *Triumph of Scipio* is in the National Gallery, London.

Scipio Aemilianus Africanus Numantinus, Publius Cornelius
(184–129 B.C.)
The younger son of the Aemilius Paullus who finally defeated the Greeks in the Third Macedonian War, he was adopted by the son of Scipio Africanus Major. He defeated Carthage in the Third Punic War, and then gained his suffix for his campaigns in Spain and destruction of Numantia. Scipio, with the orator Gaius Laelius, headed the group of young senators known as the 'Scipionic Circle' who promoted the study of Greek literature and philosophy and cultivated the friendship of the Stoic philosopher Panaetius and the Greek historian POLYBIUS. They were also patrons of the comic dramatist TERENCE. They feature in Cicero's philosophic dialogues *On Friendship* and the *Republic*, where it is clear that he admired their ideal of uniting the best in Greek and Roman civilization.

Scipio's Dream
The *Somnium Scipionis* is part of book 6 of Cicero's *Republic*, the only part known from late antiquity onwards until further fragments of the work were found in the Vatican in 1820. In it the elder Scipio Africanus appears to his grandson in a dream which the younger Scipio relates to his friends in the Scipionic Circle; the setting is 129 B.C. and the *Dream* refers to an event in his youth twenty years ago: see MASINISSA. It is a vision of the nature of the universe, based on the central power of the sun, and develops the teaching of PYTHAGORAS about transmigration of souls and immortality, and of the nine spheres which make the music of the spheres; see also POSIDONIUS. The *Dream* was known to Boethius, and through him and the commentary of MACROBIUS was also known to the author of the *Roman de la rose* and to Chaucer, who refers to it several times, and gives an epitome of it at the beginning of the *Parliament of Fowls*. Troilus's 'lighte goost' rises to the eighth sphere and hears 'sownes ful of hevenyssh melodie'. It was translated into English in 1569 and used by Shakespeare in Lorenzo's lines in *The Merchant of Venice*:

There's not the smallest orb which thou
  behold'st
But in his motion like an angel sings,
Still quiring to the young-eyed
  cherubins;
Such harmony is in immortal souls ...

Compare Milton's Nativity hymn, where the 'crystal spheres' ring out a ninefold harmony.

Scylla
(i) The daughter of NISUS, King of Megara.
(ii) A sea-monster in the Straits of Messina opposite CHARYBDIS, past which Odysseus and also the Argonauts had to sail. She was said to have six heads and a ring of barking dogs round her belly, and appears like this in vase-paintings. Later legends told by Ovid

said she was once a nymph loved by Glaucus and changed by Circe, and she was also rationalized into a rock. There is still a promontory on the Calabrian coast called Scilla, with a medieval castle and town of the same name behind. The coins of Acragas (Agrigento) showed Scylla with a crab [31.4], but her many heads and fish-eating habits described by Homer suggest the octopus or giant squid.

Sejanus, Lucius Aelius (died A.D. 31)
The Prefect of the Praetorian Guard (the regiment stationed in the capital) whose influence on the Emperor Tiberius increased until he was suspected of aiming at the throne himself, and he was executed. He is depicted as a monster of calculated evil in the early books of Tacitus's *Annals*. Ben Jonson's early tragedy *Sejanus* deals with his downfall.

Selene
A pre-Greek or eastern goddess of the moon who was identified by the Greeks with Artemis, and by the Romans with Diana or the old Italian goddess Luna, and by both with HECATE. From then on the moon was a powerful influence in sorcery and love-charms. Like Eos, the dawn, she was given horses to drive across the sky, and appeared with these on the east pediment of the Parthenon. A splendid head of one of the horses is among the Elgin Marbles.

Semele
The daughter of Cadmus, king of Thebes, and the mother of the god Dionysus, by Zeus. According to Euripides in the *Bacchae*, and to Ovid following later sources, she was persuaded by jealous Hera to test the divinity of her lover by getting him to grant her wish that he should visit her in his true shape. She was then killed by his lightning and thunderbolts, and the unborn child was taken from her body to be brought up by the nymphs (→ DIONYSUS). Her name is not Greek, and may be a form of Selene or of Zemelo, a Phrygian earth-goddess; the Greeks also knew her as Thyone. Jupiter and Semele were often painted, notably by Tintoretto, and she is the subject of an opera by Handel.

Seneca, Lucius (or **Marcus**) **Annaeus**
(*c.* 55 B.C.–A.D. 37/41)
Roman rhetorician from Cordoba in Spain, generally known as the Elder Seneca, the father of the philosopher and grandfather of the poet Lucan. His writings on contemporary history are lost, but we have about half of the anthology of rhetoric he compiled, along with a summary intended for school use of the fourth century A.D. The work consists of extracts, written from memory, of the speeches of the great orators he had heard in his lifetime, and is valuable both for the history of oratory and as an example of early literary criticism.

Seneca, Lucius Annaeus
(*c.* 4 B.C.–A.D. 65)
'The Younger Seneca' was born in Spain but spent most of his life in Rome, as a philosopher and writer, and at one time tutor and chief adviser to the Emperor Nero. It was doubtless due

to him that 'Nero's first five years' were afterwards spoken of as a period of model government. At the same time, he was attacked in the Senate for having become enormously rich through his imperial connections, and he asked Nero's permission to retire in 62. Three years afterwards he was implicated in the conspiracy of Piso and told to commit suicide. His Stoic fortitude in his last moments is described by Tacitus (*Annals* 15); a Dying Seneca standing beside his bath was painted by Rubens. Seneca's main prose works are his *Apocolocyntosis* or 'Pumpkinification' of the deified Emperor Claudius, a satire rather like Byron's *Vision of Judgement*; philosophical dialogues on ethical topics such as Friendship, Mercy and Providence; *Problems of Science*; and his *Moral Letters*, 124 in number, which are addressed to his friend Lucilius but are really essays on right conduct in the light of Seneca's Stoic beliefs.

Seneca also wrote tragedies, nine of which survive, modelled on Greek drama but very different in treatment. Among them are a *Medea*, a *Phaedra*, an *Oedipus* which leaves nothing to the imagination, and a particularly gruesome *Thyestes* (→ ATREUS for his story). They were all intended to be read rather than acted on the stage, and their mixture of rhetorical bombast and horror with passages of real poetic beauty had considerable influence on the late Elizabethan and Jacobean writers of melodrama, such as Webster and Tourneur. It was long believed that the plays were by a different Seneca, and throughout the Middle Ages, when only Cicero was better known, he was studied only as a moralist. He is frequently mentioned by Chaucer, and '*Seneca morale*' is put with Cicero and the great Greek philosophers in Limbo by Dante. He was even included in St Jerome's list of Christian saints, thanks to an apocryphal series of letters which were supposed to have passed between him and St Paul. As an essayist he had great influence on the Renaissance essay-writers Petrarch and Erasmus, Bacon and Montaigne, and is known to have been enjoyed and translated by Queen Elizabeth I. The two conflicting sides of Seneca's character were perhaps due to his health; he was an asthmatic, often ill, and certainly neurotic, so that he swings uneasily between Stoic calm and theatrical cruelty. Even in his prose style there is the feeling of stress, and on this we have the acute comment quoted in Aubrey's *Brief Lives* of Dr Ralph Kettell, D.D., who 'was wont to say that Seneca writes as a Boare does pisse, *scilicet* by jirkes'.

Septimius Severus, Lucius

(Roman Emperor A.D. 193–211)

Born a native of Lepcis Magna in north Africa, at a time when it was a prosperous seaport, Septimius was responsible for much of its splendid layout, the ruins of which are famous today. The town had a large forum, a basilica decorated with imported red granite and green marble, colonnaded streets and a great two-facing triumphal arch. Another arch stands in the forum of Rome, to commemorate victories over the Parthians. His famous *Septizonium*, an ornamental façade which served as a screen for the south-east corner of the Palatine, stood until it was pulled down and its stone used for other buildings by Sixtus V. Also in his reign a plan of Rome (the *forma urbis*) was cut in stone, several large fragments of which survive, one showing the Theatre of Pompey. Septimius's main interest was the army, and throughout his reign it took priority over the needs of the civil population. His second wife was Julia Domna, a Syrian, and a beautiful and cultivated woman who presided over a *salon* of learned people, including the physician GALEN and the philosopher Flavius Philostratus. Under her patronage, Philostratus wrote his *Life* of APOLLONIUS OF TYANA and *Lives* of the Sophists.

Sertorius, Quintus (*c.* 122–72 B.C.)
Roman popular leader and idealist, whose *Life* is written by Plutarch as an example of the admired Roman virtues of courage, leadership, and generosity towards the people he ruled. Sertorius was an opponent of the dictator Sulla, and while governor in Spain was asked by the Lusitanians to form an independent government. He set up a senate from Romans living in Spain, and schools to educate the native Spaniards, who believed that he had divine counsel and protection from Diana, and that the white fawn which always followed him was a gift from the goddess. He tried to gain support from MITHRIDATES of Pontus and it took several years of fighting with reinforced armies sent out from Rome to break his power. In the end he lost self-confidence and popularity and was murdered. He was admired by Plutarch and is the hero of one of Corneille's Roman tragedies.

Servius Tullius
Traditionally the sixth king of Rome, reigning 578–525 B.C., he is a historical figure who was responsible for building a temple to the Latin goddess Diana on the Aventine hill, and also for the original city-walls. Remains of the Wall of Servius still to be seen, however, are no earlier than the fourth century B.C.; but they are thought to follow the line of the earlier wall.

Seven against Thebes
The heroes of the episode in Theban saga described under ETEOCLES. They are listed in Aeschylus's *Seven against Thebes* and Euripides' *Suppliants* and *Phoenician Women* as: ADRASTUS, AMPHIARAUS, CAPANEUS, Hippomedon of Argos, Parthenopaeus, son of Milanion and ATALANTA, Polynices, brother of Eteocles, and Tydeus, father of DIOMEDES.

Seven Hills of Rome
The spurs of high ground above the left bank of the Tiber basin on which the city was founded are still clearly visible beneath modern buildings. They are the Capitoline, Palatine and Aventine, ringed round by the Quirinal, Viminal, Esquiline and Caelian hills.

> . . . an imperial city stood,
> With towers and temples proudly elevate
> On seven small hills, with palaces adorn'd,
> Porches and theatres, baths, aqueducts,

Statues, and trophies, and triumphal arcs,
Gardens and groves . . .

Milton (*Paradise Regained* 4.33–8) very properly mentions the aqueducts, for after these were broken by the Huns the waterless hills were abandoned. Medieval Rome grew up in the low-lying land between the hills, and it was only when the popes rebuilt the aqueducts and added to them in the sixteenth century that the great churches and palaces could be built and 'the grandeur that was Rome' reappear.

Seven Kings of Rome

These were traditionally said to be: Romulus, Numa Pompilius, Tullus Hostilius, Ancus Martius, Tarquinius Priscus, Servius Tullius and Tarquinius Superbus.

Seven Sages of Greece

These were generally said to be: THALES of Miletus, SOLON of Athens, Bias of Priene, Chilo of Sparta who brought back the bones of ORESTES, Cleobulus of Rhodes, PERIANDER of Corinth and PITTACUS of Mytilene. They were said to have had the maxims 'Know thyself' and 'Nothing too much' inscribed on the front of the Temple of Apollo at Delphi.

Seven Wonders of the Ancient World

The Pyramids of Egypt; the Mausoleum at Halicarnassus; the Hanging Gardens of Babylon; the Temple of Artemis at Ephesus; the statue of Zeus at Olympia by PHIDIAS; the COLOSSUS OF RHODES; and the Pharos of Alexandria, the great fortress and lighthouse built on a promontory of the eastern harbour which Homer knew as an island, and home of PROTEUS. It was built to the designs of Sostratus, an Asiatic Greek in the service of the Ptolemies, and was dedicated to 'the Saviour Gods' (which could cover both Castor and Pollux and the reigning king and queen) in 279 B.C. It was well over 400 feet high, topped by a 'mirror' which seems to have been part reflector, part telescope, and a statue of Poseidon, and it functioned for some time after the Arab conquest. The lantern fell in A.D. 700, and eventually earthquakes destroyed it.

Sibyl (Sibylla)

The name first used in Hellenistic Greek of an inspired prophetess, who was localized in several places, until its use became generic and there were many Sibyls; ten are listed by Varro. The most famous of these was the Sibyl of Cumae in Campania, who tells Aeneas in *Aeneid* 6 how to enter the Underworld; see the GOLDEN BOUGH. A popular story told how a Sibyl offered King Tarquinius Priscus nine books of prophecies, which he refused to buy at the price. She returned, having burnt three, and was still refused; when she had burnt another three he agreed to buy the last three at the price for the original nine. These books were kept in the charge of special priests and consulted only by order of the Senate in times of need, as we know from Livy. When they were destroyed by fire in 83 B.C. another collection was made to replace them. (There were many later additions, including Christian and Jewish forgeries, and there are still extant fourteen books of so-called sibylline prophecy.) They were last consulted in the fourth century A.D., and soon afterwards burnt by order of STILICHO.

It was because of the forged interpolations, along with Virgil's MESSIANIC ECLOGUE, in which the Sibyl is the prophet, that Sibyls come to be linked with Old Testament prophets in Christian literature and art, bridging the gap between sacred and profane prophecy. A Sibyl testifies alongside King David in the *Dies Irae*, and Sibyls are among women of the Old Testament and female Christian saints in the famous fifteenth-century carved choir-stalls in the Cathedral of Ulm [50]. Five Sibyls are painted by Michelangelo on the ceiling of the Sistine Chapel, and they also appear with angels in Raphael's Vatican paintings. A classical Sibyl was painted with Tarquin by Mantegna; with Augustus by Tintoretto; with Aeneas by Turner; and there is a solitary Sibyl by Rembrandt.

In Ovid's *Metamorphoses* the Sibyl has already lived seven generations when she is consulted by Aeneas. She tells him that Apollo had granted her request for as many years as there were grains in a handful of dust, but she had forgotten to ask him for perpetual youth as well (compare TITHONUS). Petronius adds to this in the *Satyricon* 48.8: Trimalchio claims to have seen the Sibyl hanging up in a bottle at Cumae, and when children asked her (in Greek) what she wanted, all she would say was 'I want to die.' This sinister symbol of withered hopes is used by T. S. Eliot as the epigraph to *The Waste Land*.

Sidonius Apollinaris
(*c.* A.D. 430–*c.* 480)
A noble Gallo-Roman, born in Lyon, statesman, author and Bishop of Averna (Clermont-Ferrand) in the Auvergne district of France, where he upheld his people in their resistance to the Visigoths. He was prefect of Rome for a year in 468 and wrote three verse panegyrics on the imperial family, as well as short poems to his friends, but gave up poetry when he accepted a bishopric. He was imprisoned for a short time by the Visigoths, but lived quietly on his estates for the most part, where he edited his letters for publication, in nine volumes, modelled on those of the younger Pliny. These are important for evidence about conditions in fifth-century Gaul and the break-up of the western Empire. He was later canonized as St Sidonius.

Silenus
The Sileni were originally spirits of wild nature rather like satyrs, but by the sixth century B.C. Silenus appears on the François Vase as a bearded man with horse-ears, and he becomes associated with the god Dionysus and is sometimes said to have been his tutor. He possesses special knowledge and the wisdom which is inspired by wine-drinking, and is generally drunk, as he is in the story of MIDAS. There are similar stories of his being captured and regaling his audience with wonderful tales, in Virgil's *Eclogue* 6, for example. He also becomes a rather comic drunk-

ard, and sileni are among the chorus in the comic satyr-plays; in Hellenistic art he more often appears as a fat Falstaff-type riding on a donkey than with the dignity he retains in the frescoes of the Villa dei Misteri at Pompeii. Socrates was often compared with Silenus both for his ugliness and for his god-given wisdom, and in Plato's *Symposium* Alcibiades compares Socrates with the little Silenus statuettes or boxes which opened to show the figure of a god inside, evidently popular at the time. As a symbol of things not always being what they seem and of inspirational wisdom, this was used by Renaissance writers; Rabelais in his prologue to *Gargantua* speaks of 'sileni' as small apothecaries' boxes with valuable drugs or perfumes inside, and one of the best-known *Adages* of Erasmus is *Sileni Alcibiadis*. Silenus appears in most Bacchanal paintings, notably those of Titian and Piero di Cosimo; there is a splendid drunken Silenus by Rubens in which he is being helped along by satyrs and bacchants or nymphs who are all equally drunk, and another by Géricault.

Silius Italicus (A.D. 26–101)
Roman imperial administrator and poet, who enjoyed a long cultivated retirement on his estates near Naples, collecting books and works of art, and restoring the tomb of Virgil. Most of our information about his life and death (by self-starvation to end an incurable illness) comes from a single letter by Pliny (3.7). His main work was his *Punica*, an extant 12,000-line epic on the war with Hannibal, which Pliny rightly assesses as painstaking rather than inspired.

Simonides (*c.* 556–*c.* 468 B.C.)
Greek lyric poet of Ceos, living in Athens and later in Sicily, the uncle of BACCHYLIDES and friend of THEMISTOCLES. He commemorated the Greek victories in the Persian wars, and his epigrams, drinking-songs and hymns were famous in his lifetime. The few surviving fragments of his large output include a wonderful poem on DANAË, and he is generally best known for his epitaph on the Greeks who fell at Thermopylae under LEONIDAS, which has been so often translated:

Go now, and tell the Spartans, passer-by,
That here obedient to their laws we lie.

Sinon
Not mentioned by Homer, but in the Troy legends he is the Greek who pretends to be a deserter, goes into Troy, and persuades the people to admit the Wooden Horse. He then waits till nightfall and lets out the Greeks hidden inside. He is best known from *Aeneid* 2, after which he became a byword for treachery. In Dante '*il falso Sinon greco*' (the false Greek Sinon) is in the Eighth Circle of Hell among the falsifiers of words.

Sirens
In Homer they are two sisters (the number varies later) who lure sailors to their island by their singing, and then destroy them. Odysseus takes his men safely past by stopping their ears with wax and having himself bound to the mast. The Argonauts also escape with

the help of Orpheus, whose singing surpasses the sirens'. They were traditionally associated with the *insulae Sirenusae*, the present Galli islands in the Bay of Salerno (Norman Douglas's *Siren Land*). But in the non-Homeric tradition they were originally daughters of Earth, companions of Persephone and escort to the dead; they also feed on the dead and are not unlike HARPIES. They are shown on early vases with birds' legs and wings [47], and this continues up to a wall-painting from Pompeii of the first century A.D. At the same time they become increasingly humanized as beautiful women (cf. GORGONS), and are eventually part of the conventional decoration of sarcophagi and fountains. In folklore they develop fish-tails like northern mermaids. They also lose their evil nature; in the last book of Plato's *Republic* eight sirens supply notes for the Pythagorean music of the heavenly spheres. And according to Suetonius, 'What song the Syrens sang' was no more than one of three impossible questions which the Emperor Tiberius used to put to tease his *savants*. But the popular notion of a siren is generally still one of a *femme fatale*. Her primitive pagan power reappears in E. M. Forster's *Story of the Siren*: 'Silence and loneliness cannot last for ever. It may be a hundred or a thousand years, but the sea lasts longer, and she shall come out of it and sing.'

Sisyphus

A king of Corinth and ancestor of Bellerophon; as a trickster a rival to AUTOLYCUS, and in Homer already in Hades for crimes which are variously explained by later mythographers. He was condemned to roll a huge stone uphill, though it always rolls down again; surprisingly, Titian painted him carrying the stone on his back. A 'sisyphean task' demands endless and often fruitless labour, and the title *Le mythe de Sisyphe* was chosen by Albert Camus for his essays on the absurdity of life and the futility of man's endeavours.

Socrates (469–399 B.C.)

The Athenian philosopher, traditionally son of a stone-mason, and married to Xanthippe who later became proverbial for her bad temper. In early life he had served in the army and held public office; he defied THE THIRTY TYRANTS, and when the serving generals were brought to illegal trial after the Athenian losses at Arginusae, he refused to put the motion for their conviction to the Athenian assembly. But it was a popular jury which condemned him when he was brought to trial on the charge of 'introducing strange gods' and corrupting the young, and he was sentenced to death by drinking hemlock. His defence and his last days are described by Plato in his *Apology* and *Phaedo*. Socrates believed that he had a duty (which he sometimes said was laid on him by the Delphic oracle) to teach through questioning people's beliefs, and he also called himself a midwife, not a creator, of ideas. He wrote nothing himself, and it is mainly through Plato's early dialogues and Xenophon's memoirs that we know about his teaching and personality. His famous 'Socratic irony' (pretence of ignorance) and his 'Socratic method' of skilfully directing his questions to obtain the answers he wanted could appear at first sight to produce only negative results; those he questioned were shown that their assumptions were ill-founded. But this was a necessary preliminary to the start of serious discussion with defined terms, for Socrates held that philosophy should properly be applied to conduct of life, and to be good we must know what 'good' means ('Virtue is knowledge'). Consequently he condemned the ready-made rules for success offered by the SOPHISTS. His personality attracted men of all kinds to join in the discussions which he carried on wherever he happened to be; he was perceptive, humorous and unaffected, and his intimate circle included professional philosophers from all over Greece as well as pupils as different as Plato and Alcibiades. 'Platonic love' refers to the passage in the *Symposium* where Alcibiades describes the purity of his relations with Socrates. He was caricatured by Aristophanes in the *Clouds*, but not in the many portrait-busts which show him as pug-nosed, for his ugliness was often mentioned by his contemporaries: see SILENUS. (David gave him a more heroic face in his *Death of Socrates.*) Though he was anathema to Nietzsche, who held that Socrates was an example of over-emphasis on reason, he has never lost the power to shake us out of ill-founded complacency.

Solon (*c.* 640–*c.* 560 B.C.)
Athenian statesman and legislator who was elected to end civil strife in 594. This he did by his famous reforms – cancellation of debts and the ending of serfdom by laws forbidding borrowing on the security of the person, and modification of the laws of DRACO. He also defined the duties of the popular assembly and set up the *boule*, the administrative council. Solon was also the first known Athenian poet, mainly on political themes; some fragments of his poems survive. He travelled widely in later life in Greece, Egypt and Asia Minor and was revered as one of the Seven Sages in later times. In Lydia he met CROESUS, to whom he made his famous remark that no man could be said to have lived a happy life until he was dead – which so impressed Cyrus of Persia when Croesus repeated it that Croesus was granted his life.

Sophists
The Greek word *sophistes* originally meant a wise man or an expert, but by the fifth century B.C. it had come to mean a professional teacher, usually itinerant, who gave instruction in return for fees. Famous sophists mentioned by Plato include PROTAGORAS, and Gorgias of Leontini in Sicily (*c.* 483–376 B.C.). In the absence of an adequate school-system in Greece they often gave good value for money, but their profession lost reputation in the hands of unscrupulous men (like Thrasymachus in Plato's *Republic*) who claimed to teach easy ways to success and money-making, and the technique of arguing on any point without regard for morality or truth. It was for this that Socrates condemned the sophists as a whole, and a sophistic argument has come to mean one which is specious and irresponsible.

Sophocles (*c.* 496–406 B.C.)
Athenian tragic dramatist, a genial, popular figure who was active in civic life and the friend of Herodotus and Pericles. He is known to have written 123 plays, of which seven survive: AJAX, ANTIGONE, *King* OEDIPUS, *The Women of Trachis* (→ DEIANIRA), ELECTRA, PHILOCTETES and *Oedipus at Colonus*. There are also fragments of his satyr-play, *The Trackers* (*Ichneutae*). Sophocles was an innovator in his plays; he abandoned the trilogy form, he introduced a third actor on the stage, and he was a master of dialogue as well as of logical structure of plot. He was famous for his dramatic irony, marked in *King Oedipus*, when a speaker does not realize the significance of what he says, though his audience does. He saw and exploited the dramatic possibilities within the framework of the traditional myths, and he created characters which were admired by Aristotle for being 'like ourselves only nobler'. He is the dramatist whom Aristotle most admires in the *Poetics*. Sophocles himself is quoted as saying that he created men as they ought to be, Euripides men as they are. Shelley's first love was Aeschylus, but he admired Sophocles increasingly, and in his preface to *The Cenci* grouped the two Oedipus plays with *King Lear*. A volume of Sophocles was the book found in his pocket after he was drowned.

Sophonisba
Her name is really Saphanba'al, Latinized as Sophoniba; this is the popular form. She was the daughter of a Carthaginian general, Hasdrubal, and her tragedy is told by Livy in book 30 of his history. She was already married to Syphax, king of Numidia, when he was defeated in 203 B.C. by the army of Scipio Africanus led by the exiled Numidian prince MASINISSA. He would have married her to save her having to go to Rome as a captive, but Scipio forbade it. She then took poison and died. She was painted by Mantegna, and by Rembrandt, and her romantic story was dramatized by Corneille and by several minor English playwrights in the eighteenth century. One line at least survives to be quoted from James Thomson's version: 'Oh! Sophonisba! Sophonisba! Oh!'

Spartacus
A Thracian gladiator who led a revolt in Capua in 73 B.C., and was joined by large numbers of runaway slaves, deserters from the army and renegades of all types, until his army numbered 90,000. He held out against the Roman army for two years, finding it increasingly difficult to control his followers, but was finally caught by CRASSUS and crucified with many of the rebels. Pompey killed off the survivors in 70. From Plutarch's account in his *Lives* of Crassus and Pompey it is clear that Spartacus became a legend in his lifetime. He is the idealistic hero of Arthur Koestler's historical novel, *The Gladiators*.

Sphinx
A fabulous monster, with human head and body of a lion, originating in Egypt, where the sex can be male or female. The sphinx came to Greece via

the Near East and then was always female [31.6]. In particular, a Sphinx is at the centre of the cycle of Theban legends involving the House of Oedipus. From her lair she asked her famous riddle, which has a strong element of folklore: What is it that walks on four legs in the morning, on two at noon, and on three in the evening? Anyone who failed to answer it she strangled and devoured. Oedipus answered correctly that it was Man, who first crawls on all fours, then walks upright, and in old age needs a stick as a third leg. She then leapt from a rock in fury and was dashed to pieces. Her home was traditionally on a mountain north of Thebes (below which on the railway there used to be a small station named Σφιγξ). Sphinxes were very popular in early classical art either as a decorative frieze or on the top of early grave-monuments, where they were often given wings. They gradually came to be thought of as not so much malevolent as enigmatic and mysterious, and they were humanized in art with beautiful faces and women's breasts. This is how Ingres twice painted the Sphinx with Oedipus [9]: the breasts and outstretched paw are her prominent features, as they are in the version by Moreau. A powerful image of the Sphinx is in *The Double Vision of Michael Robartes* by W. B. Yeats:

On the grey rock of Cashel I suddenly saw
A Sphinx with woman breast and lion paw,
A Buddha, hand at rest,
Hand lifted up that blest...
One lashed her tail; her eyes lit by the moon
Gazed upon all things known, all things unknown,
In triumph of intellect
With motionless head erect.

Between the Sphinx and the Buddha, intellect and heart, a girl dances; possibly intended by Yeats as a symbol of human life poised between opposites.

Statius, Publius Papinius

(*c.* A.D. 45–96)

Roman poet, born in Naples but living in Rome, where he was a popular social and literary figure, until his retirement shortly before his death. His main works are epic, but he also wrote his *Silvae*, thirty-two occasional poems addressed to friends and officials and containing some lavish flattery of his patron, the Emperor Domitian; one commemorates an equestrian statue of Domitian in the Forum, and the most famous is an *Ode to Sleep*. These were lost until a manuscript was found in 1417 by Poggio Bracciolini at Constance. Statius's reputation in the Middle Ages therefore rested on his epics, in particular his *Thebaid*, written in twelve books on the subject of Oedipus's curse on his sons and the fight between Polynices and ETEOCLES. His second epic, *Achilleid*, on the early life of Achilles (→ DEIDAMIA) was left unfinished. The *Thebaid* is the source of a medieval *Romance of Thebes*, and was even translated into Gaelic; more than seventy manuscripts existed, convincing proof of its popularity. Chaucer certainly knew Statius well and refers to him several times; in book 5 of *Troilus and Criseyde* Cassandra gives a summary of the *Thebaid*, in book 2 Criseyde and her companions are reading it, and in *The House of Fame* Statius appears on one of the pillars alongside Homer, Virgil, Ovid, Lucan and Claudian. Dante accepted the tradition that Statius was converted to Christianity by Virgil's MESSIANIC ECLOGUE: Virgil was the torch which throws light for those that follow, though its bearer is in darkness. He therefore makes Statius meet Virgil and Dante in Purgatory, and it is Statius, not Virgil, who guides Dante on the last stage of his journey and is invited to drink from the river of the Earthly Paradise (*Purgatorio* 21, 22, 33). When Dante sees Ulysses and Diomedes among the Counsellors of Fraud in the Eighth Circle of Hell, they are wrapped in a forked flame which he describes by comparison with the one from the pyre of Eteocles and Polynices in Thebes; their mutual hatred in life prevented even their flames from mingling. This he takes directly from *Thebaid* 12. Statius continued to be admired through the Renaissance, and among the Augustan poets, when he was translated by Pope and Gray. No one is likely now to class him with Virgil, but there has been awakened interest in his use of imagery since C. S. Lewis wrote of him in *The Allegory of Love* as the first allegorist poet.

Stentor

A Greek mentioned in the *Iliad* as having a 'brazen voice' equal to that of fifty men, and in later legend as having died after his defeat by Hermes in a shouting match. His name has survived in 'stentorian', meaning 'very loud'.

Stesichorus

Greek lyric poet of the early sixth century B.C., living most of his time in Magna Graecia (South Italy) or Sicily. According to SUIDAS his real name was Teisias, and this is a pseudonym. Alexandrian scholars knew twenty-six books of his collected works; only about the same number of fragments survive. But the titles of some of his poems – a *Boar-hunt*, *Oresteia*, *Geryon*, *Eriphyle* (→ AMPHIARAUS) and *Sack of Troy* – show that he gave lyric treatment to epic themes. One fragment deals with the usual legend of Helen's abduction, and is followed by another which is part of his *Palinode*, or recantation, the earliest version of the legend that she stayed in Egypt and her phantom went to Troy. He also wrote on Sicilian folklore, including the tragic love of Daphnis, and can be considered as the forerunner of pastoral poetry.

Stilicho (*c.* A.D. 365–408)

The general commanding the armies of the Roman Emperor Theodosius, a Vandal who made a career in the service of Rome. He held the Goths in check on the eastern frontiers (→ ARETHUSA), and repelled the first invasion of Italy by the Visigoth ALARIC in 403–6. He then persuaded the Roman Senate to buy the invaders off with a large subsidy of gold and to elect him a senator. This lost him popularity, and he was murdered with his family in Ravenna. His achievements were praised by CLAUDIAN who died before his downfall; but St Jerome called him 'a barbarian traitor who armed our enemies at our expense for our destruction', and his view is shared by Gibbon.

Stoics

The Stoic school of philosophy was founded by Zeno of Citium in Cyprus (335–263 B.C.), who came to Athens and taught in the Stoa Poikile, or Painted Porch. His teaching was developed by Chrysippus (*c.* 290–207 B.C.) and in the form modified by Panaetius and POSIDONIUS it reached Rome in the mid second century B.C., where it was immediately popular with the educated nobility (→ SCIPIO AEMILIANUS). In the first century A.D. its chief exponent was the younger SENECA. It also provided a philosophic basis for a group of opponents to the principle of one-man imperial rule from the time of Nero to that of Domitian; men like the senators Thrasea Paetus and Helvidius Priscus, who were admired by Tacitus and the younger Pliny, are often spoken of as a 'Stoic opposition'. After the time of EPICTETUS the most famous Stoic was the Emperor Marcus Aurelius.

The Stoics taught that nature is controlled by divine reason, and that man's reason is a spark of that divine fire. It is his moral duty to live in harmony with the rational principle, and knowledge of this truth is virtue; man is virtuous only in proportion to his wisdom, but once possessed of this virtue he is indifferent to reverses of fortune, to pain or death, he is self-controlled, and he is just towards his fellows because he is free from prejudice. In its wider aspect Stoicism taught that the divine reason was a Natural Law leading to a universal brotherhood of men, but it was easy to misrepresent the individual Stoic as lacking any warmth of sympathy or humanity: he was 'passionless, pitiless and perfect'. The whole concept was attacked by some of the humanist thinkers, notably Erasmus, by Milton in *Paradise Regained*, 4.300 ff., and latterly by T. S. Eliot as being the reverse of Christian humility. 'Stoic' or 'stoical' has now come to mean little more than a show of indifference to pain or emotion.

Strabo (*c.* 63 B.C.–A.D. 21 or later)

Greek historian and geographer from Pontus, on the Black Sea, who was wealthy enough to travel widely in Asia Minor and Egypt and to visit Rome several times. His long *Historical Studies* is entirely lost, but his geography of the Roman empire in seventeen books is almost complete, including its remarkable preface on the importance of geography as a branch of scientific inquiry. Strabo owes much to the Alexandrian geographer Eratosthenes (*c.* 275–194 B.C.) whose view that the world is a sphere he accepted, but his main interest is not physical but human geography, linked with accounts of the politics and histories of the peoples he describes.

Stymphalian Birds

Fabulous monsters which Heracles had to expel from Lake Stymphalus in Arcadia as his Sixth Labour. This he did by scaring them with bronze castanets given him by Athene. The best account of them is in Pausanias's tour of Arcadia in book 8 of his *Guide to Greece*. They were bronze-beaked and man-eating, and as big as cranes, and Pausanias describes a similar savage bird in the Arabian desert. They were somehow connected with a local cult of Artemis, for Pausanias saw a sanctuary with the birds carved in wood on the roof, and also statues of bird-legged girls (cf. HARPIES and SIRENS). APOLLONIUS RHODIUS says that they flew off from Heracles to the Black Sea, where they threatened the Argonauts. They appear on local coins and in vase-paintings, and three were carved on the metopes of the Temple of Zeus at Olympia. The castanet story was not followed by Dürer, whose only painting on a classical subject is *Hercules Killing the Stymphalian Birds*, in which Hercules is drawing a bow.

Styx

The river in the Underworld over which the souls of the dead are traditionally ferried by Charon, though it is sometimes described as a lake or swamp, as it is in Aristophanes' *Frogs*. In Dante too it is a muddy black marsh in which the Wrathful must struggle and the Sullen lie choking, and so it appears in Delacroix's picture of *Dante and Virgil Crossing the Styx*. Homer makes the gods swear their most potent oaths by Styx; and in non-Homeric legend Achilles is dipped in it to make him invulnerable. Herodotus says that the Arcadians took oath by the Infernal River which could be seen as a trickle from a rock into a basin near Pheneus, but what was generally thought to be the Styx was further west, a cascade which is still to be seen pouring down the slopes of Mount Chelmos. Its waters are as cold as any mountain torrent, and leave a black stain on the rocks. In ancient times they were thought to be poisonous; Arrian and Plutarch both report that Alexander the Great was killed by water from the Styx sent to him in a mule's hoof, though Pausanias does not commit himself. One of the artificial stretches of water in the grounds of Hadrian's Villa at Tivoli is called the Styx, a fancy which was sometimes revived by romantic classicists. In the Hellfire Caves near West Wycombe, Buckinghamshire, for example, there is a sizeable underground pool appropriately named Styx.

The famous painting *Charon Crossing the Styx* [53] by the Flemish landscape-painter Joachim Patinir shows a broad, sluggish river with its two banks in striking contrast, that of the living bathed in light and that of the dead ominously black beneath gathering storm-clouds; it is perhaps the most successful attempt at depicting a stygian atmosphere.

Suetonius Tranquillus, Gaius

(*c.* A.D. 69–*c.* 140)

Roman historian and biographer, friend and correspondent of the younger Pliny, and personal secretary to the Emperor Hadrian. All his works on natural science and antiquities are lost, and only fragments survive of his *Lives of Famous Men*, but his *Lives of the Twelve Caesars* (Julius Caesar to Domitian) is complete and became a model for biography in the Middle Ages. Einhard's *Life of Charlemagne*, for instance, is consciously modelled on Suetonius, and in its turn was copied by Asser in his *Life of Alfred*. The pattern is the same throughout: first the subject's family and early life, then his public career, his physical appearance, and finally his private life. Suetonius's interest in the colourful vices of his subjects makes lively reading and has given him the reputation of a scandalmonger, but his real fault is that he records everything he can find without any critical evaluation. He has continued to be popular in Philemon Holland's translation of 1606 and a modern one by Robert Graves.

Suidas (more accurately, 'the Suda')
This is often referred to as an authority as if it were a person, but it is in fact the name of a lexicon or literary encyclopedia compiled at the end of the tenth century A.D. The name means 'Fortress'. Its compilers evidently knew Homer and some of the dramatists, though they rely too much on late abridgements of early authors, and it contains valuable information about Greek works which would otherwise be unknown.

Sul or **Sulis**
The Celtic deity whom the Romans identified with Minerva, and the patron of the city of Aquae Sulis (modern Bath). The ruins of the temple of Sul-Minerva are less impressive than those of the great Roman Baths, fed by hot mineral springs, which were in use at least until the fourth century A.D. One of the finest fragments of Anglo-Saxon poetry is *The Ruin*, a description of a deserted Roman city generally accepted as Aquae Sulis. Nothing is more evocative of a vanished civilization:

Snapped rooftrees, towers fallen,
the work of the Giants, the stonesmiths,
mouldereth . . .

Stood stone houses; wide streams welled
hot from source, and a wall all caugh
in its bright bosom, that the baths were
hot at hall's hearth; that was fitting . . .*

Sulla, Lucius Cornelius (138–78 B.C.)
Roman general and leader of the aristocratic conservative party in the Civil War against the popular democratic leader MARIUS. Sulla's early military successes were in the East, over Mithridates of Pontus. Then after defeating Marius he made himself Dictator of Rome, with special powers, and assumed the name of Felix ('Fortunate'). He made sweeping changes in the constitution and the jury system in order to give more power to the senate and create an efficient administration, and went into retirement a year before his death. His almost regal behaviour and cruelty to his political opponents and to the Greeks were long remembered, and are recorded in Plutarch's *Life*. A modern assessment of his complex, neurotic personality is in Peter Green's historical novel, *The Sword of Pleasure*.

Sybaris
A Greek colony in south Italy, in the area known as Magna Graecia, founded in 720 B.C. on the Gulf of Tarentum,

* Michael Alexander, *The Earliest English Poems*, Penguin Books, 1966.

which monopolized trade with the Etruscans and became highly prosperous, until rivalry with neighbouring Croton ended in total destruction in 510 B.C. The Sybarites continued to be a byword for luxurious living; hence the current meaning of the epithet 'sybaritic'.

Sycophants

Greek term denoting private prosecutors in Athens, where there was no system of public prosecution. The etymology is uncertain, but probably refers to some indecent gesture connected with figs (*sykoi*), and indicates their unpopularity. Their inducement to undertake a case was often a share in fines exacted, and the system was naturally open to abuse. The worst type of professional sycophant was a blackmailer who took money to let the guilty go unpunished, and there are frequent satirical references to such men in the plays of Aristophanes. Today the epithet 'sycophantic' has come to mean servile and obsequious.

Symmachus, Quintus Aurelius

(*c.* A.D. 340–*c.* 402)

(i) Roman statesman, a member of an old noble family, and a strong opponent of Christianity, although he was a friend of AUSONIUS and recommended St Augustine for the Chair of Rhetoric at Milan. He was City Prefect of Rome in 384–5 and fought hard to retain the altar of Victory in the senate-house when pagan worship was forbidden by the Emperor Gratian. In this he was defeated by the Christian party led by St Ambrose, and lost his position; but he was later consul, and seems to have maintained good relations with successive emperors. His published letters survive in full, edited in nine books of personal and one of official correspondence like those of the younger Pliny.

(ii) His descendant of the same name was a senator and scholar, and father-in-law of BOETHIUS. He served the Gothic Emperor Theodoric, but came under suspicion of treason along with Boethius and was executed. We have Gibbon's brief account of Theodoric's later remorse and the remarkable form it took on one occasion:, (*Decline*, 4.39)

> ... His mind was humbled by the contrast of the past, and justly alarmed by the invisible terrors of futurity. One evening, as it is related, when the head of a large fish was served on the royal table, he suddenly exclaimed that he beheld the angry countenance of Symmachus, his eyes glaring fury and revenge, and his mouth armed with long sharp teeth, which threatened to devour him.

Symposium

In classical Greece a symposium was a drinking-party, though the drink was less important than the entertainment. Wine was drunk mixed with water, often one part to three; music was provided by flute-girls, garlands of flowers were worn, there were competitions for songs and riddles – all this appears in the poets (→ ANACREON), and as standard decoration on countless red-figure vases. As a literary genre a *Symposium* follows the tradition of open discussion and lively conversation at these parties. Plato's *Symposium* is a framework for a debate on love, where

'Platonic love' refers to the argument for the supremacy of non-sexual love. Xenophon's is a collection of anecdotes about Socrates, and there are serious symposia by PLUTARCH, Aulus GELLIUS and MACROBIUS, satirical versions by Lucian, and a splendid burlesque symposium in Aristophanes' *Wasps*. A symposium today is rarely helped along by wine, whether neat or watered, and generally means no more than a discussion-group or a published collection of scholars' opinions.

Syrinx
A nymph of Arcadia who was pursued by PAN and escaped by asking the earth to help her. She then turned into a bed of reeds out of which Pan made his pipes, a simple instrument of reeds of graduated lengths which in Greek is called a syrinx. In Ovid's account in the *Metamorphoses* Mercury approaches ARGUS disguised as a herdsman playing on a syrinx, and tells how the pipes were once the nymph, as a soothing story to lull Argus to sleep before killing him – a good example of Ovid's ingenuity in moving from one legend to another. Syrinx and her fate could be seen by the Renaissance as a symbol of the mystic life-through-death; or as musical inspiration coming through possession by Pan's ecstatic powers, an idea which reappears in the nineteenth-century poem by Mrs Browning, *A Musical Instrument*, once a feature of every anthology and now scarcely known beyond the opening question:

What was he doing, the great god Pan,
  Down in the reeds of the river?

He was 'Making a poet out of a man', half-beast as he is, while

The true gods sigh for the cost and pain
For the reed which grows nevermore
  again
As a reed with the reeds of the river.

Syrinx was painted with Pan by Poussin, Jordaens and Boucher among others, and her flight from Pan's pursuit is mimed in the last episode of Ravel's ballet, *Daphnis et Chloé*.

Tacitus, Cornelius (*c.* A.D. 55–*c.* 120)
The historian of imperial Rome, who was also a distinguished orator and held senatorial office, including the consulship. His circle of friends included the younger Pliny, who greatly admired him and wrote his eye-witness account of the eruption of Vesuvius for inclusion in Tacitus's *Histories*. Tacitus's earliest work, the *Dialogue on the Orators*, discusses the decline of oratory since the time of the Republic. *Agricola* and *Germania* are historical monographs on his father-in-law Julius AGRICOLA, and on the Germanic tribes whose customs and morality are contrasted with the luxurious habits of Rome (one of the earliest treatments of the theme of the Noble Savage). The *Histories* cover the period from the death of Nero to the death of Domitian, and were planned to continue to cover the reign of Trajan. The *Annals* went from the death of Augustus to the reign of Nero, but it is one of the greatest losses to historians that so much of these works is missing. Tacitus's Latin style is unique, though it owes a good deal to Sallust; intense, epigrammatic, astringent and

sometimes Virgilian, it is far removed from the rounded periods of Ciceronian prose. His outlook is pessimistic, for he shared the ancient belief that human individuals determine the pattern of history, and he saw little to admire in the emperors. The whole concept of the principate was for him a deterioration from the older, democratic virtues and contained the seeds of Rome's decay. Gibbon admired him more than any other ancient historian, and took him as his model for *The Decline and Fall of the Roman Empire*. 'The revolution of ages may bring round the same calamities, but the ages may revolve without producing a Tacitus to describe them' (Footnote to *The Decline* 36.49).

Tacitus was virtually unknown in the Middle Ages, and both the *Annals* and the *Histories* survive through the discovery of a single manuscript at the time of the Renaissance; he provided no subjects for idealized Roman qualities, and was not translated into English until the late sixteenth century. He was admired by Montaigne, but criticized by Milton for despairing of the Republic; he was also accused of influencing Machiavelli's so-called attacks on public morality. The sheer difficulty of his Latin has always been a barrier to all but his dedicated admirers.

Tantalus

Son of Zeus, king of Sipylos in Lydia, father of NIOBE and PELOPS, Tantalus is remembered for his punishment in Hades where he stands in water up to his chin and is 'tantalized' with food and water which move out of his reach whenever he tries to satisfy his hunger and thirst. He has also given his name to a case for decanters of wine and spirits such as stood on Victorian sideboards, where the drink could be seen but not enjoyed except by the owner of the key. His crimes in legend are various, the most serious being that he stole the food of the gods, and he also killed his son Pelops and cooked his flesh as a banquet for the gods, who brought the boy to life again.

Tarchon

The legendary ancestor of the Etruscan **Tarquins**, leader of the emigrants from Lydia, the founder of Tarquinii and other Etruscan cities. In Virgil's *Aeneid* 8 he joins Aeneas as an ally. Many painted tombs have been found in Tuscany (Etruria) as evidence of the advanced Etruscan culture, and at Cervetri (ancient Caere) one of the rock sepulchres in the vast necropolis is known as the 'Tomb of the Tarquins'. There were two Tarquin kings of Rome: (i) Tarquinius Priscus, traditionally the fifth king, reigning 616–579 B.C., who was believed to have brought Etruscan craftsmen to Rome, built the temples on the Capitol, and started the city's drainage and sewage system by building the Cloaca Maxima. The exit of this sewer can still be seen as it enters the Tiber, but the brickwork is much later than Tarquinius, and probably dates from Agrippa's works. It was he who bought the prophetic books from the SIBYL.

(ii) Tarquinius Superbus, the last king of Rome, who reigned traditionally from 534–510 B.C. His son Sextus Tarquinius raped LUCRETIA, the wife of his cousin Tarquinius Collatinus. After the expulsion of the Tarquins Collatinus was regarded as one of the founders of the Republic, and was elected consul with Junius BRUTUS in 509.

Tarpeia

In book I of his history Livy tells the story of the daughter of Tarpeius, the commander of the Roman garrison stationed on the Capitol at the time of the Sabine Wars, soon after the foundation of Rome. She promised to show the way up to the citadel if Tatius, the Sabine leader, would give her what his men 'wore on their shield-arms'. Instead of the gold torques she expected, their shields were used to crush her to death. This legend is clearly intended to account for the name of the Tarpeian Rock, the precipice at the south-west corner of the Capitol from which criminals were sentenced to be flung to their death. The last victim was a Roman knight accused of conspiracy against the Emperor Claudius in A.D. 43.

Tartarus

A place of punishment in the Underworld. In Homer it is only for Kronos and the defeated Titans, but later it receives all evil-doers. Hesiod describes it as being as far below earth as heaven is above, and the accounts of its torments in *Aeneid* 6 had marked effect on Dante and Christian believers in the agonies of hell.

Tecmessa

A Trojan captive assigned to Ajax; possibly wholly invented by Sophocles, who makes her a sympathetic figure in his *Ajax*, which deals with the hero's madness and death. She also appeared in lost Roman tragedies, and is in the epic poem of Quintus Smyrnaeus.

Telegonus

The legendary son of Odysseus and Circe, apparently an invention of the author of the *Telegony*, a lost epic of the sixth century B.C., in which Telegonus ultimately marries Penelope, while Telemachus marries Circe.

Telemachus

The son of Odysseus and Penelope in the *Odyssey*, where he plays a main part. In the early books he goes to inquire after his father at the courts of Nestor and Menelaus, and after being brought safely home by Athene, past an ambush laid by the suitors, he goes on hoping for Odysseus's return, meets him in the hut of EUMAEUS, and helps him to destroy the suitors. Outside Homer he is scarcely known, except in the lost *Telegony* where he ends up married to Circe. *Télémaque* is the title given by the French bishop Fénelon to a long prose romance written for the education of the grandson of Louis XIV, which was highly regarded in the eighteenth century. This describes imaginary journeyings of Telemachus and his guide, Mentor, who points the moral at every stage, and it can be taken as a satire on contemporary court life. Telemachus is Stephen Dedalus in James Joyce's *Ulysses*, where the early episodes are the counterpart of Telemachus's travels in search of his father.

Terence (Publius Terentius Afer, *c.* 185–after 160 B.C.)
Roman comic dramatist of north African origin, possibly a Berber, who came to Rome as a slave, and was freed and patronized by SCIPIO AEMILIANUS and other members of the Scipionic Circle; his enemies suggested that they wrote his plays for him. His six comedies, his sole output, are *The Girl from Andros, The Mother-in-law, The Self-Tormentor, The Eunuch, Phormio* and *The Brothers.* They are skilfully adapted from Greek New Comedy and written in lucid and elegant Latin with no concessions to popular taste. They were never appreciated by his contemporaries, and Julius Caesar is said to have summed up Terence as a 'half-size Menander'. They are really what we call 'drawing-room comedies' and demand a sophisticated audience. Terence's own prologues to the plays are of great interest, not only because they are a justification of his method of conflating his Greek sources, but also because they are one of the earliest examples known of an artist who is consciously writing about himself and his purpose. Manuscripts of Terence were carefully preserved and copied with their illustrations from the fourth century A.D. onwards, and his Latin was much admired by St Augustine and St Jerome. In the tenth century a Saxon nun, Hrotsvitha, was inspired to write in his manner on sacred subjects to provide more suitable reading for the pious. He appears, surprisingly, as a bearded elder statesman among the pagan philosophers in the fifteenth-century choir-stalls of the Cathedral at Ulm [50]. He was widely read and performed both in the original and in translation throughout the Renaissance and later into the eighteenth century, and was used as a textbook in the schools for the purity of his Latin until the reforms of Dr Arnold, who disapproved of his light-hearted treatment of young men and their love-affairs. He was probably the main influence on the Comedy of Manners in western literature, greatly admired by Congreve and by Molière, who is his true spiritual descendant. *Les Fourberies de Scapin* is closely modelled on *Phormio.*

Terminus
In Latin, a boundary mark, and in Roman religion a divinity attached locally to all such marks, important in a country of small farmers. Ovid in the *Fasti* describes how a *terminus* was set up with ceremonial offerings to its *numen*, or godhead, and describes the annual feast of the Terminalia. All local boundaries were under the general influence of a god Terminus who was believed to be the original inhabitant of the Capitol. His statue remained inside when the temple of Jupiter was built, with a hole in the roof so that he had the open sky above him.

The Renaissance humanist Erasmus chose Terminus for his emblem on a medal designed for him by Quentin Metsys; the reverse shows the god's bust on a pillar with the words *Concedo nulli* (I yield to none). Round the rim run the words in Greek 'Keep the end of a long life in view' and in Latin 'Death is the ultimate boundary of all things'. Erasmus explains in his letters that he took this both as a warning that the end of life was always at hand, and as an incentive to lead a better life, thus characteristically seeing a Christian symbol in an old pagan god.

Thales
Greek philosopher of Miletus of the late seventh century B.C., the first of the Ionian physical scientists. He tried to determine the material basis of the world and decided it was water. Herodotus says that he was able to predict within a year the solar eclipse of 585 B.C., though this is now considered unlikely, and he visited Egypt, studied the cause of the Nile floods, and found a means of measuring the height of the Pyramids. He was considered to be one of the Seven Sages of Greece, and is traditionally the absent-minded philosopher who fell down a well.

Themistocles (*c.* 528–*c.* 462 B.C.)
Athenian statesman and naval commander who persuaded the Athenians to evacuate the city after their defeat at Thermopylae, and then defeated the Persians in the naval battle of Salamis. He then persuaded the Athenians to rebuild Athens and to connect it with the port of Piraeus by the Long Walls. His policy of building up the fleet with money from the Attic silver-mines meant that the lower classes were able to play a larger part in politics, for they were needed to man the ships, but he antagonized many by his high-handed methods. He was first banished for non-cooperation with Sparta, and then condemned to death in absence for pro-Persian sympathy, at Spartan instigation. He then went over to Asia Minor and was given suitable rewards by the Persian king, and he died in a position of honour at Magnesia. Herodotus and Thucydides are the ancient authorities for his career, and his *Life* was also written by Plutarch. Napoleon compared himself with Themistocles in his letter of surrender to the English, as he threw himself on their mercy just as Themistocles did on the mercy of the Persians when he came to them as a condemned exile.

Theocritus (*c.* 300–*c.* 260 B.C.)
Greek pastoral poet of Syracuse, working mostly in Cos and Alexandria. His *Idylls* include dedicatory epigrams, court poems, mythological poems, and in *Idyll* 15 a lively picture of Alexandrian housewives at the festival of Adonis, but his great achievement was his poetry in the pastoral genre, which was to have such influence on Virgil and on all subsequent pastoral poets (→ ARCADIA). Though he writes in an artificial literary Doric dialect for a sophisticated audience, Theocritus still manages to convey his genuine feeling for the rural life of Sicily and south Italy.

Theodoric the Great
(*c.* A.D. 454–526)
Sent as a hostage to Constantinople at the age of seven, he was educated there and succeeded his father as king of the Ostrogoths in 474. After various campaigns both for and against the emperor of the East he was encouraged to come to Italy in 488, and after the surrender of Ravenna in 493 and the murder of

Odoacer (→ ROMULUS AUGUSTULUS) he reigned in Ravenna. He was responsible for building two of Ravenna's magnificent churches, San Vitale and Sant' Apollinare Nuovo, where there is a picture of his palace among the mosaics. They were planned as Arian churches and made over to the Roman Catholic Church after his death. Theodoric brought temporary peace and greater prosperity to Italy and began by encouraging literature and the arts, but as he became increasingly involved in doctrinal disputes, because of his Arian beliefs, he ended his life in disillusionment, and had already executed BOETHIUS and SYMMACHUS for suspected treason. His tomb is one of the sights of Ravenna, a ten-sided stone building of two stories with a flat dome thirty-six feet in diameter made of a single slab of stone. Theodoric is a hero of thirteenth-century German saga as Dietrich von Bern (Verona), and is mentioned as an example of the mutability of Fortune in the Anglo-Saxon poem *Deor*:

> Thirty winters Theodric ruled
> The Maering city; and many knew it.
> That went by; this may too.

Translated by Michael Alexander

Theognis
Greek elegiac poet of the late sixth century B.C., from the fragments of whose poems it can be inferred that he was a native of Megara, in love with a young man called Cyrnus, and that he looked with disillusionment on the world around him, where the traditions and privileges of his class were likely to disappear. His poems are mostly short and pithy, and were probably intended to be sung at drinking-parties (*symposia*), but it is difficult to know how much of what is attributed to him is authentic.

Theophrastus (*c.* 370–*c.* 288 B.C.)
Greek philosopher from Lesbos, the pupil of Aristotle, and after Aristotle's death the head of the Peripatetic School. From his enormous output there survive several short scientific papers and two major botanical works (the first system of botany built up on Aristotelian methods of classification by genera and species), and also the work for which he is generally remembered, his *Characters*. Here about thirty types of bad and tiresome characters are shrewdly observed and sketched with a good deal of wit and humour. The companion collection of Good Characters is lost. Some of them might be dramatic monologues, and are reflected in the characters of New Comedy; MENANDER was a pupil of Theophrastus. They also owe much to Aristotle's classification of human types in his *Ethics*. They were known in the Middle Ages and especially popular in the seventeenth and eighteenth centuries, particularly in France; their influence can be seen in La Fontaine's *Fables*, La Rochefoucauld's *Maximes*, and especially in La Bruyère's own *Caractères*, which in the first edition was prefaced by a translation of Theophrastus. They were translated several times in England, and some of the *Spectator* essays of Addison and Steele are in the same genre of character-sketch.

Thersites

The only non-heroic character in the *Iliad*, Thersites is described as ugly, low-class, mean-spirited and foul-mouthed, and he accuses Agamemnon of prolonging the war in his own interests, until he is beaten and silenced by Odysseus. In non-Homeric tradition he is of better origin, but is killed by Achilles for insulting him. In Shakespeare's *Troilus and Cressida* he is the 'deformed and scurrilous Grecian' who acts as a sardonic commentator on the play's theme of 'war and lechery'.

Theseus

The national hero of Athens, son of Aethra, a princess of Troezen, and AEGEUS or of Poseidon, who had visited Aethra in the form of a bull. He was thought to have been a contemporary of Heracles, and some of their exploits are very similar. He was brought up in Troezen, and told by Aethra to move a heavy rock under which he found a sword and sandals left for him by Aegeus. He then set out by the dangerous coast road, killing the brigands PROCRUSTES, Sinis who killed his victims by tying them between two trees which sprang apart, and Sciron who lurked on the top of the high cliffs still known as the Scironian Rocks, in order to kick travellers into the sea below. In Athens he narrowly escaped being poisoned by Medea, was set further difficult tasks, and then volunteered to go to Crete with the tribute sent to Minos. There he killed the MINOTAUR and escaped with ARIADNE, abandoned her at Dia (Naxos) and sailed on to Delos. In Plutarch's day the intricate 'crane dance' in imitation of the twists and turns of the labyrinth, which he and his men danced there, was still known. As king after the suicide of Aegeus he was said to have brought the Attic communities under the rule of Athens, and he has a part in nearly every famous legend. He took part in the Calydonian Boar-hunt, welcomed the exiled Oedipus in Athens, was the father of Hippolytus by the queen of the Amazons, and married Phaedra, sister of Ariadne. He was said to have carried off Helen before her marriage and been forced to give her back to the Dioscuri, her brothers. He took part in the battle of Lapiths and centaurs at the wedding of his close friend PIRITHOUS and went with him down to Hades in an attempt to capture Persephone, from where he was rescued by Heracles. He died on the island of Scyros, and his bones were brought to Athens in historic times and given heroic honours. He continued to protect his city, and was seen as a gigantic apparition fighting for the Greeks at the battle of Marathon.

Most of these fables are told rather uncritically by Plutarch in his *Life*, and are woven into Mary Renault's novels; → AEGEUS. Theseus is often referred to in Attic literature, especially for his love for Pirithous, and his exploits often feature on vase-paintings; there is a large fifth-century jar from Vulci now in the British Museum, which covers many of them. He also appears triumphant over the Minotaur in a fresco from Herculaneum. He has little impact on later times; *Theseus Finding his Father's Arms* was painted by Poussin, and *Theseus and the Dead Minotaur* was one of Canova's first statues in neoclassical style. Boccaccio's long verse *Teseida* was freely adapted by Chaucer for his *Knight's Tale*, the story of Palamon and Arcite who are 'sworn brothers' as the chivalrous counterpart of Theseus and Pirithous. The setting is the court of Theseus 'Duke of Athens', which Shakespeare took over for *A Midsummer Night's Dream*.

Racine in *Phèdre* saw Theseus as a man appalled by the murderous effect of his prayer to be rid of Hippolytus, but it is not until André Gide's *Thésée* that Theseus takes on symbolic significance. There he is a man who has outgrown a taste for adventure and amoral love-affairs, he has lost his wife and dearly loved son, and yet he finds fulfilment in his task of founding Athens. In his confrontation with Oedipus, his is the practical wisdom which contrasts with Oedipus's newly gained mystical insight. The subject had interested Gide for thirty years before he wrote this famous '*sotie*', in which Ariadne is the eternal woman who would keep her man tied to an apron-string, Icarus a metaphysician, and Daedalus the creator of a labyrinth which is a maze of hallucination and languorous delight from which no man wishes to escape. →→ MINOTAUR.

Thespis

Attic poet of the sixth century B.C., traditionally said to be the inventor of Greek tragedy, in that he was the first to appear on the Athenian stage as an actor separated from the chorus, and to introduce a prologue and set speeches into what had previously been a wholly choral performance. Thespis also disguised his face in order to portray a character, from which developed the tragic masks worn on the stage. 'Thespian' now refers to drama in general.

Thetis

One of the Nereids, who was fated to bear a son mightier than his father. In the legend followed by Aeschylus this was eventually revealed by Prometheus as the price of his freedom; Zeus and Poseidon then decided to marry her to a mortal. For her wedding, see PELEUS. Their son was Achilles, and late legend says that she left Peleus because he tried to stop her making Achilles immortal by dipping him in the Styx. She had also resisted having to marry him by changing her shape until she found she could not make him loose his hold. In the *Iliad* she is humanized as a mother whose only concern is her son, and she is always sadly conscious that he is doomed to early death. She comes up from the sea with her fellow-Nereids to comfort him after the death of Patroclus, and goes with them to Olympus to ask Zeus for new armour. This is the scene of *Jupiter and Thetis* painted by Ingres. Milton's list of Nereids in *Comus* is taken from Homer, and 'Thetis' tinsel-slippered feet' echoes her Homeric epithet of 'silver-footed'.

Thirty Tyrants, The

In 404 B.C., at the end of the Peloponnesian War, the oligarchs in Athens made overtures to the Spartan general LYSANDER to get help in forcing the democratic party to suspend the constitution. They then put absolute power into the hands of thirty men who let loose such a reign of terror that 'The Thirty' were long recalled with horror. (→ LYSIAS, SOCRATES.) They lasted little more than a year, after which democracy was restored, but 1,500 men were said to have been executed and many more were exiled or fled from Athens.

Thucydides (*c.* 460–*c.* 400 B.C.)
Greek historian, a general during the Peloponnesian War, who was exiled in 424 for failing to defend the important town of Amphipolis on the coast of Thrace. He did not return to Athens for twenty years. His *History of the Peloponnesian War* is in eight books, the last breaking off at events of 411, though it was his intention to carry it on to the end of the war in 404. Thucydides was the first historian to examine long-term causes and political and moral issues, to estimate the deleterious effect of war on national character, and to see all the events he records as part of a logical pattern of cause and effect. He writes terse, lucid Greek in his narrative, but is much more complex and idiosyncratic in the great dramatic speeches which serve as a medium for analysing public feeling and the issues at stake. The most famous of these are the *Melian Dialogue*, in which is debated the moral right of a strong central power to use force on a reluctant ally, if a war situation and expediency demand it, and the *Funeral Speech* delivered by Pericles, in which the Athenian contribution to civilization is magnificently set out. Thucydides was known from the Renaissance onwards from the Latin translation by Lorenzo Valla, and was translated into English in the seventeenth century by the political philosopher Thomas Hobbes. His style was too difficult for him to be read much in the original until the nineteenth century, when his account of the expanding seapower of Athens had special appeal for the British empire-builders. His great exponent was Benjamin Jowett, the famous master of Balliol College, Oxford, and along with Plato he was chosen by Dr Arnold as an author to be studied in the reformed public schools. Today, in a world in which wars and revolutions have destroyed any sense of security, we are perhaps even better equipped to appreciate the perceptive detachment of Thucydides' judgements, so that with Euripides, he is the most 'modern' of the Greeks who analysed social evils.

Tiberius (Tiberius Julius Caesar Germanicus, Roman Emperor A.D. 14–37)
Stepson of the Emperor Augustus through his wife LIVIA, Tiberius was reluctantly recognized as successor. He was in retirement at Rhodes, after an early successful military career, when he was recalled to become emperor at the age of fifty-six. He was loyal to the constitution laid down by Augustus, but his rigid economies and lack of geniality meant that he was never popular, unlike his adopted son GERMANICUS. As our main sources for his reign are Tacitus and Suetonius, one heavily biased against him, the other dwelling on personal anecdotes which are often scurrilous, it is difficult to

assess his character. He was certainly heavily dependent at first on SEJANUS, who encouraged the trials and executions for treason for which Tiberius is notorious, and his last ten years spent in close retirement on the island of Capri gave rise to rumours of orgies to which Suetonius does full justice. Local legends about 'Timberio' have added embellishments. Tacitus (*Annals* 4) says that he built twelve villas there, and the ruins of several, including the Villa Jovis, the largest, are still to be seen. After all this it is a pleasure to see him honoured in the fine triumphal arch in the French town of Orange (Roman Arausio).

Tibullus, Albius (55/48–19 B.C.)
Roman elegiac poet, the friend of Horace and of Ovid, who wrote his elegy in *Amores* 3.9. Tibullus left two books of poems addressed to his patron Valerius Messalla Corvinus, a general of the Emperor Augustus, and to his two mistresses, Delia and Nemesis. Tibullus seems to have lived quietly on his estate near Rome, writing pastoral poetry which often shows real feeling for the Italian countryside. A third book published with the other two as his contains poems by other members of Messalla's circle: an anonymous panegyric of Messalla, six rather ordinary elegies by Lygdamus, and five short, eloquent poems known as *Sulpicia's Garland*, which describe her love for an unidentified Cerinthus. Whether these are by a genuine Roman poetess it is impossible to say. Tibullus's pleasantly Ovidian poetry was known throughout the Middle Ages, and the third book was recognized by Renaissance scholars as being by various hands.

Timaeus
A Pythagorean philosopher from Locri, south Italy, the chief spokesman in Plato's late dialogue *Timaeus*, otherwise unknown, and possibly invented by Plato. The dialogue contains the first mention of ATLANTIS, and it is an attempt to reconcile the concept of a divine creation with a scientific explanation of natural phenomena. Through the Latin version of the philosopher Chalcidius (*fl. c.* A.D. 500) it was the only Platonic dialogue known in the West before the revival of Greek; it was studied throughout the Middle Ages and its Creator was often identified with the God of Genesis. It was taken up afresh in the Renaissance, particularly by the Neoplatonists in their battle against Aristotelian scholasticism. In Raphael's great painting of the *School of Athens* the two central figures are Plato and Aristotle, Plato holding a copy of *Timaeus* and pointing towards Heaven, Aristotle with his *Ethics* and a hand extended towards the earth.

Timon
A misanthrope of fifth-century Athens who may well have been legendary. Plutarch's *Life of Antony* (chapter 70) tells all that is known of him. He had been a friend of Alcibiades and was mentioned in the comedies of Aristophanes; and many anecdotes were told of him, some of which Plutarch quotes, along with his epitaph by Callimachus:

Here lies Timon who hated mankind;
let no passer-by linger.
Curse me if that is your wish, but pass,
that is all I ask.

He also appears in a dialogue by the satirist Lucian. Shakespeare's play is taken from Plutarch, in North's translation.

T(e)iresias

A Theban seer of compelling power, who is first mentioned in the *Odyssey* where he is already dead and in the Underworld. Odysseus is sent by Circe to consult him, and hears his prophecy about the strange death which will ultimately come to him. In plays of the Theban cycle he is blind, and this is variously explained by late mythographers. According to Callimachus he saw Athene bathing, and she blinded him but gave him prophetic power in compensation (→ MUSES, for their similar treatment of Thamyris). In the more popular version, followed by Ovid, he once saw two snakes mating, struck them with his staff and was changed into a woman. Seven years later he saw them and hit them again, and reverted to man's shape, a story quoted by Dante in *Inferno* 20, where Tiresias is among the sorcerers in the Eighth Circle. (Robert Graves in *The Greek Myths* refers to the belief in south India that it is unlucky to see snakes mating, and the penalty is to be made homosexual.) He was blinded in consequence, for some time after his sex changes he was called to settle a dispute between Zeus and Hera on whether men or women get more pleasure from sex, he having experienced both. He declared for women, in a ratio of nine to one. Hera was insulted and blinded him; Zeus gave him long life and the gift of prophecy in compensation. He is a key figure in Sophocles' *King Oedipus*, for he knows that the pollution in Thebes comes from Oedipus himself, and it is to prove him wrong that Oedipus starts on his searching inquiries. In Euripides' *Bacchae* he urges Pentheus to accept Dionysus at Thebes and prophesies that the god will be accommodated at Delphi; throughout the play, he is a very Euripidean mixture of inspired visionary and fifth-century rationalist, and a controversial figure.

Swinburne and Tennyson both wrote poems about Tiresias, in which the more conventional view of his blindness is taken from Callimachus, and the interest is mainly on his prophecies of the downfall of Thebes. Much more significant is his appearance in *The Waste Land*:

I Tiresias, though blind, throbbing
between two lives,
Old man with wrinkled female breasts,
can see . . .
Perceived the scene, and foretold the
rest . . .

Eliot in his notes quotes the passage from Ovid as being 'of great anthropological interest', and says that 'Tiresias, although a mere spectator and not indeed a "character" is yet the most important personage in the poem, uniting all the rest'. Tiresias also appears in the opening lines of Pound's *Cantos* and is similarly symbolic in the surrealist drama of Guillaume Apollinaire, *Les Mamelles de Tirésias*, which is still revived in its opera form by Poulenc, and was intended to be an Aristophanic comedy on the need to raise the French birthrate in spite of feminine emancipation.

Titans

In Hesiod's *Theogony* and other early Greek legends they are generally pre-Olympian gods or demi-gods, the children of Uranus and GE and often confused with the race of Giants. See KRONOS, HYPERION, PROMETHEUS.

Tithonus

Mentioned in the *Odyssey* as one of the lovers of Eos, the dawn, in later legend he is an Assyrian half-brother of Priam of Troy and, by Eos, the father of MEMNON. Eos asked Zeus to make him immortal but forgot to ask for perpetual youth for him, so that he gradually became greyer and more shrivelled until she tired of looking after him, turned him into a cicada and shut him up in a cage. Compare the fate of the SIBYL. This sinister legend was used as an illustration of the truth that '*nihil est ab omni parte beatum*' ('nothing is wholly fortunate'):

Early death snatched Achilles in his hour
of glory,
Old age dragged on to wear away
Tithonus,
And any moment may bring me the
blessing
Denied to you.

Horace, *Odes* 2.16.

In Tennyson's early poem Tithonus laments his cruel fate and prays for death, slowly consumed as he is by 'cruel immortality'.

Titus (Titus Flavius Vespasianus, Roman Emperor A.D. 79–81)

The elder son of the Emperor Vespasian, Titus had an active military career before his accession, culminating in the capture of Jerusalem in 70 (→ JOSEPHUS). This is commemorated in the Arch of Titus in the forum at Rome, which was originally topped by a bronze victory chariot. During his stay in Judaea he became the lover of BERENICE. He was universally popular, called by Suetonius 'the darling of the human race', and his short reign was remembered as a generally happy one, apart from two major disasters: the eruption of Vesuvius which destroyed Herculaneum and Pompeii in 79, and the plague and fire in Rome the following year. Titus gave generous relief to those who had suffered, and his building programme included the completion of the Colosseum and the Baths of Titus. Gluck and Mozart both wrote operas on *La clemenza di Tito*, in which he appears as merciful to a conspirator, Sextus, and to the heroine Vitellia, who is jealous of his love for Berenice.

Titus Andronicus

This peculiarly unpleasant play was probably Shakespeare's earliest; its sources are obscure, but the setting is vaguely late Roman, at the time of the Gothic invasions. Titus is listed as 'a noble Roman general against the Goths'. The rape and mutilation of his daughter Lavinia is taken from the story of PHILOMELA and ITYS, which is often referred to in the play, and the ghastly feast is modelled on Seneca's *Thyestes*. The whole has been called a 'Senecan exercise, where the horrors are all classical and quite unfelt'.

Trajan (Marcus Ulpius Trajanus, Roman Emperor A.D. 98–117)

A Spaniard by birth and a soldier by profession, Trajan was adopted as successor to NERVA but stayed to consolidate the frontiers on the Rhine before coming to Rome on Nerva's death. He was universally acclaimed, and soon given the title of Optimus Princeps which appears on his coins and monuments. He carried on the system of poor relief started by Nerva, embarked on large-scale public works, such as the Baths, Forum and Basilica of Trajan, and made good use of reliable senators like the younger Pliny as administrators. He defeated Decebalus, king of Dacia, after a series of campaigns, and made a new province out of Dacia (modern Romania). He died while still campaigning in Parthia. His achievements are commemorated on the spiral series of reliefs on Trajan's Column, which still stands in his forum; his statue on the top was replaced by one of St Peter in 1587. This is the model for the Vendôme Column in Paris, which records Napoleon's victories of 1806 to 1810 in a similar continuous spiral of reliefs. There are two well-preserved Arches of Trajan in Italy, one in Benevento and the other in Ancona, the latter of special interest because it inspired the remarkable traveller and antiquarian scholar of the fifteenth century, Cyriaco d'Ancona, to spend his life recording the surviving antiquities of Greece and Rome.

Triton

The merman of Greek myth and folklore, half man, half fish or dolphin. Pausanias was shown the pickled head of a triton in Tanagra, Boeotia, and another in Rome, just as 'mermaids' used to be exhibits at side-shows in later times. His name is connected with that of his mother, the sea-goddess Amphitrite, and is presumably pre-Greek. In ancient art tritons are little more than decorative features of marine scenes, but Triton drowns MISENUS in the *Aeneid*, and Ovid introduces him into the myth of the Flood (→DEUCALION). There he is ordered by Neptune to blow his horn or conch-shell to summon the waters to retreat, and Ovid's brief vivid description of the dripping Triton raising the great shell to his bearded lips is recalled in many fountain-figures of the Renaissance or later baroque period [39]. In Rome, for instance, there are tritons on Bernini's Trevi Fountain; one in the Borghese Gardens which used to be on the old fountain in the Piazza Navona; and a magnificent solitary Triton blowing his shell on Bernini's Triton Fountain in the Piazza Barberini. And once, at least, there is a Triton who is more than a decorative marine feature of poetry, in Wordsworth's passionate sonnet of 1807:

– Great God! I'd rather be
A Pagan suckled in a creed outworn;
So might I, standing on this pleasant lea
Have glimpses that would make me less
  forlorn;
Have sight of Proteus rising from the
  sea;
Or hear old Triton blow his wreathed
  horn.

Troilus
The son of Priam, mentioned briefly in the *Iliad* as already killed in battle. The Troilus of Shakespeare and Chaucer comes from Boccaccio: → CHRYSEIS (Cressida).

Trophonius
The god of a famous Greek oracle at Lebadeia, in Boeotia, between Athens and Delphi, where a gorge and spring and remains of the sanctuary can still be seen near modern Livadia. It was famous from the sixth century onwards, and consulted by Croesus of Lydia among countless other visitants. Pausanias describes it and its ritual in detail in his *Guide to Greece*, book 9. After complicated initiation rites the questioner was dressed like a sacrificial victim, and carrying a honey-cake to placate the infernal deities had to climb down into a pot-hole and be swept along in an underground river. In due course he was returned to the light, dazed and dejected by what he had heard from invisible speakers, and only gradually regained his senses and ability to laugh. It became a tradition to say that a gloomy person must have been consulting Trophonius. The ritual has common details with that described in *Aeneid* 6. → GOLDEN BOUGH.

Troy
The site of Troy was discovered in 1873 by the German Heinrich Schliemann, an amateur scholar of Homer with no archaeological experience, who decided that from the description in the *Iliad* it must have been on the site of modern Hissarlik in north-west Turkey, about four miles from the Dardanelles. Later excavations have distinguished between nine strata, of which Troy VIIa shows signs of destruction by fire and is generally identified with Homer's Troy, of which Priam was king. Troy was rebuilt as a Greek colony, and became the Graeco-Roman town of Ilium which flourished until the fourth century A.D.

'Tully'
An anglicized form of Tullius, the family name of Cicero, which was in general use from Chaucer's time to the nineteenth century.

Typhon
A hundred-headed monster, son of Tartarus and Ge, according to Hesiod, and sometimes said to be the father of the Chimaera and the Hydra. He was vanquished by Zeus's thunderbolts and buried, like the giants, under a volcano; in his case Mount Etna, where the eruptions were traditionally said to be due to Typhon's struggles to free himself.

Tyrants
The seventh and sixth centuries B.C. were known as 'the age of tyrants', but tyranny in this sense means authority

usurped by an individual, who was often the champion of the people, against an established aristocratic or plutocratic minority. Many of the tyrants contributed a great deal to the economic and cultural development of the city-states they ruled; see PERIANDER, PISISTRATUS, POLYCRATES. Tyranny acquired a pejorative meaning when it had been superseded by democracy, especially in fifth-century Athens, where the tyrannicides Harmodius and ARISTOGITON were glorified. For political philosophers like Plato tyranny was the worst and most irresponsible form of government, and the tyrant is analysed in the *Republic* as a man at the mercy of his baser instincts. There were indeed tyrants like this; → DIONYSIUS, PHALARIS.

Ulysses
The Latin name of ODYSSEUS.

Varro, Marcus Terentius (116–27 B.C.)
The greatest scholar of the Roman Republic, Varro was educated in Rome and Athens and followed a normal public career until he was appointed by Julius Caesar to be the first librarian of the new public library at Rome. After Caesar's death he retired to continue his studies, and is said to have written more than 600 books on an immense range of subjects. These included Menippean Satires, biographies of notable Greeks and Romans, an encyclopedia of the liberal arts, and forty-one volumes on antiquities, all of which are known only as titles or through quotations by later writers. Only his three-volume work on agriculture and parts of five out of twenty-five books on the Latin language survive.

Venus
Originally an obscure Italian deity whose name meant 'charm' or 'beauty' and is connected with the classical Latin adjective *venustus*, Venus was concerned with vegetable, not animal fertility. She was first identified with APHRODITE through the cult of Aphrodite on Mount Eryx in Sicily, which had been traditionally founded by Aeneas after the death of his father Anchises. From 217 B.C. Venus Erycina had a temple in Rome, and Venus took on all the functions and associates of Aphrodite: see ADONIS, CUPID, MARS. She was particularly important in the official state cult because the Julian family (of which Nero was the last member to be emperor) claimed descent from Aeneas who was the son of Aphrodite. In this she is Venus Genetrix, the universal mother and creator of all living things, whom Lucretius addresses in the opening words of his *De rerum natura*, and whose festival is celebrated in the late Latin poem PERVIGILIUM VENERIS.

In the Middle Ages Venus was known both as ANADYOMENE (and in rare manuscript illustrations she is still naked in the sea, as she was in classical art) and as Genetrix; but more often she is identified with the medieval sin of *luxuria* (sensuality), and pictured with her mirror as a symbol of idle dalliance to be overcome by Chastity. In the allegorical Battles of the Soul, for which the *Psychomachia* of Prudentius was the model, she is always ranged with the vices; and this is an interpretation which continues for a long time, in such pictures as Mantegna's *Triumph of Wisdom over Vice* and Perugino's *Combat of Love and Chastity*. Venus was indeed the focus of all the medieval fear of nudity and paganism. There were many tales of young men decoyed by Venus to become the prey of the devil; Tannhäuser is one of a line which stretches to Keats's *La Belle Dame sans merci*. As late as the fourteenth century it is recorded that a pagan statue of Venus was found in Siena, set up and admired, until it was thought to be the cause of a defeat by the Florentines. The Sienese then broke it up and secretly buried it in enemy territory.

A new and non-classical Venus held court in the poems of chivalry and courtly love; Gower, for instance, wrote his *Confessio amantis* in the form of a dialogue between himself as lover and the 'priest of Venus'. Chaucer's Troilus suffers and dies as her servant. It was the Italian Neoplatonists, with their belief in love as a metaphysical experience leading to awareness of the Divine, who brought back a Venus who was neither the devil's envoy nor a cruel taskmistress. Venus Genetrix is the centre of Botticelli's *Primavera* [5] as Venus Anadyomene is of his companion picture. The splendid baroque paintings in the Farnese Palace by Carracci illustrate the power of Love to transform the soul, and show Venus in her many aspects. There were also many scenes of gaiety and relaxation painted, of which perhaps Titian's *Feast of Venus* is the greatest; and when Rubens painted his *Horrors of War*, Venus and her followers are the innocent victims of Mars and the Furies. There are the beautiful individual Venuses of Giorgione, of Titian at Urbino, of Velazquez, and of Canova, whose elegant Venus has the features of Napoleon's sister, Pauline Borghese. There are also many variations of the newly interpreted distinction first drawn by Plato in the *Symposium* between Aphrodite Urania and Aphrodite Pandemos. It is unlikely that Plato meant more than a nobler, purer love and ordinary sexual love, but this was subsequently explained as Celestial or Divine Venus and Natural or Human Venus (or Sacred and Profane Love). Titian's much-discussed picture is the most famous example; but, however controversial Venus-imagery can become, Venus has remained a goddess to be welcomed, not feared.

Vercingetorix

Celtic chieftain of the tribe Averni (the Auvergne region of central France) who raised a revolt in 52 B.C. against the Roman occupation of Gaul and was only defeated after a long and heroic struggle. He was exhibited in Caesar's triumph in 46 and executed soon after. Caesar pays tribute to his ability in his *Gallic Wars*; and so does Rex Warner in his novels on Caesar. The suffix is Celtic, and appears in names of other chiefs such as Ambiorix, Cingetorix; also in that of the fictitious hero of French strip-cartoon, Astérix.

Verres, Gaius

A notorious governor of the Roman province of Sicily, who is remembered largely through the speeches of Cicero when he prosecuted him on behalf of the Sicilian cities in 70 B.C. The charges were extortion, embezzlement of tax money, looting of works of art, corruption by bribery, and general misgovernment over a period of three years, with a total disregard for the interests of the provincials. Only one of the six speeches was delivered, as Verres went into voluntary exile at Marseilles, and was fined and outlawed in his absence. Juvenal, however, implies that he took most of his loot with him, and he was executed in 43 because, it was said, Antony coveted his possessions. This was Cicero's first major triumph against the celebrated advocate Quintus Hortensius, who was his forensic opponent on many subsequent occasions. When the eighteenth-century parliamentary orator Edmund Burke impeached Warren Hastings for misgovernment of India he modelled his speeches explicitly on the Verrines, and this would have been well appreciated by his hearers.

Vespasian (Titus Flavius Vespasianus, Roman Emperor A.D. 69–79)

The first of the Flavian Emperors after the murder of Nero and the year of Civil War which saw Galba, Otho, Vitellius and Vespasian successively hailed as emperor by the armies they commanded. Vespasian had been sent by Nero to put down the Jewish revolt, but left his son TITUS to carry on in Judaea and started his march to Rome. He was a provincial Italian with a countryman's virtues, thrift, shrewd common sense and a blunt tongue, and if Suetonius's tales are true, he had a rather coarse but pithy wit. Vespasian brought peace to a harassed city and stability to the empire. He filled up vacancies in the Senate with Italians like himself, and kept strict control over his administrative officials, so that he left Rome solvent and was one of the few emperors to die in his bed and be universally regretted. He started the building of the Temple of Peace and of the great Flavian amphitheatre in the grounds of Nero's Golden House, later known as the Colosseum after the huge statue of Nero near it, where so many Christian martyrs were burned or flung to the lions. It has remained one of the marvels of Rome for visitors ever since the days of medieval pilgrims, although it is 'reduced to its naked majesty', as Gibbon puts it. He quotes a Latin proverb or prophecy which is known from writings ascribed to Bede in the eighth century: 'As long as the Colosseum stands, Rome shall stand; when the Colosseum falls, Rome will fall; when Rome falls, the world will fall.'

Vesta

The Roman hearth-goddess, the counterpart of the Greek Hestia, who was worshipped in every household and also officially in a temple in the Roman forum; this held a fire said to have been brought from Troy, which must never be allowed to go out. The fire was tended up to the late fourth century A.D. by the **Vestal Virgins**, priestesses who were six in number in historical times, and served for thirty years under the control of the High Priest (Pontifex Maximus). Their punishment if they lost their virginity was to be buried alive, and this was recorded as having been carried out on two Vestals by Domitian. Otherwise they were held in high honour and enjoyed many privileges. The round base of the temple of Vesta and remains of the *Atrium Vestae*, where the Vestals lived, can be seen in the forum, and near by is the square cistern of the Spring of Juturna, a local water nymph, from which the Vestals drew their water, as they were ritually forbidden to use piped water. (In this spring Castor and Pollux were traditionally said to have washed and watered their horses after the battle of Lake Regillus.) There are also fragments of some of the statues of the Vestals which stood round the courtyard. Hestia/Vesta is scarcely personified at any time, but is an ancient symbol of fire as the source of life, while the hearth signified personal security, as it does in all primitive societies. The public cult of Vesta probably arose out of the feeling that the hearth of the king was of special importance for his people. Every town had its temple of Vesta built round its sacred fire, and the circular temple at Tivoli, with its distinctive Corinthian capitals of the first century B.C., was copied by Sir John Soane in the eighteenth century for the circular corner of the Bank of England in London. Small round temples of this pattern were often set up in the landscaped gardens of the same period.

Victory

The goddess of Victory is 'Nike' in Greek, 'Victoria' in Latin, and according to Hesiod, Nike was honoured by Zeus for fighting on the side of the Olympians in the war with the Titans. She was sometimes identified with Athene, as she is in the small temple of Athena-Nike on the Acropolis at Athens (the Temple of Wingless Victory), which was built after the Propylaea to fit between it and the bastion. Parts of its frieze showing the Greeks victorious over the Persians were brought to London with the Elgin Marbles and are in the British Museum. Nike appears in a relief carved on the balustrade, already with the thin swirling drapery which is a characteristic of later Victory statues. There is a famous Victory at Olympia, a marble contemporary copy of a bronze original by the late-fifth-century sculptor Paeonius, but the best known of all Victories is probably the Winged Victory of Samothrace [55], which now stands eight feet high on the main staircase of the Louvre. It originally showed Victory alighting on a ship's prow and stood in a great basin of water where it was reflected, to commemorate a naval victory, and dates from about 190 B.C. When it was found in 1813 it was broken into over a hundred marble pieces, which fitted together to form the familiar windswept figure with great wings outstretched. In Rome Victory had a temple on the Palatine and was naturally worshipped by the army, but her most sacred symbol was the altar of Victory in the senate-house. For its disappearance, → SYMMACHUS.

Virgil (Publius Vergilius Maro, 70–19 B.C.)

Roman poet, born near Mantua, where he is honoured in a medieval statue, who was educated at Cremona and

Milan, and then came to Rome where he joined the circle of MAECENAS and became a close friend of Horace. Apart from his juvenilia of doubtful authenticity, his first work was the *Eclogues* or *Bucolics*, ten pastoral poems modelled on those of Theocritus, but giving some personal information; we know from these that his modest family property had been confiscated in 42 when land was needed for retired veterans of the Civil Wars, but was afterwards returned, possibly by intervention of the future Emperor Augustus. Then came the GEORGICS. For the last ten years of his life he lived at his country home near Naples working on the AENEID. He intended to finish revising it and then to study philosophy, but in 19 he set out on a tour of Greece, fell ill, and died at Brindisi. His body was brought to Naples and buried outside the city, with the epitaph said to have been written by Virgil himself:

Mantua brought me life, Calabria
  death, and now I lie
In Naples, the poet of flocks
  and farms and heroes.

Within a century his tomb was honoured as a shrine (→ SILIUS ITALICUS) and his works were a textbook in Roman schools.

In the Middle Ages he was hailed both as a prophet of Christianity in his 'MESSIANIC ECLOGUE' and as a wonder-working magician. Gower, for instance, writes of Virgil's Mirror, which was supposed to reflect approaching enemies from a distance of thirty miles. And fortune-telling by means of the *Sortes Virgilianae*, opening a volume of Virgil at random, as an alternative to the Bible, was common all over Europe. Rabelais makes Panurge have recourse to it in his *Third Book*, and it lingered on at least until the seventeenth century, when Charles I is recorded as trying it. Local tradition found his tomb in a Roman columbarium above the old Grotto di Posilippo, which is in fact the remains of a Roman tunnel through the rock, but there Virgil was said to practise his magic arts. It was visited by Petrarch, who planted a laurel and saw the epitaph, but found the tomb already in ruins. Today Virgil is commemorated in that pleasant green oasis in Naples, the Virgilian Park.

He was admired by Chaucer, who gives an outline of the *Aeneid* in *The House of Fame*, and for Dante he was '*il nostro maggior poeta*' ('our greatest poet'), who was his guide through Hell. From the Renaissance onwards Virgil has been a major influence on all writers of literary epic. He has always been considered one of the world's greatest poets, and Poussin rightly drew him being crowned by Apollo on the title-page of the Royal Virgil of 1641. Today we think of him less as Tennyson did as

Wielder of the stateliest measure
  Ever moulded by the lips of man

and more as the poet for whom *sunt lacrimae rerum*; there are tears at the heart of life itself. His sensitivity to words and imagery can produce an inner tension in his symbolism which has hitherto defied translators. But there have been many attempts, notably Dryden's; and it was R. J. Thornton's translation of 1821 which produced an *Eclogues* tenderly illustrated by Blake [49].

Virgil was known to have a streak of melancholy which was analysed in a study of PALINURUS, and his reluctance to have the *Aeneid* published in its unrevised form prompted the remarkable poetic novel, *The Death of Virgil*, written in 1945 by the Austrian Hermann Broch. This turns on the poet's decision at the moment of his death to destroy his manuscript, because he realizes that truth and beauty of language are inadequate to cope with human suffering and the advance of barbarism, or indeed with reality itself. As he crosses into death he experiences what is 'incomprehensible and unutterable for him: it was the world beyond speech'.

Virginia

In one of the legends of early Rome told by Livy in book 3 of his history, she is killed by her father Virginius in order to save her from the designs of Appius Claudius, one of the Board of Ten (*decemviri*) which had been elected to draw up a code of laws. This led to a plebeian revolution in 449 B.C. which overthrew the *decemviri*. It is not known whether the story was invented to account for some historic disturbance or whether it was aimed at building up a legend of tyranny round Appius by people who disliked the patrician family of the Claudii, of which the notorious CLODIUS was a member. Virginia is the heroine of the Elizabethan tragedy *Appius and Virginia*, and of one of Macaulay's *Lays of Ancient Rome*.

Vitellius, Aulus

The third of the Roman emperors in the year A.D. 69, after his defeat of Otho. He was in command of the legions on the Rhine frontier when news came of Nero's death, and posed as his successor, but he was idle and incompetent, and dependent on his more efficient legionary commanders. When they were defeated at Cremona by the army of Vespasian, Vitellius was brutally murdered in Rome.

Vitruvius Pollio

Roman architect and engineer, a surveyor for the Emperor Augustus, famous for his *De architectura* in ten books. This is a treatise which covers all types of Greek and Roman building, civic and domestic, town-planning, water-supplies, civil engineering, geometry and astronomy, and methods of decoration in stucco and fresco – the only book of its kind to survive from antiquity. It was obviously in use as a textbook of planning when the north African towns of Dougga and Timgad were built. It was copied several times in the Middle Ages, but Vitruvius was best known to the architects of the Renaissance from the edition published in 1486, when it had great influence on men like Bramante, who designed St Peter's, and Palladio, who built Vicenza and the Palladian villas of Venetia. Alberti, the architect of San Francesco, Rimini, had read a manuscript and wrote his own *Ten Books of Architecture* in Latin, with Vitruvius for his model. Vitruvius can thus be said to have fixed the classical style for Europe, and later on for England in the designs of such architects as Inigo Jones and Christopher Wren; and still later for the United States in Thomas Jefferson's University of Virginia.

'Vitruvian man' refers to his explanation of his theory of ideal human proportions by means of a square related to (not inside) a circle, and there are many drawings made to illustrate this. The most famous is perhaps that of Leonardo da Vinci, but the most beautiful is Blake's *Glad Day* in the British Museum, of which it has been said that 'geometrically perfect man is given back some of Apollo's lost vitality' [56].

Vulcan

The Roman god of fire, identified with HEPHAESTUS and sometimes called Mulciber, 'the smelter'. Vulcan with the Cyclopes working at the forge provided a popular subject for painters, and there are many minor examples as well as the famous pictures by Tintoretto and Velazquez; and H. V. Morton in *The Fountains of Rome* describes a hydraulic marvel in the gardens of the Quirinal Palace, dating from the late sixteenth century – a cavern with life-size marble figures which used to bring their hammers up and down on an anvil when the water ran freely to work the mechanism. But the most remarkable pictures of Vulcan are those in the series by that unique painter, Piero di Cosimo. These he based on his reading of LUCRETIUS and of the passage in Vitruvius, book 2, which describes the primitive origins of civilization before the discovery of fire, and adds the odd notion that Vulcan had been brought up by apes. Two pictures show Piero's conception of a Stone Age, one *The Forest Fire*, one shows Vulcan as a youth who has just fallen on Lemnos and is being welcomed by nymphs (though this could also show the story of Hylas), and the fifth Vulcan as a blacksmith hammering at a horseshoe, while horses wait and the god Aeolus blows a primitive bellows. In the background people are constructing wooden huts, such as Vitruvius describes, watched by a placid giraffe. These are pictures of genuine sympathy with the ancient myths, comparable with his *Discovery of Honey by Bacchus*, which was suggested by Ovid's *Fasti* 3; see BACCHUS.

The Wooden (*or* Trojan) **Horse**

This famous stratagem whereby the Greeks sent a party of men into Troy hidden in a hollow wooden horse was part of the cycle of Troy sagas known to Homer, though in the *Iliad* nothing is said of it. Its builder, Epeius, is mentioned only as a champion boxer. In *Odyssey* 4 Menelaus reminds Helen how once the horse was inside the walls she had walked round patting it and calling out the names of the men she suspected might be inside; evidently the horse cannot have been imagined as unduly large. She was being used as a decoy, for she had a Trojan prince, Deiphobus, with her, but Odysseus had prevented anyone from answering. In *Odyssey* 8, at the court of Alcinous, Odysseus asks the minstrel to sing of how Epeius made the horse with Athene's help, and how it was got into Troy through Odysseus's ingenuity, so that Homer is able briefly to tell of the sack of Troy and bridge the gap between the two epics. In *Odyssey* 11 Odysseus tells the shade of Achilles in the Underworld that his son Neoptolemus had been one of those chosen to go in it. But all the details which Virgil makes use of in *Aeneid* 2 are taken from lost minor epics: SINON persuades the Trojans that the Greeks have given up and sailed away for good, leaving behind the horse as an offering to Athene, and LAOCOÖN tries in vain to stop the Trojans from dragging it into the city. Then Sinon lets the Greeks out at night, and the gates are opened to the main army. This horse is immense, 'like a mountain'. Greek scholars, including Pausanias, sometimes tried to account for the horse by saying that it was a horse-shaped siege tower brought up to the walls, or a postern gate marked by a horse's head, but it is far too good a story to be explained away in a learned commentary. It is shown on early vase-paintings, and a particularly fine painting from Pompeii is as dramatic in its way as the two paintings by Tiepolo in the National Gallery, London [54].

Xenophanes (*c.* 570–480 B.C.)
Greek poet and philosopher who left his native Ionia to live in south Italy and Syracuse, where he devoted himself to attacking the current anthropomorphic gods of Homer and Hesiod. Few fragments of his verse survive. He taught the relativity of religious ideas and the impossibility of gaining knowledge of the gods, but he had profound faith in a supreme deity who controls everything by reason; and he can be called the first philosophic theologian, whose influence on later Ionian philosophers was considerable.

Xenophon (*c.* 428–*c.* 354 B.C.)
Greek historian, in his youth a follower of Socrates, who features in his *Memoirs* and *Symposium*. Later he greatly admired the elder CYRUS and the Spartan king Agesilaus, and wrote idealized biographies of both. Most of his life he lived in his estates at Scillus near Olympia, which had been given him by the Spartan government. He was a prolific writer on a wide range of subjects, and his treatises on hunting and estate management, horsemanship and finance are still extant, as well as his two major historical works: his *Hellenica*, a history of Greece from 411 (where Thucydides breaks off) to 362, and the *Anabasis* or *Persian Expedition*, on his adventures with the 10,000 mercenary soldiers enlisted by the younger CYRUS.

Xerxes
King of Persia 485–465 B.C., the son of DARIUS and Atossa. Xerxes assembled an enormous fleet and army in order to avenge his father's defeat by the Greeks at the battle of Marathon. He crossed the Hellespont on a pontoon bridge, dug a canal through the Mount Athos peninsula, and invaded Greece. He forced the pass at Thermopylae (→ LEONIDAS) and occupied Athens (→ THEMISTOCLES). But when his fleet was defeated at Salamis he had to withdraw, and his commander Mardonius was decisively defeated at the battle of Plataea. This ended Xerxes' designs on Greece. Little is known of his later life; he is the King Ahasuerus of the book of

Esther in the Old Testament. Herodotus mentions several colourful details about Xerxes which were often referred to by later classical writers: his reliance on dreams; his punishment of the Hellespont after a storm by ordering it three hundred lashes (later a symbol of futile anger); his decorating with gold ornaments a plane tree near Sardis which he thought particularly beautiful; his amazement when he heard that the Greeks competed at their games for no more than an olive-wreath; his tears, when he reviewed his army, at the thought of man's brief life; and how he watched his defeat at Salamis from the base of Mount Aegaleos on the mainland, which Byron recalls in *The Isles of Greece*:

A king sate on the rocky brow
  Which looks o'er sea-born Salamis;
And ships, by thousands, lay below,
  And men in nations;—all were his!
He counted them at break of day—
And when the sun set, where were they?

Only Handel, however, seems to have developed the dramatic possibilities of these episodes in his rarely sung opera *Xerxes*.

Zenobia
The wife of a Syrian nobleman, Odaenathus of Palmyra, who led his own army and from A.D. 262 to 267 the Roman army of the East as well, and was virtually ruler of the Eastern Empire. This was the heyday of the great city, built at an oasis on the trade-route between Syria and Babylonia. The ruins of its temple of Bel, colonnaded streets and necropolis are famous. After her husband's murder, which she may have organized herself, Zenobia ruled alone as queen in Palmyra, a woman of great intelligence but overmastering personal ambition. Her armies overran Asia Minor and Egypt until the Emperor Aurelian marched against them, led a series of successful campaigns, and besieged Zenobia in Palmyra. After her capture in 272 she was exhibited in Aurelian's triumph and then pensioned off to live in a villa at Tibur. Chaucer tells her story fairly accurately under the name of Cenobie, wife of Odenake, in the *Monk's Tale*, which he took from Boccaccio's *On the Fates of Famous Men and Women* (though he attributes it to Petrarch). Here Zenobia is grouped with Hercules, Alexander, Julius Caesar and Nero along with several biblical characters as an illustration of the truth that

But ay Fortune hath in hire hony galle;
This myghty queene may no while
  endure.
Fortune out of hir regne made hir falle
To wrecchednesse and to mysaventure.

Zephyrus
In Greek mythology, the west wind, who like all the winds (→ BOREAS) was originally imagined in horse form. In the *Iliad* he is the father of Xanthus and Balius, the wonderful talking horses of Achilles which had been a wedding present from Poseidon to Peleus. Some of the poets make him the husband of IRIS (through association of rain-bringing wind and rainbow). He is also said to have deflected the discus which

killed the boy HYACINTHUS, another association of west wind and spring. In Italy a west wind is generally mild and heralds the spring, so that for the Romans Zephyr (and his Latin counterpart, Favonius) comes to mean a gentle, warm breeze, and this is the convention in the poets from Chaucer onwards. He appears in Botticelli's pictures breathing life into FLORA [5] and wafting VENUS ANADYOMENE to the shore.

Zeus

'The father of gods and men' in Homer, with whom the Romans identified their supreme god JUPITER. The name of Zeus is found in some form in most Indo-European languages meaning 'sky', and his earliest cults are connected with mountain tops and the bringing of rain and thunderstorms. He retains his attribute of the thunderbolt in Homer, but he has also become the protector of the king and his rightful authority, and of families, guests and suppliants. His dethronement of KRONOS and battle against the Titans represent the triumph of the Olympians over the pre-Greek deities. He has few popular or local cults in Greece, though the story of his being a son of Kronos and brought up by AMALTHEA is Cretan legend. His authority is based on power, not on morality, and so, as well as all his legitimate children in Olympus (Athene, Apollo, Artemis, Ares, Dionysus), he has many other loves and children; → ANTIOPE, CALLISTO, DANAË, IO, LEDA, SEMELE. These have provided interest individually at all times, and also collectively as 'The Loves of Jupiter'. The tapestry shown to Britomart in book 3 of Spenser's *Faerie Queene*, which depicts several of his amours, has its counterpart in sets of Italian tapestries and frescoes for the palaces of the nobility from the sixteenth century onwards, and some of the sets of engravings designed by such painters as Giulio Romano and circulated for private enjoyment, must have had a good deal of pleasurable pornographic interest for the ducal connoisseurs who commissioned them.

In classical times Zeus became the supreme civic god as the protector of law and justice, as he is in the plays of Aeschylus. His temples were of special grandeur; in the Temple of Zeus at Olympia, for example, there was the great gold-and-ivory statue seated on a throne, the work of Phidias, which Pausanias saw and described. Later on his name was used by the STOICS as synonymous with the divine principle.

Zeuxis

Greek painter of the late fifth century B.C., a native of Heraclea in south Italy, but also working in Athens. None of his work survives, but he was much praised in antiquity for his subtle use of shaded colour and his faithful representations; his still-life of grapes was said to have been pecked at by birds. His most famous picture was a portrait of Helen, painted for the south Italian town of Croton. Cicero and the elder Pliny say that he chose five of the local girls and painted the mouth of one, nose of another, and so on. (The same tale was later told of Raphael.) The theory behind this is not so much that the sum of perfect parts must make a perfect whole, but that the artist is working on an idea, an Ideal Form in the Platonic sense (→ PLATO). Here then is the germ of the theory of Ideal Art which develops into the geometric man of VITRUVIUS, Dürer's theories on the ideally proportioned man, and the ennoblement of the human form which was one of the aims of the Neoclassicists of the late eighteenth century.

Table of Main Dates

Greece	*Rome*	*Near East*
	B.C.	
***c.*1000** Dorian invasion of Peloponnese		*trad.* **1184** Fall of Troy
776 First Olympic Games	*trad.* **753** Foundation of Rome	**650–600** Rise of tyrants in Ionia
***c.*700** Possible date for Homer in Ionia *trad.* **621** Draco's law code at Athens		**612** Assyria falls to Babylonia and Media; Nineveh destroyed
594 Reforms of Solon **561** Pisistratus first seizes tyranny at Athens		**549** Cyrus of Persia defeats Media **546** Cyrus defeats Croesus of Lydia; Ionia falls to Persia
508 Democratic reforms at Athens **490** ⚔ Marathon: Darius of Persia defeated by Athenians **480** ⚔ Salamis: Xerxes of Persia defeated by combined Greeks	*trad.* **510** Expulsion of Tarquinius Superbus, last king of Rome. Foundation of Republic	**538** Cyrus takes Babylon; Jews return to Jerusalem **516** Temple at Jerusalem rebuilt **521–486** Darius King of Persia
	trad. **451** Codification of law: XII tables	**485–465** Xerxes King of Persia
445–431 Age of Pericles Parthenon, etc. built **431–404** Peloponnesian War **415** Sicilian expedition of Athenians **405** ⚔ Aegospotami **404** Athens surrenders to Sparta		**444** Nehemiah appointed governor of Judaea; walls of Jerusalem rebuilt **401** Expedition of Cyrus and March of the Ten Thousand
399 Trial and death of Socrates		
338 ⚔ Chaeronea: Philip of Macedon gains control of Greece	**387** Gauls sack Rome	
336 Death of Philip. Alexander the Great elected general of the Greeks **331** Foundation of Alexandria **323** Death of Alexander		**334–323** Campaigns of Alexander against Persia, Babylonia and North India **332** Jews recognize Alexander as emperor **320** Ptolemy of Egypt takes Jerusalem
	279–275 Pyrrhus in Italy	
267 Athens falls to mercenary army of the Macedonian Antigonus	**264–241** First Punic War against Carthage **218–201** Second Punic War: Hannibal invades Italy	
197 Rome declares freedom of the Greeks after defeating Philip V	***c.*155** Scipionic Circle promotes Greek culture	**168** Rebellion of Judas Maccabeus against Seleucid Kings of Syria

Greece	*Rome*	*Near East*
	B.C.	
147 Annexation of Macedonia by Rome	**149–146** Third Punic War: Carthage destroyed	
146 Destruction of Corinth: Greece subject to Rome		
86 Athens falls to Sulla in his war with Mithridates	**133–123** Attempted social reforms of Tiberius and Gaius Gracchus	
	82–79 Sulla dictator of Rome	**63** Jerusalem taken by Pompey
	59 First Triumvirate, (Caesar, Pompey, Crassus)	**53** ⚔ Carrhae; Roman defeat by Parthia
	49 Civil war: Caesar *v.* Pompey	
	48 ⚔ Pharsalus: Pompey defeated	
	44 Caesar assassinated	
	Second Triumvirate (Antony, Lepidus, Octavian)	**40** Herod declared king of Judaea by Rome
	31 ⚔ Actium: Octavian defeats Antony	
	27 Octavian first emperor (Augustus)	
	A.D.	
		30 Crucifixion of Christ
	43 Claudius invades Britain	
	61 Rising of Boadicea	**47** Paul's first missionary journey
	66–73 Jewish–Roman War	**70** Destruction of Jerusalem by Rome
	68 Death of Nero	**73** Fall of Massada
	117–80 Antonine emperors	**113–117** Trajan's campaigns in Parthia
	212–17 Caracalla emperor: extension of citizenship	
	293 Diocletian's reforms: two emperors, of East and West	**131–4** Jewish rebellion put down by Hadrian
	313 Edict of Milan giving toleration to Christians	
	323 Constantine sole emperor: Byzantium (Constantinople) capital of Empire	
	410 Visigoths (Alaric) capture Rome	
	451 Attila defeated	
	455 Vandals sack Rome	
	476 Romulus Augustulus, last emperor of the West, deposed	
	493–518 Theodoric King of of Italy	

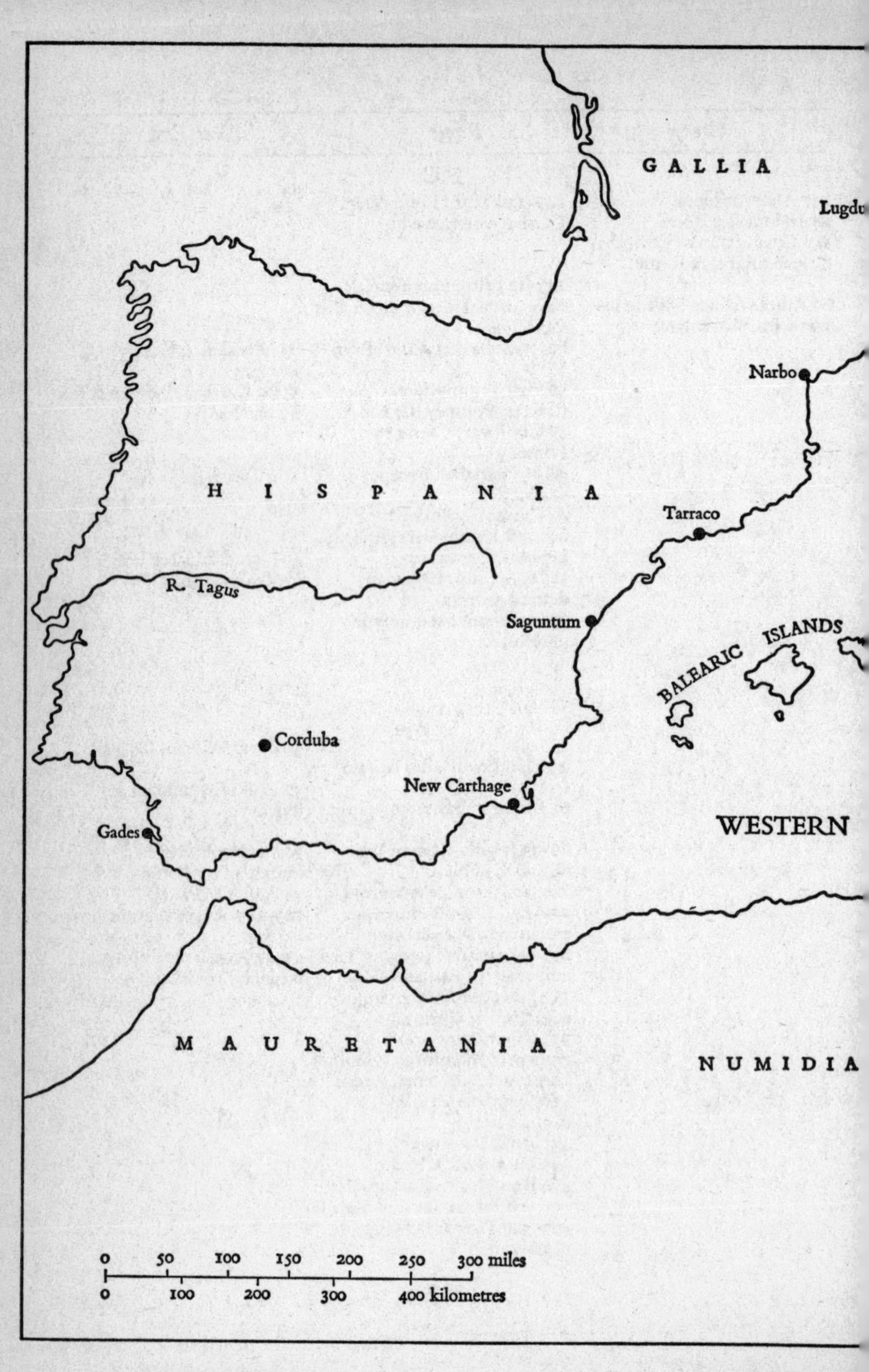
GALLIA
Lugdu
Narbo
HISPANIA
Tarraco
R. Tagus
Saguntum
BALEARIC ISLANDS
Corduba
New Carthage
Gades
WESTERN
MAURETANIA
NUMIDIA
0 50 100 150 200 250 300 miles
0 100 200 300 400 kilometres

TRANSALPINE GAUL
Aquileia
Verona
Mediolanum
Cremona
Mantua
R. Po
CIS'ALPINE GAUL
Ravenna
ETRURIA
R. Tiber
Ancona
ILLYRIA
ilia
Forum Julii
Lake Trasimene
UMBRIA
PICENUM
ADRIATIC SEA
LATIUM
Rome
CORSICA
Ostia
SAMNIUM
Cannae
Asculum
APULIA
Capua
CAMPANIA
Brundisium
Puteoli
Tarentum
Pompeii
Heraclea
Paestum
Sybaris
SARDINIA
Thurii
ETRUSCAN SEA
Croton
CALABRIA
IONIAN SEA
Messana
Rhegium
AEGADIAN ISLANDS
Segesta
Mt Etna
DITERRANEAN
Enna
Agrigentum
Syracuse
Utica
Carthage
Hippo Regius
Malta
Zama
Thapsus
AFRICA
Djerba
Lepcis Magna

R. Danube
Tomis
MOESIA
ILLYRIA
R. Strymon
R. Hebrus
THRACE
Dyrrhachium
MACEDONIA
BOSPORUS
Pella
Philippi
Amphipolis
Byzantium
Thessalonica
CHALCIDICE
THASOS
Nicomedia
EPIRUS
Mt Olympus
SAMOTHRACE
HELLESPONT
Sestus
Abydos
Cyzicus
CORCYRA
R. Peneus
Pharsalus
LEMNOS
Troy
Mt Ida
Dodona
AEGEAN SEA
Pergamum
Actium
THESSALY
LESBOS
Mytilene
IONIAN SEA
ACARNANIA
AETOLIA
SCYROS
ASIA
ITHACA
CHIOS
Sardes
ACHAEA
Athens
Symrna
R. Maeander
ELIS
SAMOS
Ephesus
Laodicea
Olympia
Mantinea
R. Alpheus
ARCADIA
DELOS
ICARIAN SEA
Miletus
Sparta
PAROS
MESSENIA
LACONIA
NAXOS
Halicarnassus
COS
R. Eurotas
LYCIA
Cnidos
CYTHERA
Xanthus
RHODES
CRETE
Knossos
EASTERN MEDITERRANEA
Cyrene
Alexandria

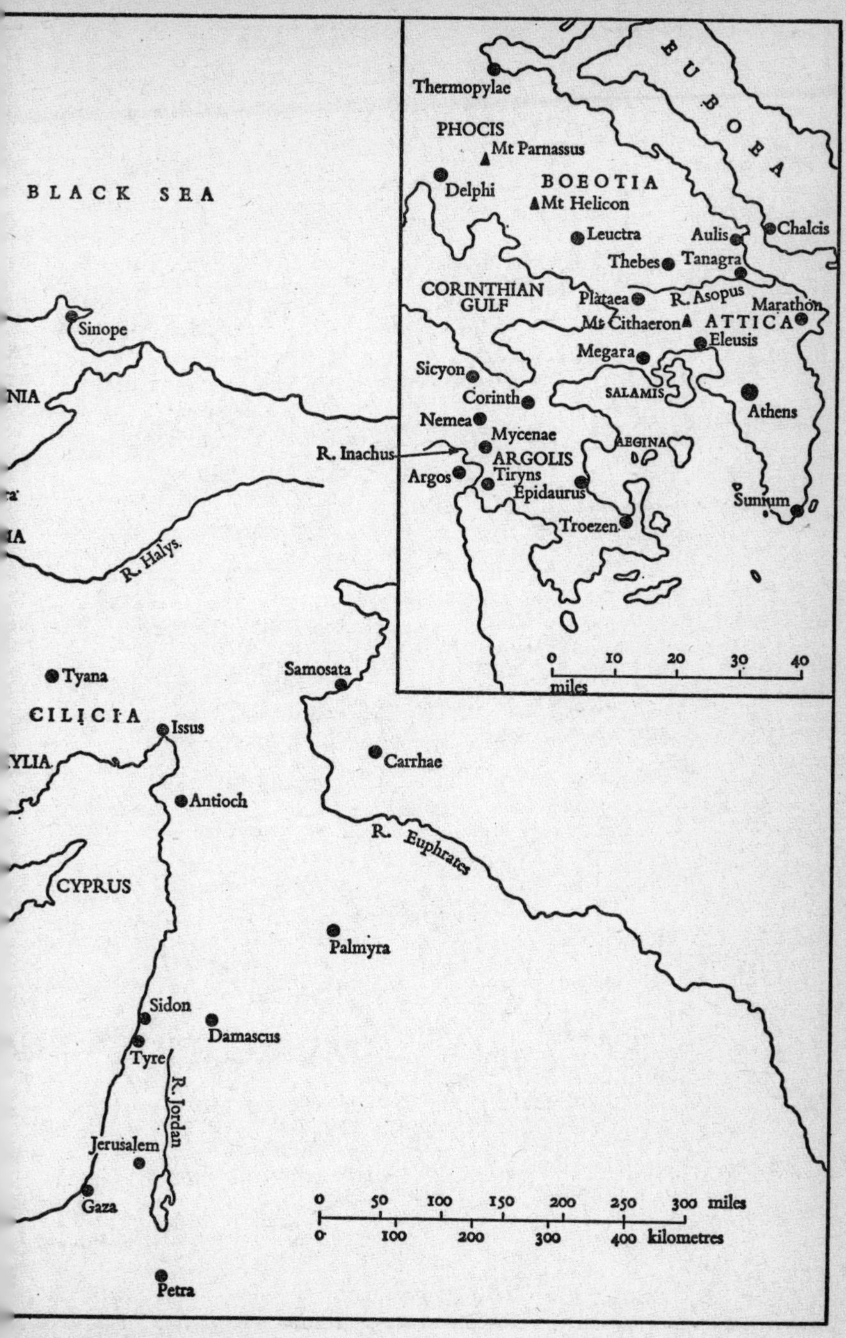

BLACK SEA
Sinope
NIA
IA
R. Halys
Tyana
CILICIA
Issus
YLIA
Antioch
CYPRUS
Samosata
Carrhae
R. Euphrates
Palmyra
Sidon
Damascus
Tyre
R. Jordan
Jerusalem
Gaza
Petra
0 50 100 150 200 250 300 miles
0 100 200 300 400 kilometres
R. Inachus
EUBOEA
Thermopylae
PHOCIS
Mt Parnassus
Delphi
BOEOTIA
Mt Helicon
Leuctra
Aulis
Chalcis
Thebes
Tanagra
CORINTHIAN GULF
Plataea
R. Asopus
Marathon
Mt Cithaeron
ATTICA
Eleusis
Megara
Sicyon
SALAMIS
Corinth
Athens
Nemea
Mycenae
AEGINA
ARGOLIS
Argos
Tiryns
Epidaurus
Sunium
Troezen
0 10 20 30 40
miles

INDEX

Notes

1. **Bold** figures indicate main entries.
2. a = first column, b = second column.
3. Dates 'B.C.' are so indicated, otherwise 'A.D.' is implied.